LONELY PLANET'S

WHERE TO GO WHEN EUROPE

THE ULTIMATE TRIP PLANNER FOR EVERY MONTH OF THE YEAR

CONTENTS

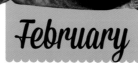

January
P8–31

February
P32–55

March
P56–79

April

P80-103

May

P104-127

June

P128-151

CONTENTS

October

P224-247

November

P248-271

December

P272-295

INTRODUCTION

'I've heard Scandinavia is very expensive.'

'The Canaries? Packed with tourists.'

'The Alps are only for winter sports enthusiasts.'

Sound familiar? It's all too easy to decide that somewhere is, or isn't, for us. And while generalisations often stem from a kernel of truth, one of the great beauties of travel is this: nowhere is the same all year around. St Moritz might be a playground for the jetset in January, but arrive in August and there'll be verdant mountains and wildflowers, idyllic lakes to sunbathe beside and not a ski boot in sight.

And it's not just the seasons that affect our experience of a place. Is there a festival filling the streets with colour and energy? Is the ferry running this month, or will those picturesque islands be tantalisingly out of reach? Might you glimpse puffins in the Faroe Islands at this time of year, or the tracks of lynx through Romanian snow? Are the sights aflood with visitors or wonderfully quiet?

This last is an ever-growing concern. Nobody wants to spend their big trip jostling against hundreds of selfie sticks. Which is why this book gives the inside scoop on not just where to go but when, for the best possible experience of that place: whether it's an off-season, springtime jaunt to the Algarve to see the almond blossom (p60) or an atmospheric road trip across the Scottish Highlands in November (p263). We've included destinations all over Europe, including those in the Caucasus where two great continents converge.

If you're looking for trip inspiration, this is a perfect place to start. Perhaps you've got set dates for your next holiday, and

© Rastislav Sedlak SK / Shutterstock

(L) Hallstatt, Austria in summer; (R) Sunrise at Quiraing on the Isle of Skye; (B) Surf's up on Portugal's Algarve

need to find a destination that ticks all your boxes, whether that's good value, winter sunshine, wildlife-spotting, peace and quiet – or a finely-tuned combination of them all. Or maybe you've got a once-in-a-lifetime bucket list experience in mind, and want to know when best to take the plunge. (There's no point arriving in Finnish Lapland in May, for instance, hoping to see the Northern Lights: they're only visible September to April.)

One thing's for sure: every traveller is unique, and there's no one-size-fits-all approach to travel. So the advice in this book is designed to give you a plethora of options – and perhaps make you consider places you've never considered before. The book is divided into 12 chapters, one for each month. At the start of each is a flowchart. Answer the questions and follow the strands to find the trip you want. There are also monthly charts detailing annual events and the value and family-friendliness of each destination – all tools designed to ignite your wanderlust and help you make informed decisions to answer that most important of questions: where to go when?

By Jessica Cole

January

WHERE TO GO WHEN

CHALLENGE MYSELF →

I WANT TO

TAKE ME OUT FOR...

FOOD
- RIGA, LATVIA P23
- BILBAO, SPAIN P27

DRINK
- VIENNA, AUSTRIA P17

Prost! Savour Vienna's famous coffee houses

Zagreb celebrates quirky culture and an offbeat art scene

TAKE ME TO TOWN

ART & CULTURE
- UMEÅ, SWEDEN P23
- ZAGREB, CROATIA P14

NIGHT-LIFE & HEDONISM
- LONDON, ENGLAND P29
- MONTE CARLO, MONACO P15

RELAX/ INDULGE

Teeter along Chornohora Ridge in the Romanian Carpathians

Take a soak in Budapest's Széchenyi Baths

DIAL IT DOWN

WELLNESS
- BUDAPEST, HUNGARY P19

CHILLING
- SANTORINI, GREECE P21
- CARPATHIANS, ROMANIA P13

Tuck into a plate of *sardeles pastes*, served up fresh from a fishing boat in Greece

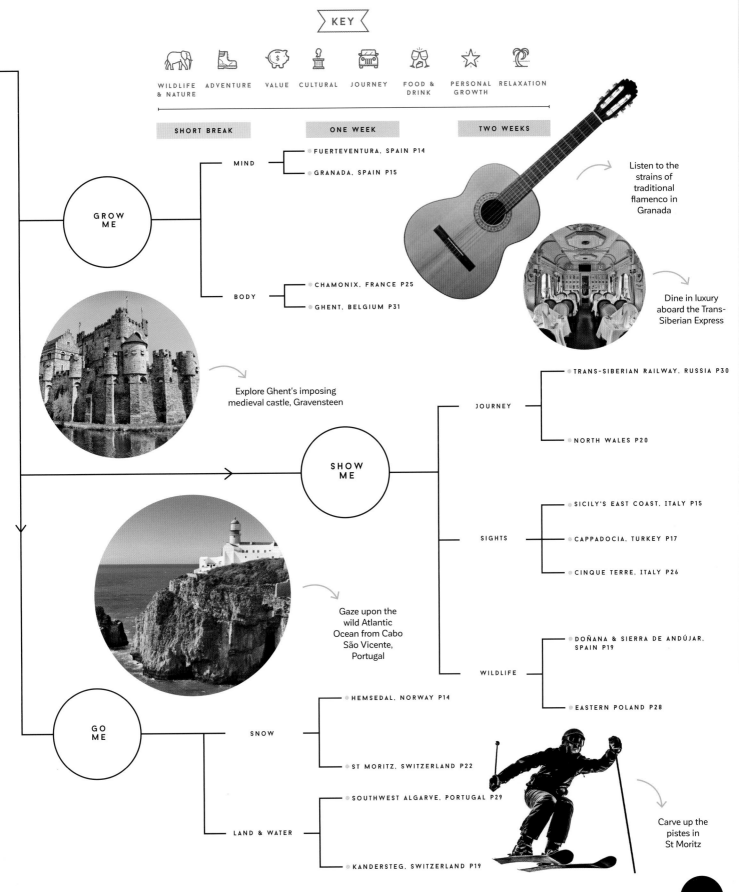

KEY

WILDLIFE & NATURE   ADVENTURE   VALUE   CULTURAL   JOURNEY   FOOD & DRINK   PERSONAL GROWTH   RELAXATION

SHORT BREAK   ONE WEEK   TWO WEEKS

GROW ME

MIND
- FUERTEVENTURA, SPAIN P14
- GRANADA, SPAIN P15

BODY
- CHAMONIX, FRANCE P25
- GHENT, BELGIUM P31

Listen to the strains of traditional flamenco in Granada

Dine in luxury aboard the Trans-Siberian Express

Explore Ghent's imposing medieval castle, Gravensteen

SHOW ME

JOURNEY
- TRANS-SIBERIAN RAILWAY, RUSSIA P30
- NORTH WALES P20

SIGHTS
- SICILY'S EAST COAST, ITALY P15
- CAPPADOCIA, TURKEY P17
- CINQUE TERRE, ITALY P26

WILDLIFE
- DOÑANA & SIERRA DE ANDÚJAR, SPAIN P19
- EASTERN POLAND P28

Gaze upon the wild Atlantic Ocean from Cabo São Vicente, Portugal

GO ME

SNOW
- HEMSEDAL, NORWAY P14
- ST MORITZ, SWITZERLAND P22

LAND & WATER
- SOUTHWEST ALGARVE, PORTUGAL P29
- KANDERSTEG, SWITZERLAND P19

Carve up the pistes in St Moritz

9

EVENTS
IN JANUARY

UP HELLY AA
Lerwick, Shetland, Scotland
Guizers in Viking garb carry a ship through the streets before setting it aflame in this dramatic fire festival.

SCHEVENINGEN NEW YEAR'S DIVE
The Hague, Netherlands
Join 10,000 intrepid swimmers as they splash into the chilly North Sea on New Year's Day.

CABALGATA DE REYES MAGOS
Bilbao, Spain
The Kings' Parade celebrates the arrival of the Three Wise Men with an evening cavalcade of floats and fancy-dress.

KIRUNA SNOW FESTIVAL
Kiruna, Sweden
Brave the Arctic chill to admire ice sculptures as well as paintings, dog sledding and figure-skating.

INTERNATIONAL CIRCUS FESTIVAL
Acrobats, jugglers, clowns, horse-riders and more perform at this long-running carnival of circus arts.
Monte Carlo, Monaco

THE NORTHERN LIGHTS FESTIVALS
Ten days of top tunes – from opera to orchestras, chamber music to jazz, Norwegian to international – played out (with luck) under the dancing aurora.
Tromsø, Norway

BALL SEASON
Don tux or gown and prepare to waltz. The ZuckerBäcker (Confectioners') Ball in mid-January is among the more accessible.
Vienna, Austria

VOGEL GRYFF
A griffin, a wild man and a lion chase away winter in a traditional performance dating from the 16th century.
Basel, Switzerland

Inner ring (clockwise from top)
- 1 January — $
- 5 January — $
- 13, 20 or 27 January — $
- January and February — $$$
- Third Sunday in January — $
- 11 days from third Thursday in January — $$
- Five days in late January — $$
- Last Tuesday in January — $

VERY
FAMILY
FRIENDLY

- HEMSEDAL, NORWAY

- KANDERSTEG, SWITZERLAND

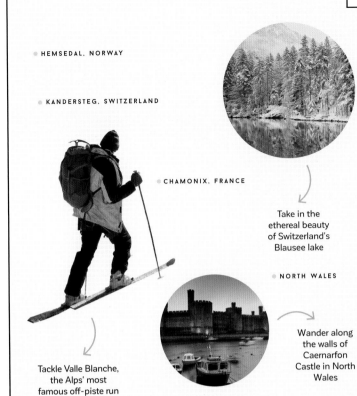

Get a bird's-eye view of Cappadocia's fairytale chimneys

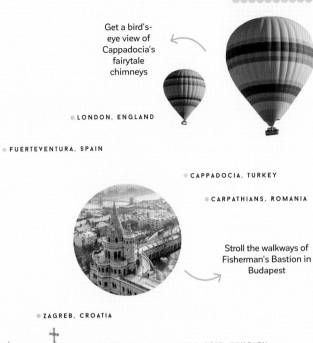

- LONDON, ENGLAND

- FUERTEVENTURA, SPAIN

- CAPPADOCIA, TURKEY

- CHAMONIX, FRANCE

- CARPATHIANS, ROMANIA

Take in the ethereal beauty of Switzerland's Blausee lake

Stroll the walkways of Fisherman's Bastion in Budapest

- NORTH WALES

Wander along the walls of Caernarfon Castle in North Wales

- ZAGREB, CROATIA

- BUDAPEST, HUNGARY

Explore pretty Santorini without the crowds

- SOUTHWEST ALGARVE, PORTUGAL

- SANTORINI, GREECE

Tackle Valle Blanche, the Alps' most famous off-piste run

- UMEA, SWEDEN

EXPENSIVE
BUT WORTH IT

GOOD
VALUE

- BILBAO, SPAIN

- RIGA, LATVIA

- CINQUETERRE, ITALY

Gabled houses along the serene waterways of Ghent

- EASTERN SICILY, ITALY

- BIALOWIEZA, POLAND

- VIENNA, AUSTRIA

- GRANADA, SPAIN

Warm yourself up with apple strudel in Vienna

- GHENT, BELGIUM

Lose yourself amid the Moorish wonders of the Alhambra

- TRANS-SIBERIAN RAILWAY, RUSSIA

- MONTE CARLO, MONACO

Try to spot the elusive Iberian lynx in Cordoba

Watch Russia roll by from the comfort of the Trans-Siberian Express

Rocket down the world's oldest bobsleigh track in St Mortiz

- DOÑANA, SPAIN

- ST MORITZ, SWITZERLAND

LEAVE
THE KIDS
AT HOME

12

CARPATHIANS
ROMANIA

Why now? Bag a bargain ice-bed.
Rocking up in Romania's Carpathians in winter is a little like walking into a Christmas card: this is a landscape of sparkling-white summits, snow-heavy forests, horse-drawn carts and crooked chimneys wafting woodsmoke above maze-like medieval towns. To add to the fairytale feel, as well as creepy castles, there's also a Hotel of Ice. Built afresh each December using frozen chunks cut from glacial Lake Balea, this seriously cool bolthole offers ice rooms and igloos strewn with blankets and animal furs; there's an ice bar that pours glasses of hot sparkling wine and a restaurant that serves local delicacies on frozen platters. Best of all, Romania's ice hotel is significantly cheaper than a night in its Scandinavian counterpart. During your stay, warm up with snowshoeing, ski-touring and tubing excursions, head out hiking with a guide to follow wolf tracks in the snow, or visit nearby Sibiu to see the old Saxon city's walls, towers, churches and cafés at their most romantic and tourist-free.

Trip plan: The nearest airports are Bucharest or Sibiu. Allow a week; spend two nights at the Hotel of Ice, adding on time in Sibiu and perhaps handsome Sighișoara.

Need to know: Wrap up warm – the mercury can drop to -20°C (-4°F) in the high mountains during midwinter.

Other months: Dec-Mar – Hotel of Ice open, snow activities; Apr-Jun – spring wildflowers; Jul-Aug – hottest, cooler in mountains; Sep-Nov – autumn colours.

A brown bear in the Carpathian Mountains

ZAGREB CROATIA

→ **Why now?** Enjoy tourist-free sites and city skiing.

Yes, it'll be chilly – barely above freezing – but pay a visit to Croatia in winter and you'll see how the locals actually live. Capital city Zagreb continues about its business – just with fewer tourists, cheaper prices and possibly a smattering of snow. The city mixes a relaxed Med vibe with northern European spunkiness: there's a good line in alternative music, bars and fringe fashion. For more conventional exhibitions, head for Mimara art museum, a neo-Renaissance manor packed with treasures, or MSU, Zagreb's huge Museum of Contemporary Art. Ivy-cloaked Mirogoj cemetery is especially atmospheric on a cold, frosty day. And there's skiing within a 20min drive of Zagreb: head to Mt Medvednica's Sljeme resort for a downhill dash, a hike or a fiery shot of Croatian rakia at the slope-top tavern.

Trip plan: Allow two or three days. Add a day trip to Plitvice, to see the lakes and cascades in full frozen splendour.

Need to know: Špica, the custom of donning glad-rags and lingering in cafés around the main square, is a Saturday morning ritual. To fit in, dress smartly.

Other months: Nov-Mar – cold, quietest; Apr-May – warm, uncrowded; Jun-Jul – hot; Aug – locals decamp to the coast; Sep-Oct – balmy.

FUERTEVENTURA CANARY ISLANDS

→ **Why now?** Ride the waves (or just relax) under winter sun.

The dramatic, volcanic and Martian-like landscapes of the second-largest Canary Isle are extremely appealing in winter. While much of the rest of Europe shivers under grey skies, here there are seven hours of sunshine a day and average highs of 21°C (70°F), making it one of the only spots on the continent where you can truly have a January beach break. And what beaches: the biggest and best in the Canaries are here – try 3km-long (2 mile) Playa del Matorral, offbeat and isolated Cofete and the endless dunes of protected Parque Natural de Corralejo. But Fuerteventura is also a good choice for wellness: maybe some alfresco yoga, t'ai chi, qigong or meditation in earshot of the ocean, breathing in lungfuls of negative-ion-charged sea breeze (which is conducive to better sleep).

Trip plan: Hire a car – there are some spectacular drives, such as the route between Betancuria and Pájara on the FV-30, via volcanic peaks and lava fields.

Need to know: Fuerteventura is a playground for surfers, and from November to February there are consistent 2–2.5m (6–8ft) swells. Wind and surf tend to be stronger on the west coast than the east.

Other months: Dec-Feb – mild, busy; Mar-Jun – lovely weather; Jul-Aug – hottest; Sep-Nov – still balmy, cooler evenings.

HEMSEDAL NORWAY

→ **Why now?** Find reliable snow on unmobbed pistes.

The Hallingdal mountains – aka the Scandinavian Alps – are less well known than their more southerly counterparts. But that's all the better for the skiers and snowboarders that seek them out. The 50-plus slopes around the resort of Hemsedal, which offer some of the best skiing in Norway, feel far less busy than Austria or France, but still offer a good variety of runs for all levels, from beginner-friendly to scary-black, as well as a range of off-piste possibilities. And at this more northerly latitude, the snow is super reliable, usually dumping in November and making good early-season skiing a cert. Days are shorter, but there's floodlighting on some slopes on darker afternoons. The quality ski school and selection of easier runs make it a good place for kids to learn; activities such as sledding, dog-mushing and horse-riding will add variety for youngsters, too. Bombing about by snowmobile (adults only) is a fun way to see more of the mountains.

Trip plan: Daily express buses run between Oslo and Hemsedal (via Oslo Airport) year-round. Trains run from Oslo and Bergen to Gol, from where you can pick up buses or taxis to Hemsedal.

Need to know: Hemsedal's Mountain Village offers accommodation right on the slopes. The resort town of Hemsedal itself, 2.5km (1.5 miles) below, has more options and slightly livelier nightlife.

Other months: Nov-May – skiing and winter sports; Jun-Oct – summer activities.

GRANADA SPAIN

→ **Why now? Learn the lingo without getting hot and bothered.**

Resolved to learn a new skill this New Year? Then head to Granada to study Spanish in a city that might well leave you briefly speechless. January, when the mercury here hovers around 10°C and the surrounding Sierra Nevada is capped in snow, offers a good temperature for concentration; also, the streets are likely to be filled with more Spanish voices, as opposed to tourists – good for full cultural immersion. Sign up at a language school for either group or one-to-one lessons, and consider staying in a local home so you can practise your new skills over the dinner table. You could also enroll for extra classes in cooking or flamenco while you're here to really tick-off some resolutions. Do allow time to explore outside the classroom. Granada was the last stronghold of the Moors and you can feel their influence everywhere, from the cosy teahouses and narrow lanes of the Arabic Albayzín quarter to the hilltop Alhambra, the city's breathtaking palace-fortress, which is at its quietest during the winter months.

Trip plan: Allow a week or two, and consider intensive learning – it's said that one week of one-to-one lessons can advance your skills as much as four weeks of group classes. Book sessions in the mornings to leave afternoons free for sightseeing.

Need to know: In winter it's possible to combine a city stay with skiing in the Sierra Nevada mountains, just 32km (20 miles) from central Granada.

Other months: Nov-Feb – mild; Mar-May & Oct – warm, pleasant; Jun-Sep – baking hot.

SICILY'S EAST COAST ITALY

→ **Why now? See the sights in peace, and ski an active volcano.**

A winter escape to the Mediterranean's largest island is unconventional, but might just work. While many coastal resorts close down (the average highs of around 16°C/61°F are a little cold for swimming), the towns and cities are still functioning, and the ancient sites are crowd-free and more comfortable to explore. Prices tend to be lower too. Amble the Greek and Roman ruins of Unesco-listed Syracuse, once a colossal city of the ancient world. Feel the undiminished energy of gloriously gritty Catania, Sicily's second-biggest city. And take a peek at the sublime seaside resort of Taormina – annoyingly shut-up or blissfully free of summer hordes, depending on your perspective. Taormina's impressive Teatro Greco, with even more impressive sea views, is open year-round. For bragging rights, add a trip up the 3326m (10,913ft) snow-smothered slopes of Mt Etna, where the resorts of Piano Provenzana and Nicolosi offer cheap skiing – though they might have to shut suddenly if the volcano starts to erupt...

Trip plan: Several airlines fly into Catania. Alternatively, take a ferry from mainland Italy over to Messina. Hiring a car is the easiest way to explore.

Need to know: Look out for seasonal produce, including sea urchins and artichoke-like carduna.

Other months: Nov-Mar – cool, some coastal resorts closed; Apr-Jun – good weather, reasonable prices; Jul-Aug – hot, busy; Sep-Oct – mild, good value.

MONTE CARLO MONACO

→ **Why now? Get a sneak peek of rally fever.**

The world's second-smallest country might be better known for the Grand Prix that roars around its avenues each May. But in off-season January (expect a chilly-but-mild average of around 11°C/52°F), a much older auto event comes to town. The Rallye Automobile Monte-Carlo, running since 1911, sees cars from across the continent race 1400km (870 miles) around the principality and surrounding countryside, including treacherous sections on the snow-cloaked Hautes-Alps. It ends with fanfare in Monte Carlo itself in late January. Even for non-petrolheads, Monaco is a good option for adding some much needed glamour to an often dour month. Hotel prices will be a fraction lower, leaving more to spend/lose at the famed Casino. Also worth a visit are the clifftop old town of Le Rocher (home to the royal palace), the fishy spectacle of the Musée Océanographique and, for a cheering bloom of winter colour, the bright Jardin Exotique.

Trip plan: Hotels can be expensive even in winter, so consider staying in nearby Nice. A day or two is enough for Monte Carlo's sites; add time to explore further along the Riviera by train.

Need to know: Don't miss the Marché de la Condamine, the covered market (heated in winter), where Provençal delights are sold every day throughout the year.

Other months: Nov-Feb – mild, off-season; Mar-Apr & Sep-Oct – lovely weather; May – Grand Prix buzz; Jun-Aug – hot, crowded.

Vienna's Karlskirche,
iced by a blanket
of snow

VIENNA AUSTRIA

Why now? Whirl through wintry streets during ball season.

The Austrian capital bewitches at any time of year, its melange of Baroque and Art Nouveau architecture, imperial grandeur and classic café culture endlessly appealing. But to see the city resplendent in its very finest finery, visit during ball season – which peaks January into February – when some 450-plus balls entertain tux- and gown-clad socialites waltzing the night away. And though events sport names such as the Doctors' Ball and the Jägerball (Hunters' Ball), many are open to everyone: simply buy a ticket, dress up for the occasion and prepare to be dazzled by the atmosphere and music. Of course, the city doesn't just wake at night. It continues to bustle under a chilly cloak of snow each day, with much to explore: don't miss the imperial Hofburg palace, the Kunsthistorisches (Art History) Museum or the bling Baroque palaces of Schloss Schönbrunn and the Belvedere. With warming coffee and excellent cake beckoning from atmospheric cafés on every corner, and hip bars and restaurants lining streets around the city, Vienna is a culinary delight, too.

Trip plan: Allow three or four days. Ball tickets can sell out months in advance – book early.

Need to know: Strict dress codes apply at most balls: tuxedo or dinner jacket for men, gowns for women. These can be hired at various stores in the city.

Other months: Nov-Mar – cold, ball season; Apr-May – mild, less crowded; Jun-Aug – hottest, busiest, festivals; Sep-Oct – quieter, warm.

Balloons fly high over Cappadocia's winter wonderland

© Ayhan Altun / Getty Images

CAPPADOCIA TURKEY

Why now? Find fairy chimneys sprinkled with snow.

Mother Nature must have been in a whimsical mood when she sculpted the Central Anatolian region of Cappadocia. Here, the soft tuff rock has been carved into a fantastical confection of ravines, tablelands and turrets. And it all looks extra pretty under a sprinkle of Turkish snow – somehow a dusting of the white stuff adds an extra dimension to the landscape's natural formations and the ancient houses and churches that have been cut out of the rock. As it's off-season, room rates drop and crowds are low in January, making for cheaper and more comfortable exploring around sites such as the monastery at Keşlik, the labyrinthine underground city of Kaymaklı and the fresco-slathered cave churches of the Göreme Open-Air Museum. And because so many of the sites are subterranean or rock-hewn, it's easy to escape bad weather – though on crisp days, wintry walks down the Ihlara Valley beckon, thawing out afterwards in a steamy hamam or around a hot stove with a bowl of rich lentil soup. Retreat each night to the womb-like comfort of one of Cappadocia's boutique cave hotels.

Trip plan: Two airports serve Cappadocia: Kayseri (75km/46.6 miles from Göreme) and Nevşehir (40km/25 miles). Both are a 2hr flight from Istanbul.

Need to know: Flights aboard hot air balloons are massively popular in Cappadocia. They operate year-round, though cancellations are more likely in winter – stay longer to increase your chances of a successful takeoff.

Other months: Nov-Mar – cold, snow possible; Apr-Jun & Sep-Oct – warm, sunny; Jul-Aug – very hot.

(A) Blausee lake near Kandersteg; (L) Budapest's Gellért baths; (R) Flamingos at the National Park of Doñana, Andalucia

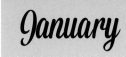

KANDERSTEG
SWITZERLAND

Why now? Take a fairytale trip back in time.

Chocolate-box Kandersteg, a small cluster of wooden chalets resting in the Bernese Oberland's Kander Valley, is like the Switzerland of yesteryear – and never more so than in January, when the little village briefly turns the clock back a century. Towards the end of the month, Belle Époque Week takes over: gentlemen don top hats and vintage tailoring, ladies swish through the snow in long skirts and horse-drawn carriages glide by. The ice rink hosts retro-dressed skaters and old-fashioned curling matches, and there are bob races in historic sleds, nostalgic games and music, plus a formal Belle Époque Ball. Even outside the festival, wintry Kandersteg remains magical. More than 50km (30 miles) of trails make it heaven for cross-country skiing (lessons are available). Snowshoeing, curling, tobogganing, ice-fishing and ice-climbing are all possible too. For the biggest thrill, ride the gondola ride up to the Oeschinensee, a dazzling lake set within a bowl of mighty mountains, where you can walk across the ice. Warm up afterwards in one of Kandersteg's fine family-run hotels – pick one with a sauna, heated pool and bar serving mulled wine.

Trip plan: Allow a week to try a range of activities, as well as time for relaxing in the winter sunshine.

Need to know: The closest airport is Zürich. The train to Kandersteg takes 1hr 30min, with a change in Bern. The Geneva–Kandersteg train takes just over 3hr.

Other months: Dec-Apr – winter, snow sports; May & Nov – shoulder months; Jun-Oct – warm, excellent hiking.

BUDAPEST
HUNGARY

Why now? Work up a sweat in the city of thermal baths.

Hungary's elegant capital won't leave you with cold feet, even in January. The land on which it's built is peppered with more than 120 hot springs, many of which are open to the public as thermal baths – from the Turkish-style Rudas Baths to the art nouveau gem at the Gellért and vast Széchenyi, where those iconic pictures of elderly chess-playing men chest-deep in steaming water were shot. Perfect for winter warming. The city itself is glorious at any time, the medieval marvels of Buda's Castle Hill contrasting with the Secessionist glory of Pest. And with buzzing nightlife ranging from grunge-chic ruin bars to a performance at the magnificent neo-Renaissance State Opera House, there's plenty to keep you entertained through the long, dark evenings.

Trip plan: The main decision to make is whether to stay on the west bank of the Danube in Buda, dominated by the medieval sights of Castle Hill, or in Art Nouveau Pest on the opposite bank. Exploring's easy on the comprehensive metro, train and tram network.

Need to know: Not all baths open every day, and a few are men- or women-only on some days – check details in advance. You're usually allowed to stay for 2hr on weekdays, 90min on weekends.

Other months: Nov-Feb – cold to chilly, snow possible; Mar-Jun – warming, blooming, spring festivals; Jul-Aug – hottest; Sep-Oct – pleasant.

DOÑANA
AND SIERRA DE
ANDÚJAR SPAIN

Why now? Go wild and mild.

It's not just humans who like the cool of the Andalucían winter. The wildlife is keen too, which means that in southern Spain in January, you can combine pleasant climes (16–18°C/61–64°F) with super sightings. The Sierra de Andújar Natural Park, part of the Sierra Morena range, is virtually the last redoubt of the endangered Iberian lynx (only around 200 individuals remain). January is a good time to try and see them as the lynx are active during the cool daytime, searching for mates; when it's warmer they become more nocturnal. But it's not just lynx: this forested, rocky park also harbours species such as wolves, black vultures, golden eagles, wild boar, deer and mouflon (wild sheep). A little south, lynx might also be seen amid the flat grasslands and pine forests of Coto Doñana National Park, which promises excellent birding as well as big-cat tracking. Doñana's *marismas* (marshes) tend to dry out as the temperature climbs, but in winter they hold plenty of water, attracting large numbers of flamingos, herons, storks, ibis and other charismatic species.

Trip plan: Spend a few nights in Seville, then hire a car: Doñana is a 1hr drive west, Andújar 3hr east.

Need to know: The most atmospheric base near Doñana is the village of El Rocío, where the vibe is more 'Wild West' than southern Spain: its sandy streets are lined with white houses, and horses are still the primary form of transport.

Other months: Nov-Mar – wet and cool; Apr-May & Sept-Oct – warm, peak time; Jun-Aug – hot, dry.

Twr Bach Lighthouse, Anglesey

NORTH WALES

➜ **Why now? Drive by quiet castles and romantic isles.**

Welsh weather can be unpredictable at any time, so best to just get on with enjoying the sites, skies be damned. Explore by car and you're protected from the elements, making a road trip along the North Coast Way a good choice. Running for 120km (74 miles) from the border town of Mold to the island of Anglesey, it passes bracing sea coast, big beaches, bucolic Clwydian hills and medieval castles, with the mountains of Snowdonia – likely covered in namesake snow – visible to the south. Stop at the half-timbered town of Ruthin, the revitalised prom at Colwyn Bay, Victorian Llandudno's MOSTYN contemporary art gallery and the mighty castles of Conwy and Caernarfon. Cross the Menai Strait via the 19th-century suspension bridge to reach Anglesey – home to Beaumaris

castle, good surf (best in winter) and the wild South Stack cliffs. Finish on Llanddwyn Island (actually a peninsula) at the ruins of St Dwynwen's Church. Patron saint of lovers, and Wales's answer to St Valentine, St Dwynwen is said to be buried here, and is celebrated on 25 January.

Trip plan: Allow four to six days for the drive. Cadw membership affords free entry to selected historic sites, including many castles.

Need to know: Consider combining this with another driving route. The Cambrian Way intersects with the North Wales Way in Llandudno and runs south to Cardiff; the Coastal Way runs from the Llŷn Peninsula (south of Anglesey) to Pembrokeshire.

Other months: Nov-Feb – coldest, bracing; Mar-May – daffodils, wildlife; Jun-Aug – warmest, busiest; Sep-Oct – pleasant.

© Ian Brown / Alamy Stock Photo

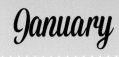
Oia's picture-
perfect coastline in
Santorini

SANTORINI
GREECE

→ **Why now? Sidestep the crowds and save some cash.**

Santorini is a victim of its own gorgeousness. This idyllic confection of whitewashed houses tumbling down the sides of the sea-sunken caldera has graced a gazillion postcards – and, come summer, drowns in tourists. But winter, particularly January and February, are a different story. Fewer ferries arrive, no cruise ships come, occupancy is at about 10%. There's a real chance it might be just you and the locals sharing the world's best sunsets. Of course the weather's not much good for the beach (January average maximums are around 14°C/57°F) but the chance to stroll freely without the throng is a delight. Much remains open in the towns of Oia and especially Fira, with local life bumbling along, so these make the best bases; being located on the caldera edge, they also have the most dramatic views. While many hotels do close for winter, increasing numbers are staying open, often offering significant reductions on astronomical summer rates.

Trip plan: Ferries and high-speed catamarans link Santorini with Athens' main port of Piraeus year-round, taking around 8hr; there's usually only one service a day in winter. Few international flights land at Santorini in January, but there are flights to Athens year-round.

Need to know: In winter it's best to stick to Santorini – ferries are too infrequent for easy island-hopping.

Other months: Nov-Mar – cool, sleepy; Apr & Oct – mild, quieter; May-Jun & Sep – hot, busy; Jul-Aug – very hot, very busy.

ST MORITZ
SWITZERLAND

→ **Why now? Mix glamorous skiing and a scary sled-track.**

To discover skiing at its very best, come to where it all began. The ski holiday was born in St Moritz, in eastern Switzerland's Engadine Valley, a little over 150 years ago – and it's still one of the world's best spots for winter sports, with 350km (217 miles) of slopes to tackle across four main areas: Corviglia, Corvatsch (with great glacier descents), Diavolezza/Lagalb and Zuoz. Cheap, it isn't – this chichi resort is a magnet for the wealthy and want-to-be-seens. But in January, there's really nowhere better to barrel down a black run. Some 160km (100 miles) of groomed trails take cross-country skiers into the spectacular surrounding woodlands, and you can soak those weary muscles in a thermal spa bath too. St Moritz also offers a near-unique opportunity to really test your mettle: the infamous Cresta Run ice toboggan track, on which the pros can reach speeds of 129kph/80mph over its total length of 1.2km (0.7 miles). First built in 1884, the Cresta part-opens from late December, with riding from the very top starting in mid-January; it closes in March. With nerves of steel, even novices can lie on a skeleton bob and hurtle down its terrifying bends.

Trip plan: The closest international airport is Zürich, a 4hr train ride away.

Need to know: Beginner slots on the Cresta Run are limited – book well ahead. Over 18s only; women by invitation only.

Other months: Dec-Apr – winter ski season; May & Nov – shoulder months; Jun-Oct – summer activities, hiking, biking.

A sled hurtles down the bobsleigh run at St Moritz

Rīga and its Art Nouveau buildings dazzle under a dusting of snow

RIGA LATVIA

→ **Why now? See the prettiest cityscape without the crowds.**

Whether you find it blue-sky crisp or grey and storm-broody, Rīga in winter delivers, despite the chill. Though days are short, long nights are fun: the city has the liveliest after-dark scene in the Baltics, with cosy cafés and underground bars aplenty serving strong shots of local tipple Black Balsam. The artsy Miera iela neighbourhood is the hippest place to head, but with its cobblestones and spires, the medieval Old Town looks especially lovely when frosty: the best rooftop lookout is the tower of St Peter's Church. Rīga's New Town provides a smart contrast. Wander its wide boulevards and visit the Art Nouveau Museum for insight into the district's turn-of-the-century facades. The Central Market, housed in former Zeppelin hangars, is the place to refuel with everything from traditional doughnuts to steamy ramen. If there's a decent amount of snow, head across the Daugava River to Victory Park for cross-country skiing in sight of the city; or take a train to Sigulda (1hr 15min) for longer trails amid pine forests and old castles.

Trip plan: Allow two days for a city break, four to head into the countryside.

Need to know: Trains connect to cities such as Moscow (16hr) and Minsk (11hr); cheap buses run to Tallinn and to Vilnius (both 4hr). Ferries sail over the Baltic to Stockholm (18hr).

Other months: Nov-Mar – cold but quiet; Apr-Jun – festivals, pleasantly warm; Jul-Aug – heaving; Sep-Oct – mild to cool.

UMEÅ SWEDEN

→ **Why now? Seek Sami insight and Scandi chic.**

Umeå might be perched on the Bothnian Coast, only 400km (248 miles) south of the Arctic Circle, but it's no frozen-in-time backwater. This is Sweden's fastest-growing city, with a huge student population, a strong cultural bent and a growing foodie reputation – expect a constantly changing menu of places to eat, running from cheap noodle bars to classy joints doing fancy things with reindeer. In short, it's a living, breathing hub that doesn't shut down when the snow falls, and which offers a mix of Scandi urban cool, Sami history and easy access to winter wilderness. In the city, visit the Väven cultural centre (home to Sweden's first Museum of Women's History) and the Västerbottens Museum, which traces the region's development since prehistoric times. Spend time café-hopping around Storgatan and browsing Umeå's trendy shops. Then quit the 'city of the silver birches' for the countryside: options include ice-fishing, snowmobiling, skiing, husky-sledding and a night watching the skies glow from an Aurora Teepee. Lake Nydalasjön is popular with Northern Lights hunters; there's also a 10km (6 mile) illuminated trail around the lake.

Trip plan: Umeå Airport is served by daily flights from Stockholm. Allow a couple of city days before heading out to the snow.

Need to know: Musos shouldn't miss Guitars – the Museum, Europe's greatest collection of vintage guitars.

Other months: Nov-Mar – cold, snow activities; Apr & Oct – shoulder months, cool; May-Sep – warmest, lightest (midsummer celebrations Jun).

CHAMONIX
FRANCE

🐘 🥾 ☆

→ **Why now? Gallivant about on a great glacier.**

Chamonix is a veritable winter playground – even non-skiers will find fun aplenty around this spirited hub-town of the Mont Blanc massif. January is a good pick: the snow has reliably dumped and seasonal facilities (cable cars, museums) have reopened, but there are generally fewer tourists than in February or March. The downhill skiing is super. But those that don't fancy the slopes can try something else: there are opportunities to cross-country ski, husky-sled, fat-bike, ice-skate, toboggan, take biathlon lessons or shop for all your outdoor kit. The vertiginous cable car up the 3842m (12605ft) Aiguille du Midi is in full operation too, allowing big views of Mont Blanc at its most sparkling. Or ride the historic cog railway to Montenvers – especially scenic in winter – to stay at the alpine-chic refuge and gaze at the Mer de Glace, France's largest glacier. Learn about glaciers in the Ice Cave and hit the snowshoe trails that riddle the surrounding forests. Ice climbing, for beginners and pros, is possible too.

Trip plan: Chamonix is about 1hr 15min by road from Geneva airport; private shuttle buses offer transfers. The valley is well served by buses and trains.

Need to know: Mont Blanc Unlimited passes cover access to ten ski areas (including slopes in Italy and Switzerland) as well as benefits like entry to the pool, skating rink, museums and wellness centre.

Other months: Dec-Apr – good snow, busy; May & Nov – shoulder months, quiet; Jun-Oct – warm, summer sports.

(L) Off-piste skiers, Vallée Blanche;
(R) Mont Blanc peaks

CINQUE TERRE
ITALY

→ **Why now?** Live like a local, admire an enormous nativity.

We challenge anyone to find a more knock-your-socks-off set of villages, anywhere in the world, than the Cinque Terre. The five medieval cliff-clinging fishing hamlets of Monterosso al Mare, Vernazza, Manarola, Corniglia and Riomaggiore teeter on the Ligurian Riviera, tumbling to the water's edge with pastel-hued picturesqueness. Trouble is, they're tiny and terribly popular – in summer, the villages, and the 120km (74 miles) of hiking trails that wriggle between them, are heaving. Visit in winter, however, and you'll get a taste of what this coast was like before everyone found it. True, much shuts down. But the hotels that are still open will be cheaper, and there is always at least one bar and restaurant serving in each village, filled with locals. Inclement weather can close trails, but on average there are only eight rainy days a month in winter (compared to five in summer) so odds are still in your favour. Relish the moody skies, dramatic waves and empty lanes.

Trip plan: Book accommodation in which you can self-cater with goodies from local markets rather than relying on restaurants. Don't stay in Corniglia – as the least-visited village, fewer facilities remain open in the off-season.

Need to know: From early December to the end of January, Manarola's hillside hosts the world's largest *presepe* (nativity scene), a masterwork of 300 characters made from recycled materials, lit up by 15,000 solar-powered lights. Quite a sight.

Other months: Nov-Mar – cool, path closures more likely; Apr-May & Oct – warm, less crowded; Jun-Sep – increasingly hot, increasingly heaving.

Manarola hunkers down under winter skies

© Justin Folkes / Lonely Planet

Sample some Basque Country pintxos

BILBAO SPAIN

→ **Why now? Take a spirited city break.**
Bilbao can be cool and rainy in winter – maxing at around 12°C/54°F – but that doesn't dampen its spirits. The formerly down-at-heel Basque capital is one of the continent's greatest regeneration stories – so much so that the 'Bilbao effect' is now a recognised term. These days, the city's combination of grit, graft, glamour and gastronomy makes it shine even if skies are grey. Plus, the lively Cabalgata de Reyes Magos parade (5 January) of floats and fancy-dressed performers keeps the mood festive, while lower accommodation rates leave more spending money for pintxos, Basque finger-food. Excellent indoor entertainment includes Frank Gehry's ground-breaking Guggenheim Museum and the Museo de Bellas Artes – less showy, but with a more varied collection of art. Azkuna Zentroa, an old wine warehouse transformed into an exhibition space by Philippe Starck, hosts all sorts, and its cool rooftop pool is open year-round. Most fun is ambling the Old Town, from the cafés and produce stalls of the Art Deco Mercado de la Ribera to the medieval Siete Calles (Seven Streets) – there's hours of browsing to be done along these narrow lanes. Nearby Plaza Neuva has the biggest pick of pintxos bars.

Trip plan: Bilbao is a great gateway to the Basque region. From here, catch a bus to foodie San Sebastián (1hr 20min) or historic Guernica (45min).

Need to know: For bracing sea air, ride the metro to the coastal suburb of Getxo, with its tiny old fishing village, beach and promenade of grand fin de siècle mansions.

Other months: Dec-Mar – mild, damp; Apr-May – warm; Jun-Sep – hottest, driest, busiest; Oct-Nov – cooler, rainy.

Wolf in the wild,
eastern Poland

EASTERN POLAND

→ **Why now? Track wolves and lynx through epic wintry wilderness.**

Here be giants: wisent, or European bison, are the continent's largest land mammal, standing up to 1.8m (6ft) high and weighing in at nearly a tonne. The stronghold of the bison is Białowieża National Park, a sprawling reserve that's part of the primeval Białowieża Forest spanning the borders of Poland and Belarus. Wisent were reintroduced here in 1929 after becoming extinct in Europe in 1919; more than 500 now live free in the Polish part of the forest. Midwinter is the time for a thrilling expedition tracking bison, wolf and elk (moose) footprints through the snow, and watching for boar, lynx and pine martens. If you don't catch a glimpse of wild bison, be awed by captive-bred beasts at the show reserve. Nearby Biebrza National Park is another winter wonderland, a marshy valley where the big draw is elk – head out to track one of the reserve's 600 resident moose, and you might also enjoy encounters with otters, boars or wolves. Days end in log cabins with hot and hearty bowls of *bigos* (stew).

Trip plan: Fly to Warsaw before heading east to Białowieża and Biebrza national parks – allow at least four days for the trip to Białowieża alone, a week to include both parks.

Need to know: Temperatures average about -5°C (23°F) in January, and may drop much lower – pack warm clothes.

Other months: Dec-Feb – good for tracking; Mar-Jun – spring budding; Jul-Aug – warm, dense foliage, hard to see animals; Sep-Nov – autumn colours, deer rutting.

LONDON
ENGLAND

→ **Why now? Soak up Dickensian atmosphere and Scrooge-worthy prices.**

Like New York, London never sleeps: there are always millions of people, hundreds of happenings. But if there is a slightly drowsier time, January is it. This is the least hectic month, and with that comes some of the lowest hotel rates, airfares and ticket prices – the annual Get Into London Theatre promotion, which offers discounts on West End shows, runs 1 January to mid-February. January is also prone to being damp and dismal, which sounds unappealing but can add a dash of the Dickensian – a chance to taste the much-romanticised London of yore. Join a nighttime Jack the Ripper walk to hear gruesome tales amid the streets of Whitechapel and Spitalfields, and follow the Darkest Victorian London tour, which recreates a time of prostitutes and pickpockets, wending via a 19th-century prison and a paupers' burial ground. You might also visit authentically 18th-century Dennis Severs' House; the thrice-weekly Silent Night slots, when the house flickers by candlelight, are most atmospheric on winter evenings.

Trip plan: Foreign visitors can buy a Visitor Oyster card before arrival. These are the cheapest ways to pay for bus, Tube, DLR, tram and river-bus journeys; they also offer discounts on some attractions.

Need to know: Seek out a pub where Dickens drank. Many make the claim, but Fleet Street's maze-like Ye Olde Cheshire Cheese still feels like he only just left.

Other months: Jan-Feb – cold, rainy; Mar-Apr & Oct-Nov – mild, shoulder season; May-Sep – hottest, most crowded; Dec – pre-Christmas busy.

Sizing up the swell in the southern Algarve

© Westend61 / Getty Images

SOUTHWEST ALGARVE PORTUGAL

→ **Why now? Ride wide waves on mild seas.**

Portugal's southwestern tip is swell in winter. The coastline at the corner of the Iberian Peninsula has a wide swell window, and can pick up wave surges from almost any direction; in winter, that's often big nor'westers, which slap Cabo de São Vicente and Sagres, and wrap right into the coves beyond. This means impressively gnarly waves for experienced riders – fun to watch even if you don't want to get into the water. And there's always a protected bay somewhere that will be suitable for beginners; local surf schools operate year-round. While it's hardly bikini weather, it's pleasant for winter: the air averages 13°C, the water no less than 14°C, so you won't need more than a 4/3 wetsuit. It's also relatively tourist-free – this bit of the Algarve has more of a friendly, laid-back local vibe, especially in the off-season. Head for a chilled-out surfer town like Sagres, where you'll find cheap cafés and an outdoorsy vibe.

Trip plan: Sagres is around 120km (74 miles) west of Faro airport. It's easiest to get there by car; or you can take the train from Faro to Lagos, then a bus to Sagres.

Need to know: Beware of ocean currents. Check beaches' flags: chequered means it's unsupervised, red means it's unsafe, yellow means paddle but don't swim, and green means swimming is safe. Blue means the beach is safe and clean.

Other months: Oct-Mar – mild climes, big waves; Apr-Sept – warm to hot (heat and crowds peaking Jul-Aug).

TRANS-SIBERIAN RAILWAY RUSSIA

Why now: See Siberia at its most Siberian – from a heated railway carriage.

Sure, it's cold outside – expect the mercury to dip to at least -25°C (-13°F) in some places – but isn't that the point? You don't travel to Siberia for sun and sand: this is the land of endless fir forests and grasslands, both of which look far better under a forgiving blanket of snow. Usually, when folks talk about the Trans-Siberian, they mean the Trans-Mongolian, which loops south from Irkutsk through the Mongolian capital Ulaanbaatar before reaching Beijing, providing glimpses of nomads' yurts on the grassy steppes and of the stark Gobi Desert – so long Europe! But whichever route you choose, you'll spend most time crossing Siberia, stopping at Perm, Yekaterinburg and Irkutsk on the shores of Baikal – the world's deepest freshwater lake, glitteringly frozen in January. Bring a good book and a ready smile for the strangers with whom you'll share carriages (and vodka).

Trip plan: Choose between the seven-night Moscow–Vladivostok Trans-Siberian Railway, the six-night Trans-Mongolian to Beijing via Ulaanbaatar, or the six-night Trans-Manchurian to Beijing via Harbin.

Need to know: As well as the clean, comfortable public trains, several luxurious, pricey private services run the route – for example, the Golden Eagle.

Other months: Nov-Mar – freezing; Apr-May – thaw, flowers; Jun-Aug – long days, good for window-gazing; Sep-Oct – fewer people, milder climes.

Luxury awaits aboard the Trans-Siberian Express

© Vostok / Getty Images

GHENT BELGIUM

→ **Why now? Resolve to go meat-free in this veggie-friendly city.**

It's that time when thoughts turn to New Year's resolutions. And if going meat-free is one of your vows, it's a good time to get thee to Ghent. This fine Flemish city purports to be one of Europe's most veggie friendly, with proportionally more meat-free restaurants than London or Paris. It was also first to adopt Donderdag Veggiedag – Thursday Veggie Day – when every restaurant in the city offers vegetarian dishes, or goes fully veggie, for 24 hours. Fill up at a budget spot like Lekker GEC, a pay-by-weight vegan buffet, or opt for the pure-veg tasting menu at fancy, Michelin-starred Vrijmoed.

This is all good fuel for exploring Ghent's river port, which wears its considerable medieval charm well – it still feels like a real city rather than a tourist fairytale. If the weather is brisk, shelter inside St Bavo's Cathedral (to admire the van Eyck brothers' *Adoration of the Mystic Lamb* altarpiece), the edgy SMAK museum of contemporary art and the spooky 12th-century Gravensteen (Castle of the Counts).

Trip plan: Take a wintry flit through more of Flanders, using trains to reach Bruges' warming beer and chocolate, and the fashion boutiques of arty Antwerp.

Need to know: If you fancy a non-veggie feed, try *waterzooi*, a Flemish seafood soup traditionally made with pike, carp or bass and thickened with eggs and cream.

Other months: Nov-Mar – cold, cheaper; Apr-May – warming; Jun-Aug – warmest, busiest, events; Sep-Oct – quieter, warm.

The Korenlai cuts a watery swathe through the riverside walk of Ghent

© Arterra Picture Library / Alamy Stock Photo

BEYOND GHENT

DEURLE · 14KM (7 MILES) · Upmarket village with galleries and restaurants dotted along shady lanes

BRUGES · 50KM (30 MILES) Fairytale medieval town with cobblestones, canals and market squares

BRUSSELS · 57KM (35 MILES) · A cosmopolitan metropolis with excellent museums, architecture and gastronomy

ANTWERP · 60KM (37 MILES) · Belgium's biggest port and capital of cool

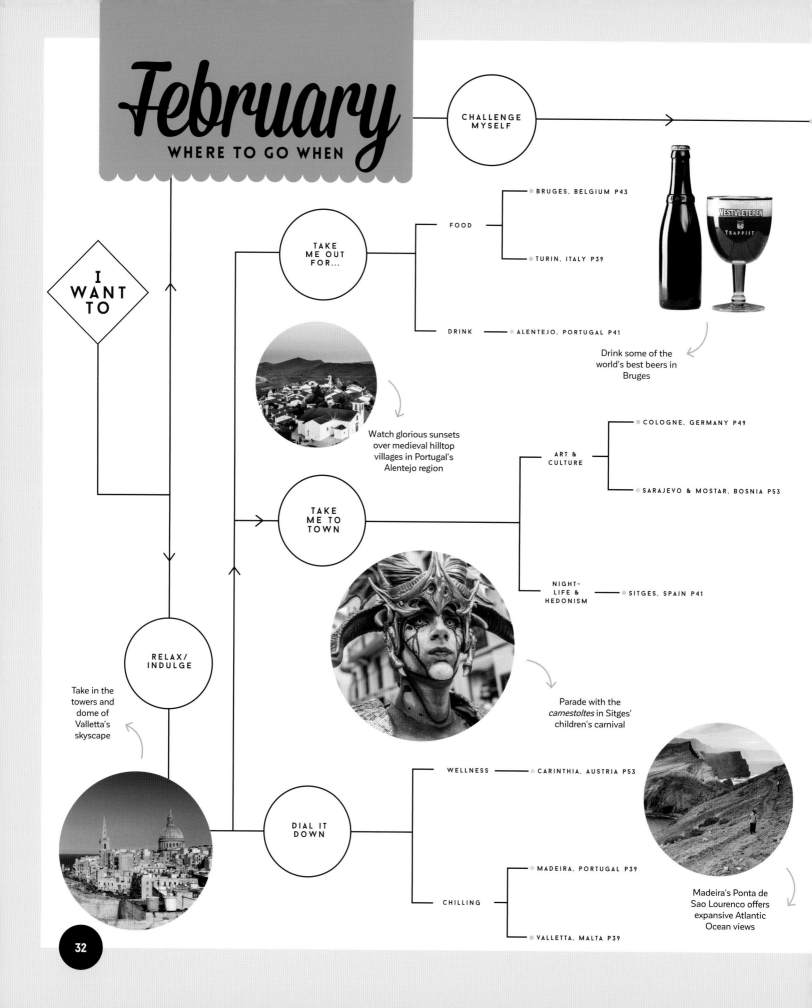

February
WHERE TO GO WHEN

I WANT TO

CHALLENGE MYSELF

TAKE ME OUT FOR...

FOOD
- BRUGES, BELGIUM P43
- TURIN, ITALY P39

DRINK
- ALENTEJO, PORTUGAL P41

Drink some of the world's best beers in Bruges

Watch glorious sunsets over medieval hilltop villages in Portugal's Alentejo region

TAKE ME TO TOWN

ART & CULTURE
- COLOGNE, GERMANY P49
- SARAJEVO & MOSTAR, BOSNIA P53

NIGHT-LIFE & HEDONISM
- SITGES, SPAIN P41

Parade with the *carnestoltes* in Sitges' children's carnival

RELAX/INDULGE

Take in the towers and dome of Valletta's skyscape

DIAL IT DOWN

WELLNESS
- CARINTHIA, AUSTRIA P53

CHILLING
- MADEIRA, PORTUGAL P39
- VALLETTA, MALTA P39

Madeira's Ponta de Sao Lourenco offers expansive Atlantic Ocean views

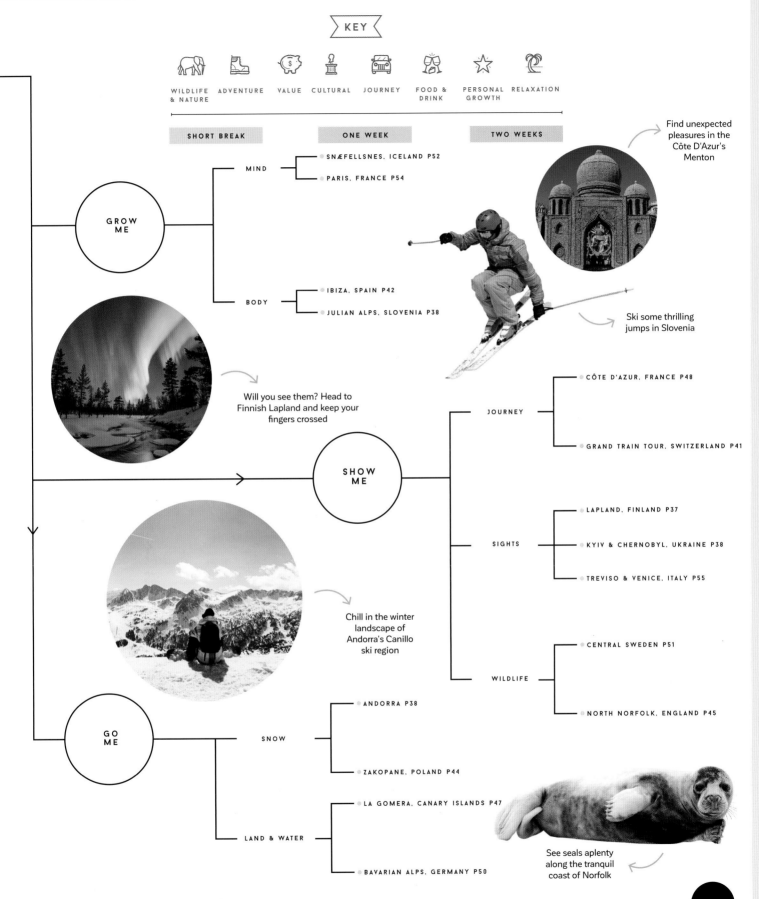

KEY

| WILDLIFE & NATURE | ADVENTURE | VALUE | CULTURAL | JOURNEY | FOOD & DRINK | PERSONAL GROWTH | RELAXATION |

SHORT BREAK **ONE WEEK** **TWO WEEKS**

GROW ME

MIND
- SNÆFELLSNES, ICELAND P52
- PARIS, FRANCE P54

BODY
- IBIZA, SPAIN P42
- JULIAN ALPS, SLOVENIA P38

Find unexpected pleasures in the Côte D'Azur's Menton

Ski some thrilling jumps in Slovenia

Will you see them? Head to Finnish Lapland and keep your fingers crossed

SHOW ME

JOURNEY
- CÔTE D'AZUR, FRANCE P48
- GRAND TRAIN TOUR, SWITZERLAND P41

SIGHTS
- LAPLAND, FINLAND P37
- KYIV & CHERNOBYL, UKRAINE P38
- TREVISO & VENICE, ITALY P55

WILDLIFE
- CENTRAL SWEDEN P51
- NORTH NORFOLK, ENGLAND P45

Chill in the winter landscape of Andorra's Canillo ski region

GO ME

SNOW
- ANDORRA P38
- ZAKOPANE, POLAND P44

LAND & WATER
- LA GOMERA, CANARY ISLANDS P47
- BAVARIAN ALPS, GERMANY P50

See seals aplenty along the tranquil coast of Norfolk

EVENTS
IN FEBRUARY

FESTIVAL DE JEREZ

Spain
Visit Jerez to immerse yourself in flamenco-focused festivities at this music and dance event spanning two weeks.

BRUGES BEER FESTIVAL

Bruges, Belgium
Sample more than 350 top-notch tipples from 80-plus breweries in the home of super-strength beer.

VINTERJAZZ

Various venues, Denmark
Nod and jive to top jazz musicians playing more than 600 concerts in venues across the country.

MASLENITSA

Moscow, Russia
Binge on blinis (pancakes) and the carnival atmosphere at Russia's colourful pagan-throwback coming-of-spring festival.

ST VALENTINE'S DAY

Terni, Italy
Celebrate the most romantic saint with performances, poetry, painting, street art and more in his Umbrian birthplace and resting place.

BERLINALE

Berlin, Germany
Check out the hottest forthcoming movies in the German capital at one of Europe's oldest and most prestigious film festivals.

LEMON FESTIVAL

Menton, France
Some 140 tonnes of the versatile citrus adorn sculptures, floats and gardens during this two-week fruit-fest on the Côte d'Azur.

CARNIVAL

Venice, Italy
Pre-Lent festivities throng Europe, notably in Nice, Binche (Belgium), Cologne and Sitges – but Venice's masques are arguably most photogenic.

Inner ring labels:
- End of February
- Start of February
- Three weeks from first Friday in February
- 14 February
- From mid-February
- To Shrove Tuesday (usually late February)
- 10 days in late February
- Week before Shrove Tuesday

Price markers: $$, $, $$, $$, $, $, $, $$

See migrating geese and more in the bird reserves of Norfolk

LAPLAND, FINLAND

The dancing lights of the Aurora Borealis

COLOGNE, GERMANY

NORFOLK, ENGLAND

CARINTHIA, AUSTRIA

BAVARIA, GERMANY

Admire the turrets of Bavaria's Neuschwanstein Castle

When in Turin, *bicerin*! It's a mix of espresso, drinking chocolate and milk

TURIN, ITALY

The pretty wooden Jaszczurowka Chapel in Zakopane

JULIAN ALPS, SLOVENIA

ZAKOPANE, POLAND

Scale Valletta's Basilica of our Lady of Mount Carmel for far-reaching views

ANDORRA

Take in Andorra's dramatic peaks

VALLETTA, MALTA

Enjoy the mild microclimate of Nice in winter

CÔTE D'AZUR, FRANCE

SWITZERLAND

Waffle your way through breakfast in Bruges

BRUGES, BELGIUM

PARIS, FRANCE

TREVISO & VENICE, ITALY

CENTRAL SWEDEN

WEST ICELAND

Stark pleasures: monochrome landscapes and buildings make Iceland unforgettable

MADEIRA, PORTUGAL

Take a taste of Madeira's famous poncha

SARAJEVO & MOSTAR, BOSNIA

IBIZA, SPAIN

LA GOMERA, SPAIN

Sitges knows how to party, especially at carnival time when *carnestoltes* come out to play

PARIS, FRANCE

ALENTEJO, PORTUGAL

Wander the abandoned amusement park in Pripyat

SITGES, SPAIN

CHERNOBYL, UKRAINE

LAPLAND
FINLAND

Why now? Go on a hunt for the Northern Lights.

The Arctic Circle sparkles at this time of year, with the landscape buried under a duvet of snow and the lakes frozen solid. Polar night (the period of 24hr darkness) is finally over, and the sun puts in ever-longer appearances. And the magical Northern Lights are quite likely to dance: premium times to look for the aurora are February– April and September–October. This is also a great time for everyone – young, old, families, couples – to get into the great outdoors. Though still chilly, temperatures are starting to rise, and wilderness lodges offer full programmes of activities that are guaranteed to warm you up: husky-sledding, snowmobiling, sleigh rides, snowshoeing, cross-country skiing. If all else fails, a visit to a traditional Finnish sauna will top up your inner heat.

Trip plan: Airports at Rovaniemi (right on the Arctic Circle) and Ivalo (further north) offer access to Finland's Lapland region. Spend four or more nights at a wilderness lodge to maximise chances of seeing the aurora, and to pack in plenty of snowy fun. Lodges away from settlements and light pollution will provide the best dark skies.

Need to know: Many lodges offer automatic 'aurora alert' systems or the option to ask for a wake-up call if the lights come out so you don't sleep through the show.

Other months: Dec-Apr – snow activities (aurora Sept-Apr); May-Aug – long days, warmest; Sep-Nov – brief autumn, cooling.

Reindeer and the Northern Lights; just two Saariselkä attractions

JULIAN ALPS
SLOVENIA

Why now? Hit good-value pistes, ideal for beginners.

Slovenia's slopes are often overlooked by Alps fans, but there are some fine pistes to be found across this handsome country's chunk of the range, for a fraction of the prices at French or Swiss ski resorts. Snow is more reliable later in the season, making February a good choice. Vogel, one of Slovenia's highest resorts, is a great all-rounder. With just 22km (13.6 miles) of well-groomed runs, it's small but varied, and especially suits families and beginners, with plenty of English-speaking ski and snowboard instructors. It also has an enviable natural setting within Triglav National Park, offering big views over pristine mountains and down to Lake Bohinj; iconic Lake Bled is only a short drive away too. The landscape also offers possibilities for spectacular ski touring through virgin snow. The resort of Kranjska Gora is a livelier choice, with 18 pistes of varied difficulty, activities such as sledding and ice-climbing, a more active après-ski scene and plenty of events, including various ski jumping championships (usually held in February and March).

Trip plan: The closest airport is Ljubljana – the drive to Vogel takes around 1hr 20min, and around 50min to Kranjska Gora.

Need to know: Both Vogel and Kranjska Gora offer a free Ski Bus service, which runs between select hotels and the slopes.

Other months: Jan-Apr – skiing; May-Oct – hiking, rafting, outdoor activities; Nov-Dec – colder, anticipating snow.

KYIV & CHERNOBYL
UKRAINE

Why now? Combine snowy domes and surreal scenes.

If you're prepared to wrap up warm, now's the time to experience Ukraine with a big dose of atmosphere. Cool capital Kyiv (formerly Kiev) will be glistening under a pall of snow, so it's a bracing time to stroll the Dnipro River, admire the golden globes of St Sophia's Cathedral, ride the world's deepest metro to Pecherska Lavra (the Monastery of the Caves, Ukraine's holiest of holy sites) and feel the creative energy around the hip (and cheap) bars and coffee houses. Most striking of all, though, is a visit to Chernobyl, the site of the world's worst nuclear accident. Entering the Exclusion Zone and seeing the concrete-wrapped reactors and abandoned town of Pripyat in the bleak midwinter adds to the dark mood. You can see everything – from the rusting fairground to the tumbling school – laid bare without the obstructive fuzz of spring-summer nature or many other tourists. Look for prints in the snow, too – animals such as elk, wolves, bears and bison are flourishing in the human-free landscape.

Trip plan: Spend a few days exploring Kyiv, including a visit to the Chernobyl Museum. Chernobyl itself, 100km (62 miles) north, can be visited on a long day-trip or as an overnight excursion, with a night spent inside the Exclusion Zone. Over 18s only.

Need to know: Winter is the safest season to visit Chernobyl: the snow acts as a shield, keeping radiation levels at their lowest.

Other months: Nov-Mar – cold to freezing, quiet; Apr-Jun – green, warm; Jul-Aug – hot, long days; Sep-Oct – warm, autumn colours.

ANDORRA

Why now? Learn to ski on reliable mid-season snow.

Tucked into the Pyrenees between France and Spain, the diminutive principality of Andorra is basically all mountains – so it's no surprise that skiing is a big deal here. Indeed, Andorra offers some of the best skiing in the Pyrenees: it has modern chairlifts, top-notch ski schools, a good mix of accommodation and excellent slopes for beginners and intermediates. Being so small, all its main resorts are close, so you can easily move between them if you get bored: its huge Grandvalira ski area is split into six sectors, but one pass covers unlimited access to them all. Prices are reasonable too in all the resorts. February is a good choice – expect clear skies, and virtually guaranteed snow dusting the resort summits, which all top out at over 2500m (8200ft). Away from the piste, the après-ski is enjoyable and, thanks to low VAT, the shopping inexpensive.

Trip plan: Grandvalira encompasses 210km (130 miles) of linked slopes. The six sectors each have a different feel: Pas de la Casa has the liveliest après-ski; Grau Roig is more remote and low-key; Canillo is good for beginners, with lots of gentle blue runs; Soldeu has more intermediate slopes and off-piste options; El Tarter and Encamp both have a charming village vibe.

Need to know: Andorra doesn't have an international airport – the best access is via Toulouse (France) or Barcelona (Spain).

Other months: Dec-Apr – ski season; May-Sep – warm, best for hiking/biking; Oct-Nov – cool, off-season.

MADEIRA
PORTUGAL

→ Why now? Have outdoor fun in the winter sun.

Madeira is an island without climatic extremes, but with plenty of topographical ones. Adrift in the Atlantic, closer to Morocco than to its Portuguese motherland, there's barely any flatland to be found – every inch seems dramatically ruptured – but the sun shines all year round. Suffice to say, in February, when most of Europe shivers, Madeira can bask in temperatures of up to 20°C (68°F); even if it rains, there are so many microclimates that you can travel to a different spot and find better weather.

The mild winter is ideal for strolling the island's network of *levadas* (old irrigation channels) or simply for relaxing with a *poncha* (sugarcane-spirit cocktail) in an ocean-view bar. Capital Funchal has plenty to divert: the ornate Sé; the Art Deco Mercado dos Lavradores; the cable car up to Monte, where the Monte Palace Tropical Gardens bloom year-round; or taking an elegant afternoon tea at Reid's Palace hotel. Or base yourself in the pretty fishing village of Câmara de Lobos, favoured bolthole of Winston Churchill. Madeira promises numerous activities, too, from trail running to mountain-biking and canyoning.

Trip plan: Madeira's airport is a 25min drive east of Funchal. Driving can be nerve-wracking – use buses and tours to make forays across the island.

Need to know: Carnival, one of the island's biggest events, falls in February/March (40 days before Easter). As well a grand parade through Funchal, events take place around the island during Carnival week.

Other months: Oct-Apr – mild, wetter; May-Sep – hotter, driest.

VALLETTA MALTA

→ Why now? Search out heat and history.

Malta's harbour-hugging capital, Valletta, looks much as it did 400 years ago when it was founded by the Knights Hospitaller. The Baroque palaces, churches, narrow lanes and beefy fortifications are so well-preserved that the city is Unesco-listed in its entirety, and was named European Capital of Culture in 2018. While February isn't hot (with highs of around 15°C/59°F), it's perfectly pleasant for wandering Valletta's old streets, browsing the National Museum of Archaeology and being dazzled by the Baroque St John's Co-Cathedral. And check out Malta's contemporary edge at the MUŻA art museum and Renzo Piano's bold new Parliament Building. If the elements are unkind, seek refuge at the Hal Saflieni Hypogeum, an astonishing subterranean prehistoric burial site. For the best views of the city, head to the Upper Barrakka Gardens. Or to admire Valletta from water-level, sail across the Grand Harbour in a traditional *dgħajsa* (open rowing boat). Disembark at tiny Vittoriosa, one of the three cities facing Valletta, and get lost in its labyrinthine backstreets.

Trip plan: Allow three days. Stay in a converted palazzo in the centre; the city is compact and all the main attractions are within easy walking distance.

Need to know: If you're planning to visit several historic sites and museums, consider a Heritage Malta multisite pass, which covers entrance to 25 sites over 30 days.

Other months: Dec-Mar – mild, quiet; Apr-Jun & Oct-Nov – warm, uncrowded; Jul-Sep – hot, dry, busiest, festivals.

TURIN ITALY

→ Why now? Pig out beneath snow-capped peaks.

Elegant, culturally thriving and delicious, Turin is just the place for a sophisticated winter break. For a start, February may be cold but it's one of Turin's driest months. And the Alps, which surround the city, provide a splendid snowy backdrop – get a breathtaking view from the 85m/278ft-high deck of the Mole Antonelliana tower. But mostly, gorge yourself. Graze at Eataly Lingotto, a converted factory selling a vast array of sustainable edibles – the global Slow Food movement began here. The European love affair with chocolate also originated in Turin – the first chocolate houses sprang up here in the 17th century. Seek out one of the city's Art Nouveau cafés and order a traditional *bicerin* (coffee with bitter chocolate, topped with cream) or browse the many chocolate shops (cioccolateria) for gianduja, the city's hazelnut-choc invention. Still hungry? Make the most of apertivo time. In Turin many bars lay on a substantial free buffet – anything from cheeses to pies and pasta – to accompany that early evening Cinzano. The boho bars of the studenty San Salvario neighbourhood are good places to look for big portions.

Trip plan: Allow at least three days. Make time for the Museo Egizio's Ancient Egyptian artefacts, the wonderful wheels of the Museo Nazionale dell'Automobile and the hillside Basilica di Superga.

Need to know: Apertivo runs roughly 6-9pm; during this time you pay a little more for your drinks, but the buffet is free.

Other months: Dec-Mar – cold, skiing; Apr-May – warming, quiet; Jun-Aug – hot; Sep-Nov – warm, harvest.

© Matt Munro / Lonely Planet

(L) Portugal at its most picturesque in Evora; (R) It's carnival time in Sitges; (B) The famous red livery of the Bernina Express

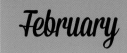

ALENTEJO
PORTUGAL

Why now? Take a winter wine wander.

On a crisp, blue-sky February day, there's little finer than sipping a big, beefy, warming red amid the vines from which it sprang. The Alentejo is a deliciously under-touristed wine region at any time, but it's particularly alluring in winter, when the skies are often clear and the landscape of rolling hills, cork forests, traditional quintas (wineries) and Moorish architecture gleams in the low sunlight. Évora's Unesco-listed walled Old Town makes a good base; as well as an impressive cathedral, a pretty town square, the Templo Romano (one of Iberia's best-preserved Roman monuments) and a lively vibe, it's home to the HQ of the Rota dos Vinhos do Alentejo (Wine Route of the Alentejo), where you can taste a few tipples and plan a winery tour. Northeast, head to the Serra de São Mamede region for full-bodied fruity reds, while smoother reds and fruity whites can be tried nearer Évora, in the hilltop town of Estremoz and the medieval village of Monsaraz.

Trip plan: Évora is a 2hr train ride from Lisbon. From Évora, make day-trips to the surrounding wineries; many offer hearty Alentejan cuisine and tastings. Some of the vineyards offer characterful accommodation too (prices are lower in winter).

Need to know: Order *caldo verde*, a traditional winter-warmer soup typically served with pork sausage and cornbread.

Other months: Nov-Mar – cooler, off-season; Apr-Jun & Sept-Oct – warm/hot; Jul-Aug –baking, busiest.

SITGES SPAIN

Why now? Have a gay old time.

Some 2000 years ago, the Romans built the settlement of Subur on Spain's Costa Daurada; Sitges, which now occupies the same spot, has lost none of their bacchanalian spirit. Long a bohemian hangout, the picture-perfect town has become the country's LGBTQ capital, with an open and uninhibited feel, a pumping nightclub and bar scene, and a lively social calendar. The hottest diary date comes at the end of winter: Carnival. Usually falling in February, this week of revelry sees extravagant parades of bespangled drag queens, naked flesh, glitter and booming tunes culminating in outrageous masked balls and boozy all-night parties. This time of year tends to be rain-free, with temperatures of 13–18°C/55–64°F, but there's no chance of getting chilly with all these shenanigans going on. If you miss Carnival, no matter. Promenade the Passeig Maritim, wander the whitewashed Old Town and stroll around the Modernista mansions on the headland; the former home of Catalan Modernisme pioneer Santiago Rusiñol now holds the Museu del Cau Ferrat, hung with Rusiñol's art alongside pieces by contemporaries such as Picasso. Then gird your loins for a wild night out on Sitges' Carrer del Picat ('Sin Street').

Trip plan: Combine relaxing and raucous Sitges with fresh air in surrounding Garraf Natural Park, or head for the big-league sights of Barcelona (45min by train).

Need to know: Local food is good. Look out for *arròs a la sitgetana* (a risotto-like meat and seafood stew) and *xató* (salad with salt cod, tuna, anchovies and olives).

Other months: Dec-Feb – mild, dry; Mar-Jun – warm, sea chilly (Gay Pride Jun); Jul-Aug – hot, busy; Sep-Nov – warm, quieter.

GRAND TRAIN TOUR
SWITZERLAND

Why now? Effortless travel through sparkling landscapes.

The Swiss rail network doesn't give a jot about winter. Trains remain well-heated and punctual even after a dumping of snow. And the routes are some of the most scenic in the world, delving between icy mountains, over gravity-defying viaducts and around frozen lakes. The biggest adventure is the Grand Train Tour, which covers around 1280km (795 miles) split into eight sections, using some premium trains and historic tracks. Ride the route in February and the panoramic carriages will be looking out onto a Narnian wonderland. Highlights include the city-to-summits Lucerne–Interlaken Express; the GoldenPass service from Interlaken's peaks to French-feel Montreux; the narrow-gauge Glacier Express between Zermatt and St Moritz, which glides past the mighty Matterhorn; and the St Moritz–Lugano Bernina Express, which surges south towards Italian-speaking Switzerland on the Unesco-listed Rhaetian Railway, the highest transalpine railway of them all.

Trip plan: A Swiss Travel Pass covers train, bus and boat journeys across Switzerland on three, four, eight or 15 consecutive days. Allow at least eight days to ride all sections of the Grand Train Tour; two weeks gives enough time to explore stops en route or add on some fantastic skiing.

Need to know: Seat reservations are mandatory on some services (such as the Glacier Express) even if you have a pass. The Glacier Express doesn't run mid-October to mid-December.

Other months: Nov-May – winter timetable, snow scenes, spring wildflowers; May-Oct – summer rail timetable, warm to hot.

(L) Watching the sunset over Es Vedra; (B) Pretty Ibiza town

© Annapurna Mellor / Lonely Planet

IBIZA SPAIN

→ **Why now? Boost your fitness in warming climes.**

For the antithesis of Balearic hedonism, come to Ibiza now. This island, so well known for its wild summer clubbing scene, is a far quieter prospect off-season, when it's a good choice for a more cleansing, abstemious break. Indeed, as devotion to New Year's resolutions inevitably starts to wane in February, boost up with a fitness-focused Ibizan escape, taking advantage of the relatively mild winter temperatures (10–16°C/50–60°F). The island has become something of a wellness hub, and there are heaps of villas and gurus specialising in healthy holidays; many are located near good running and cycling trails, and offer optional extras such as visits from personal trainers and chefs who cook up creative, waistline-friendly, vegan/veggie/intolerance-kind dishes. There are also yoga retreats that operate year-round. Or you can work-out on your own: this beautiful island of pine forests, pretty coves, craggy clifftops and whitewashed hamlets is ideal for trail runs and downward-dogging out in nature. The February explosion of almond blossom is an added bonus.

Trip plan: Book a remote villa for a proper escape. Visit capital Ibiza Town, where many restaurants remain open and full of locals.

Need to know: Many bars and almost all nightclubs close from October to May.

Other months: Nov-Mar – mild; Apr-May – warm, pleasant; Jun-Aug – hot, busy; Sep-Oct – winding down, club closing parties.

(L & B) Gorge on fine chocolate and medieval architecture in Bruges

BRUGES
BELGIUM

→ **Why now? For beer, chocolate, chips – and romance.**

Bruges is a beauty, especially in winter. Mist-hung canals wend around narrow lanes, step-gabled houses and fire-warmed taverns, and when darkness falls, lights twinkle on the waterways. It's a dreamy spot for Valentine's month, that's for sure, with the chilly temperatures (around 5°C/41°F) forcing couples to cuddle up. Another way to keep warm is to refuel constantly. Come early in the month and you might catch the Bruges Beer Festival, when more than 300 different beers are on offer over one hop-happy weekend. Otherwise, simply crawl around some of the city's many bars, sampling the many Belgian styles, from strong amber Kwak to sour-cherry Lambic. A tour at the Half Man Brewery comes with guided tastings in the cellars. Soak up the grog with some frites (here, traditionally fried in beef fat) before learning more about the potato at the Frietmuseum. Then it's time for something sweet. Bruges is the self-professed chocolate capital of the world, with more than 50 chocolatiers trading here. Explore the history of cacao at the Choco Story museum before hitting the shops – there are lots on Katelijnestraat, selling some of Belgium's best truffles.

Trip plan: Spend three days gorging on Bruges. If you're still hungry, add on equally foodie Brussels (1hr 10min by train).

Need to know: Seek out Oud Huis Deman bakery, source of fine dentelle de Bruges (lace biscuits) for the last 130 years.

Other months: Nov-Feb – cold (Christmas markets Dec); Mar-May & Sept-Oct – mild, shoulder months; Jun-Aug – hotter, busy.

© Annapurna Mellor / Lonely Planet

© Matt Munro / Lonely Planet

© Predrag Jankovic / Shutterstock

ZAKOPANE
POLAND

→ **Why now? Whizz down the slopes of two countries.**

Tucked into the foothills of the Tatras mountains and dotted with handsome wooden villas, Zakopane is Poland's winter-sports capital. It's also almost in Slovakia – head up 1985m (6512ft) Mt Kasprowy and, at the top, you can plant one ski boot in Poland, the other over the border. That opens up multiple mountain possibilities in one trip: from Zakopane, learn downhill skiing at the beginner-friendly Nosal Ski Centre, practise snowboard tricks at the Witów Ski snow park, or have a go at dog-mushing and take a dip in the thermal pools at Bukowina Tatrzańska. Then hop over into Slovakia for snowshoeing and cross-country skiing around the picturesque Štrbské Pleso lake. As a bonus, this is one of Europe's cheapest ski areas too, with good-value lift passes and even better value après-ski.

Trip plan: Krakow airport is about 1hr 30min drive or bus ride north of Zakopane – allow a few days in the medieval city before heading into the mountains.

Need to know: The Zakopane area can also be accessed from Poprad in Slovakia, which has an airport. From Poprad, regular buses and trains take about 30min to reach Tatras resorts such as Smokovec and Tatranska Lomnicá; funicular railways continue into the mountains.

Other months: Jan-Mar – skiing; Apr-Jun – wildflowers (skiing on highest slopes Apr); Jul-Aug – hiking, festivals; Sep-Oct – uncrowded, hiking still possible; Nov-Dec – quiet, first snows (Christmas festivities Dec).

Gasienicowa Valley is one of Zakopane's majestic attractions

© Chris Herring / Alamy Stock Photo

NORTH NORFOLK ENGLAND

Come in winter to
see Holkham Bay in
a new light

→ Why now? Witness a wealth of wildlife.

The North Norfolk coast is never better than in winter: its big skies are bigger, its birdlife is in profusion, its beaches are wild and empty. Start the day at RSPB Snettisham, where 10,000-strong flocks of pink-footed geese take flight at dawn; numbers peak January and February. Next, take a bracing walk along the coast path, perhaps striding across the vast sands of Holkham, like Gwyneth in *Shakespeare in Love* – a most romantic Valentine stroll. Have lunch in Brancaster, where you can eat local mussels (in season September–April) while gazing over the tidal marshes; you might see the fishermen bringing in their catch. In the afternoon, take a shingly walk or boat trip out to Blakeney Point, where the colony of grey seals – the largest in England – is

coming to the end of pupping season; you might still spot some. When darkness falls, head to Wiveton Downs, a certified Dark Sky Discovery site, for out-of-this-world stars.

Trip plan: North Norfolk has a number of boutique hotels and gastropubs. Good bases include the villages of Burnham Market, Thornham and Wells.

Need to know: Trains from London to Norwich and King's Lynn take 2hr. From these hubs there are connections to the coastal towns of Cromer and Hunstanton. Coasthopper buses service North Norfolk year-round, though services are reduced in winter.

Other months: Nov-Feb – coldest, seal pups, overwintering birds; Mar-May – warm, good birding; Jun-Aug – warmest, busiest; Sep-Oct – migrating birds, deer ruts.

LA GOMERA
CANARY ISLANDS

→ Why now? Lace up for wonderful winter walking.

It rains very little on the jagged volcanic outcrop of La Gomera. But if the skies do open, it's usually in December and January, leaving drier February lush and lovely, with burgeoning wildflowers and highs of about 21°C (70°F): perfect for walking. And that's why most people come to this more offbeat Canary Island, which lacks golden sands (beaches here are black) but makes up for it with swathes of ancient laurel trees, precipitous *barrancos* (ravines), cloud-swirled peaks and a network of 250 hiking trails. Explore small but colourful capital San Sebastián. Then hike to the top of 1487m (4879ft) Alto de Garajonay, the island's highest point; stroll amid the fruits and flowers of the Vallehermoso; and head southwest for walks in the verdant Valle Gran Rey. Finish up with classic Canarian dishes: fresh seafood, hearty stews and *patatas arrugadas* (wrinkly potatoes); in February, wild mushrooms will also be on the menu.

Trip plan: There are several daily flights (30min) between La Gomera's airport and Tenerife Norte, as well as ferries to Tenerife (50min) and La Palma (2hr). Hiring a car is the easiest way to explore; book ahead as there are a limited number available. The island has a comprehensive bus network.

Need to know: The waters off Valle Gran Rey are a cetacean superhighway; dolphins and whales can be spotted year-round.

Other months: Dec-Jan – cooler, wettest; Feb-May – warm, wildflowers; Jun-Aug – hottest, driest; Sep-Nov – warm seas.

(L) Look out towards Tenerife from the Mirador de Abrante; (R) The densely forested Garajonay National Park

CÔTE D'AZUR
FRANCE

→ **Why now? It's quiet, mild and extra zesty.**

How times change. Hitting the glitzy Côte d'Azur in February is now considered an off-season choice – a good time to avoid the summer crowds. But it was the winter visitors (such as Queen Victoria) who first made this Mediterranean stretch so fashionable in the 19th century. They came for the microclimate that gives the French Riviera – roughly from Menton to St Tropez – such pleasantly mild winters (February highs average 14°C/57°F). They also came for the oh-so-blue waters, scattered offshore islands and dramatic green hills. And then a host of artists descended for the special clarity of the light. All these attractions remain, but the masses now prefer to wait for bikini weather. Let them keep it. Come now for crowd-free coves, emptier coast roads and quieter explorations of the fine old town in Nice and Monaco's moneyed harbour. If it's crowds you want, add on a visit to Menton – each February the town hosts a two-week Lemon Festival, which involves huge floats and the creative use of some 145 tonnes of citrus fruit.

Trip plan: Fly to Nice and explore the Côte by car – traffic/parking is less hellish in winter. Trace the Corniches (the Riviera's most scenic roads), café-hop in Cannes and visit the art galleries of hilltop St-Paul de Vence.

Need to know: Nice will be jam-packed during its huge two-week Carnival (February/March) – check dates before travelling.

Other months: Nov-Jan – some businesses close; Feb-May – quiet, warm; Jun-Sep – glorious, heaving; Oct – changeable weather.

Quintessentially Côte: Nice's Promenade des Anglais and Menton's Fête du Citron

© bellena / Shutterstock

© Giancarlo Liguori / Shutterstock

COLOGNE
GERMANY

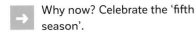

→ **Why now? Celebrate the 'fifth season'.**

The historic and high-spirited Rhineland city of Cologne doesn't just celebrate Carnival – it creates a whole new time period for it. The 'fifth season' officially starts on 11 November, but the party really kicks off the following February, on the Thursday before Lent. Then ensue the 'crazy days', between Fat Thursday and Ash Wednesday, when parading, masquerading, drinking, dancing and general revelry take over the streets. It's raucous good fun, and not at all out of character for Cologne, which is known for its liberalism, elan and generous number of traditional beer halls serving local-brewed Kölsch, hearty food and liberal dollops of *gemutlischkeit* (aka hygge, German-style). There's plenty to see, too: the gargantuan twin-spired cathedral and the rambling lanes of the riverside Altstadt (Old Town), the modern art at Museum Ludwig and Cologne's Roman heritage at the Römisch-Germanisches Museum. A particularly moving way to move around the city is by following the Stolpersteins – brass plaques memorialising victims of the Nazis, part of

Old meets new: Hohenzollern Bridge leading to Cologne Cathedral

© quill23 / Getty Images

a project by Cologne-based artist Gunter Demnig; they're especially dense in the Belgisches Viertel (Belgian Quarter), which is also one of the hippest hangouts, with lots of bars and boutiques.

Trip plan: Allow at least two days to explore, more if you plan to be nursing a Carnival hangover.

Need to know: Consider buying a MuseumsCard, which covers admission to many museums on two consecutive days.

Other months: Nov-Mar – cold (Christmas markets Dec); Apr-Jun & Sep-Oct – warm, less crowded; Jul-Aug – hottest, festivals.

BEYOND COLOGNE

BONN • 30KM (19 MILES) • erstwhile capital of West Germany; birthplace of Beethoven

DUSSELDÖRF • 40KM (25 MILES) • Great nightlife, architecture and shopping

EIFEL NATIONAL PARK • 60KM (37 MILES) • Protected forest park, home to wild cats, beavers, kingfishers and owls

ANTWERP • 200KM (125 MILES) • Dutch capital of cool, renowed for its vibrant fashion and entertainment scene

BAVARIAN ALPS
GERMANY

→ **Why now? See fairy-tale castles sparkle in the snow.**

Winter doesn't stop explorers in the beautiful Bavarian Königswinkel region, just north of the Austrian border on the edge of the Alps. Here, snow-clad mountains, glittering lakes and a clutch of castles render the place like Disney's *Frozen* made real – not least at Schloss Neuschwanstein, the architectural fairytale created by eccentric King Ludwig II in the late 19th century, and the model for virtually every cartoon castle since. Seeing Neuschwanstein and the area's other castles – Versailles-influenced Linderhof or Gothic-style Hohenschwangau – under a patina of ice adds an extra sprinkle of magic. Medieval Füssen, one of Bavaria's highest towns, makes a good base. Explore its old centre, visit St Mang's Abbey and warm up with a drink in a Bavarian *bierstube*. Then head onto the network of gentle trails in boots or snowshoes (conditions dependent); if it's cold enough, you can skate on the lakes. The crowds are long gone, the air is pure, and the forests and foothills offer total tranquillity.

Trip plan: Füssen is a 1hr 30min train journey from Munich. Spend a week here castle-hopping (there are useful buses), hiking and visiting sites such as Oberammergau, an historic village known for its long-running Passion Play and its exuberant painted facades.

Need to know: The castles are open year-round (except Christmas and 1 January). Combination tickets are available – a 14-day Bavarian Palace Department pass covers entrance to 40-plus sights.

Other months: Dec-Feb – snow; Mar-Apr – warming; May-Jun & Sep-Oct – warm, uncrowded, Jul-Aug – hottest, busiest.

© Andrew Montgomery / Lonely Planet

Schloss Neuschwanstein was the model for Disney's *Sleeping Beauty* castle

CENTRAL SWEDEN

→ **Why now? Brilliant birds against brilliant-white backdrops.**

A smidgen north of Stockholm, swathes of rural, frozen central Sweden prove prime twitching territory in winter. With lakes iced over, trees heavy with snow and berries bright against a blanket of white, the stage is picturesquely set to show off some charismatic birds hunting and foraging in the stillness: golden and white-tailed eagles, pretty waxwings, crossbills and bullfinches, forest grouse and goshawk. Parts of this region are especially good for hawk owls – the birds tend to pick a spot and stay put in winter, making them easier to locate, before they head north to their breeding grounds in March. There are opportunities to sled or snowmobile to bird hides, to add extra adventure. From these sheltered spots, photography opportunities are excellent, particularly as daylight hours slowly increase from February. Other species that might be seen include elk, deer, fox and hare – look for their tracks in the snow.

Trip plan: The Svartådalen (Black River Valley) in Västmanland is a good spot for winter birding; it's around a two-hour drive northwest of Stockholm. Alternatively, seek out wilderness lodges in Hälsingland, around three or four hours' drive away. Combine with a sparkling stay in Stockholm itself.

Need to know: Wrap up warm, with plenty of layers: sitting still in hides is chilly business, and temperatures will be well below zero – the February average is around -6°C.

Other months: Nov-Mar – cold, snowy; Apr-May, Sept-Oct – good birding, warmer; Jun- Aug – warmest, long days.

Monochrome set:
Budir Black Church
and the frozen
Kirkjufellsfoss

© Jonathan Gregson / Lonely Planet

© Jonathan Gregson / Lonely Planet

SNÆFELLSNES
ICELAND

→ **Why now? Capture aurora and orca on camera.**

Iceland in February might sound like a cold and gloomy prospect, but this is far from the truth. The Gulf Stream keeps this northerly isle on a par with New York City, while by month's end, the sun is up before 9am and doesn't set until after 6pm. Fortunately, this still leaves a good amount of darkness against which to see – and snap – the Northern Lights. The western Snæfellsnes Peninsula, known as 'Iceland in miniature' for its mix of volcanic features, caves and gorges, waterfalls, glaciers and fishing villages, is ideal for aurora photography. There's little light pollution and a range of scenery to add plenty of foreground and background interest – for instance, around free-standing Mt Kirkjufell (to capture the lights above the peak and reflected in the water), the hamlet of Hellnar (for the lights behind the little church) and mighty Snæfellsjökull Glacier (of Jules Verne's *Journey to the Centre of the Earth* fame). There's a chance to practise wildlife photography too: during the winter months, orca hunt herring around the peninsula.

Trip plan: Snæfellsnes is a 2hr drive from Reykjavík. Good bases include the villages of Grundarfjörður and Stykkishólmur.

Need to know: Pack a wide-angle lens (55mm or less), a tripod to keep the camera stable for long exposures and a swimming costume so you can warm up in the peninsula's natural hot springs.

Other months: Oct-Mar – cold, dark, aurora possible; Apr-Sep – more tours, warmer.

CARINTHIA
AUSTRIA

 **Why now? Indulge in a dose of winter wellness.**

The air might be brisk, but the sky is bright and the water warm in Austria's southern Carinthia region. Not only does it enjoy 100 hours more sunshine during the winter months than regions north of the Alps, this land of lakes – numbering 1270 in total – is also a land of thermal activity. Even in Roman times the area around the city of Villach was renowned for its hot springs; today, more than 60 curative spas are located nearby, offering aqua-therapy of all sorts. Families can find heated outdoor pools with fun slides. There are slick and contemporary spas with fancy treatments and late-night saunas. And there are elegant 19th-century resorts where visitors were coming to seek 'wellness' long before it became a modern buzzword. Some resorts have a decidedly medical bent, with minerals in the hot springs alleging to aid a range of ailments. There are also heated pools beside the lakes of Millstätter, Wörthersee and Turracher, where you can swim year-round with marvellous mountain views.

Trip plan: Come for a relaxing week of spa treatments, and Carinthian cuisine such as polenta, buckwheat cake and hearty *kärntner nudeln*, a sort of super-sized filled pasta pocket. Head to the Bad Kleinkirchheim region to segue straight from the thermal spas to the ski slopes.

Need to know: Klagenfurt Airport is the main gateway. Klagenfurt and Villach are the hubs for trains from elsewhere in Europe.

Other months: Jan-Mar – snowy, skiing; Apr-May & Oct-Nov – shoulder seasons, quiet; Jun-Sep – hottest, hiking, cycling, swimming.

SARAJEVO & MOSTAR
BOSNIA & HERCEGOVINA

The elegant Stari Most bridge of Mostar

 **Why now? Find crowd-free culture and skiing at a snip.**

Sarajevo is not a city that is subdued by winter. If anything, it embraces it. One of the country's key cultural events, Sarajevska Zima has been held from early February to late March since 1984, and has become a symbol of freedom and multiculturalism. Sarajevo also has a fascinating old centre, Baščaršija, and plenty of excellent museums, such as war-confronting Galerija 11/07/95, and the History Museum of BiH, which looks at the end of the Yugoslav dream (and has a Tito-themed bar). For lighter relief, there's always a cheap underground restaurant or cosy café serving strong coffee and *begova čorba* (a clay-pot-cooked chicken soup). Plus, this month also sees snow on the surrounding mountains, offering bargain skiing and accessible snowshoeing. Combine the capital with Mostar, Bosnia's biggest draw, which gets overrun in summer; in winter you can wander the higgle-piggle Ottoman-era Old Town and iconic Stari Most bridge – originally built in the 16th century, destroyed in 1993, rebuilt in 2004 – without the crowds.

Trip plan: Spend a few days in each city. Sarajevo–Mostar is a 1hr 30min drive via the Neretva Canyon, or 2hr by train.

Need to know: Many facilities in Mostar shut down in the off season, but those that stay open offer heavily reduced rates.

Other months: Dec-Feb – snow, skiing; Mar-May & Sep-Nov – quieter, cool, flowers/autumn colours; Jun-Aug – hot, busiest, lots of festivals.

PARIS FRANCE

→ **Why now? Expand your horizons and enjoy some romance.**

The 'city of love' is an obvious choice for Valentine's month, and of course there are plenty of opportunities for canoodling along the Seine. But Paris in February offers more than amour. Not only are there shorter queues at the museums, there are also exotic celebrations: the French capital has multiple Chinatowns, and around Chinese New Year (usually February) big events are staged in the 13th arrondissement, home to Europe's largest Chinatown, as well as the Marais, Belleville and Ménilmontant districts. Focusing a trip on these latter three easterly arrondissements is to see Paris at its most multicultural. The maze-like Marais has must-see sites – romantic Place des Vosges, the Picasso Museum – but also the excellent Enfants Rouges covered food market, a glut of hip bars and boutiques, and thriving gay and Jewish communities. Adjacent Ménilmontant has the best nightlife, as well as Cimetière du Père Lachaise, the beautiful cemetery where many celebs have been laid to rest. Belleville is an offbeat melting pot – shop at Chinese supermarkets, Egyptian spice stores, kosher delis, African grocers and colourful street markets; and hilly Parc de Belleville offers some of the best views of the city, without the crowds.

Trip plan: Spend three to four days exploring. There are many accommodation options in the Marais, spanning all budgets.

Need to know: The Marais is flat, but Ménilmontant and Belleville are steeper – save energy by riding the Metro eastwards and walking downhill towards the Marais.

Other months: Nov-Mar – coldest, cheaper; Apr-Jun & Oct – warm, less crowded; Jul-Sep – hot, busy.

Elegant architecture, pavement cafes and baguettes galore... welcome to Paris

© Rrrainbow / Getty Images

© Matt Munro / Lonely Planet

© Adrienne Pitts / Lonely Planet

TREVISO & VENICE ITALY

→ **Why now? Discover alternative off-season canals.**

Venice steals the headlines in Italy's Veneto region with good reason. 'La Serenissima' is an overwhelming jumble of historical, architectural and aqua-tectural treasures; even in February, when it can be grey, chilly and prone to floods, the city looks atmospheric, with the bonus that tourist numbers are lower and most cruise ships stay away. However, travel half an hour north and you'll find a similarly waterway-riddled city where you can escape ALL the crowds – especially good to know if Venice Carnival is on (the hugely popular pre-Lenten spectacular often falls in February). Treviso's handsome walled centre is a maze of arcaded streets, willow-tickled canals, frescoed facades and traditional *osterie* (taverns), where you can eat red radicchio (a local speciality, in season December–March) and creamy tiramisu (invented here). The excellent Luigi Bailo modern art museum is also worth a look. It's all far lower-key than Venice, but all the more authentically Italian for it. You can always pop to Venice for the day, or consider excursions to other overlooked hubs such as ancient Padua, home to the glorious Basilica of St Anthony and the Cappella

The ultimate pick-me-up: tiramisu was invented in Treviso

© Susan Wright / Lonely Planet

degli Scrovegni's Giotto frescos, or to the Palladian city of Vicenza.

Trip plan: Treviso is 30min from Venice by train. Trains to Vicenza and Padua take around 1hr.

Need to know: The balls, parades and fireworks of Venice Carnival take over the city for ten days in February/March (check dates). Hotels will be busy during this time.

Other months: Nov-Apr – cold/cool, quietest (Carnival Feb/Mar); May-Jun & Sep – warm; Jul-Aug – hot, heaving.

BEYOND VENICE

PADUA • 40KM (25 MILES) • Awesome art galleries

CORTINA D'AMPEZZO, DOLOMITES • 160KM (99 MILES) • Winter skiing

LAKE GARDA • 160KM (100 MILES) • Water sports, Roman remains and gorgeous gardens

ROME • 550KM (342 MILES) • Only three hours to the capital by high-speed train

March
WHERE TO GO WHEN

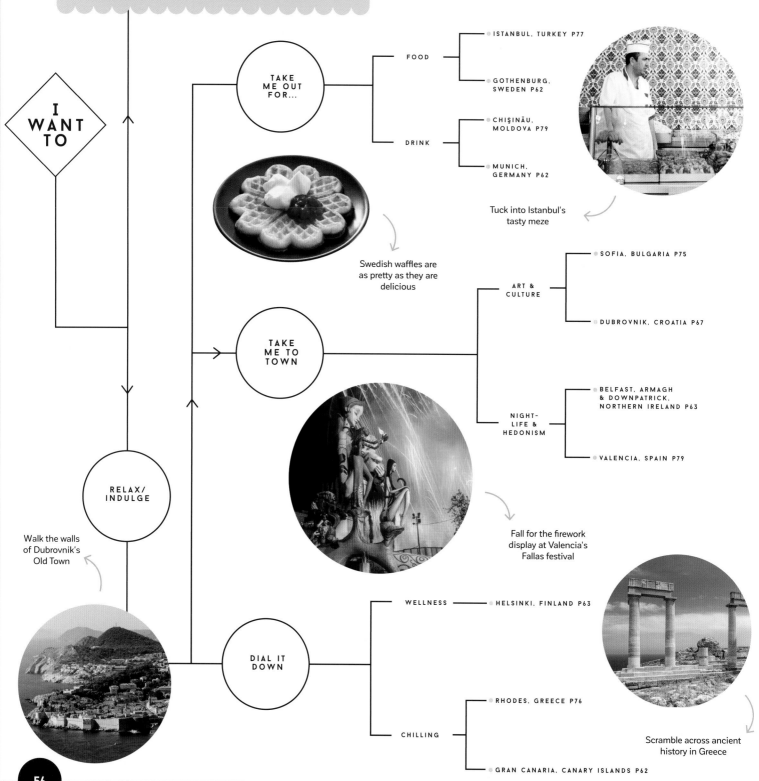

I WANT TO

CHALLENGE MYSELF

TAKE ME OUT FOR...

- FOOD
  - ● ISTANBUL, TURKEY P77
  - ● GOTHENBURG, SWEDEN P62
- DRINK
  - ● CHIŞINĂU, MOLDOVA P79
  - ● MUNICH, GERMANY P62

Tuck into Istanbul's tasty meze

Swedish waffles are as pretty as they are delicious

TAKE ME TO TOWN

- ART & CULTURE
  - ● SOFIA, BULGARIA P75
  - ● DUBROVNIK, CROATIA P67
- NIGHT-LIFE & HEDONISM
  - ● BELFAST, ARMAGH & DOWNPATRICK, NORTHERN IRELAND P63
  - ● VALENCIA, SPAIN P79

Fall for the firework display at Valencia's Fallas festival

RELAX/ INDULGE

Walk the walls of Dubrovnik's Old Town

DIAL IT DOWN

- WELLNESS ——— ● HELSINKI, FINLAND P63
- CHILLING
  - ● RHODES, GREECE P76
  - ● GRAN CANARIA, CANARY ISLANDS P62

Scramble across ancient history in Greece

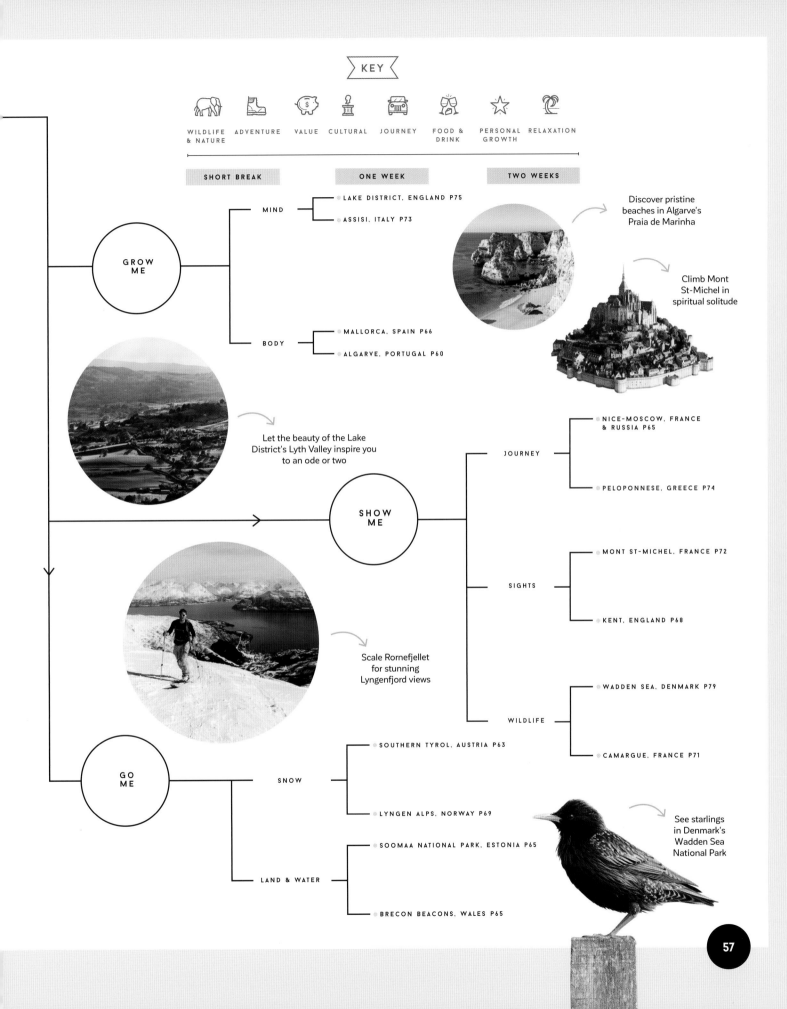

KEY

🐘 WILDLIFE & NATURE
🥾 ADVENTURE
🐷 VALUE
🏛 CULTURAL
🚙 JOURNEY
🥂 FOOD & DRINK
⭐ PERSONAL GROWTH
🌴 RELAXATION

SHORT BREAK

ONE WEEK

TWO WEEKS

GROW ME

MIND
- LAKE DISTRICT, ENGLAND P75
- ASSISI, ITALY P73

BODY
- MALLORCA, SPAIN P66
- ALGARVE, PORTUGAL P60

Discover pristine beaches in Algarve's Praia de Marinha

Climb Mont St-Michel in spiritual solitude

Let the beauty of the Lake District's Lyth Valley inspire you to an ode or two

SHOW ME

JOURNEY
- NICE–MOSCOW, FRANCE & RUSSIA P65
- PELOPONNESE, GREECE P74

SIGHTS
- MONT ST-MICHEL, FRANCE P72
- KENT, ENGLAND P68

WILDLIFE
- WADDEN SEA, DENMARK P79
- CAMARGUE, FRANCE P71

Scale Rornefjellet for stunning Lyngenfjord views

GO ME

SNOW
- SOUTHERN TYROL, AUSTRIA P63
- LYNGEN ALPS, NORWAY P69

LAND & WATER
- SOOMAA NATIONAL PARK, ESTONIA P65
- BRECON BEACONS, WALES P65

See starlings in Denmark's Wadden Sea National Park

EVENTS
IN MARCH

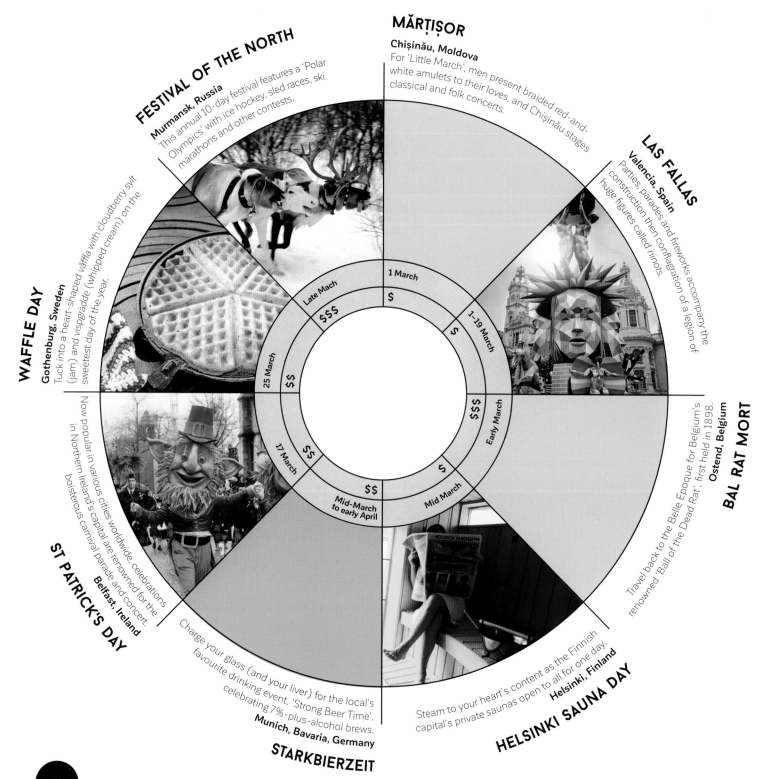

FESTIVAL OF THE NORTH
Murmansk, Russia
This annual 10-day festival features a 'Polar Olympics' with ice hockey, sled races, ski marathons and other contests.

MĂRȚIȘOR
Chișinău, Moldova
For 'Little March', men present braided red-and-white amulets to their loves, and Chișinău stages classical and folk concerts.

LAS FALLAS
Valencia, Spain
Parties, parades and fireworks accompany the construction then conflagration of a legion of huge figures called ninots.

WAFFLE DAY
Gothenburg, Sweden
Tuck into a heart-shaped *våffla* with cloudberry sylt (jam) and vispgrädde (whipped cream) on the sweetest day of the year.

BAL RAT MORT
Ostend, Belgium
Travel back to the Belle Epoque for Belgium's renowned 'Ball of the Dead Rat', first held in 1898.

ST PATRICK'S DAY
Belfast, Ireland
Now popular in various cities worldwide celebrations in Northern Ireland's capital are renowned for the boisterous carnival parade and concert.

HELSINKI SAUNA DAY
Helsinki, Finland
Steam to your heart's content as the Finnish capital's private saunas open to all for one day.

STARKBIERZEIT
Munich, Bavaria, Germany
Charge your glass (and your liver) for the local's favourite drinking event, 'Strong Beer Time', celebrating 7%-plus-alcohol brews.

Inner wheel labels:
1 March — $
1–19 March — $
Early March — $$$
Mid March — $
Mid-March to early April — $$
17 March — $$
25 March — $$
Late March — $$$

VERY FAMILY FRIENDLY

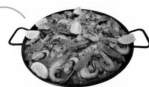

The Lake District springs into life in March

SOUTHERN TYROL, AUSTRIA

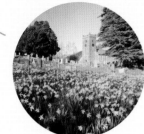

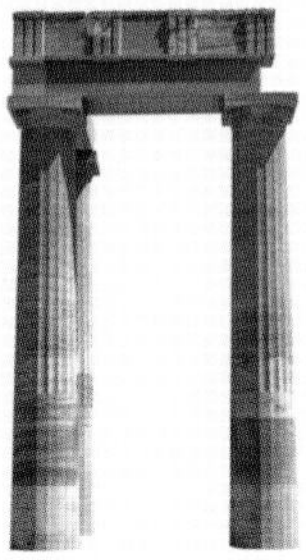

LAKE DISTRICT, ENGLAND

WADDEN SEA, DENMARK

Look out across the waters from the eyrie of Mont St-Michel

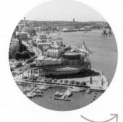

MONT ST-MICHEL, FRANCE

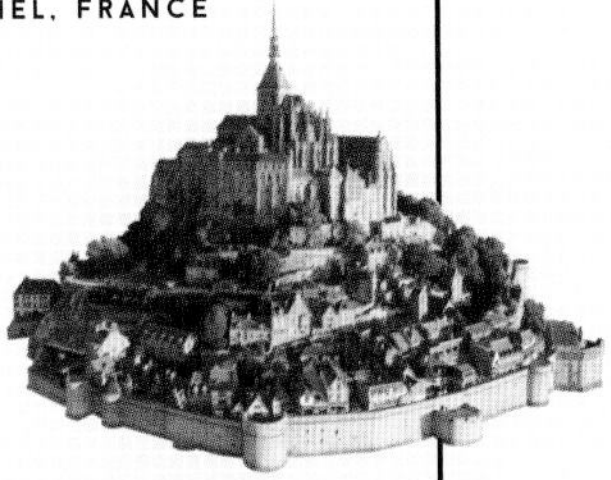

Take in a tune or two at Gothenburg's opera house

GOTHENBURG, SWEDEN

GRAN CANARIA, SPAIN

KENT, ENGLAND

BRECON BEACONS, WALES

MALLORCA, SPAIN

RHODES, GREECE

Find perfect paella in Mallorca

Explore ancient sites on Rhodes

DUBROVNIK, CROATIA

SOOMAA, ESTONIA

VALENCIA, SPAIN

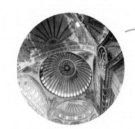

ALGARVE, PORTUGAL

Worth getting a crick in your neck for: the dome of Istanbul's Aya Sofya

ISTANBUL, TURKEY

EXPENSIVE BUT WORTH IT

GOOD VALUE

CAMARGUE, FRANCE

No rose-tinted specs needed to see the pink flamingos of the Camargue

HELSINKI, FINLAND

BELFAST, ARMAGH & DOWNPATRICK, NORTHERN IRELAND

Good workouts are guaranteed in the Lyngen Alps

LYNGEN ALPS, NORWAY

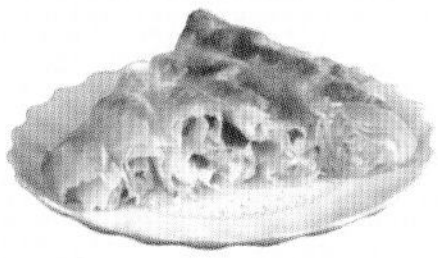

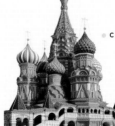

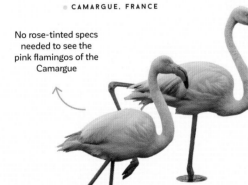

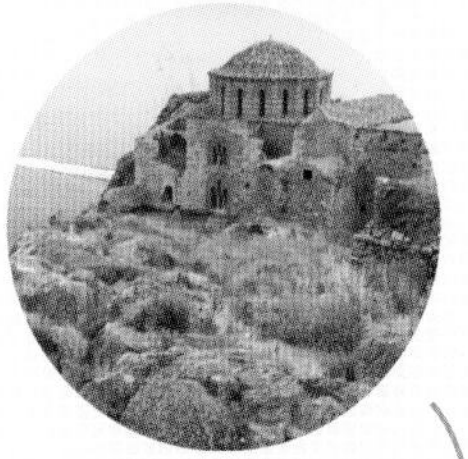

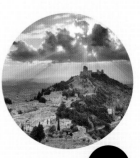

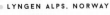

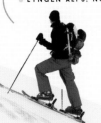

Light floods into Munich's Nymphenburg Castle

MUNICH, BAVARIA

SOFIA, BULGARIA

PELOPONNESE, GREECE

Sample baked *banitsa* for breakfast in Sofia

The colourful turrets of St Basil's cathedral in Moscow

CHIŞINĂU, MOLDOVA

Gorgeous colours characterise the Peloponnese in spring

NICE-MOSCOW, FRANCE & RUSSIA

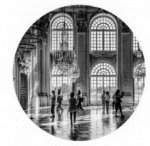

The fortress of Rocca Maggiore looms over Assisi

ASSISI, ITALY

LEAVE THE KIDS AT HOME

ALGARVE
PORTUGAL

Why now? Nurture body and mind in the season of new growth.

Spring comes early to the Algarve, mainland Portugal's most southerly, sunniest and driest region. The mercury nudges toward 20°C (68°F) and rainfall declines, while blossom falls from the almond trees and wildflowers bloom: now's the time to shake off the winter torpor and stretch out limbs and psyche alike. Yoga retreats are clustered along the Algarve's southern coast and up towards the border with the Alentejo, offering classes and longer courses; many augment yoga and meditation techniques with other aspects of mindfulness and, in many cases, surfing. As the high season hasn't really kicked in yet, March offers good value and availability of accommodation and other activities – golf courses, for example, start filling up as the month goes on. It's also prime time for walking the dramatic trails north along the Atlantic Coast, and exploring the historic old towns of Faro and Lagos.

Trip plan: Fly to Faro; buses and trains run west along the coast to Albufeira, Portimão and Lagos, from where buses continue to Sagres, where nearby Cabo de São Vicente marks the very western tip of the Algarve, and the most southwesterly spot in Europe.

Need to know: For more pampering, head inland to Caldas de Monchique, where thermal waters have attracted spa-goers since Roman times.

Other months: Nov-Feb – cooler, wetter, lower prices; Mar-May & Sep-Oct – pleasantly warm; Jun-Aug – very hot, busy.

Praia da Marinha, one of the Algarve's most beautiful beaches

GOTHENBURG
SWEDEN

➜ **Why now?** Indulge in Swedish *fika* in peak waffle season.

Nowhere does cosy café culture quite like Sweden, which even has a special word for the perfect coffee break with friends and cake: *fika*. March is the time to experience *fika* in Sweden's second city, when temperatures rise reliably above freezing, daylight hours stretch and lovers of sweet treats celebrate Waffle Day. Tucking into a heart-shaped *våffla* loaded with cloudberry *sylt* (jam) and *vispgrädde* (whipped cream) is de rigueur on 25 March, but any time is perfect for popping into the tempting cafés in the 17th-century suburb of Haga, just south of the city's historic centre; intersperse your grazing by browsing the independent shops among Haga's wooden houses. Back in Gothenburg's centre, roam around historic churches, museums and innovative galleries, and seek out the finest cuisine in this foodiest of cities: visit the unique Feskekörka (Fish Cathedral) for fresh prawns, or tuck into giant cinnamon buns at Café Husaren.

Trip plan: Allow two or three days for a visit – more to explore the fishing villages and wildlife-rich shores of the Gothenburg Archipelago's 20-plus islands, or the Bohuslän Archipelago further north.

Need to know: Alcohol (particularly wine) isn't cheap in Sweden. Stick to coffee or bring plenty of kronor – but if you're here at Christmas time, do sample the *glögg* (spiced mulled wine) at festive markets.

Other months: Oct-Mar – cold; Apr-Jun & Sep – warm, less crowded; Jul-Aug – sunny, packed festival calendar.

MUNICH
GERMANY

➜ **Why now?** Raise a glass to Bavaria's plus-strength beer.

In Bavaria, an alternative holy trinity has been revered for 500 years: water, barley and hops – the only ingredients permitted in beer, according to the purity law (Reinheitsgebot) adopted by the southern German state in 1516. More than 6 million people descend on Munich in September to chug and carouse during Oktoberfest – but that's not the only beer bash in town. The Starkbierzeit ('Strong Beer Time') in March is the locals' favourite, celebrating 7%-alcohol-plus tipples with ominously potent names such as Animator, Maximator and Triumphator, originally brewed by monks during Lent to make culinary abstinence more bearable. And unlike the stag-party-heavy autumn affair, held in the purpose-built tent city on Theresienwiese meadows, the spring event is spread across venues that include big Munich breweries and promises live music, competitions and various other cultural events. Accommodation and beer are cheaper in March, too.

Trip plan: Don't lose your entire trip to beer: spare at least two days to explore Munich's historical highlights – the ducal complex known as the Residenz, the spectacular Schloss Nymphenburg, or BMW Welt.

Need to know: Shake off the hangover with surfing – catch the artificial break on the Eisbach River in the English Gardens, right in the city centre.

Other months: Nov-Feb – very cold (Christmas markets Dec); Mar-Apr & Sep-Oct – cool; May-Aug – warm, frequent rain.

GRAN CANARIA
CANARY ISLANDS

➜ **Why now?** Get a sneak preview of summer with beaches and blooms.

It's Spain, but it's Africa: Gran Canaria has the Spanish vibe and cuisine, the sand dunes and climate of Morocco, plus a variety of landscapes and experiences to enthral all comers. March marks the start of spring, when days are lengthening and temperatures are reliably above 20°C (68°F) – the perfect time to visit, whether you're looking to sunbathe or to strike out onto the trails. Wildflowers bloom on the flanks of the *cumbres* (summits) in the central highlands, which rise to nearly 2000m (6562ft). Here you can hike among forests, *barrancos* (ravines) and delightful villages such as Artenara, the island's highest, with its ancient troglodyte dwellings. Back at sea level, the beaches beckon – with over seven hours of sunshine daily, March is a great time to relax on the sand. Las Palmas, the island's capital, is a best-of-both-worlds place, with the broad sweep of Las Canteras beach and the atmospheric Vegueta district, first established in the 15th century.

Trip plan: Base yourself in Las Palmas for sand and city life, Maspalomas for lively beach action and vast sand dunes, Puerto de Mogán for a picturesque harbour, or the interior and north of the island for hiking.

Need to know: Take a boat trip from Puerto Rico in the island's south to spot dolphins and, if you're lucky, pilot, sperm, humpback and possibly even blue whales.

Other months: Nov-Feb – cool, some rain, (Carnival Feb); Mar-May & Sep-Oct – pleasantly warm; Jun-Aug – very hot.

SOUTHERN TYROL
AUSTRIA

→ **Why now?** Some of the best late-season skiing.

In the high-altitude resorts of the Austrian Tyrol region, spring doesn't have to signal the end of skiing. The valleys south and west of Innsbruck – the Stubaital, Ötztal, Tuxertal and Paznauntal, in particular – are blessed with glaciers and lofty, north-facing slopes that hold the snow well into March and beyond. There's variety here, too: the pretty, traditional village of Obergurgl has pistes suitable for beginners and intermediates, while nearby Sölden has more challenging runs and two glaciers, guaranteeing skiing into May. High-level Ischgl is known for its excellent Snowpark, with jumps, boxes and funtubes, and for its very lively après-ski, while the slopes of the Stubaital include good off-piste options as well as traditional groomed runs. There are alternative activities galore, too: snowshoeing, winter hiking, tobogganing, ice-climbing and skating, and the James Bond exhibition on the Gaislachkogl mountain in Sölden adds some 00-oooh to proceedings. Oh, and the food and drink are both high-calibre, too.

Trip plan: The international airport at Innsbruck, capital of the Tirol, is well served by flights from across Europe, with good transport links to the resorts.

Need to know: If you absolutely, positively have to ski outside of the winter season, Hintertux is the place to head – skiing on the glacier is possible year-round.

Other months: Dec-Apr – ski season (some ski areas open through May); May & Oct-Nov – cool; Jun-Sep – warm, good hiking.

BELFAST, ARMAGH & DOWNPATRICK
N IRELAND

→ **Why now?** Celebrate Ireland's patron saint in his festival month.

To be sure, St Patrick is feted each 17 March in New York, Boston, even Buenos Aires – but to really immerse yourself in the craic, you need to be in Ireland. The whole island erupts with parades and parties, outdoor ceílís (folk dances) and concerts on the saint's day, but for an alternative experience, eschew the busier spots such as Dublin and head to Northern Ireland, where Patrick began his converting mission in the fifth century. The towns of Armagh – where the saint built his first great stone church in AD 445 – and Downpatrick, reputed site of his arrival and burial, combine for the ten-day Home of St Patrick Festival each year in mid-March, featuring music, talks, comedy, theatre and film. Belfast, unsurprisingly, hosts a boisterous carnival parade and concert – but the city is set up for partying year-round, with countless traditional pubs and buzzing bars, particularly in the Cathedral Quarter and around Grosvenor Road.

Trip plan: Base yourself in Belfast, which has plentiful accommodation and good transport links to Armagh and Downpatrick (both about 1hr away by bus, less by car).

Need to know: Had enough Guinness? County Armagh is famed for its cider – savour alcoholic apple juice from local cider-makers including Long Meadow, Toby's, Mac Ivors and the Armagh Cider Company.

Other months: Oct-Mar – cool; Apr-Jun – spring, warm, fairly dry; Jul-Sep – summer.

HELSINKI
FINLAND

→ **Why now?** Let off steam in the sauna capital of the world.

It's said that Finland has more than two million saunas – you can't move without tripping over a pine-clad, steam-filled cabin. Even in its bustling capital, with its Art Nouveau architecture, magnificent boulevards and edgy art, you're surrounded by places to heat up when the mercury's way down outside. You can strip off in one of the public saunas like traditional, wood-fired Kotiharjun, where punters have been sweated and scrubbed since 1928; or opt for a private venue on Helsinki Sauna Day: for one day each March, usually off-limits saunas open their doors to the average Jo(e) free of charge. But don't hide inside all day: in March you can make the most of the rapidly expanding daylight hours by enjoying city ice-skating and cross-country skiing nearby, as well as exploring groundbreaking street art – head north of the centre to the Pasila district, where ambitious artworks decorate walls, staircases and bridges. At night you'll want to retreat indoors, not least because Helsinki's bar and club scene is fabulous.

Trip plan: Allow at least three days to explore the city and its historic fortress island of Suomenlinna.

Need to know: Consider combining with a visit to Tallinn, Estonia's marvellously medieval capital, just 2hr away by ferry.

Other months: Dec-Feb – sub-zero skating and skiing; Mar – temperatures hover at zero; Apr-Jun – warmer, festivals; Jul-Aug – warm, long days, busy; Sep-Nov – autumn colours, berries.

(A) Boats crowd the harbour in Nice; (L) Snow and lambs in the Brecon Beacons; (R) Estonia's Soomaa waterscape in spring

NICE-MOSCOW
FRANCE & RUSSIA

→ **Why now? Take a classic train trip for this quirky twin-centre break.**

Europe's sleeper trains are an endangered species, but those that survive offer unforgettable experiences. The two-day, two-night odyssey between the French Riviera and the Russian capital is one such epic ride – and March is a prime time to enjoy it. Start in Nice where, by March, spring is aspringing in earnest and temperatures are among the highest in Europe. Drink in the coastal scenery as the train chugs through Monaco, Menton, San Remo and Genoa before heading inland to Milan and Verona, and crossing the Alps during the night. You'll hit Vienna for breakfast, and traverse the Czech Republic and Poland through the second day before changing gauges at Brest and powering through Belarus by night, arriving in Moscow mid-morning. Though March in the Russian capital is mostly sub-zero, it's also dry and bright – a fine time to photograph the Kremlin, Red Square and St Basil's Cathedral.

Trip plan: Russian Railways' night train 18 departs Nice Ville station on Sunday morning, arriving at Moscow Belorussky on Tuesday morning; in the other direction, train 17 departs Moscow on Thursday evening, arriving in Nice on Saturday evening. As an alternative, train 24 departs Paris Gare de l'Est on Thursday evening, arriving in Moscow on Saturday morning. Trains operate year-round.

Need to know: Check visa regulations before travelling. A Belarus transit visa and Russia visa are usually required.

Other months: Nice: Oct-May – pleasant; Jun-Sep – hot. Moscow: Nov-Mar – sub-zero; Apr-May & Sep-Oct – cool; Jun-Aug – warm.

BRECON BEACONS
WALES

→ **Why now? Outdoor pursuits among daffodils and spring lambs.**

Springtime in Wales: newborn lambs gambol on verdant hillsides sprinkled with clusters of butter-yellow daffodils. For once, reality matches cliché; though sunshine is never guaranteed here, the Welsh countryside is glorious in March. This is a great time to dust off wintry cobwebs and explore some of the UK's less visited corners, not least because on 1 March, St David's Day, Wales celebrates its patron saint. The Brecon Beacons, though popular with hikers, still boasts countless kilometres of near-empty trails on rolling mountains. At 886m (2907ft), angular Pen-y-Fan presents the classic challenge, but Black Mountain to the west and Sugar Loaf in the east also offer epic hiking. For a history fix, climb to Carreg Cennen castle – it opens for the year on 1 April, but its setting on a limestone scarp is sensational at any time of the year.

Trip plan: Bed down and fuel up in Crickhowell, Brecon or Abergavenny, all ideal bases from which to stride out – the latter in particular boasts a number of top-notch restaurants. Abergavenny is served by regular trains to Cardiff and Newport with connections to English destinations.

Need to know: Warm up after a hike with a bowl of traditional cawl (pronounced 'cowl'), a hearty, thick lamb and vegetable soup.

Other months: Nov-Feb – cold; Mar-Oct – spring to autumn, driest and warmest (Crickhowell Walking Festival Mar, Abergavenny Food Festival Sep).

SOOMAA NATIONAL PARK
ESTONIA

→ **Why now? Experience the 'fifth season' in the Baltic wilderness.**

Only four seasons? Spring, summer, autumn, winter? So passé! In the wetlands of 390 sq km (150 sq mile) Soomaa National Park in southwest Estonia, villagers welcome the so-called 'fifth season' from around late March. Snowmelt and runoff from heavy rain in nearby uplands send water levels soaring by up to 5m (16ft), transforming the landscape from merely boggy to a glistening watery wonderland. The swamps and meandering river are inundated by floods, leaving meadows submerged, forests eerily reflected in still waters and tussock mounds morphed into isolated islands. Bog-walking, using snowshoe-like footwear, is the usual way of navigating Soomaa, but in the 'fifth season' exploring by boat is really the only way to get around. Join a guided tour in a *haabja* (traditional dugout canoe) or kayak through the forest, scouring treetops for eagles and marsh edges for capercaillie, black grouse and corncrakes. Look out for beaver and listen for wolves – bear and lynx roam the region too, though you'd be lucky to spot them.

Trip plan: Hire a car to reach the National Park Visitor Centre at Kõrtsi-Tõramaa. Kayaking trips run on the river outside the 'fifth season'.

Need to know: 'Fifth season' floods usually occur for a couple of weeks in late March or early April, but can vary in extent year to year. From late April to late June, bog-walking is restricted to protect nesting birds.

Other months: Sep-May – cold, best wildlife-watching; Jun-Aug – warm.

The warm red rooftops of walled Dubrovnik

MALLORCA SPAIN

March sees Mallorca's almond trees blossom

Why now? Escape the crowds under cover of almond blossom.

The 'snow of Mallorca' still blankets the hillsides of this Balearic island in March – not actual, frozen-water snow, you understand; rather, it's the pinky-white blossom of countless almond trees that give Mallorca its distinctive icing-sugar coating at the start of the year. And as the blossoms fall in early March, so the increasingly warm weather makes exploring a delight – before the arrival of masses of package tourists, but with plenty of sunshine to enjoy the beaches, roam traditional honey-hued towns and villages such as Deià, Fornalutx and Sóller, and hike the heights of the Serra de Tramuntana. Don't discount Palma, either; though

sometimes unfortunately conflated with nearby party resorts such as Magaluf, the capital's Old Town is a charming historic district, with wonderful palaces, museums, squares and the monumental cathedral.

Trip plan: Ample domestic and international flights serve Palma, and with reasonable car hire and efficient public transport, it's easy to organise a weekend break or a longer tour of the island.

Need to know: Mallorca is a magnet for cyclists. Several pro teams train on its well-maintained mountain roads in winter – bring your bike and join them.

Other months: Dec-Feb – winter, mild with showers; Mar-Apr & Nov – warm; May-Oct – hot.

DUBROVNIK
CROATIA

→ Why now? Promenade the 'pearl of the Adriatic' without the summer crowds.

A crescent of terracotta roofs curling round to embrace an azure corner of the Adriatic, ever-beguiling Dubrovnik has been assailed many times through the centuries: besieged by Saracens, taken by Venetians, then devastated by the 1667 earthquake, by Napoleon and then by the war of 1991–92. Today, its alluring thoroughfares are invaded each summer by hordes of cruise-ship passengers – but arrive in March, at the cusp of spring and before the waves of day-trippers arrive, and you'll mostly enjoy the sunshine and historic grandeur in the company of locals. Start by making a circuit of the Old Town's walls, visiting the medieval forts built to defend the city, then delve into the labyrinth of gleaming limestone streets in the timeless core. For a different perspective, take the cable car up Mt Srd, or head around the bay to peaceful Cavtat, founded by Greek settlers who fled Slavic attack to build the more famous Dubrovnik in AD 614.

Trip plan: Reasonably priced accommodation in Dubrovnik's Old Town is limited; you'll find more in Lapad, a mile or so to the west.

Need to know: The cable car on Mt Srd runs year-round, though the last departure is earlier in March than in high summer. Ferries to Cavtat run Apr–Oct, and some tourist facilities may be closed in March.

Other months: Nov-Mar – cool, few tourists, many facilities closed; Apr-Oct – warm, clear days.

Ightham Mote, a medieval manor house in the Kent countryside

© RMAX / Getty Images

KENT ENGLAND

➜ **Why now?** See spring-spruced stately homes in the Garden of England.

Many of the UK's greatest historic buildings, owned or managed by the National Trust, are closed over winter for some vital conservation TLC. Spring's a great time to visit, just as the dustsheets are cast off and the doors flung open, allowing you to discover these newly spruced-up time machines in all their magnificence.

A cluster of properties in Kent are prime examples. Knole, the Trust's largest house, boasts an array of 400-year-old showrooms, and is set in a vast medieval deer park that's a delight to roam in spring. At Chartwell, country home of British statesman Winston Churchill, you can visit 'Winnie's' painting studio and admire his art. Nearby, timber-framed Ightham Mote is arguably England's most romantic medieval manor house, dating from the 14th century. Take a long weekend to explore all three (or more – there are plenty of other wonderful NT houses to visit nearby); or tick off two in a day by walking a delightful 6.5km (4 mile) section of the Greensand Way footpath, which runs directly between Ightham Mote and Knole.

Trip plan: Sevenoaks, which has a railway station served by trains from London, makes a convenient base for exploring all three properties.

Need to know: Exact opening dates and time vary – check www.nationaltrust.org.uk for the latest details.

Other months: Nov-Mar – many National Trust properties closed (some open limited areas pre-Christmas); Apr-Oct – most properties open.

High above the Arctic Circle, a skier tours the Lyngen Alps above the Lyngenfjord

© Lachlan Bucknall / Alamy Stock Photo

LYNGEN ALPS NORWAY

→ Why now? Ski-tour the mountains during the *kornsnø* season.

Norwegians have many different words for snow, from freshly fallen flakes (*nysnø*) and the best type for snowballs (*kramsnø*) to fresh powder (*puddersnø, pulversnø, finsnø*). But according to aficionados, the best snow for ski-touring is compact-grained spring fall known as *kornsø*. And for the finest ski-touring in Norway, head to the Lyngen Alps, a jagged ridge looming up to 1833m (6014ft) along the rocky

finger sandwiched between the Ullsfjord and the Lyngenfjord, far north of the Arctic Circle. Challenging, sure, but ski-touring is a thrilling step up from cross-country, offering the chance to traverse pristine snow off-piste and far from busy resorts and crowds. March is the ideal time to strap on those skis and explore the Lyngen Alps, as rapidly increasing sun and that grainy *kornsø* provide excellent conditions; make for the slopes of Rundfjellet, which offer a safe introduction to the sport.

Trip plan: The nearest airport is Tromsø, 50km (31 miles) to the west, which has plenty of connecting flights to international destinations via Oslo. You'll need to hire a car or book a tour to reach the Lyngen Alps.
Need to know: Sightings of the Aurora Borealis (Northern Lights) often peak around the spring equinox – keep an eye on the sky during cold, clear nights.
Other months: Oct-Feb – cold, dark; Mar-Apr – ideal for ski-touring; May-Jun – Midnight Sun; Jul-Sep – wonderful hiking.

CAMARGUE
FRANCE

Why now? Watch pink flamingos, white horses and black bulls on gleaming wetlands.

Designated as a Unesco Biosphere Reserve, this salty 1930 sq km (745 sq mile) expanse of wetland at the mouth of the Rhône River is a unique habitat of marshes, lagoons and grassland that hosts about one-third of all European bird species in the course of each year. It's also home to saltmakers, *gardians* ('cowboys') riding white horses and herding black bulls, and countless pink flamingos that perform elaborate courtship displays over the winter. The trick is to time your visit right. March is a sweet spot: the flamingos are still dancing, migratory birds are starting to arrive and the mercury's rising, but it's just early enough to avoid the summer plagues of insanity-inducing mosquitoes. To watch the birds in action, visit the Parc Ornithologique du Pont de Gau, amble the nature trails – try La Capelière, Domaine de la Palissade or Digue à la Mer – and perhaps saddle up for a horse-ride. Don't miss the walled medieval city of Aigues-Mortes ('dead waters') to the west, and the extraordinary Roman remains and Van Gogh sites of Arles.

Trip plan: Base yourself in Arles and spend two or three days exploring the city sights, making day-trips to the bird-bustling wetlands, Aigues-Mortes and the seaside town of Stes-Maries-de-la-Mer.

Need to know: Avignon is less than 20min by train from Arles, so you can see the immense Palais des Papes – the world's largest Gothic palace – on an easy day-trip.

Other months: Nov-Mar – dancing flamingos; Apr-Nov – mosquitoes!

Find wild horses and pink flamingos in France's Camargue

71

MONT ST-MICHEL FRANCE

→ **Why now? Watch spring tides gallop toward this magical medieval marvel.**

It's over 13 centuries since the Archangel Michael ordered Bishop Aubert of Avranches to build his church on a rocky island between Brittany and Normandy, his edifice rapidly becoming a popular pilgrimage destination for devout Christians. Today, the great confection of pinnacles, ramparts and turrets constructed over the following centuries – like a giant wedding cake designed by Peter Jackson – attracts upwards of 2.5 million visitors each year. Most, though, arrive in summer: come in March, and you can gawp at the extraordinary Romanesque-Gothic church and its 13th-century Merveille ('Marvel') service wing unhindered by the hordes. In addition, time your visit for just after the March full moon and you can witness the natural spectacle of the *grandes marées* – Europe's highest spring tides, rising up to 15m (49ft) and charging in across the bay 'as swiftly as a galloping horse', according to Victor Hugo.

Trip plan: Most hotels and restaurants on the mount itself are overpriced and underwhelming – better stay near Genêts to the east, where some accommodation options have views across the bay to the rock-top abbey.

Need to know: If the Grande Rue – the main street winding up to the abbey – gets too hectic, dodge the crowds by taking to the path along the medieval ramparts. Check tide timetables at www.ot-montsaintmichel.com.

Other months: Nov-Mar – cold; Apr & Sep-Oct – moderate crowds, high tides (bay walks Apr-Oct); May-Aug – warm, crowded.

Mont St-Michel, rising like a mirage from the coastal sands

ASSISI ITALY

→ **Why now? Find quiet-season peace in St Francis' birthplace.**

St Francis, patron saint of animals, famously renounced the trappings of worldly wealth. His hometown, Assisi, hasn't quite done likewise – today, it's machine-tooled to cater to the hordes of tourists and pilgrims who descend to pay homage at Francis' namesake medieval basilica, packed with astonishing 13th- and 14th-century art. Yet there's no denying the spiritual essence of the place, particularly in this quiet month when tourists are (relatively) sparse, and several venues in and around Assisi offer meditation retreats at which you can recharge your metaphysical batteries. Don't neglect the historic marvels, though: the mighty Francesco Basilica promises frescoes by Giotto in its Basilica Superiore, and by Cimabue, Martini and Lorenzetti in its Basilica Inferiore. Otherwise, check out the Roman amphitheatre and the church of San Damiano, where St Francis is said to have heard the voice of God in the early 13th century. Oh, and treat yourself to a drop of fine local Orvieto or Grechetto white – the younger, hellraising Francis would certainly approve.

Labyrinthine medieval streets in Assisi

© Matt Munro / Lonely Planet

Trip plan: If you're not joining a residential retreat, book accommodation well in advance, or consider staying in nearby Spello. Alternatively, a week or two road-tripping around Umbria's hill towns – Gubbio, Trevi, Todi and so on – would be time well spent.

Need to know: Assisi is busy all year, but gets hectic during Easter, the Calendimaggio festival (early May) and Festival of St Francis (3–4 Oct).

Other months: Dec-Mar – cool; Apr-May & Oct-Nov – warmer; Jun-Sep – hot.

BEYOND ASSISI

 PERUGIA • 25KM (15 MILES) • Town with a pristine medieval centre and an international student population

 SAN MARINO • 160KM (100 MILES) • Landlocked micronation with ramparts and hilltop views

 PIANO GRANDE • 170KM (105 MILES) • Vast upland plain renowned for its springtime wildflowers

 **FLORENCE • 180KM (110 MILES) •** World-class art, jaw-dropping architecture and gourmet Tuscan cuisine

Methoni's
15th-century
Venetian fortress

PELOPONNESE
GREECE

→ **Why now? Cool ruins, warm sunshine.**

Inexplicably, though this hand-shaped peninsula has some of Greece's finest beaches, best-preserved ancient and medieval sites, most appealing mountains and the original Arcadia, it sees only a fraction of the tourists that besiege other corners of the country. March promises sparse crowds but clement temperatures for walking, plus good availability and prices for accommodation. Must-sees include Olympia, where the Olympic Games were held for over a thousand years; the citadel of Mycenae, swirled by Homeric legends; Epidaurus' 14,000-seater amphitheatre; and the Byzantine port of Monemvasia. The wild Mani peninsula offers fine hiking, particularly around Výros Gorge, as well as alluring villages, while the west coast has some of Greece's best sand. Food is fresh and fabulous: Kalamata is famed for its plump olives, while aubergines, fish and honey feature in many local treats; look out, too, for Agiorgitiko red wines.

Trip plan: From Athens, cross onto the Peloponnese via ancient Corinth, and visit nearby Mycenae, Epidaurus and the pretty seaside town of Nafplio with its Venetian houses – doable in a few days. With longer, head south to Monemvasia and the Mani, then back north via the west coast and Olympia.

Need to know: Athens is 85km (53 miles) by road from Corinth (driving time around 1hr); buses, trains and ferries run from near Athens to the Peloponnese. Check bus times: services may be reduced outside high season.

Other months: Nov-Feb – cold; Mar-May – warming, flowers; Jun-Aug – hot, busy; Sept-Oct – warm, quieter.

SOFIA BULGARIA

Why now? Bring in the spring while snow beckons on the ski slopes.

In Bulgaria, March is a lady – well, a grumpy old woman, Baba Marta, with fickle moods. On the first of her month, following an ancient pagan tradition, Martenitsa – red-and-white bracelets – are exchanged in tribute to 'Grandma March', hoping for sunny weather. But Bulgaria's capital is a buzzing place to explore whether Baba Marta is sunny or sullen, packed with history, east-meets-west culture and chompable cuisine. On warm spring days, it's a treat to wander between ancient Roman sites, Thracian relics in the dazzling Archaeological Museum, fresco-daubed medieval churches, gilded Russian-style domes and Communist-era monuments. But if the skies cloud over, head to a cinema – Sofia International Film Festival screens some fantastic independent movies during March. And for an adrenaline boost, there's accessible skiing on the city's local peak, Vitosha, or in the Rila Mountains a little further south; good snow lingers into April, but slopes are less crowded than in the thick of winter. For aprés, hop between the traditional pubs and chic bars around Vitosha Boulevard.

Trip plan: Central Sofia is eminently walkable, and is reachable from the airport on Metro Line 1 in under 20min. For taxis, use a reputable company with metered fares such as OK-Supertrans.

Need to know: For a quick, tasty morning snack between sightseeing stops, grab a *banitsa* (traditional flaky cheese pastry), sold at bakeries across the city.

Other months: Dec-Feb – skiing on Vitosha; Mar-May & Nov – cool; Jun-Aug – hot; Sep-Oct – pleasantly warm.

© Helen Smith / Getty Images

Sunshine-bright daffodils cluster in dappled woodlands

LAKE DISTRICT ENGLAND

Why now? Be uplifted and inspired by a host of golden daffodils.

The poet William Wordsworth loved the Lake District, settling at Dove Cottage (now open to visitors) in Grasmere, and finding inspiration in the surrounding fells: it was after a daffodil-blessed walk in spring 1802 that he produced his most famous work, *I Wandered Lonely as a Cloud*. Spring in the Lakes might make anyone feel lyrical. Newborn lambs bleating, daffodils nodding, the hills an extraordinary shade of green. The first serious waves of tourists arrive in April, so in March the region's roads, campsites and honeypot towns are quieter. Holiday cottages are also easier to book and generally more affordable, while facilities such as boat services across the lakes are becoming more frequent. And there's heaps of great hiking and cycling; yes, the weather can be unpredictable, but then it always is year-round. Prepare for cold and rain, hope for sun, set out to be inspired.

Trip plan: Base yourself at Windermere or Ambleside for Lake Windermere, Coniston Water and Grasmere. Keswick is gateway to the northern lakes and the valleys of Borrowdale and Buttermere. Scafell Pike, England's highest summit (978m/3209ft), is in the west.

Need to know: Lakeland peaks aren't too high but should not be underestimated – go prepared, and choose trails suited to your experience.

Other months: Nov-Feb – coldest, snow possible; Mar-May & Sept-Oct – quieter; Jun-Aug – warmest, busiest.

RHODES GREECE

→ Why now? Chase the sun in the brightest corner of Greece.

Tucked away off the south coast of Anatolia, the easternmost of the Dodecanese islands is also among the sunniest in Greece, and has a sizeable year-round community that ensures plenty to do even out of the main tourist season. True, the water's chilly in March, but as the beautiful sandy swathes in the northeast (such as Anthony Quinn beach) are empty of the crowds that plague them in high summer, you might be tempted to take a brisk dip. But mostly, this is a time to explore the historic sites and gorgeous landscapes in peace. Rhodes Town's historic core, guarded by massive stone walls and encompassing the imposing inns and palaces of the cobbled Knights' Quarter, is a must. But don't miss the white 17th-century houses and ancient Acropolis of Lindos, and the medieval monasteries and valleys in the south.

Trip plan: Fly to Rhodes; spend a night or two in Rhodes Town, but allow several days to explore the rest of the island – and do include a night in Lindos. Consider sailing to Halki, just off Rhodes' west coast, for an even more low-key island escape.

Need to know: Direct flights and ferry timetables thin out or stop completely over winter, so check in advance if planning to combine Rhodes with other islands.

Other months: Nov-Mar – off season, some businesses closed; Apr-May & Sep-Oct – pleasantly warm; Jun-Aug – hot, though the meltemi provides cooling breezes.

© Chris Ridley / Getty Images

(A) The Acropolis of Lindos on St Paul's Bay; (B) The elegant Old Town of Rhodes

© Matt Munro / Lonely Planet

ISTANBUL
TURKEY

→ **Why now? Discover bazaars, ancient wonders and culinary secrets in peace.**

You might debate which is the greatest treasure of the former Constantinople: the incredible sixth-century basilica-mosque-museum of Aya Sofya? Sprawling, opulent Topkapı Palace? The domes, minarets and ornate azure tilework of the Blue Mosque? Wander among them all to decide for yourself, by all means – and in March, as things begin to warm up towards the end of the low season, you can enjoy discounts, smaller crowds and more forgiving weather. But save some time for the greatest legacy the Ottomans left the world: food! Why else would the Spice Bazaar be so huge and bustling? From simple kebabs to meze feasts and the luscious aubergine masterpiece, *imam bayaldi*, there are few cuisines as indulgent as Turkish. Over the past couple of decades a roster of excellent food-themed walking tours and cookery schools has sprung up in Istanbul, providing the opportunity to combine a spring city break with a culinary reboot.

Trip plan: Base yourself in the Sultanahmet district, on the west (European) side of the Bosphorus, for easy access to the Grand Bazaar, Spice Bazaar and most historic sites.

Need to know: Turkish etiquette decrees that you shouldn't point your finger or the sole of your foot towards anyone.

Other months: Nov-Feb – cold, damp; Mar-May & Sept-Oct – mild, quiet; Jun-Aug – hot, busy.

A cruise along the Golden Horn is a great way to see Istanbul's sights

© Viacheslav Lopatin / Shutterstock

BEYOND ISTANBUL

 **PRINCES ISLANDS • 20KM (12 MILES) •** An escape from the city with oceanfront dining and tiny coves for paddling

 EDIRNE • 240KM (150 MILES) • A bustling border town with mosques as fine as almost any in Istanbul

 BUCHAREST • 445KM (277 MILES) • Connect with the Romanian capital via the overnight Bosphorus/Balkan Express

 EPHESUS • 540KM (335 MILES) • One of the greatest surviving Graeco-Roman cities

Floats at Valencia's Las Fallas festival

A murmuration of starlings in the Wadden Sea at Jutland

VALENCIA
SPAIN

→ **Why now?** Sample Spain's finest paella in the springtime sunshine.

Spain's third city heats up in March – meteorologically and culturally. This is the month when legions of huge figures called *ninots* are constructed in Valencia's centre, then burned in a vast conflagration accompanied by the fireworks and festivities of Las Fallas. Aside from the pyrotechnics, though, March is a great time to explore the city's culinary variety, reflecting the fertility of the surrounding La Huerta farmlands. Valencia is the home of paella, and nowhere else is the rice feast prepared so magnificently – head to the wetlands of nearby Albufera National Park to see the lush rice fields, and take a cookery class to learn how to prepare the perfect paella yourself. Spare time to explore the city's historic, warren-like Barrio del Carmen, visit its multiple museums and admire its magnificent Gothic cathedral and futuristic La Ciudad de las Artes y Ciencias cultural complex, largely designed by renowned Valencian architect Santiago Calatrava.

Trip plan: Valencia is served by flights from most major European cities.

Need to know: Valencia gets full to bursting for the climax of Las Fallas (15–19 March) – it's a great time to be in town, but book transport and accommodation well in advance.

Other months: Jan-May – mild, pleasant; Jun-Sep – very hot, busy; Oct-Dec – autumn: cooler, rainy.

WADDEN SEA
DENMARK

→ **Why now?** Marvel at the 'Black Sun' murmurations.

Early in the evening, as the sun dips into the calm waters of the Wadden Sea, a strange shape appears in the sky: billowing, streaming, even dancing – a cloud made of tens or even hundreds of thousands of starlings, arriving to find safety in their nocturnal roosts on the marshes near Ribe and Tønder. The sight of a starling murmuration is mesmerising wherever it occurs, but in early spring and autumn off the southwest coast of Jutland, it has a special power – here, it's known as the Sort Sol: the 'Black Sun'. March is also a great time to discover the wonders of this watery national park, a crucial feeding stop for over 12 million birds on their bi-annual migrations; join their shellfish quest by wandering out on the tidal mudflats to gather, shuck and slurp oysters; the season spans from mid-October to the end of April.

Trip plan: Base yourself in Ribe, Denmark's oldest town, dating from the ninth century; its cobbled streets are lined with charming medieval buildings and dominated by an ancient cathedral.

Need to know: Book a tour or learn more about the history and ecosystems of the area's Unesco-listed mudflats and saltmarshes at the groundbreaking Wadden Sea Centre near Ribe.

Other months: Nov-Feb – cold; Mar-Apr & Sep-Oct – cool, murmurations (common seals rest on sandbanks Jul-Oct); May-Aug – warm.

CHIŞINĂU
MOLDOVA

→ **Why now?** Toast the impending spring with a cultural blossoming.

Winters in Moldova are dark and mostly sub-zero between December and February – so when spring comes, it's welcomed with pizzazz. On 1 March – Mărţişor ('Little March') – men present braided red-and-white amulets to their loves, and in the capital, Chişinău, classical and folk concerts and dances are staged during the ten-day Mărţişor Music Festival. Part of the Soviet Union for half a century, Chişinău boasts its fair share of Brutalist blocks, but they're interspersed with cultural nuggets (don't miss the National Art Museum or the Moorish-style Ethnographic and Natural History Museum). The biggest surprise, though, is the wine: Moldova has been creating gluggable tipples since at least the third millennium BC. If a wet day hits, wine-bar-hop to sip quality pinot noirs and cabernets, along with wines made with local grape varieties such as Fetească Neagră. Or pay a visit to one of the world's two largest wine cellars, Mileştii Mici and Cricova, which have a combined total of some 320km (200 miles) of ancient subterranean tunnels, kept to a constant temperature year-round and stocked with more than 2.5 million bottles of wine.

Trip plan: Allow two days to explore the city, which can be roamed happily on foot, but add extra for visits to wineries such as Mileştii Mici and Cricova outside Chişinău's centre.

Need to know: Feeling fragile after all that wine? The traditional hangover cure is a bowl of *zeama*, fragrant chicken noodle soup.

Other months: Nov-Mar – cold; Apr-May – warming (Victory Day celebrations 9 May); Jun-Oct – warm, bright but often rainy.

April

WHERE TO GO WHEN

I WANT TO

CHALLENGE MYSELF

TAKE ME OUT FOR...

- FOOD
  - ESTREMADURA, PORTUGAL P87
  - SOUTH TYROL, ITALY P84
- DRINK
  - PTUJ & MARIBOR, SLOVENIA P101
  - PLOVDIV, BULGARIA P86

Down a *ginja de Óbidos* in Portugal

No filter needed: the Rainbow Lake in Italy's South Tyrol

TAKE ME TO TOWN

- ART & CULTURE
  - METZ, FRANCE P93
  - ROME, ITALY P103
- NIGHT-LIFE & HEDONISM
  - MAASTRICHT, NETHERLANDS P99
  - GALWAY, IRELAND P87

Feel the echoes of ancient crowds in Rome's Colosseum

RELAX/ INDULGE

Cyprus' Aphrodite's rock and Romiou beach are at their best in spring

DIAL IT DOWN

- WELLNESS —— ÎLE DE RÉ, FRANCE P89
- CHILLING —— WESTERN CYPRUS P93

Slurp down oysters on Île de Ré

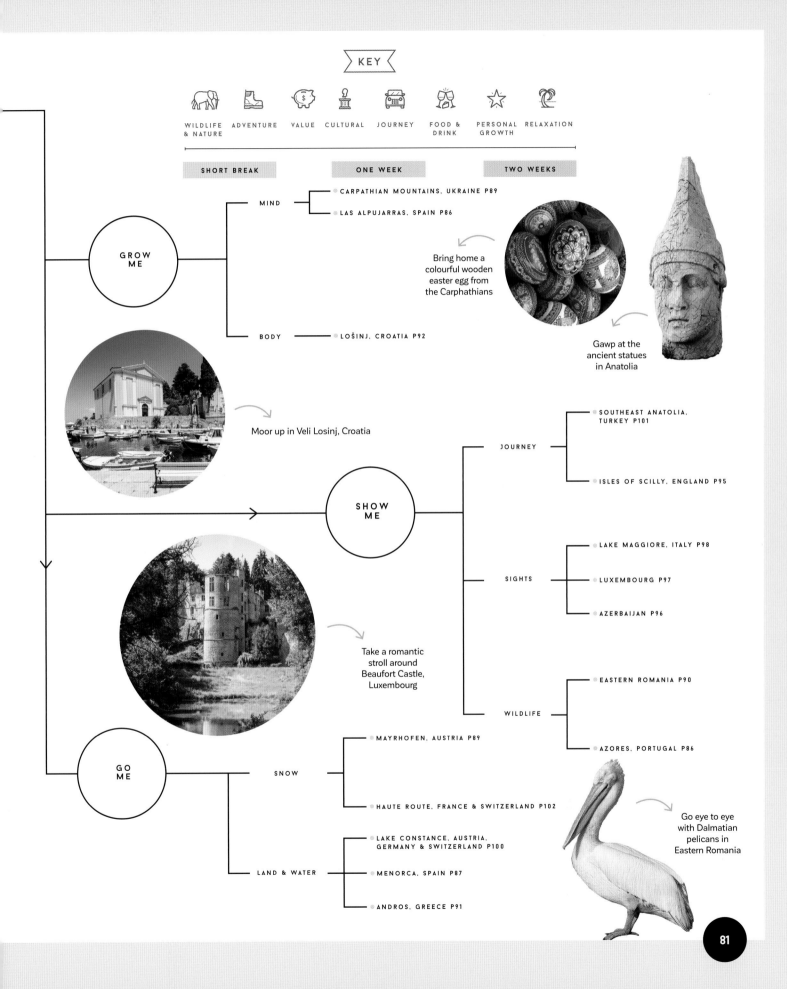

KEY

🐘	🥾	🐷	🏛	🚙	🥂	☆	🌴
WILDLIFE & NATURE	ADVENTURE	VALUE	CULTURAL	JOURNEY	FOOD & DRINK	PERSONAL GROWTH	RELAXATION

SHORT BREAK | **ONE WEEK** | **TWO WEEKS**

GROW ME

MIND
- CARPATHIAN MOUNTAINS, UKRAINE P89
- LAS ALPUJARRAS, SPAIN P86

BODY
- LOŠINJ, CROATIA P92

Bring home a colourful wooden easter egg from the Carphathians

Gawp at the ancient statues in Anatolia

Moor up in Veli Losinj, Croatia

SHOW ME

JOURNEY
- SOUTHEAST ANATOLIA, TURKEY P101
- ISLES OF SCILLY, ENGLAND P95

SIGHTS
- LAKE MAGGIORE, ITALY P98
- LUXEMBOURG P97
- AZERBAIJAN P96

WILDLIFE
- EASTERN ROMANIA P90
- AZORES, PORTUGAL P86

Take a romantic stroll around Beaufort Castle, Luxembourg

GO ME

SNOW
- MAYRHOFEN, AUSTRIA P89
- HAUTE ROUTE, FRANCE & SWITZERLAND P102

LAND & WATER
- LAKE CONSTANCE, AUSTRIA, GERMANY & SWITZERLAND P100
- MENORCA, SPAIN P87
- ANDROS, GREECE P91

Go eye to eye with Dalmatian pelicans in Eastern Romania

EVENTS
IN APIL

WALPURGISNACHT

Thale, Germany

On the night when witches gather in the Harz Mountains, join the throngs on the Hexentanzplatz (Witches' Dance Square) for music and merriment.

INTERNATIONAL CHOCOLATE FESTIVAL

Óbidos, Portugal

Admire and inhale the delectable confectionary, used to create monumental sculptures during Óbidos' annual extravaganza.

SEMANA SANTA

Seville, Spain

Easter parades are most dramatic in the Andalusian capital, with floats and processions of brotherhoods sporting pointed hoods.

SNOWBOMBING

Mayrhofen, Austria

Ski or board by day, dance by night during the Tyrol's funkiest week-long music-and-snowsports festival.

KING'S DAY

Amsterdam, Netherlands

Orange is ubiquitous during this day of royal revelry, with street parties and general mayhem across the country.

PANIGIRAKI

Arachova, Greece

The most renowned of the Greek festivities on the Feast of St George involves parades, sports and other celebrations.

NATALE DI ROMA

Rome, Italy

Celebrate the birthday of the Eternal City – reputedly founded on 21 April 753BC – with events, illuminations and extravagant firework displays.

FESTIVAL INTERNATIONAL DES JARDINS

Château de Chaumont-sur-Loire, France

Nurture your horticultural imagination at the International Garden Festival, bringing together the best of garden design for three decades.

Inner wheel labels

- Easter Week, usually early April — $
- Mid-April — $$$
- From mid-April — $$
- 21 April — $
- 23 April — $
- 27 April — $
- Late April — $
- 30 April — $$

ISLES OF SCILLY, ENGLAND

Glimpse puffins on
the Isles of Scilly

SOUTH TYROL, ITALY

LAKE CONSTANCE

LUXEMBOURG

Sunrise over
Luxembourg City

Marvel at Rome's
ancient sites

ROME, ITALY

WESTERN CYPRUS

Aphrodite's Rock
and Beach in
Western Cyprus

Jamón Ibérico is
a staple in Las
Alpujarras

ESTREMADURA, PORTUGAL

LAS ALPUJARRAS, SPAIN

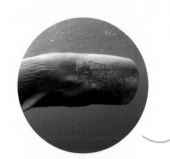

Watch sperm whale mothers
diving with their calves in
the Azores

ÎLE DE RÉ, FRANCE   AZORES, PORTUGAL

MAASTRICHT, NETHERLANDS

METZ, FRANCE

Find a medieval marvel in the
cathedral of Saint Stephen in Metz

GALWAY, IRELAND

LAKE MAGGIORE, ITALY

A statue on Isola
Bella overlooks
Lake Maggiore

MAYRHOFEN, AUSTRIA

HAUTE ROUTE, FRANCE & SWITZERLAND

SOUTH-EAST ANATOLIA,
TURKEY

Pretty wooden boats
crowd the harbour of
Losinj, Croatia

LOSINJ, CROATIA   ANDROS, GREECE

AZERBAIJAN

EASTERN ROMANIA

PTUJ & MARIBOR, SLOVENIA

Try your hand
at painting a
Ukrainian
Easter egg

CARPATHIANS, UKRAINE

Wonder at Plovdiv's
amphitheatre

PLOVDIV, BULGARIA

MENORCA, SPAIN

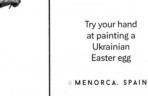

SOUTH TYROL ITALY

→ Why now? Pamper your palate with spring specialities.

In Alto Adige you're likely to be greeted not with a 'buongiorno' but a 'grüss gott', reflecting the historic heritage of the area also known as Südtirol. Formerly part of Austria, this spectacular region on the southern slopes of the Alps became part of Italy after WWI, and today it's a gastronomic mélange of the two. In April, orchards around Bolzano (Bozen) glow pink and white and the air is scented with apple blossoms, while in Terlano (Terlan), restaurants celebrate the start of the asparagus season with special meals and special events. Scoot or hike verdant valleys between picturesque Alpine villages and into the foothills of the Dolomites, pausing at traditional Buschenschänke and Hofschänke (farm inns) to savour strudel, speck (cured ham) and *schlutzkrapfen*

(local ravioli) with fine Südtirol wines. Feeling energetic? The Adige Cycle Route follows the Roman Via Augusta alongside the Adige River, with enticing side-trails.

Trip plan: Bolzano is around 2hr from Verona or Innsbruck (the nearest airports), and on a busy railway line between Germany and the rest of Italy. Find a farmstay or guesthouse and roam for a tasty long weekend – by bike, car or the quintessentially Italian Vespa.

Need to know: As well as German and Italian, you might hear a third language spoken in South Tyrol: Ladin, an ancient tongue derived from historic Latin.

Other months: Dec-Mar – cold, Dolomites skiing; Apr-May & Oct-Nov – pleasant, fairly dry; Jun-Sep – warm, wetter.

Picture perfect: Lake Braies in the Prags Dolomites of South Tyrol

AZORES
PORTUGAL

→ **Why now?** Watch migrating whales in the mid-Atlantic.

The nine islands of the Azores are remote indeed, scattered 1500km (932 miles) west of their Portuguese motherland. Created by up-thrusting seabed volcanoes, this mid-Atlantic archipelago is a playground of gnarled rocks, black sands, lava tubes, crater lakes and soaring cones – yet it's also endlessly green, and produces excellent wines. April brings spring blossoms – the azaleas are incredible – and mesmerising marine wildlife: 24 of the world's 80 whale species are seen off the Azores. One species you're less likely to encounter is the tourist: April is wonderfully quiet. Join a boat tour to spot the oceanic behemoths, or watch from clifftop *vigias* – former whale-hunters' lookout towers, repurposed for eco-tourists. You could also head to Pico Island to bag Portugal's highest peak (2351m/7713ft), hike around lakes and enjoy birdwatching and flowers on Flores, or plan a cycling trip on Terceira, the 'lilac isle'.

Trip plan: Ponta Delgada International Airport is on São Miguel. Base yourself on one island – São Miguel is largest, with the most tours. Or spend a week or two island-hopping: Pico, Faial and São Jorge ('The Triangle') are easily combined by ferry.

Need to know: To watch beaked whales and swim with manta rays off Pico, come between July and September.

Other months: Nov-Mar – rainy, reduced services; Apr-Jun – sunny, flowers, whales; Jul-Aug – warmest, whales, diving; Sept-Oct – warm, whales.

LAS ALPUJARRAS
SPAIN

→ **Why now?** Explore quiet villages, blooming hillsides and local delicacies.

A string of white-painted villages speckle the southern foothills of the Sierra Nevada – the region known as Las Alpujarras, which provided a haven for the Moors expelled from Granada in 1492. Still more Moroccan than Spanish in many ways, this region is typified by its traditional farming villages. April is the ideal time to visit, whether you want to relax in warm spring sunshine, hike tantalising trails through blossoming orange groves, or perhaps learn local cuisine – various places offer lessons or courses where you can master everything from almond and garlic soup to rich stews. Semana Santa (Easter) celebrations, usually in April, bring huge parades, and there's still the chance to snow-shoe in the high Sierra above. A string of fine beaches – much quieter before the summer peak – are just a hop away to the south.

Trip plan: Málaga, Almería or Granada are the nearest airports; there's no convenient train station in the Alpujarras. Explore from a base in one of the charming Alpujarran villages, perhaps Mairena, Válor, Cádiar, or Yegen, former home of writer Gerald Brenan.

Need to know: Some of Spain's finest *jamón serrano* (dry-cured ham) is produced in the lofty village of Trevélez – visit producers to see the production process and buy direct.

Other months: Nov-Feb – mild winters; Mar-May & Oct – warm, pleasant; Jun-Sept – baking hot.

PLOVDIV
BULGARIA

→ **Why now?** Absorb past glories and bargain wine in Bulgaria's historic hub.

The ancient Thracians settled it some 7000 years ago. Alexander the Great's father, Philip II of Macedon, renamed it Philippopolis after himself in the fourth century BCE. Then the Romans remodelled it, the Goths plundered it and Bulgars, Byzantines, Crusaders and Ottoman Turks took it and developed it over the following centuries. Today, Plovdiv cherishes its chequered past, but the culture and nightlife of this vibrant student town is far from fusty – particularly since the city was named European Capital of Culture 2019, and following renovations in the Kapana creative quarter and Tsar Simeon Gardens. The mellow spring days of April, before May's rains and the summer crowds arrive, are ideal for an offbeat city break: explore Roman remains, stately Nationalist Revival mansions and innovative art exhibitions by day, then hop between buzzing bars by night. Surrounded by the sprawling vineyards of the Thracian Plain, Plovdiv is the place to taste fine Mavrud reds and some of the country's most appealing restaurants – all reassuringly inexpensive.

Trip plan: Plovdiv has an international airport, though Sofia receives more flights and is a little over 2hr away by bus or train, less by car. Allow three days to explore the city and take a trip to Bachkovo Monastery, surrounded by vineyards and hike-friendly hills.

Need to know: Prices rise during the festival-heavy months of May and September.

Other months: Dec-Feb – cold; Mar-Apr & Oct-Nov – cooler; May-Sep – warm, busy.

MENORCA
SPAIN

Why now? Complete a circuit of this peaceful Balearic island.

The scent of orange blossom and wild jasmine wafting on warm breezes, the shush of waves against deserted shores, the empty prehistoric sites and paths – April brings the best out of Menorca's historic coastal trail. Reputedly created during the Middle Ages for horse-mounted knights patrolling the shore, the Camí de Cavalls traces a gently undulating, 185km (115 mile) waymarked circuit, accessible to hikers, mountain-bikers and – for budding knights – horse-riders. Menorca has plenty of fascinating historic sites, too: the old centres of the capital Maó and former capital Ciutadella, plus a scattering of megalithic sites, some dating from 2000BCE. Fuel up on local specialities such as *sobrasada* (paprika sausage), *caldereta de langosta* (lobster stew) and artisan Mahón cheese, and cool off with an iced gin and lemon – legacy of 18th-century British occupation.

Trip plan: Menorca Airport is 5km (3 miles) southwest of Maó, served by regular buses. If not completing the Camí de Cavalls, pick one or two bases from which to spend a week exploring – perhaps attractive Ciutadella in the west, and Maó in the east.

Need to know: Ferries between Ciutadella and Alcúdia in northern Mallorca make the short crossing at least daily, enabling a twin-island break. Some accommodation and businesses may not open till May.

Other months: Dec-Mar – cool, wet; Apr-May – warming, drier; Jun-Aug – very hot, dry; Sep-Nov – warm, wet.

© Gonzalo Azumendi / Getty Images

GALWAY
IRELAND

Why now? Absorb craic and culture galore.

The Republic of Ireland's fourth-largest city doesn't lag behind in terms of nightlife. The bars and restaurants of Galway are legendary, from classic pubs such as The Crane, O'Connor's, Tigh Neáchtain and Tig Coílí – where you can drink to a soundtrack of *bodhrán* (drum), flute and pipe – to contemporary music in the Roísín Dubh and stylish venues where you'll sip cocktails rather than the black stuff. The food's fabulous, too, from Michelin-starred eateries to the bustling market, best on Saturdays; try the famed Galway Bay oysters – April's the end of the season for these succulent shellfish. This month you can alternate revelry with culture: during the Cúirt International Festival of Literature, the city is awash with poetry, theatre, film and more. Get your retail fix on the aptly named Shop Street, admire the city's historic sites – the 16th-century Spanish Arch and Lynch's Castle, and even older St Nicholas Church and Hall of the Red Earl – then craic on into the night with a bar-hopping adventure.

Trip plan: The two closest commercial airports, at Knock to the north and Shannon to the south, are both 1hr away by road. Galway is served by long-distance buses and trains from Dublin and other cities.

Need to know: A Galway Hooker isn't as dubious as it sounds – the traditional black-wood boat used to transport goods, the name's also been adopted by a well-loved County Galway brewery.

ESTREMADURA
PORTUGAL

Why now? Savour chocolate and cherry liqueur, and surf big waves.

In 1282, Princess Isabel of Aragon was so smitten with the enchanting hilltop settlement of Óbidos that her new husband, 'poet king' Dom Dinis of Portugal, presented it to her as a wedding gift. This timewarp town is sweeter still today – not least in April, when the International Chocolate Festival floods Óbidos with delicious treats, including monumental sculptures made from the delectable brown stuff. Can't time your visit for the festival? Not to worry – you can enjoy chocolate here year-round, some of it in the form of cups from which the nationally famous sour-cherry liqueur Ginja de Óbidos is traditionally drunk. First, absorb the historic highlights: Moorish walls, medieval castle, blue-tiled churches, 16th-century aqueduct and labyrinthine cobbled alleys lined with flower-bedecked whitewashed houses. Then hop west to the Estremadura coast, where a string of appealing ports and resorts – Ericeira, Peniche, Nazaré – offer excellent seafood, fine beaches and some of Portugal's biggest and most in-demand surf breaks.

Trip plan: Buses from Lisbon to Óbidos take around 1hr, a bit longer to the coast. Explore the medieval town for a day or two before heading for shore and surf.

Need to know: Óbidos gets very busy at weekends and during festivals – book accommodation well in advance.

Other months: Nov-Feb – cooler but pleasant; Mar-May & Oct – warm; Jun-Sep – hot, busy.

(A) Tyrolean
Mayrhofen;
(L) Carpathian
pysanka Easter eggs;
(R) Île de Ré oysters

88

MAYRHOFEN
AUSTRIA

→ **Why now?** Hurtle down the slopes for noisy high-jinks.

The ski season might be winding down in most resorts by April, but in Mayrhofen the party's just getting started. For a week this month, the hills are alive with the sound of music – dance music, mostly, with big-name acts and DJs bringing the noise to various venues and mountain stages, forests and even igloos for the annual Snowbombing festival: ski (or board) by day, rave by night (and also day). But even if the so-called 'Ibiza in snow' doesn't tickle your musical tastebuds, the surrounding Zillertal region has a ring to it at all times – there's music-making along the whole valley, with bands playing huts and bars pretty much throughout the year, while Mayrhofen has an enviable array of aprés-ski options. Skiers won't want for variety: some 140km (87 miles) of piste and 58 lifts offer access to everything from family-friendly slopes to black runs – including the Harakiri, reputedly Austria's steepest piste.

Trip plan: Mayrhofen is a 1hr drive or 2hr train or bus ride from Innsbruck, the nearest airport. Munich and Salzburg airports are also accessible.

Need to know: Accommodation prices tend to be lower outside central Mayrhofen, particularly during Snowbombing; within the ski area, try villages along the valley such as Hippach, Finkenberg and Lanersbach.

Other months: Dec-Apr – ski slopes open; May & Nov – lifts and many businesses closed; Jun-Oct – generally sunny, lifts open for summer season.

CARPATHIAN MOUNTAINS
UKRAINE

→ **Why now?** Learn elaborate egg-painting, Hutsul-style.

Nowhere does Easter quite like Ukraine. Painting ornate designs on eggs is popular across Eastern Europe, but in the wooded Carpathian foothills of western Ukraine, the most extraordinary *pysanky* are created by the region's Hutsul peoples, who have preserved a colourful folk culture and are renowned for their mastery of handicrafts. You can explore their unique traditions at the Museum of Hutsul Folk Art inwwwthe appealing regional hub, Kolomyya, where there's also a vast, egg-shaped Pysanky Museum. But to get hands-on, head for the hills to a village such as Kosmach, where you can learn to use a stylus, beeswax and coloured dyes and create intricate, symbolic designs on your own pysanka, bake paska Easter bread and even create cheese toys – another unique Hutsul tradition. Activity climaxes in the weeks before Easter – join a host family at a homestay in April to experience Hutsul arts, music, dance and lifestyle first-hand.

Trip plan: The nearest international airport is at Lviv, about 3hr 30min from Kolomyya by train. Realistically, the best option is to book a guided tour through the Hutsul villages, including an egg-painting class.

Need to know: Though temperatures climb during April, nights in the mountains can be very cold, often sub-zero – bring warm clothes. Kolomyya's museums are closed Mondays.

Other months: Dec-Mar – cold, skiing available; Apr-May – warming; Jun-Aug – very hot; Sep-Nov – pleasant, grape harvests.

ÎLE DE RÉ
FRANCE

→ **Why now?** Sooth your skin with some seaside therapy.

'The sea washes away all the ills of men', said Greek dramatist Euripides in the 5th century BCE – and the idea really caught on. Over the past century or so, thalassotherapy – treatments based on seawater, particularly focusing on the skin – have become hugely popular. Pretty Île de Ré, off the west coast of France, is the place to come for a salty spring pick-me-up, with several thalasso spas. And in April, the chances of sunshine are good, the island's famously tasty oysters are plump and the beaches are gleaming; you'll also find peaceful hiking and cycle trails, and cafés not yet packed with the Parisian masses that descend in high summer. If the sun declines to shine, explore the island's rich history, from pretty village churches to the imposing 17th-century fortifications ringing the main town, St-Martin-de-Ré, where you can also take shelter in a vibrant covered market selling piles of fresh seafood and local cheese.

Trip plan: Nearby La Rochelle airport receives many international flights, some summer only. La Rochelle is 3hr from Paris by train. There's a range of accommodation in St-Martin-de-Ré and around the island, including hotels and campsites, most open in April.

Need to know: A 3km (1.8 mile) toll bridge connects Île de Ré with the mainland; toll rates for cars halve outside high season (June-September), but it's free for pedestrians and cyclists year-round.

Other months: Nov-Mar – cool, some businesses closed; Apr-May & Oct – pleasantly warm; Jun-Sep – hot, busy.

See Dalmatian pelicans
swoop and swirl in the
Danube Delta

EASTERN ROMANIA

➜ **Why now? Admire spectacular birds and painted monasteries.**

Fangs but no thanks: though wildlife-watchers and culture vultures gravitate to Transylvania, there's another wild side to Romania – in the east. The Danube Delta is a great glistening wetland spanning over 4000 sq km (1544 sq miles), hosting more than 300 bird species among its reedbeds, channels and islands, along with wolves, otters, wildcats and wild boar. Spring marks the start of the birding season, when the delta welcomes white and Dalmatian pelicans, glossy ibis and pygmy cormorants in vast colonies; board a boat from Tulcea to explore the endless waterways. Then travel north into the historical regions of Moldova and Bucovina, where 15th- and 16th-century monasteries are decorated with colourful frescoes – don't miss the

'Sistine Chapel of the East', Voroneţ, where the detailed paintings covering the exterior include the Last Judgment, the Tree of Jesus and the Ladder of St John. Make time to savour blooming wildflowers and fine Moldovan wines, too.

Trip plan: Constanţa, nearest airport to the delta, is 3hr 30min from Tulcea by bus; Bucharest–Tulcea is a 4hr 30min journey. Explore by ferry or join a birding tour, then head north to Bucovina; fly out from Iaşi or extend your trip into Transylvania.

Need to know: Schedules for delta ferries, run by Navrom, vary by season and may be less frequent in April before the high season kicks in. They tend to depart at 1.30pm.

Other months: Nov-Mar – very cold, geese and eagles in the Delta; Apr-May – warm, pelicans; Jun-Aug – hot, wetter; Sep-Oct – pleasant.

Find an uncrowded Cyclades on the Greek island of Andros

ANDROS
GREECE

→ **Why now? Enjoy quality hiking on an uncrowded isle.**

Andros, second-largest of the Cyclades, isn't like other Greek islands. With tourism kept in check by the wealthy shipping magnates who make their homes here, its rugged interior and Aegean beaches remain largely undeveloped, while year-round rivers and springs keep the landscape unusually lush. It has also been designated a Leading Quality Trails island by the European Ramblers Association in recognition of its remarkable 170km (106 mile) network of footpaths, former mule tracks restored by the volunteer-run Andros Routes project. Warm but not-too-hot spring (highs of 18–20°C/64–68°F) is perfect: ravines and terraces bloom with wildflowers and fruit trees, and businesses reopen for the season. The headland-clustered capital, Hora (aka Andros), with its fine mansions and museums of archaeology and contemporary art, is a good base – from here, mount day-walks to Panachrantou Monastery, the ruins of 13th-century Faneromeni castle or the healing spring at Apikia. Or pick up the 100km (62 mile) cross-island trail, taking in tiny villages, highlands cloaked with fragrant shrub, the remains of the ancient former capital Palaiopolis, and the low-key resort of Batsi.

Trip plan: Ferries to Andros sail from Rafina (20min from Athens airport); the crossing takes 2hr. Buy an Andros Routes map to support the trail-rehabilitation project.

Need to know: The summer *meltemi* wind can be very strong. Pack a tight-fitting hat and take care on exposed trails.

Other months: Nov-Mar – mild, wet, quiet; Apr-May – warm, lush, uncrowded; Jun-Aug – very hot, windy; Sept-Oct – warm air and seas.

© milangonda / Getty Images

LOŠINJ
CROATIA

→ **Why now? Inhale spring on the 'Island of Vitality'.**

Feeling jaded after the long, dark winter? We prescribe a spring visit to Croatia's 'Island of Vitality'. Since the late 19th century, physicians have recognised the healing properties of Lošinj – a potent brew of sunshine (more than 2500 hours annually), pellucid water and clear air scented with pine and medicinal herbs. The elite of Vienna and Budapest (including Austrian Emperor Franz Joseph) built stately villas and hotels on Lošinj, and today its beaches are packed in July and August – but in April you can have the historic ports, pine forests, fishing villages, seafood restaurants and gorgeous Adriatic-lapped Čikat Bay pretty much to yourself. Various hotels have spas focusing on wellness and health, but it's easy to DIY: roam around more then 250km (155 miles) of hiking and cycling trails, inhaling pine-tinged air in the forest parks of Pod Javori and Čikat, and the aromas of the Garden of Fine Scents in Mali Lošinj. Keep an eye out for dolphins at sea, and pop across to neighbouring Cres island to watch magnificent griffon vultures. See? You feel better already.

Trip plan: Pula and Zadar are the most convenient airports, both within easy distance of catamaran services to Lošinj (journey time 3hr). Base yourself in either Mali Lošinj or Veli Lošinj, and strike out on foot or by bike.

Need to know: Some businesses, including dolphin-watching boat tour companies, may not operate till May.

Other months: Nov-Mar – cold; Apr-May & Sep-Oct – pleasantly warm; Jun-Aug – hot, good swimming, increasingly busy.

A bird's-eye view of Mali Lošinj on Croatia's 'island of vitality'

© zeleno / Getty Images

METZ FRANCE

→ **Why now? Raise a glass to stained-glass in marvellous Metz.**

Few cities are better set up for a spring break than Metz (pronounced 'mess'). Sunny? Roam the old French quarter, its streets lined with charming buildings of golden Jeumont stone, then board a cruise boat to drink in the sights or loll alongside the Plan d'Eau, a kind of pseudo-lake in the Moselle River. Rainy? Delve into the historic covered market to pick up delectable patisserie, and step back in time with a visit to the Roman baths and medieval collections at the Musée de la Cour d'Or. Contrast with contemporary art at the Centre Pompidou-Metz and gaze at the peerless array of stained-glass windows in the Cathédrale St-Étienne, some dating from the 13th century. Whether under umbrella or parasol, roam the winsome streets of the Imperial Quarter, built during German occupation in the late 19th century. And then relax in a leafy square – maybe pedestrianised Place Saint-Jacques – for a glass of local Lorraine wine or a Mojito à la Mirabelle (made with the famed local plum) to kick off a night of revelry.

Trip plan: Metz is around 1hr 30min by train from Paris, and 1hr from Luxembourg, the most convenient international airport. Stay in the old French Quarter to explore with ease.

Need to know: Among Metz's gastronomic delights (aside from the internationally famed quiche Lorraine), tuck into a Paris-Metz – a macaron sandwich filled with crème anglaise and fresh raspberries.

Other months: Nov-Mar – cool; Apr-May & Sep-Oct – warm; Jun-Aug – hot.

The sea stack of Aphrodite's Rock

© Anton Zelenov / Shutterstock

WESTERN CYPRUS

→ **Why now? Find good food, good weather and the Goddess of Love.**

According to myth, Aphrodite was born on Cyprus, emerging from a surge of sea foam at rocky Petra tou Romiou beach. It's a popular spot, but you'll likely have it mostly to yourself in April – chilly swimming weather, but with highs over 20°C (68°F), low rainfall, and sunshine and wildflowers enough to please the goddess of beauty and love. Start in Pafos, a European Capital of Culture in 2017. Walk the ancient Tombs of the Kings, absorb the Roman villas and exquisite mosaics at the Archaeological Park, and stroll both the laid-back promenade and the lanes of Upper Pafos, where interesting relics and colonial buildings are interspersed with modern blocks. For sea and surf, the best local spot is Sandy Beach near Chloraka.

Then drive to the spectacular Avgas Gorge, lush Akamas Peninsula (home to the Baths of Aphrodite), the traditional villages of the Akamas Heights plateau dotted with little stone churches and folk museums, and lovely Latchi Beach. Also seek out spring specialities like *kleftiko* (oven-baked lamb) and Easter *flaounes*, savoury pastries made with herbs and cheese.

Trip plan: Pafos has an international airport. Car hire is cheap, especially outside peak season.

Need to know: Seek out The Place, a Cypriot crafts centre in Upper Pafos where you might see icon-painters and leathersmiths at work; joining in is encouraged.

Other months: Nov-Mar – mild, wettest; Apr-May – warm; Jun-Aug – hot, busiest; Sep-Oct – quieter, warm.

ISLES OF SCILLY
ENGLAND

Why now? Arrive with the spring at England's westernmost outpost.

This tiny archipelago – 140 islets and skerries, just five of them inhabited – lying 45km (30 miles) off the western tip of Cornwall is England's warmest enclave. Spring comes first to Scilly, and with it the return of ferry services, as well as the puffins that nest here each April. Crowds, though, are still sparse, and life delightfully slow – so it's pretty much the ideal month to explore, sailing from the biggest island, St Mary's, to the other inhabited isles. Wander gleaming beaches and snorkel with seals from St Martin's; explore the subtropical Abbey Gardens on Tresco; roam the windswept trails of rugged Bryher; discover Bronze Age Obadiah's Barrow and the gin distillery on St Agnes; and visit Iron Age sites and taste delicious seafood on St Mary's.

Trip plan: Fly to St Mary's by Skybus plane from Exeter, Newquay or Land's End, or by helicopter from Penzance to St Mary's or Tresco. The Scillonian ferry sails to St Mary's from Penzance daily from mid-March to October. Base yourself on one of the five inhabited islands or spend a week hopping between all of them.

Need to know: Bad weather can delay or cancel flights or ferry departures – build some flexibility into your travel plans in case of hold-ups.

Other months: Nov-Mar – cool, many businesses close, ferries don't sail; Apr-Oct – warm, sunny, busy.

(L) Bryher's wonderfully named Droppy Nose Point; (R) The white sands of Tresco's Pentle Bay

95

A mud voclano of
Qobustan

AZERBAIJAN

→ **Why now? Explore the 'Land of Fire'
as it warms up in spring.**

In this former Soviet republic, east meets
west – and north nudges in, too. Long a
trading hub on the Silk Road routes, there's
also a hint of Russia here, thanks to nearly
two centuries under Moscow's thumb.
Today's Azerbaijan is an oil-rich state
where shiny new buildings rub shoulders
with ancient fortresses, mosques and
caravanserais (traditional inns), particularly

in the rapidly developing capital, Baku.
Sandwiched between icy Caucasus winters
and scorching summers, April is a fine time
to explore, with wildflowers exploding into
bloom. After gawping at Baku's contrasting
architecture, gaze into the 'flaming
mountain' of Yanar Dağ on the Absheron
Peninsula, visit plopping mud volcanoes
and 12,000-year-old petroglyphs in nearby
Qobustan, then head to the heights. Hike
mountain trails from traditional villages
such as Lahic, and finish in historic Şəki
with a visit to the magnificent 18th-century
Xan Sarayı (Khan's Palace).

Trip plan: Fly to Baku and allow at least
a week to explore the east and north.
Combined tours visiting Georgia and
Armenia are popular.

Need to know: Most visitors require a visa;
e-Visas are usually valid for stays up to 30
days and are available via www.evisa.gov.az.
Travel to the disputed region of Nagorno-
Karabakh (Artsakh) and the border with
Armenia is not advised.

Other months: Nov-Mar – cold, skiing in
Shahdag; Apr-Jun & Sep-Oct – pleasantly
warm; Jul-Aug – very hot at lower altitudes,
good mountain trekking.

Picturesque Luxembourg – a great hiking base

LUXEMBOURG

→ **Why now? Check out chateaux and crags in spring sunshine.**

Squeezed between France, Belgium and Germany, little Luxembourg – just 82km (51 miles) long and 57km (35 miles) wide – is often overlooked by travellers. Yet this compact Grand Duchy encompasses some of the best elements of all three: the Ardennes forests of the north, shared with Belgium; the stately chateaux and language of France; and the excellent wines produced in the Moselle Valley, where the river forms the border with the famous German wine region. Spring brings warm days, blossoms and budding foliage, but crowds remain sparse (outside the capital, anyway) and prices moderate. There's plenty to fill a long weekend in Luxembourg City, its historic core picturesquely perched on a cliff: visit a host of exceptional museums, elegant Notre-Dame Cathedral and the Palais Grand-Ducal – if you happen to be here on Easter Monday, buy a Péckvillercher (whistling clay bird), sold only on that day. But stretch your horizons roaming the craggy Müllerthal gorges or trails of the Ardennes forest, and marvel at castles in Clervaux, Vianden and Beaufort.

© Dado Daniela / Getty Images

Trip plan: Frequent buses link the airport with Luxembourg City, which is also a major rail hub. If not hiking, base yourself in the capital and explore via the excellent train and bus network.

Need to know: All public transport in Luxembourg has been free since March 2020. Several museums within the Museumsmile network offer free entry on various weekday evenings; check in advance.

Other months: Nov-Feb – winter, often sub-zero; Mar-Apr & Oct – cool; May-Sep – pleasantly warm.

BEYOND LUXEMBOURG

BOUILLON • 92KM (57 MILES) • Crusader castle and kayaks across the Belgian border

LIEGE • 160KM (100 MILES) • Boisterous big-city action

REIMS • 195KM (120 MILES) • The heart of the Champagne region

PARIS • 370KM (230 MILES) • Reach the French capital by TGV in just two hours

LAKE MAGGIORE
ITALY

➜ **Why now?** Explore fantastic gardens without the crowds.

Northern Italy's not short on gorgeous lakes: Como, Garda, Lugano, Iseo – each has unique charms, and all have lured travellers since before the days of the Grand Tour. As the elite built grand villas on their shores, competitive construction led to the creation of some truly spectacular landscapes – formal or classical, floral or verdant. But none comes close to the wedding-cake extravagance of Isola Bella on Maggiore where, in the 17th century, Count Borromeo created a 10-tiered, 37m/121ft-high garden for his wife Isabella; come in April, just after it opens for the year but before the hordes intensify, to absorb its Baroque excess in relative peace. This is a great month to visit Maggiore in general, as the lake's delightful towns awaken – Cannobio, Stresa and Verbania, where you can admire the lavish botanic gardens at Villa Taranto, open from April.

Trip plan: Milan's Malpensa, the nearest international airport, is around 1hr by train from Maggiore. Stresa is the hopping-off point for Isola Bella, and a good place to stay; Cannobio, further north along the western shore, makes another appealing base.

Need to know: Little Lake Orta, some 20km (12 miles) west of Maggiore, is also a charmer – visit the lovely cobbled, pastel-hued village of Orta San Giulio and sail to Isola San Giulio to admire its 12th-century basilica.

Other months: Nov-Mar – cold, businesses closed; Apr-May & Oct – warm, not too busy; Jun-Sep – hot, lots of tourists.

© Yadid Levy / Robert Harding

Borromeo Palace statues gaze out from Isola Bella

MAASTRICHT
NETHERLANDS

Why now? Mix history and hedonism as the nation toasts King's Day.

On 27 April, the Netherlands turns an even deeper shade of orange as the monarch is celebrated with noisy revelry across the country. But rather than joining the throngs packing Amsterdam, make this the month for Maastricht: it hosts a massive free party in the Stadspark on the big day of the Konigsdag, but enjoys buzzing nightlife at all times. Almost more Belgian or French than Dutch, and with a huge student population fuelling its vibrant bar scene, this historic city is a delightful blend of ancient sites and hip hedonism. Explore medieval gates and walls, the Roman fort of St Pieter and the vast network of tunnels beneath – but also wander café-crammed squares such as Vrijthof, Markt and Onze Lieve Vrouweplein, the last with its fabulous ancient basilica, and bar-hop the cobbled streets either side of Sint-Servaasbrug footbridge spanning the Maas River.

Trip plan: Maastricht is best visited by train – connect via Eindhoven (Netherlands), Liège (Belgium) or Aachen (Germany). Stay central – accommodation is clustered around the main Markt square – and spend a weekend roaming on foot. Bars and eateries stud the old town and the lively Wyck district east of Sint-Servaasbrug.

Need to know: The hills around Maastricht are striped with some of the Netherlands' oldest vineyards, planted by the Romans – try Pinot Noir, Riesling and Müller-Thürgau here. The city erupts during the pre-Lenten Carnival, while the last weekend in August sees the huge 't Preuvenemint food festival.

Other months: Nov-Mar – cold; Apr & Oct – cool; May-Sep – warm.

Colourful Lindau's
Little Harbour

© Maurizio Rellini / Four Corners

LAKE CONSTANCE
AUSTRIA, GERMANY & SWITZERLAND

Why now? Three countries, two wheels, one blooming marvellous ride.

Epic adventures don't come much easier: pedal around one of Europe's largest lakes, traversing three countries along a largely flat, well-surfaced cycle path that provides a safe route for most of the 270km (168 mile) circuit. Lake Constance (Bodensee in German), 63km (39 miles) long but just 14km (9 miles) wide, is bookended by the Alps at its eastern (Austrian) end and the roaring Rhine Falls to the west. In April it's flanked by blooming flowers – particularly on the castle-garden island Mainau – but few other cyclists enjoying early spring sunshine. Start in Germany, in Konstanz's medieval core; scoot past Mainau, then admire the cathedral at Überlingen, the Merovingian castle at Meersburg – pausing for a drop of local wine amid the vineyards at Hagnau – and the flamboyant Gothic architecture in the Bavarian town of Lindau. Then it's into Bregenz, where the Austrian Alps cool their toes in the lake, and west into Switzerland along Constance's southern shore. Refuel with fine chocolate in fresco-daubed Stein am Rhein and tour the medieval monastic island of Reichenau before completing the loop.

Trip plan: Lakeside Friedrichshafen Airport serves a handful of international destinations. The direct train from Zurich Airport to Konstanz takes about 1hr. Allow six days to cycle the circuit at a relaxed pace.

Need to know: Traditionally, cyclists circuit the lake in a clockwise direction.

Other months: Nov-Mar – cold; Apr-May – warming, spring flowers; Jun-Aug – hot, lakeside trail busy; Sep-Oct – mellow, ripe fruit.

PTUJ & MARIBOR
SLOVENIA

→ **Why now? Tackle a tipple-tastic twin-city break.**

For most visitors, the combination of coast, crags, caves and cities tips the balance in favour of Slovenia's western half – which leaves tourism delightfully sparse in the east. Here, the historic cities of Ptuj and Maribor are within wine-spitting distance of one another, and make the perfect pairing for a short two-for-one break in springtime, when the mercury rises but May's rains are still around the corner. Ptuj's history stretches back to Roman times, though its core is a charming blend of medieval and Baroque, Gothic and Renaissance – roam its cobbled alleys to visit the hilltop castle, magnificent Minorite monastery and central plaza of Slovenski trg. Maribor, Slovenia's second city, has a regional museum inside its castle, as well as a fine 13th-century cathedral and what's claimed to be the world's oldest vine, reputedly over 400 years old. Both cities are viticulture hubs, their cafés and bars filling glasses with local vintages – to visit the vineyards, head out along the Jeruzalem–Ljutomer wine route or into the hills around Maribor.

Trip plan: The nearest international airport is Graz, over the border in Austria, around 1hr from Maribor by bus or train; Ljubljana airport around 1hr 30min by rail or road.

Need to know: Frequent trains link Ptuj and Maribor in about 40min so it's convenient to base yourself in one city and visit the other for a day – Maribor is bigger and livelier, Ptuj is quieter but with ample history and wine culture.

Other months: Nov-Mar – cold; Apr & Sep-Oct – pleasant, fairly dry; May-Aug – hot, often wet.

The colossal heads of Nemrut Dağı

SOUTHEAST ANATOLIA TURKEY

→ **Why now? Travel back in time through Anatolia.**

Turkey's not short on historic wonders: Ancient Greek Ephesus, Istanbul's Byzantine and Ottoman marvels, Ani's Armenian churches. But relatively few explore the sites of southeastern Anatolia, some dating back over 10,000 years. Embark on your expedition in April, between chilly winter and stifling summer. A rewarding semi-circuit starts in Gaziantep (famed for finger-licking pistachio baklava) with visits to the medieval *kale* (citadel) and astonishing Zeguma Mosaic Museum. Then it's north via the humpbacked Cendere Bridge, built by the Romans in the 2nd century AD, to Nemrut Dağı, a mountain topped by colossal statues with eerily blank stares, part of a tomb complex built by an ancient King of Commagene in the first century BCE. (Note that the peak may still be clad in snow in early April.) Turn south to Göbekli Tepe, where rings of megaliths date back some 11,000 years, and Harran, to roam among ancient beehive houses. Finally, lose yourself in Şanlıurfa's bustling bazaar, overlooked by its mighty *kale*.

Trip plan: Gaziantep and Şanlıurfa receive flights from Istanbul for international connections. Allow at least a week to see the big sites. To get the most out of your visit, join a tour or hire a car and knowledgeable driver.

Need to know: The UK Foreign and Commonwealth Office advises against travel to regions close to the Syrian border. Destinations covered here were not considered a risk at the time of press, but check the latest advice before travel.

Other months: Nov-Mar – cool, wetter; Apr-May & Oct – pleasantly warm; Jun-Sep – very hot.

HAUTE ROUTE
FRANCE & SWITZERLAND

→ **Why now? A prime time to tackle a classic Alpine ski-tour.**

The 120km (74 mile) Haute Route links Chamonix and Mont Blanc with Zermatt, at the base of the Matterhorn, via some of the Alps' finest terrain. En route it ticks off two countries, skirts beneath most of the range's highest summits, crosses cols, traverses lakes and descends glaciers. Simply put, it is the crème de la crème of ski-touring, and it's only suitable for those with experience: long days at high altitude (it tops out at 3796m/12,454ft Pignes d'Arolla) make it a challenging prospect. The main Haute Route ski-touring season runs from mid-March to late April: this is when the glaciers are safely covered in powder, the weather is generally milder and the mountain huts are open, heated and cooking up hearty hot meals. What if you don't ski? Come back in summer to tackle it on foot – equally epic, just less icy.

Trip plan: Skiing the Haute Route takes around six days, but allow time to enjoy lively Chamonix and Zermatt at either end. Both towns are accessible by public transport from Geneva and Zurich (the most convenient airports), as well as scenic train routes: the narrow-gauge Mont Blanc Express runs up to Chamonix from Martigny, while Zermatt is the end of the line for the Glacier Express from St Moritz.

Need to know: You will need both euros (France) and Swiss francs (Switzerland).

Other months: Nov-Feb & May – Haute Route conditions not ideal; Mar-Apr – best snow conditions; Jun-Sept – route hikeable.

Zermatt Valley and the Matterhorn at dawn; après-ski later in the day

© anshar73 / Getty Images

© Matt Munro / Lonely Planet

Imagine the roar of 50,000 spectators at the Colosseum

ROME ITALY

→ **Why now? Enjoy stress-free springtime sightseeing.**

The cry on the lips of history buffs in April: happy birthday, Rome! The Eternal City was (reputedly) founded back in 753 BCE on 21 April, and every year it celebrates with events, illuminations and truckloads of fireworks. Festivities aside, April is a delightful time to visit. Rome is a city for sightseeing, which is far better enjoyed in milder spring climes (15–20°C/59–68°F) than in the depths of winter or the heights of summer – the largely shadeless Roman Forum being particularly unforgiving on the hottest days. It's also less busy (and a little cheaper), though seasonal attractions are open; for instance, atmospheric after-dark tours of the Colosseum run from April to October. To top it all, menus start to feature tasty spring produce, such as artichokes and asparagus – vignarola, a Roman speciality combining peas, fava (broad) beans, lettuce and artichokes, is the season's signature dish.

Trip plan: Rome warrants several days of exploring, ideally on foot. As well as visiting its famed ruins and piazzas, take a walk along the Via Appia (the first Roman road), which is particularly lush in spring.

Need to know: Free drinking water is available from 18th-century *nasoni* (public fountains) across the city – but letting your lips touch the spout might attract a fine; instead, follow the locals and cup your hands to direct water into your mouth.

Other months: Nov-Mar – cool, wet; Apr-May & Sept-Oct – manageable weather, quiet; Jun-Aug – sweltering, busiest.

© Justin Foulkes / Lonely Planet

BEYOND ROME

 CASTELLI ROMANI · 20KM (12 MILES) · A getaway in the Alban Hills well-loved for its fine wines and excellent food

 OSTIA ANTICA · 32KM (20 MILES) · Well-preserved ruins dating back to the 4th century BCE

 POMPEII · 240KM (150 MILES) · Europe's most compelling archaeological site

 NICE · 700KM (435 MILES) · Connect to the French Rivieria in eight hours by high-speed train via Milan

May

WHERE TO GO WHEN

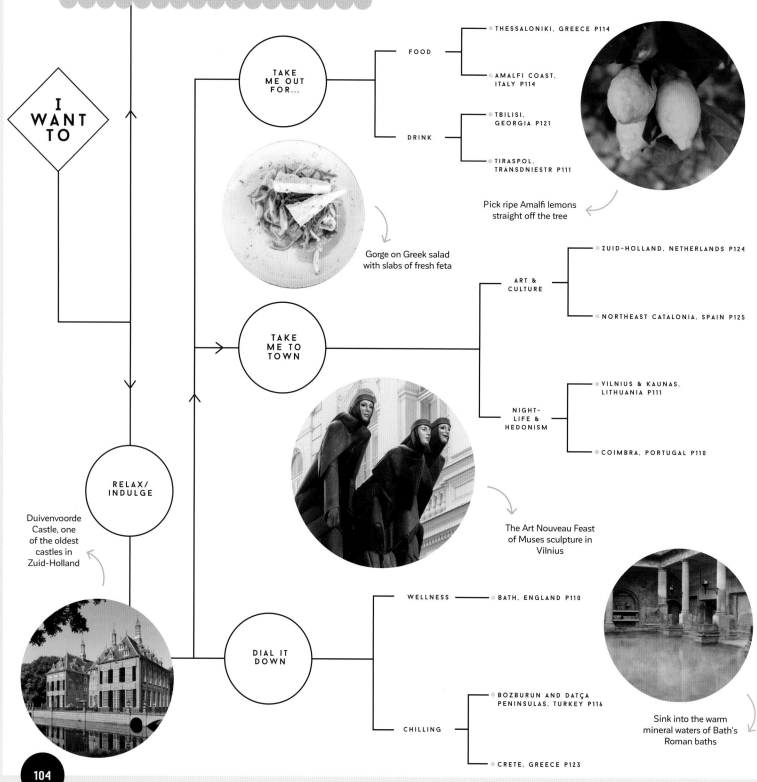

I WANT TO

CHALLENGE MYSELF

TAKE ME OUT FOR...

FOOD
- THESSALONIKI, GREECE P114
- AMALFI COAST, ITALY P114

DRINK
- TBILISI, GEORGIA P121
- TIRASPOL, TRANSDNIESTR P111

Pick ripe Amalfi lemons straight off the tree

Gorge on Greek salad with slabs of fresh feta

TAKE ME TO TOWN

ART & CULTURE
- ZUID-HOLLAND, NETHERLANDS P124
- NORTHEAST CATALONIA, SPAIN P125

NIGHT-LIFE & HEDONISM
- VILNIUS & KAUNAS, LITHUANIA P111
- COIMBRA, PORTUGAL P110

The Art Nouveau Feast of Muses sculpture in Vilnius

RELAX/INDULGE

Duivenvoorde Castle, one of the oldest castles in Zuid-Holland

DIAL IT DOWN

WELLNESS — BATH, ENGLAND P110

CHILLING
- BOZBURUN AND DATÇA PENINSULAS, TURKEY P116
- CRETE, GREECE P123

Sink into the warm mineral waters of Bath's Roman baths

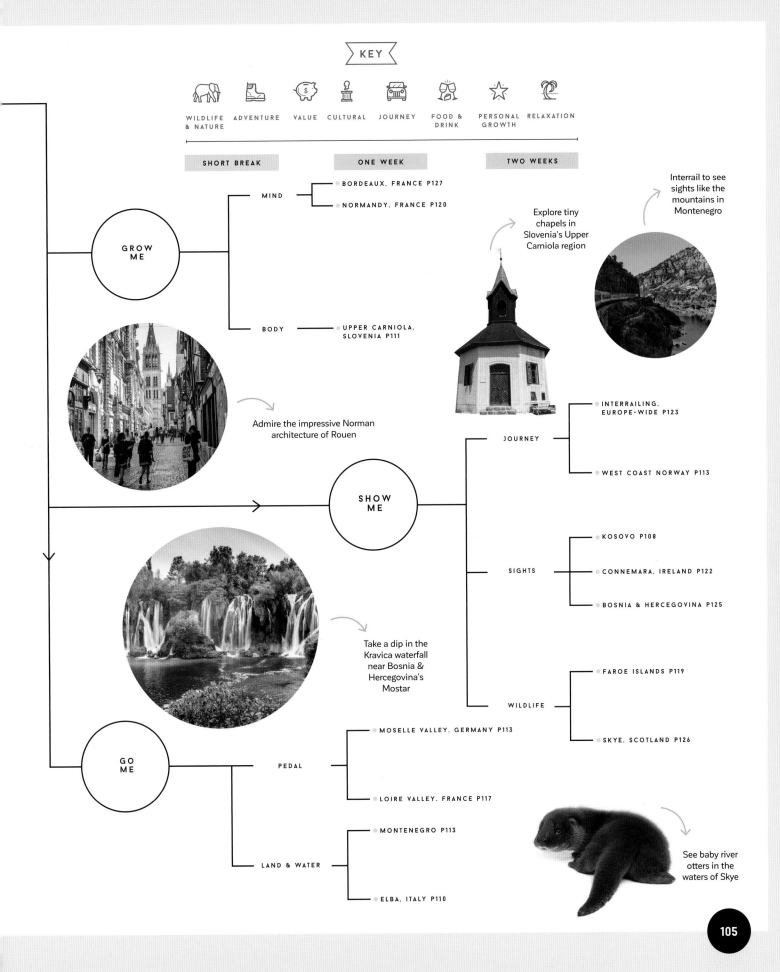

KEY

🐘	🥾	💰	🏛	🚙	🥂	⭐	🌴
WILDLIFE & NATURE	ADVENTURE	VALUE	CULTURAL	JOURNEY	FOOD & DRINK	PERSONAL GROWTH	RELAXATION

SHORT BREAK   **ONE WEEK**   **TWO WEEKS**

GROW ME

MIND
- BORDEAUX, FRANCE P127
- NORMANDY, FRANCE P120

BODY
- UPPER CARNIOLA, SLOVENIA P111

Explore tiny chapels in Slovenia's Upper Carniola region

Interrail to see sights like the mountains in Montenegro

Admire the impressive Norman architecture of Rouen

SHOW ME

JOURNEY
- INTERRAILING, EUROPE-WIDE P123
- WEST COAST NORWAY P113

SIGHTS
- KOSOVO P108
- CONNEMARA, IRELAND P122
- BOSNIA & HERCEGOVINA P125

WILDLIFE
- FAROE ISLANDS P119
- SKYE, SCOTLAND P126

Take a dip in the Kravica waterfall near Bosnia & Hercegovina's Mostar

GO ME

PEDAL
- MOSELLE VALLEY, GERMANY P113
- LOIRE VALLEY, FRANCE P117

LAND & WATER
- MONTENEGRO P113
- ELBA, ITALY P110

See baby river otters in the waters of Skye

EVENTS
IN MAY

QUEIMA DAS FITAS
Coimbra, Portugal
Traditional music echoes around this university city as parties and parades mark the end of term 'Burning of the Ribbons'.

LA DUCASSE
Mons, Belgium
A parade of saintly relics and an outing for a golden carriage precede a battle between George and the dragon.

OIL-WRESTLING FESTIVAL
Selçuk, Turkey
Burly blokes tussle in contests made trickier with the addition of copious quantities of olive oil.

PÉLEGRINAGE DES GITANS
Les Saintes-Maries de la Mer, France
Gitans ('gypsies') gather to honour patron saint Sara 'the Black', parading her to the sea at the end of festivities.

FERIA DEL CABALLO
Jerez de la Frontera, Spain
Join the crowds enjoying food, drink, music and of course livestock during the historic week-long Horse Fair.

CORSA DEI CERI
Gubbio, Italy
Three teams race through the Umbrian city carrying giant 'candles' (wooden pillars) topped with saints in a nine-century-old tradition.

VICTORY DAY
Tiraspol, Transdniestr
In former Soviet states, Victory Day commemorates the effective end of the war against Nazi Germany with grand military parades.

PRAZSKE JARO
Prague, Czech Republic
Enjoy three weeks of quality classical music and opera performances in the Czech capital during 'Prague Spring'.

Inner wheel labels:
Trinity Sunday (late May/early June) — $
First week of May — $
First Sunday in May — $
Early to mid-May — $
9 May — $$
From mid-May — $$
15 May — $
24-25 May — $

106

Don't miss the
Loire's Château de
Chenonceau

• LOIRE VALLEY, FRANCE

• NORMANDY, FRANCE

• SKYE, SCOTLAND

• TUSCAN NATIONAL PARK, ELBA, ITALY

• AMALFI COAST, ITALY

Catch sight of
sea eagles over
the waters of
Skye

• CONNEMARA, IRELAND

Sunset in Amalfi

Square up to a
bull in Heraklion's
archeology museum

• CRETE, GREECE

The medieval market
square of the Moselle's
Bernkastel-Kues

• CARNOLIA, SLOVENIA

• MONTENEGRO

• BOZBURUN AND DATÇA
PENINSULAS, TURKEY

Mostar's Stari
Most in Bosnia &
Hercegovina

• MOSELLE RIVER, GERMANY

• BOSNIA HERCEGOVINA

• NORTHERN CATALONIA, SPAIN

A koulouri (sesame seed
bread ring) is a Greek
speciality

• THESSALONIKI, GREECE

• BATH, ENGLAND

Bath's abbey and
Roman statues add
to its historic appeal

• ZUID-HOLLAND,
NETHERLANDS

• FAROE ISLANDS

• BORDEAUX, FRANCE

A Bordeaux beauty:
the Pont de Pierre
bridge over the
Garonne

• COASTAL NORWAY

Take to the
waters to see
Norway's
coastline at
its best

Go hiking in the Prokletije
mountain range on the
Kosovo-Montenegro border

• KOSOVO

A Georgian
treat:
khachapuri
with cheese
and egg

• VILNIUS & KAUNAS,
LITHUANIA

• TBILISI, GEORGIA

• INTERRAILING

• COIMBRA, PORTUGAL

• TIRASPOL, TRANS-DNIESTER,
MOLDOVA

Moldova's Soviet past looms large
with this statue of Lenin in Tiraspol

KOSOVO

Why now? Find fine climes for offbeat exploring.

An independent country only since 2008 (and still not recognised as such by several nations, including Serbia), Kosovo is about as far-out a European destination as you'll find. But this mountainous, landlocked little Balkan rewards those who visit, and mild May, with average highs around 22°C/73°F, is a great time. Capital Pristina has a youthful energy and a lively cultural scene; spend a few days sipping macchiatos in hip cafés and grazing the multi-ethnic streetfood stalls of Shadervan, the main square. West of the capital, head to spectacularly frescoed Visoki Dečani Monastery (where you can buy wine and cheese made by the monks), and out to the Rugova Mountains, great for hiking. South lies the Rahovec Valley, Kosovo's main wine region, and the mosque-dotted old town of Prizren, with its ruined hilltop citadel. In the southwest, the quirky Dragash region promises mountain villages such as Brod, its streets lined with Ottoman houses and its surrounding meadows alive with spring wildflowers.

Trip plan: The only airport is just outside Pristina. Hiring a car is possible; booking a tour will be more relaxing.

Need to know: If you entered Kosovo via another country (eg Albania) and plan to continue into Serbia, think again: as Serbia doesn't recognise Kosovan independence, border guards won't admit you. You'll need to exit Kosovo via a third country and enter Serbia from there. If you entered Kosovo from Serbia, returning to Serbia isn't a problem.

Other months: Nov-Mar – cold, potential for snow; Apr-Jun – pleasant; Jul-Aug – hot; Sep-Oct – warm.

Nature at its most glorious on the Kosovo-Montenegro border

COIMBRA
PORTUGAL

→ **Why now? See student high-jinks and spring sunshine.**

Dating from 1290, Coimbra University is Portugal's first and most prestigious academic institution, and is among the oldest in the world. It dominates the city physically, lording it on a hilltop above the old cobbled alleys and Mondego River, and it also affects Coimbra's mood: the students add youthful dynamism to the city's cheap bars and cafés. And never more so than in May: the first week of the month is given over to the Queima das Fitas – the 'Burning of the Ribbons' – when traditional fado music floats around the cathedral square, parades wend through the streets and books are forgotten in favour of all-night partying. Many of Coimbra's main attractions lie in the university area and the upper reaches of the Old Town. Visit the Romanesque 'old' cathedral from 1184 and its 'new' counterpart, built between 1598 and 1698; the Baroque Biblioteca Joanina; the grand Sala dos Capelos; and the Torre da Universidade, climbing its 180 steps for the best city views.

Trip plan: Trains run from Coimbra to Lisbon (2hr) and Porto (1hr 15min).

Need to know: To skip the steep climb up to the university, head to the market square and take the Elevador do Mercado, a lift and funicular connected by a walkway.

Other months: Nov-Mar – cool, wet, lively; Apr-May – warm, end-of-term events; Jun-Aug – hottest, dry, no students; Sep-Oct – warm, quiet.

BATH
ENGLAND

→ **Why now? Make like the Romans and sink into this elegant Georgian spa city.**

Ludicrously good-looking Bath becomes even more beautiful in May – its Unesco-listed honeystone centre glows under late-spring sunshine and its girdle of hills are lush, leafy and pungent with wild garlic. With its drapery of trees, lazy waters, towpath flowers and chirruping birds, Bath's Kennet and Avon Canal is as therapeutic as any wellness treatment: take an easy stroll toward equally lovely Bradford on Avon. That said, an actual wellness treatment at the Thermae Bath Spa should be high on the list. Fed by Britain's only natural thermal waters, the complex has a range of saunas and a rooftop pool overlooking the city and countryside; go early evening (it's open until 9.30pm) to watch the sun set. Combine this with a visit to the Roman Baths complex, where you can't bathe but you can see where the Romans did when they founded the city 2000 years ago.

Trip plan: Bath is 1hr 30min by train from London. The nearest airport is Bristol (1hr by bus). Consider a Spas Ancient & Modern package, which includes entrance to the Roman Baths, the Thermae spa and lunch at the elegant Pump Room, once frequented by Jane Austen.

Need to know: The ten-day Bath Festival (mid-May) brings an eclectic programme of music, literature, comedy and theatre.

Other months: Nov-Mar – cold (Christmas market Nov-Dec); Apr-Jun – warm; Jul-Aug – busy, hottest; Sep-Oct – cool, quieter.

ELBA
ITALY

→ **Why now? Send yourself into uncrowded exile.**

Napoleon might have been eager to escape Elba (he was exiled here in 1814), but most visitors don't feel the same urge. The largest island in the Tuscan Archipelago – which also comprises uninhabited Montecristo and five others – is a gem: just 28km by 19km (17 by 12 miles) of turquoise-lapped white sand, sheer cliffs, dense woods, acclaimed vineyards, olive and citrus groves and Mediterranean maquis scrub, rising up to 1019m (3343ft) Monte Capanne. In high summer, Elba's lovely little roads are frustratingly clogged. But in spring you'll find warm weather without the crowds. You might also catch some celebrations: 5 May is Napoleon Day, celebrated with a special mass at the Chiesa della Misericordia in fortified Portoferraio, Elba's biggest town. Also, April and May see the Tuscany Walking Festival, with guided walks across the archipelago's highlands and coast. Relaxation can be found on wonderful beaches such as the sandy-pebble coves of Morcone, Pareti and Innamorata, the crystal-clear duo of Sorgente and Sansone (perfect for snorkelling and kayaking) and the golden sands of Fetovaia.

Trip plan: Ferries run from Piombino on the Italian mainland; the crossing takes around 1hr. Elba also has a tiny airport with direct links to some foreign and Italian cities.

Need to know: The easiest way to get around is by hire car from Portoferraio or Marina di Campo. The most scenic drives are on the southwest coast.

Other months: Nov-Mar – coldest, driest, quiet; Apr-Jun – warm, uncrowded, lush; Jul-Aug – hot, busy; Sep-Oct – warm, harvest.

UPPER CARNIOLA
SLOVENIA

→ **Why now? Big up the bees.**
Beekeeping is a big deal in Slovenia. The 18th-century apiarist Anton Janša, born in the Carniolan village of Breznica, is considered the father of modern beekeeping, and the country is renowned for its apiculture traditions and high-quality honey. It was Slovenia that first proposed World Bee Day, which is now celebrated on 20 May – Janša's birthday. The country's apicultural heartland is in the Alpine region of Gorenjska (Upper Carniola). Here, beneath the looming Karavanke Mountains, a handful of small towns and villages offer an insight into apiculture: see Janša's shed-size memorial apiary in Breznica, buy honey wine and perfume at family-run Noč Beekeeping in Žirovnica and visit the Beekeeping Centre of Gorenjska (which runs tours, tastings and workshops). In the medieval Old Town of Radovljica, the Museum of Apiculture houses a unique collection of gorgeous antique painted beehive panels, and the local restaurants serve honey-infused menus. And at Beekeeping Ambrožič, near Lake Bled, you can even try apitherapy (relaxing inside a beehive), allegedly beneficial for those with respiratory problems.

Trip plan: Radovljica is 48km north of Ljubljana; buses and trains link the two. Local tourist offices can arrange api-experiences.

Need to know: The Lectar Inn in Radovljica has a Gingerbread Museum where you can watch traditional heart-shaped honey-biscuits being made.

Other months: Nov-Apr – cold, snow possible; May-Jun – warmer, summer activities begin; Jul-Aug – busiest, hottest; Sep-Oct – warm, autumn colours.

TIRASPOL
TRANSDNIESTR

→ **Why now? Toast Victory Day with fine brandy in a breakaway state.**
One of the most unusual countries in Europe, Transdniestr isn't a nation at all – at least, in the eyes of most of the world. This sliver of land wedged between Ukraine and Moldova declared independence from the former Soviet republic in 1990 and today operates as a de-facto state, with its own currency, army and flag (the only one that still sports a hammer and sickle). Spring is the ideal time to explore Transdniestr's unique capital, sampling its famous *divin* (cognac-style brandy), caviar at a sturgeon farm, or Moldovan-Russian-Ukrainian cuisine in a local restaurant. And on 9 May, Tiraspol rumbles with rolling tanks and marching boots as Victory Day commemorates the effective end of the war with Nazi Germany: it's a display of pomp with poignance, as locals carry pictures of lost family, but also with a carnival atmosphere. There's history, too, from the peculiar mix of Soviet and imperial Russian iconography adorning Tiraspol's streets and squares to its fascinating Noul Neamţ Monastery and the Ottoman fort at nearby Bendery.

Trip plan: Fly to Chişinău in Moldova, then arrange a driver into Transdniestr; from the airport, it's a 1hr 15min drive to Tiraspol.

Need to know: Transdniestran rubles are the only accepted currency; banks will exchange US dollars, Euros, Russian rubles and Moldovan leu, but only in-country. A visa isn't usually required.

Other months: Dec-Feb – sub-zero; Mar-May & Oct-Nov – chilly; Jun-Sep – warm.

VILNIUS & KAUNAS
LITHUANIA

→ **Why now? Gaze at green shoots and quiet sights.**
Around 40% of the Lithuanian capital is green space – from parks to leafy squares and riverbanks – making spring an especially lovely time to visit Vilnius. Days are long, too, giving plenty of time for seeing the sights: the elegant Palace of the Grand Dukes (a replica of the 17th-century original), the neoclassical Cathedral, the maze-like cobbled alleys of the Old Town, the courtyards of the historic university and castle-topped Gediminas Hill. More harrowing are the Museum of Genocide, which tells the stories of those who died during the Soviet occupation, and chilling displays of the Holocaust Museum. The city can fill several days – and nights, as there's a lively bar and music scene. But it's also easy to combine Vilnius with Kaunas, Lithuania's second city, an inexpensive train ride away. Located at the confluence of the Nemunas and Neris Rivers, Kaunas isn't as grand, but it has a compact and comely Old Town, a 14th-century castle, a die-hard (and cheap) party spirit and some excellent galleries. It's also undergoing a facelift ahead of its 2022 stint as European Capital of Culture.

Trip plan: Trains between Vilnius and Kaunas take 1hr 30min.

Need to know: The town of Trakai, home to two medieval castles, makes a good day-trip from Vilnius (30min by train).

Other months: Nov-Feb – freezing, Christmas markets (Dec); Mar-Apr & Oct – chilly, good birding; May & Sep – warm, uncrowded; Jun-Aug – hot, busy, festivals.

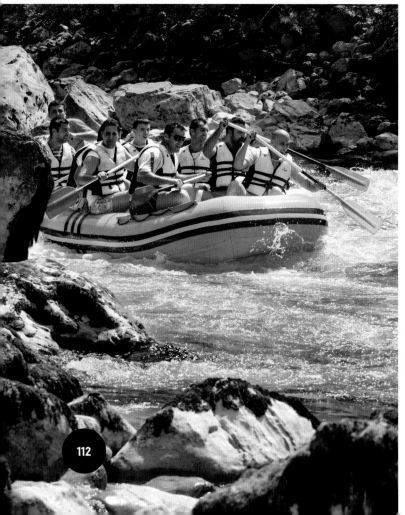

(A) Cruising the calm waters of Geirangerfjord; (L) White-water rafting in Montenegro; (R) A Moselle vineyard

WEST COAST NORWAY

→ **Why now?** Sail sublime fjords in the sunshine.

Operating 365 days a year, Hurtigruten ferries ply all 2400km (1491 miles) of Norway's west coast, from southerly Bergen to Arctic Kirkenes. They are a lifeline for people living along this wild, fjord-serrated seaboard, so they always depart, whatever the conditions. That said, May is a good time to jump aboard and visit this rugged part of Norway. The weather is generally mild and days extraordinarily long; by mid-May, the sun doesn't set at all in far-north Tromsø, so you can watch jaw-dropping scenery glide by all night long. Better weather and more light makes it easier to hop off for activities, too. The Hurtigruten serves 34 ports of call in all; disembark to admire the Art Nouveau architecture of Ålesund, sniff the fragrant air of Molde (named the 'Town of Roses' for its rich soil and abundance of greenery), fish in the craggy-peaked Lofoten Islands, meet Sami people at North Cape, hike near the iconic Geirangerfjord. And as May sees a round of festivals in pretty Bergen, allow extra time here before you sail.

Trip plan: A Bergen-Kirkenes-Bergen round-trip voyage takes 12 days; shorter cruises and numerous excursions are possible.

Need to know: Compared to big cruise ships, Hurtigruten boats have very few frills – cabins are functional rather than fancy, there is little choice of dining and virtually no entertainment.

Other months: Oct-Apr – cool to cold, aurora possible; May-Jun & Sep – warm, long days; Jul-Aug – warmest, most expensive.

MONTENEGRO

→ **Why now?** Raft wild rivers, laze on quiet shores.

Diminutive and diverse Montenegro is a great place to mix it up – a bit of beautiful beach, a bit of high adventure. And as it's so compact, it pays to visit before peak season hits, when the roads get clogged up and accommodation is scarce. In May, temperatures on the coast can get as high as 25°C (77°F) and the sea warms up, so you can happily dally in dazzling Adriatic spots. Cliff-hugged Kotor is a plum choice, with its walled medieval Old Town of Venetian palaces, museum and churches, twisting alleys and café-lined squares. Pick of the nearby beaches is shimmering Dobreč, at the end of the Luštica Peninsula and only accessible by sea; taxi-boats run from Herceg Novi or you can join a kayak tour. For a different kind of watery fun, head inland toward the mountains. May sees the start of rafting season through the Tara Canyon, one of the deepest and longest in Europe. Bubbling with snowmelt, the Tara River is lively but safe; the most thrilling section, via rapids, waterfalls and impressive rock walls, is between Brštanovica and Šćepan Polje.

Trip plan: Spend a week combining coast and interior. Several companies offer guided day-long and overnight rafting trips.

Need to know: There are airports in Tivat and the capital, Podgorica. Buses run into Montenegro from Dubrovnik (Croatia).

Other months: Nov-Mar – cold, skiing possible; Apr-Jun & Sep-Oct – warm, less crowded; Jul-Aug – hot, busy.

MOSELLE VALLEY
GERMANY

→ **Why now?** Cycle alongside one of Germany's most beautiful rivers.

A gorgeous ribbon of water snakes through Germany, its banks striped with vineyards and overhung by ridges topped with fairytale castles. No, not the Rhine – rather, its pretty tributary, the Moselle, which enjoys most of the former's attributes, but without its hefty cargo ships and heavy tourist traffic. Flowing in from Luxembourg near Trier, an ancient city blessed with Roman remains, the Moselle winds between castle-topped medieval towns such as Bernkastel-Kues, Traben-Trarbach, Beilstein and Cochem before meeting the Rhine at Koblenz. May is a lovely time to ride beside the Moselle: the vines, twisted into a traditional heart-shape hereabouts, are beginning to bud; the wine festival season is already underway and vineyards are open for tastings; the temperature averages a cycle-friendly 19°C (66°F), but the crowds haven't yet descended. It's a wonderfully easy ride, suitable for families, with wide, well-paved and traffic-free bike lanes hugging every meander of the Moselle, often on both banks of the river.

Trip plan: The full cycle route, between Thionville (France) and Koblenz is 275km (171 miles). Both ends of the trail are reachable by train.

Need to know: Between May and October, scheduled boat services link towns along the Moselle several times daily; bikes can be transported for an extra charge. Bikes can also be taken on trains (outside rush hour) and buses (pre-booking required).

Other months: Nov-Mar – winter, many facilities closed; Apr-Jun – warmer, quieter; Jul-Aug – hottest, busy; Sep-Oct – warm, grape harvest.

THESSALONIKI GREECE

The church of St
Paul and, beyond it,
Thessaloniki

➜ **Why now? Feel this ancient city
spring to life.**

Ancient Thessaloniki, founded in 315 BCE,
feels young at heart. There's a palpable
buzz to Greece's second city, and in May
that buzz moves outside when locals
– including a huge student population –
start hanging out in Navarinou Square,
sipping strong coffee and *tsipouro* (grape
brandy) at pavement cafés, and filling the
rooftop bars as they begin to open for
the season. With average highs of 24°C
(75°F), it's even warm enough to pop
to the beach: Blue Flag Epanomi is only
25km (15 miles) south, and the famed
turquoise waters of the Halkidiki Peninsula
are a 2–3hr bus journey away. Take a dip,
too, into Thessaloniki's neighbourhoods.
Egnatia, built on a Roman road, is the
main thoroughfare; around it are Roman
monuments (including the ruined palace

and Arch of Galerius), interesting churches
and stalls selling *koulouri* (pretzel-like
sesame rings). The waterfront, home to the
city's iconic White Tower, was regenerated
in 2013, and is a wonderful place to stroll
or cycle. It ends at the port – home to the
Macedonian Museum of Contemporary Art
– and Ladadika, the former bazaar district,
packed with restaurants and late-night
action. Ano Poli is the Upper Town, a messy,
atmospheric tumble of old Ottoman alleys.

Trip plan: Spend two or three days in the
city. Add a day-trip to Pella (45min by bus),
birthplace of Alexander the Great.

Need to know: Browse the old markets of
Modiano and Kapani, stuffed with fresh
fish, creamy cheeses, olives and spices.
Small tavernas and bars line the edges.

Other months: Nov-Mar – cool, wettest;
Apr-Jun – warm, lively; Jul-Aug – hot; Sep-
Oct – warm, uncrowded, festivals.

© Andrei Bortnikau / EyeEm / Getty Images

Vertigo-inducing but worth it: the Amalfi Coast

AMALFI COAST
ITALY

→ **Why now? Add extra zest to la dolce vita.**

The sparkling azure sea! The cliff-tumbling towns! The serpentine coast roads! The hellish traffic jams! Wait a minute... On the Sorrentine Peninsula south of Naples and in sight of Mt Vesuvius, the Amalfi Coast oozes Italian seaside glamour – you'll picture 1950s starlets in catseye sunglasses wherever you look. But in high summer, the picturesque little roads grind to a standstill with chic-seeking tourists. Come in spring instead, and driving between honeypot towns such as Sorrento, Positano and Ravello is less onerous but the weather is still a delight (average highs 24°C/75°F). The rugged Sorrentine is also famed for its luscious lemons (arguably the world's best), and the hillsides will be fruit-heavy, fragrant and cheerily yellow right now. Book into a traditional *agriturismo* (working farm) to learn to make pizza dough and limoncello, and sleep within scent of the groves.

Trip plan: Enjoy the foodie delights of Naples (birthplace of pizza) before heading south to Amalfi, via Pompeii's astounding archaeology. For extra glitz, sail over to Capri for the day.

Need to know: Naples to Sorrento takes about 1hr by road or rail. Ferries to Capri depart from Naples (from 50min) and Sorrento (from 25min).

Other months: Nov-Mar – off-season, coolest, businesses close; Apr-Jun – pleasant, quieter; Jul-Aug – hot, heaving; Sept-Oct – warm, less crowded.

© Mark Read / Lonely Planet

The ruins of Knidos, famous for statues of Dionysus and Athena

BOZBURUN & DATÇA PENINSULAS
TURKEY

→ **Why now? Seek some solitude at ancient sites and calm coves.**

So you're dreaming of soaking up the late-spring rays and dunking yourself in the dazzling blue Aegean – fair enough. But you're not the only one. By May, when sea temperatures reach dipping point but before the sun hits brain-melting levels, many Med resorts are beginning to bustle and hotspots such as Marmaris are mayhem. Relax: there are still old boatbuilding villages, hidden coves and peaceful beaches where you can find a semblance of solitude. Head for the Datça and Bozburun peninsulas stretching west from Marmaris, the two gnarled fingers where you'll also find charming Ottoman villages – try Eski Datça, just inland from that more lively port town – and ancient remains, including the 2400-year-old Dorian port city of Knidos, the Hellenistic acropolis at Hydas and the hillside amphitheatre of Amos. Feeling energetic? Hike a section of the Carian Trail, wending through pine and almond groves and past blue beehives and monumental tombs.

Trip plan: Dalaman is the most convenient international airport, about 1hr 30min drive east of Marmaris. That journey is served by buses, but transport on to the peninsulas is best by taxi. Turunç, Selimiye and Datça or Bozburun towns all make fine waterfront bases.

Need to know: If exploring on foot, trails can be confusing and maps poor – best to find a local guide.

Other months: Oct-Apr – cooler, wetter, some businesses closed; May-Sep – very hot.

Turrets triumph in the 14th-century château of Sully-sur-Loire

LOIRE VALLEY FRANCE

 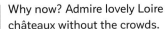

Why now? Admire lovely Loire châteaux without the crowds.

No river is as resplendent as the Loire. Draped in weeping willows, lined by vineyards and flanked by a parade of châteaux, palaces and pretty towns, it's in a class of its own. There's plenty of history, from Joan of Arc links in Orléans to the royal tombs at Fontevraud's abbey, and wonderful wine and food at Michelin-starred restaurants or simple family auberges – plus, in May, markets are full of strawberries and asparagus. Any overindulgence can be offset by delightful canoe paddles, and strolls or cycles along the riverbank. This calibre of destination attracts crowds, but May is much quieter than high summer. You can admire the valley's cavalcade of castles – enormous Chambord, river-spanning Chenonceau, exquisitely furnished Cheverny – before things get seriously busy, or plump for off-the-beaten-track châteaux such as Brissac, Brézé and Beauregard. Don't disregard the gardens either, which will be looking splendid in spring; at Château de Chaumont-sur-Loire, the grounds are reinvented in mid-April each year for the Festival International des Jardins.

Trip plan: Concentrate on the central Loire, from Orléans to Angers, and include a night at a château hotel. Multi-château passes are available; for individual visits, pre-purchase tickets to avoid queues.

Need to know: Trains link the Loire Valley to Paris; journey time to Orléans is around 1hr.

Other months: Nov-Mar – cold, damp; Apr-Jun & Sept-Oct – mild, quieter; Jul-Aug – hot, crowded, river levels low.

© Viacheslav Lopatin / Shutterstock

117

FAROE ISLANDS

→ Why now? Explore Viking remains and vast seabird colonies.

There's nowhere quite like the 'Land of Maybe', as this climatically unpredictable subarctic archipelago has been dubbed. A cluster of 18 small basalt skerries rearing up from the North Atlantic, the Faroe Islands is a place of human and natural drama, of sheer cliffs and plunging waterfalls, remote fishing villages, grass-roofed farmsteads and the remains of ancient Viking settlements. In May, as the weather becomes drier and more clement, the islands awaken from winter torpor: migratory seabirds arrive in their millions to breed – puffins, gannets, razorbills, fulmars, shags, kittiwakes, guillemots – and attractions reopen. Venture to the raucous seabird colonies at Mykines and Vestmanna, wander the fishing harbour and medieval core of tiny capital Tórshavn, and venture to remote settlements such as Saksun, where the fascinating farm-museum reveals how tough life has been for the Faroese over the centuries. Most of all, though, simply drink in the views: of soaring sea stacks, of high moors trilling with the calls of whimbrels and curlews, of fjords and coastal hamlets and roaring cascades. It'll probably rain. Then sun. Then mist over. Then sun some more. And it'll be all the more magical for it.

Trip plan: Fly to the Faroes' only international airport, Vágar, then hire a car or – if you're feeling intrepid – bike: most roads are fairly quiet and distances relatively short, though hills are steep, winds strong and tunnels scary.

Need to know: Weather changes rapidly and ferry or helicopter departures may be delayed, so a flexible schedule is best.

Other months: Oct-Apr – colder, wetter, many facilities closed; May-Sep – warm, drier, long days.

Wildlife rules the roost in the Faroes, where sheep vastly outnumber humans

NORMANDY
FRANCE

→ **Why now? Venture right into a Monet masterpiece.**

Normandy is literally pretty as a picture. The Impressionist movement began right here, amid the region's fertile fields, Gothic and Romanesque towns, willowy riverbanks and chalk-cliff coast. And it was here that Claude Monet, founder of the movement, created some of his finest works. Follow an Impressionist's trail through the region. Start in Giverny, where Monet spent his last decades; in May, his house and its glorious gardens will be a riot of rhododendrons, wisteria, peonies and poppies. Next, trace the Seine northwest to Rouen. Its medieval centre is dominated by the Gothic cathedral which Monet painted repeatedly, while the Musée des Beaux-Arts has the second-largest collection of Impressionist works in France. Continue to the Alabaster Coast; Etretat, with its mighty rock arches, was a favourite subject. The port of Le Havre seems industrial, but its delicate light drew many artists, and its Musée Malraux museum contains more fine Impressionist works. Wake early for sunrise: this is where Monet painted *Impression, soleil levant*, the work that gave the movement its name. Finish at pretty Honfleur, where the mast-clanking quay and antique streets provided much Impressionist inspiration.

Trip plan: Le Havre, Dieppe and Cherbourg are Normandy's main ports. Trains run from Paris to Vernon (45min), from where shuttlebuses run to Giverny.

Need to know: If visiting Giverny on a Saturday, arrive in Vernon early to browse the local market (8am-1pm).

Other months: Nov-Mar – chilly, Monet's house closed; Apr-Jun – pleasant, peak gardens; Jul-Aug – hot, crowded, waterlilies; Sep-Oct – warm, quieter, dahlias.

Boats bob in the calm waters of Honfleur's harbour

TBILISI GEORGIA

→ Why now? Raise a glass to the genial weather.

May is just right in the Georgian capital: not too hot, not too cold. Which, along with a glut of festivals, lends a buzzing atmosphere to a city that has grown into the cool, cosmopolitan capital of the Caucasus. There's a lot to like, from the striking valley setting and handsome architecture to the vibrant cultural scene and new wave of hip cafés, clubs, parks, galleries and hotels that lend Tbilisi a modern edge. And it's still fun to get lost in the Old Town, with its twisty alleys, balconied houses, churches, bathhouses and ancient Narikala Fortress. The wine has always been good here. The surrounding slopes comprise one of the world's oldest viticulture regions; Georgia's traditional *qvevri* winemaking method has even been recognised by Unesco. Tbilisi has plenty of wine bars and cellars, and early May heralds the New Wine Festival, when tipples from over 200 wineries can be sipped in Mtatsminda Park. To drink more deeply, take a day trip to the scenic Kakheti region to taste wines by the vines.

Trip plan: Tbilisi airport is 15km (9 miles) east of the city. Use buses, *marshrutky* (minibuses) and the Tbilisi metro to get around.

Need to know: Some diary dates: 9 May is Victory Over Fascism Day, when uniformed veterans gather in Vake Park; 26 May is Independence Day (also a public holiday), celebrated with parades, fireworks and concerts.

Other months: Nov-Mar – dry, chilly; Apr-Jun – warm, lively; Jul-Aug – hot, humid; Sep-Oct – wine harvest, cooling.

Fortify yourself with a *khachapuri* before climbing to Tbilisi's Narikala Fortress

BEYOND TBILISI

 **UPLISTSIKHE · 60KM (38 MILES) ·** The remains of an ancient pagan settlement with hundreds of cave dwellings

 KHAREBA WINERY · 140KM (87 MILES) · Sprawling hillside winery with wines stored in a Soviet-era tunnel

 KUTAISI · 230KM (140 MILES) · City of ancient monasteries; a gateway for outdoor pursuits

BAHUMI · 370KM (230 MILES) · Relaxing seaside getaway on the Black Sea

CONNEMARA
IRELAND

→ **Why now?** Explore a very emerald isle without the crowds.

Wild and wonderful Connemara has a bit of everything: glittering lakes (loughs), sea islands and inlets, heathery bogs, craggy mountains and imposing castles (some of which are fancy hotels), not to mention a thriving Irish culture. Here, you can mix activities, scenic drives, traditional pubs and historic sites as you see fit. May is clement enough – one of Ireland's driest months, with highs of around 15°C (59°F) – to enable indoor and outdoor exploring. Following the Sky Road, which cuts through Connemara from Clifden, provides views of the dramatically incised coast; the R334, along the Lough Inagh Valley, gives views of the Maumturk mountains on one side, the Twelve Bens on the other. Do make frequent stops as you tour around: at Kylemore Abbey, with its Gothic church, Victorian garden and lakeside grounds; at steep-sided Killary Harbour, to see otters frolicking in the water or weavers at work in the Sheep & Wool Centre; and at the galleries of Roundstone village. Make time for a hike, too, maybe up Errisbeg or along the Gleann Chóchan Horseshoe, and consider taking the ferry to tiny Inishbofin, for a rocky retreat and traditional folk music.

Trip plan: Hiring a car offers the most flexibility. Bus services can be irregular – some operate May-September, some July-August only.

Need to know: Connemara offers good salmon fishing. The seasons on the Corrib and Ballynahinch rivers run March-Sept, but the best time is May-August.

Other months: Nov-Mar – coldest, wettest; Apr-May – warmer, uncrowded; Jun-Aug – busy, warmest, most expensive; Sep-Oct – cooling, quieter.

Get expansive coastal views from Diamond Hill in Connemara National Park

INTERRAILING
EUROPE-WIDE

➡ **Why now?** Go everywhere, before everyone else does.

Can't pick one European country? Pick them all! The Interrail pass was first introduced in 1972 to encourage passengers up to the age of 21 to explore the continent. Now, anyone of any age can purchase one of a range of passes and plot an epic rail adventure. Perhaps Paris one day, Munich the next; a few days in the Alps, an overnight trundle to the Balkans; over to Italy, up to Scandinavia… Poring over timetables and potential ports of call is almost as thrilling as arriving in a different place every day. And given the diversity of potential destinations, a spring-cheery shoulder-season month like May is ideal: hotels, sites and train carriages won't be too crowded; the weather should be pleasant everywhere – from 16°C/61°F in Oslo to 24°C/75°F in Rome.

Trip plan: Currently, the Interrail Global Pass is valid for travel within 31 European countries: Austria (including Liechtenstein), Belgium, Bosnia & Hercegovina, Bulgaria, Croatia, the Czech Republic, Denmark, Finland, France (including Monaco), Germany, Great Britain, Greece, Hungary, Ireland, Italy, Lithuania, Luxembourg, North Macedonia, Montenegro, Netherlands, Norway, Poland, Portugal, Romania, Serbia, Slovakia, Slovenia, Spain, Sweden, Switzerland and Turkey.

Need to know: Continuous Travel passes can be used every day within a set period (from 15 days to three months). Flexible passes allow limited travel within a set period (eg five days within one month).

Other months: Nov-Mar – coldest, potential train disruption and restricted services; Apr-Jun – quieter; Jul-Aug – warmest, busiest; Sep-Oct – less crowded.

CRETE
GREECE

➡ **Why now?** Gambol down gorgeous gorges, sink into super seas.

Greece's largest island makes the perfect spring break, when the weather (average highs of 24°C/75°F) is warm enough to enjoy the glorious beaches, but cool enough for visiting ancient ruins or hiking coastal trails and the White Mountains. The countryside is still green, too, and pungent with wild herbs. With fine Venetian architecture and an excellent Archaeological Museum, buzzy capital Iraklio is close to both vineyard-strewn wine country and the remarkable Minoan palace of Knossos. On the south coast, the former hippie hangout of Matala is a good base for visiting ancient Gortyna, Phaestos and Agia Triada, as well as swimming – by late May, the water is delicious. Further west lies pretty Preveli Beach; northwest is the town of Rethymno, with its winding Venetian alleys. The countryside of western Crete is well worth exploring: stay in the mountain village of Argyroupoli or hike through plunging Samaria Gorge. From Agia Roumeli, at the gorge bottom, boats run to whitewashed Loutro and also to Hora Sfakion, for connecting to handsome Hania, with its Venetian harbour, historic townhouses and handicraft shopping.

Trip plan: Allow two weeks. Flights land at Iraklio (Heraklion) and Hania (Chania). Ferries sail to Crete from Piraeus (around 9hr), Santorini (2hr 30min) and other islands.

Need to know: Samaria Gorge is susceptible to flash flooding and only opens May-October.

Other months: Nov-Mar – cool, some facilities close; Apr-Jun – fine weather, quiet; Jul-Aug – hot, crowded; Sep-Oct – pleasant, crowds thinning, seas warm.

Zuid-Holland seen from on high... unsurprisingly, it's inspired many artists

ZUID-HOLLAND
NETHERLANDS

Why now? Get into the Golden Age.
Throughout the 17th century there was no more exciting or enlightened place to be than Zuid-Holland (South Holland). International trade brought great wealth, the spoils of which can be seen in a cluster of fine cities; Holland's artists were also particularly inspired, creating some of the greatest masterpieces during this Golden Age. May is a marvellous time to explore the region, when the weather is mild, the countryside is coming to life and the tulips are blooming. It would be remiss to miss Amsterdam, ever-alluring capital and home to the Rijksmuseum and Rembrandt's former residence. Then explore other Golden Age centres: walk in the footsteps of Dutch Master Frans Hals amid the Dutch Renaissance architecture of Haarlem; visit Leiden, birthplace of Rembrandt and home to many fine museums; make a beeline for Den Haag, the seat of government, where the Mauritshuis' formidable collection of Golden Age art includes Vermeer's *Girl with a Pearl Earring*; and amble exquisitely preserved medieval Delft, climbing the tower of the Nieuwe Kerk for the best views. Add on a visit to cheesy Gouda – perhaps Holland at its most uber-Dutch: every Thursday (Apr-Aug), the touristy but tasty *kaasstad* (cheese market) takes over this canal-encircled town.

Trip plan: Trains serve all the main towns, and a tram connects Den Haag and Delft. Cycle paths also crisscross the region.

Need to know: A Holland Pass (valid for one month) offers free and discounted entrance to 100-plus museums and attractions, plus skip-the-queue access.

Other months: Nov-Mar – cold, rainy; Apr-Jun – tulips, Gouda cheese market; Jul-Aug – mild, festivals; Sep-Oct – cooler.

NORTHEAST CATALONIA
SPAIN

→ **Why now? Tour the Dalí triangle in the artist's birthday month.**

A century ago, artists, writers, filmmakers and other creative types were pushing the boundaries of the real in their work – and no one made a more profound mark on the Surrealist movement than Salvador Dalí. Couches like puckered lips, lobster telephones, melting clocks: the mind-bending images he conjured are as bemusing and enchanting today as they were when he made waves in the art world last century. The month of the artist's birth (and before peak season), May is the ideal time to explore the 'Dalí triangle' in his corner of northeast Catalonia. There's his (relatively) understated home by the sea in Port Lligat, created from an old fisherman's hut near the lovely harbour town of Cadaqués and now the Casa Museu Dalí; his OTT Teatre-Museu Dalí in Figueres, home to a career-spanning collection of his art and, in an adjacent annex, jewellery; and most quirky and memorable, Castell de Púbol, the medieval bastion Dalí bought and renovated for his wife Gala. And while you're here, sample the region's delectable cuisine (don't miss the seafood soup-stew, *zarzuela de mariscos*), visit the Greco-Roman remains at Empúries, and enjoy the dramatic coastline and fine beaches.

Trip plan: Fly to Girona or Perpignan (France), then hire a car or tour the Dalí sights by public transport – the region is well served by buses. Cadaqués makes an attractive base.

Need to know: The Dalí museums are closed most Mondays outside of July–September.

Other months: Dec-Feb – coolest; Mar-May – warm, quieter; Jun-Sep – hot, dry; Oct-Nov – cooler, still mostly pleasant.

© Jan Wlodarczyk / Alamy Stock Photo

Ottoman-style Sebilj Fountain in Sarajevo's Old Town

BOSNIA & HERCEGOVINA

→ **Why now? Mix wild rivers, warm weather, empty sites and high-jinks.**

If travellers make it to Bosnia & Hercegovina, they make it mainly to Mostar. Which is great – the Ottoman city and its iconic bridge are splendid. But this still largely offbeat Balkan has far more going for it than just Mostar, especially in May, when the flowers are blooming and the average high is around 18°C (64°F). Start in the south, in the walled old town of Trebinje, or in hillside Počitelj, a small, picturesque but uncrowded medieval centre; impressive Kravica Waterfall – Hercegovina's Niagara – is nearby. Do visit Mostar, then continue north, perhaps to the mountain village of Lukomir, where you'll encounter traditional dress, food, houses and hospitality. After a couple of hedonistic nights in capital city Sarajevo, make for the lakes, waterfall and historic centre of Jajce. Further north still,

the Una River roars – snowmelt makes the water super-exciting in May, great for rafting and canoeing trips around Bihać.

Trip plan: If starting in Trebinje, consider flying into Dubrovnik, only 30km (19 miles) away (45min by bus). If finishing in Bihać, the nearest major airport is Zagreb (170km/106 miles; 3hr). Bosnia & Hercegovina has a cheap and comprehensive bus network, but hiring a car will of course allow more flexibility.

Need to know: The most adventurous way to travel between Dubrovnik and Mostar is the 160km (100 mile) Ćiro cycling trail, a former Austro-Hungarian railway line turned bike path that passes through fine scenery and deserted towns.

Other months: Dec-Mar – skiing; Apr-Jun – warm, rivers in full flow; Jul-Sep – hot, lively festivals; Oct-Nov – cooler, autumn colours.

SKYE
SCOTLAND

→ **Why now? Embrace long days on the invigorating western isle.**

If you're blessed with good weather on Scotland's second-largest island, you're blessed indeed. Skye's lochs sparkle, the mountains blush, the moors glow green. If you have bad weather, well, that's OK too – the Cuillin range in cloud or mist holds plenty of atmospheric allure. That said, May – statistically one of the driest months – is a good choice. This is when bluebells carpet the woods, lambs gambol and innumerable seabirds return to the island's towering cliffs. It also offers really long days (sunrise before 4am, sunset after 11pm), which leaves plenty of time for castles, crofting museums, pretty Portree and the striking rock formations of the Trotternish Peninsula. Come early in the month if you can – western Scotland is plagued by microscopic but maddening midges from mid-May to September (though they're worst July-August). Note, though, that midges don't like wind, so a breezy ridge or coast hike should help to keep them away.

Trip plan: Skye is a 5hr drive from Glasgow (break the journey in Fort William). Stay as long as you can. Base yourself in Portree, the largest town, and make forays to Trotternish and the Cuillins and book a sea cruise to see eagles. And don't forget to taste the Talisker whisky.

Need to know: Skye is connected to mainland Scotland by a road bridge (with a total span of 2.6km/1.5 miles) and by ferry from Mallaig (30min).

Other months: Nov-Mar – dark, cold, aurora possible; Apr-Jun & Sep-Oct – quieter; Jul-Aug – peak season, midges.

Skye's most westerly headland and Neist Point lighthouse

© Martin M303 / Shutterstock

BORDEAUX
FRANCE

Why now? Cook up a storm with fine fresh produce.

The phrase joie de vivre could have been coined for Bordeaux. This port city on the Garonne river is surrounded by vineyards – and not just any old vineyards: viticulture has been practised here for millennia, and no other region in the world produces as much fine wine. The food is excellent, with many Michelin-starred restaurants, plus food trucks, experimental bistros and good coffee shops. Bordeaux itself is also delicious, with much of its homogenous 18th-century centre recognised as a World Heritage Site. It's also a city for learning. Take a cookery course – perhaps at the Côté Cours school at Michelin-starred St James Hotel, just outside Bordeaux – and learn to cook like a local. This is an ideal time: in May, food markets – such as the historic Marché des Capucins – overflow with fresh goodies, from baby carrots to raspberries and rhubarb. Then learn about wine. Start at the architecturally audacious Cité du Vin, a wine museum befitting Bordeaux's brilliant viticultural traditions; inside are exhibits, workshops and tastings. Then head out into the vineyards for a guided tasting.

Trip plan: To secure a table at a Michelin-starred joint, book at least three months in advance; make weekend reservations at popular restaurants several days ahead.

Need to know: Local specialities include entrecôte à la Bordelaise (beef in red wine sauce), Aquitaine caviar (from the sturgeon of the Garonne) and dunes blanches de Bordeaux (choux buns filled with cream).

Other months: Nov-Mar – coldest, wettest; Apr-Jun – warm, less busy, blooming; Jul-Aug – hottest, crowded; Sept-Oct – warm, harvest.

The Pont de Pierre over the Garonne river

© Justin Foulkes / Lonely Planet

BEYOND BORDEAUX

SAINT-ÉMILION • 50KM (30 MILES) • Unesco-listed medieval village perched alluringly above vineyards

DUNE DU PILAT • 65KM (40 MILES) • Colossal sand dune that's spreading eastwards at 4.5m per year

BIARRITZ • 200KM (125 MILES) • Half ritzy coastal resort, half summer surfers' hang-out

TOULOUSE • 245KM (150 MILES) • One of provincial France's most vibrant and animated cities

June

WHERE TO GO WHEN

I WANT TO

CHALLENGE MYSELF →

TAKE ME OUT FOR...

    FOOD
- SEGOVIA, SPAIN P148
- PUGLIA, ITALY P133

    DRINK
- VENETO, ITALY P150

A must for Puglians: freshly opened sea urchins

Drink in the beauty of the Veneto valley's vineyards

TAKE ME TO TOWN

    ART & CULTURE
- RAVENNA, ITALY P137
- BERLIN, GERMANY P145

    NIGHT-LIFE & HEDONISM
- REYKJAVÍK, ICELAND P135
- LISBON, PORTUGAL P151

Swim in Berlin's River Spree

RELAX/ INDULGE

Feel the weight of prehistory under Lewis's Callanish Standing Stones

DIAL IT DOWN

    WELLNESS
- OUTER HEBRIDES, SCOTLAND P138
- FRISIAN ISLANDS, NETHERLANDS P141

    CHILLING
- HVAR, CROATIA P140
- BORNHOLM, DENMARK P135

Tuck into a *pastel de nata* in Lisbon

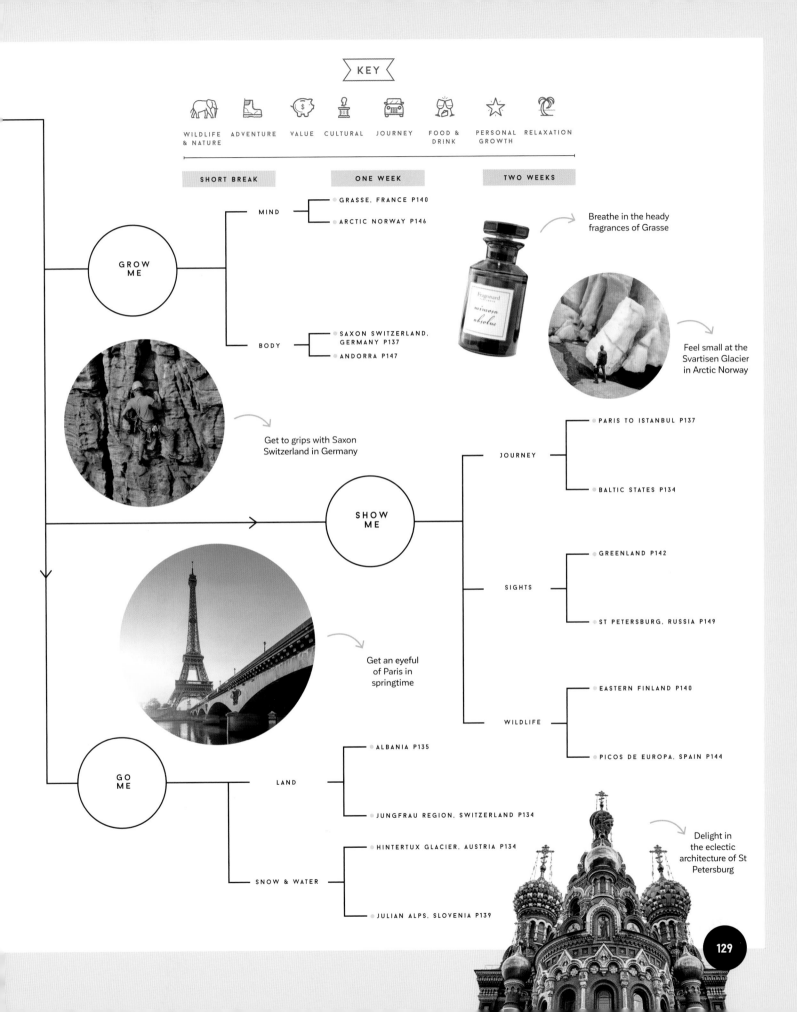

WILDLIFE & NATURE

ADVENTURE

VALUE

CULTURAL

JOURNEY

FOOD & DRINK

PERSONAL GROWTH

RELAXATION

SHORT BREAK

ONE WEEK

TWO WEEKS

GROW ME

MIND
- GRASSE, FRANCE P140
- ARCTIC NORWAY P146

BODY
- SAXON SWITZERLAND, GERMANY P137
- ANDORRA P147

Breathe in the heady fragrances of Grasse

Feel small at the Svartisen Glacier in Arctic Norway

Get to grips with Saxon Switzerland in Germany

SHOW ME

JOURNEY
- PARIS TO ISTANBUL P137
- BALTIC STATES P134

SIGHTS
- GREENLAND P142
- ST PETERSBURG, RUSSIA P149

WILDLIFE
- EASTERN FINLAND P140
- PICOS DE EUROPA, SPAIN P144

Get an eyeful of Paris in springtime

GO ME

LAND
- ALBANIA P135
- JUNGFRAU REGION, SWITZERLAND P134

SNOW & WATER
- HINTERTUX GLACIER, AUSTRIA P134
- JULIAN ALPS, SLOVENIA P139

Delight in the eclectic architecture of St Petersburg

EVENTS
IN JUNE

HVAR SUMMER FESTIVAL
Croatia
Enjoy a packed roster of alfresco music and other cultural events on this alluring Dalmatian island.

BATALLA DEL VINO
Haro, Spain
Folk in this Rioja town celebrate St Pedro's day with a Battle of Wine, hurling red plonk at each other.

FEAST OF ST ANTHONY
Lisbon, Portugal
The capital's 'matchmaker' patron saint is honoured with parades, love poems and the aroma of grilled sardines across the city.

LAJKONIK
Kraków, Poland
A hero in Tatar costume rides a hobby horse through town in a centuries-old traditional procession.

Three months from 1 June
$$
29 June
$
Thursday after Corpus Christi
$
12 June
$
21 June (usually)
$
Mid-June
$$
23–24 June
$
17 June
$$

SUMMER SOLSTICE
Stonehenge, England
Thousands of New Agers congregate among the monumental 4500-year-old Neolithic stone circle to greet the dawn.

PINKPOP FESTIVAL
Landgraaf, Netherlands
International bands and artists rock the crowds at the Netherlands' big summer music gig.

JAANIPÄEV
Tallinn, Estonia
Bonfires, beer and barbecues fuel pagan-style hedonism on St John's Eve in an all-night affair (sleeping discouraged).

REGATTA OF ST RANIERI
Pisa, Italy
Crews representing the four quarters of this historic Tuscan city compete in a boat race in honour of Pisa's patron saint.

BORNHOLM, DENMARK

FRISIAN ISLANDS, NETHERLANDS

OUTER HEBRIDES, SCOTLAND

Bring a camper and bikes
to reach every corner of the
Outer Hebrides

The Ameland
Lighthouse in
Frisian Islands

ANDORRA

Wild horses in
the mountains
of Andorra

HINTERTUX GLACIER, AUSTRIA

REYKJAVÍK, ICELAND

Hallgrímskirkja in
Reykjavík

SAXON SWITZERLAND,
GERMANY

A spot for serious
climbers in Saxon
Switzerland

PUGLIA, ITALY

The tiny trulli houses
of Puglia

PICOS DE EUROPA, SPAIN

Climb La Picota
in Picos De
Europa for views
of Lake Enol

BERLIN, GERMANY

Berlin's historic
Brandenburg Gate

JULIAN ALPS, SLOVENIA

LISBON, PORTUGAL

SEGOVIA, SPAIN

Hop aboard Lisbon's
Glória funicular

GRASSE, FRANCE

HVAR, CROATIA

ESTONIA, LATVIA
& LITHUANIA

Escape Hvar's midday heat at
its Franciscan monastery

VENETO, ITALY

ARCTIC NORWAY

If you go down to
Finland's boreal
forest today –
watch out for
brown bears

EASTERN FINLAND

JUNGFRAU REGION,
SWITZERLAND

RAVENNA, ITALY

PARIS-ISTANBUL,
VARIOUS

Istanbul's
hotting up; stop
for lots of meze
breaks

ST PETERSBURG, RUSSIA

Delight in the
colour palette
of Greenland's
Tasiilaq

GREENLAND

Revel over
Ravenna's
mosaics

ALBANIA

Find this pretty
church at the heart
of Albania's Theth
National Park

PUGLIA
ITALY

Why now? Enjoy a trulli tasty Pugliese break.

Down at heel? Yes and no. Largely agricultural Puglia, the stiletto of the Italian boot, is one of the country's least wealthy regions; traditional Pugliese cuisine is known as *cucina povera* (loosely, food of the poor). However, it's also a richly satisfying destination – the 'poor' food is delicious, and historic little towns, baroque piazzas, olive groves and sandy shores are abundant. In June, Puglia is the place to lose the crowds before the high season really kicks in, enjoying warm sunshine and long, dry days. Now's also the time to indulge in both seasonal bounty such as cherries, celebrated particularly in the region, and year-round local specialities – Burrata cheese, *orecchiette* ('little ears') pasta, seafood and endless breads – the Salento region alone has more than 100 types. Hunker down in a converted *masserie* (fortified farmhouse) or, better still, one of Puglia's *trulli* – mysterious conical limestone dwellings that pepper the peaceful countryside, offering cool sanctuary from the rising heat of summer.

Trip plan: Allow one to two weeks, taking in the Baroque beauty of Lecce, so-called Florence of the south, plus 13th-century Castel del Monte, the Grotte di Castellana cave network, the unspoilt beaches and forests of the Gargano promontory, the white town of Ostuni and the 1500-odd *trulli* of Alberobello.

Need to know: There are international airports at both Bari and Brindisi.

Other months: Nov-Apr – cool/cold, wettest; May & Sept-Oct – warm, quieter; Jun-Aug – hottest, busiest.

(L): The Baroque Puglian town of Locorotondo; (R): Making orecchiette by hand

BALTIC STATES

Why now? Take an end-to-end expedition during endless summer days.

Lithuania, Latvia and Estonia often get lumped together, but each has a unique vibe: consider the Baroque splendour of Vilnius, Rīga's Art Nouveau marvels and Tallinn's medieval Old Town. Compare and contrast the three on one legendary summer road trip, making the most of June's long days and cultural events. Start in Vilnius, Lithuania's forward-looking capital, exploring its cathedral and Old Town; then head west to the magnificent island castle of Trakai and on to Klaipėda, gateway to the sandy beaches and dunes of the vast Curonian Spit National Park. Skirt the coast into Latvia and lively port Ventspils before delving inland to Rīga for history both ancient and modern, notably the occupations by Nazi Germany and the Soviet Union. Into Estonia, taste Tartu's student-focused nightlife, roam the pine forests and heaths of Saaremaa island then stroll Tallinn's cobbled streets. Plan for a night or two of pagan-style hedonism on Midsummer's Eve and St John's Day, celebrated with beer and bonfires across all three countries.

Trip plan: Fly into Vilnius and out of Tallinn, allowing 10 days to two weeks for a road trip – longer if cycling. It's also possible to travel between Vilnius, Rīga and Tallinn by train – a cheap and interesting alternative.

Need to know: All three Baltic States are EU members and Schengen signatories, but you'll need visas if entering neighbouring Russia or Belarus.

Other months: Nov-Mar – cold, dark, snowy; Apr-May & Sep-Oct – cooler, colourful landscapes; Jun-Aug – summer, relatively warm and dry.

HINTERTUX GLACIER
AUSTRIA

Why now? Get your ski fix in summer

It's never too early to get in ski-shape for winter... even if it's the longest day. So shake the dust off your sticks and wax up: on the Hintertux Glacier in Austria's central Tyrol region, you can glide down groomed snow year-round. Even in high summer, at least 10 of the ski area's 20 lifts are usually open, and with slopes topping out at 3250m (10,662ft) and dropping to around 1500m (4921ft), there's reliable white stuff blanketing up to 20km (12 miles) of active slopes. This isn't the spot for really pushing yourself – with 50% red runs and just 10% black – but it's ideal for beginners and families, or for keeping yourself sharp between seasons. If freestyle's your bag, time your visit when Betterpark Hintertux is open (April to early June and mid-September to December), for a half-pipe and five lines of different levels. Of course, this being the Alps, there's magnificent hiking in the valleys below; spa and wellness options abound, too.

Trip plan: The nearest airport is Innsbruck, from where it's a 1hr drive to Mayrhofen and the turn-off for the Tuxertal valley, gateway to Hintertux. There's a variety of accommodation options in Hintertux village and in other settlements east along the valley.

Need to know: In summer, it's best to hit the slopes in the early morning, when snow conditions are at their best before the sun heats up.

Other months: Dec-Feb – cold; Mar-Apr & Oct-Nov – cool; May-Sep – warm.

JUNGFRAU REGION
SWITZERLAND

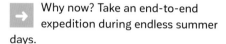

Why now? Hike Europe's best one-day route before it gets busy.

Is the (un)holy trinity of peaks in central Switzerland the most epic skyline in Europe? Soaring up to around 4000m (13,123ft), the Eiger ('Ogre'), Mönch ('Monk') and Jungfrau ('Maiden) are certainly three of the most dramatic characters you'll encounter. For a face-to-north-face meeting, lace up those hiking boots – but don't worry: you don't need to tackle vertiginous climbs. Arguably the finest day-walk on the continent, the 15km (9 mile) Faulhornweg is a relatively gentle amble from the top of the cog railway at Schynige Platte to First, above Grindelwald. Admire jaw-dropping vistas across Interlaken, flanked by twin meres, and south to those three mammoth mountains and the snaggle-toothed range running east. Alternatively, the views from the 5.6km (3.4 mile) Panorama Trail are almost as spectacular, and the meadows and mountainsides throughout the Jungfrau are laced with trails and rails.

Trip plan: Trains serve Interlaken, the main hub for this area, from Geneva and Zurich airports. Mürren, Wengen, Grindelwald make appealing bases for exploring on foot.

Need to know: The cog railway from Wilderswil to Schynige Platte runs early June to late October. The Jungfraujoch railway from Kleine Scheidegg runs year-round.

Other months: Dec-Apr – winter, pistes open; May & Nov – cool; Jun-Oct – warm, good hiking weather.

ALBANIA

→ **Why now?** Hike the Accursed Mountains in blessed weather.

It's still possible to escape the 21st century in Europe – possible, and even delightful. The traditional mountain lifestyle you feared swallowed by the modern world survives today in the rugged range around the villages of Theth and Valbona, amid the lofty crags known as the Accursed Mountains (aka, the Albanian Alps). In June, warm days bring sunshine to the alpine meadows, and a trek through the forested valleys of this delightfully rural region provides immersive insights into rural Albanian culture. Start at a homestay in Theth to experience everyday life in an Ottoman-era house, overlooked by the stone lock-in tower in which villagers sought sanctuary during the era of blood feuds, and head out onto trails among peaks rising to nearly 2700m (8858ft). Then explore the south of the country, from glistening Lake Ohrid and the Ottoman architecture of Gjirokastra to the charms of the Mediterranean coast, including the ancient Greek and Roman remains at Butrint and the white-sand beaches along the Albanian Riviera.

Trip plan: Start out in the capital, Tirana, and head north to the Accursed Mountains via the historic lakeside city of Shkodra; from Theth or Valbona, you could also pop across into Kosovo. To the south, Korça's Museum of Medieval Art and walks in Llogora National Park are worthy add-ons to the Riviera beaches, Butrint and Gjirokastra.

Need to know: When asking a question, be aware that in Albania, a shake of the head means yes, while a nod means no.

Other months: Nov-Mar – winter, good snowshoeing; Apr-Oct – warm, mostly dry.

BORNHOLM
DENMARK

→ **Why now?** Beat the crowds to this laidback Baltic bolthole.

Get there quick – then relax. Beautiful little Bornholm island is at its best in early June, when you can explore forests, craggy cliffs, thatched fishing villages, round churches and bright-blonde beaches before the crowds and elevated prices of high summer hit. Rent a cottage by the fine sands at Dueodde and do nothing but watch the waves; or pedal some of the 235km (146 miles) of bike trails; Route 10 (105km/65 miles) circumnavigates the whole island. Bornholm is Europe's first World Craft Region, and you can watch artisans making textiles, pottery, art and glassware at the gallery in Hasle. The thriving food scene focuses on local, seasonal produce, nurtured by the island's sunny microclimate. Eat at a Michelin-starred beach shack or seek out historic *røgeri* (smokehouses). On the last Saturday in June, Gudhjem harbour sees chefs battling to make the winning Sol over Gudhjem, a traditional dish of smoked herring, raw egg, chives and radish on fresh-baked rye bread.

Trip plan: Cycling is the best way to explore. There are bike rental outlets in most major towns. Bikes can be taken on public buses for a small charge.

Need to know: Flying time from Copenhagen to Bornholm is 35min. The quickest ferry crossing (1hr 20min) is from Ystad in Sweden.

Other months: Nov-Feb – cold, quiet, cheap; Mar-May – spring blooming, longer days; Jun-Sept – warm, long days (busiest in Jul); Sept-Oct – mild, uncrowded.

REYKJAVÍK
ICELAND

→ **Why now?** Watch whales during peak viewing season.

There's really no bad time for a city break in Iceland's quirky, always-innovating capital – but to combine bar-hopping and cultural insights with the best chance of seeing cetaceans, come in June, when long days, dry weather and the biggest whale populations converge. Minke whales and porpoises live around Iceland year-round, but you're more likely to spot killer whales, plus humpback, sperm and even mighty blue whales, off the west coast in June. As a bonus, puffins return to breed on coastal islands in summer. Back onshore, make time to roam the capital's attractions: the historic sights of Old Reykjavík ('haunted' guided walks are memorable); the astonishing white church, Hallgrímskirkja, with its statue of Viking adventurer Leifur Eiríksson; and the array of museums, including the pun-inducing Phallological Museum.

Trip plan: International flights arrive at Keflavík Airport, 48km (30 miles) southwest of Reykjavík and connected by regular buses. Allow at least three days to explore the capital and take a whale-watching excursion.

Need to know: Close to the airport, the geothermal Blue Lagoon is Iceland's most famous natural spring complex, but you can soak in thermal waters for a fraction of the price at Reykjavík's Laugardalslaug pool.

Other months: Oct-Apr – cold, dark, aurora sightings possible; May & Sep – cooler, pleasant; Jun-Aug – warmer, drier.

(A): The dramatic Bastei Bridge in Saxon Switzerland; (L): Marvel at Ravenna's stunning frescoes; (R): Cross a continent from Istanbul to Paris

SAXON SWITZERLAND
GERMANY

→ **Why now?** Get some peak practice in the birthplace of climbing.

Germany's far east, between Dresden and the Czech border, is the pinnacle of climbing – or, rather, pinnacles. Dubbed Saxon Switzerland (Sächsische Schweiz) by Romantic artists, it's even more dramatic than that moniker suggests, its dense woods interspersed with the 1100-plus sandstone pillars and crags that inspired 19th-century climbers, prickling up like a vast fossilised forest on the banks of the river Elbe. Today, the region is a hub for chalky-fingered adventurers lured here by some 20,000 climbing routes, and it's a great place to learn the basics of rock climbing, with a number of excellent schools offering lessons – ideal in June, with steady weather but before the high summer rush. If you'd rather explore at ground level, try hiking the 112km (70 mile) Painters' Way, pedal the riverside Elberadweg cycle route and admire historic bastions such as Königstein, Hohnstein and Felsenburg Neurathen – the last a 13th-century rock-top ruin accessed via the astonishing Basteibrücke (Bastei Bridge) between soaring crags. Combine with a couple of days exploring the restored Baroque and neo-Renaissance monuments of lively Dresden.

Trip plan: The most convenient airport is Prague, from where is a 1hr 30min train ride to Bad Schandau – a convenient base for exploring Saxon Switzerland – and 2hr by rail to Dresden.

Need to know: Classic paddle-steamers chug along the Elbe in Dresden, with special cruises through Saxon Switzerland on selected dates between April and September.

Other months: Nov-Mar – cold, wet; Apr-May & Oct – cooler, fewer visitors; Jun-Sep – sunniest months.

RAVENNA
ITALY

→ **Why now?** Make Byzantine-style mosaics in festival season.

To say that Ravenna has a tempestuous past would be a serious understatement. A key Roman port under Augustus, it became the capital of the Western Roman Empire in AD 402, and then of the Ostrogothic kingdom; for a few glorious centuries, it was the major Byzantine city in Italy. And boy, did those Byzantines like mosaics: today, Ravenna is packed with masterpieces from that era. Once you've explored the historic centre, called at Dante's final resting place and admired the astonishingly intricate pieces at the finest sites – the sixth-century basilicas of San Vitale and Sant'Apollinare Nuovo, and the Neonian Baptistry, for example – try your hand at creating a mosaic yourself: several schools offer courses for beginners. June is a great time to visit: it's warm but generally not sweltering, and from the beginning of the month a symphony of classical, opera, folk and other music serenades the city during the Ravenna Festival, which continues into mid-July.

Trip plan: The nearest airport is Bologna, around 1hr away by train or car. Demand for affordable accommodation is keen, particularly during the festival – book ahead.

Need to know: On hot summer days, the lure of the sea is strong – fortunately, the bustling Adriatic resort of Rimini, with its vast sweep of sand and vibrant nightlife, is a mere 1hr train ride from Ravenna.

Other months: Nov-Mar – cool, wet; Apr-May & Oct – warm; Jun-Sep – hot, dry.

PARIS TO ISTANBUL

→ **Why now?** Traverse Europe by train in timeless style.

In 1883, the first Compagnie Internationale des Wagons-Lits service chugged out of Paris Gare de Lyon en route to Constantinople (now Istanbul), transporting passengers in luxury through Strasbourg, Munich, Vienna, Budapest, Belgrade and Sofia to the very edge of Europe – the original Orient Express. Today, though you can't trace that epic route on one convenient train (unless you splurge thousands on the uber-luxe Venice Simplon-Orient-Express), and though overnight sleeper services are being eaten away by easy-access low-cost flights, it's still possible to follow in the footsteps of those Belle Époque adventurers. June is a great time to do so, with lots of trains running and good weather outside. Catch a day-train from Paris to Munich, then the sleeper to Budapest; explore its Art Nouveau glories (perhaps taking a dip in the Gellért thermal baths), then bed down on another train to Bucharest, taking in the Romanian capital before your final nocturnal ride to Istanbul. Time to spare? Countless diversions and stop-offs beckon: the medieval heart of old Strasbourg; art, café-culture and regal Baroque palaces in Vienna; or Belgrade's fortress and buzzing underground bars.

Trip plan: The journey from Paris to Istanbul takes a minimum of three days, but best plan for stops and allow at least five or six. For expert advice, visit www.seat61.com.

Need to know: Most travellers need a visa to enter Turkey; ideally, buy an e-visa online before departing from home.

Other months: Nov-Mar – cold; Apr-May & Oct-Nov – cool; Jun-Sep – warmest.

Ageing rock stars on the Isle of Lewis: the Callanish stones

© Julian Elliott / Robert Harding

OUTER HEBRIDES SCOTLAND

 Why now? Roam dazzling white sands on the sunniest days.

Forget the Caribbean or Aegean: the finest beaches in the world, lapped by the clearest turquoise waters, are in Scotland. The west coasts of the Outer Hebrides, also known as the Western Isles (Na h-Eileanan an Iar in Gaelic), gleam with white shell fragments – and the long days of June are perfect for roaming these vast, empty beaches before high season (for both humans and midges). On Berneray you might spot otters, seals and puffins; on North Uist the hairs on the back of your neck will stand up at the 5000-year-old tomb of Bharpa Langass and Pobull Fhinn stone circle, and you might hear the cicada-like calls of corncrakes at Balranald RSPB Reserve. Lewis has the main town, Stornoway, plus traditional crofters' blackhouses and

Callanish stone circle, while 11th-century Kisimul Castle guards Barra. Throughout, you'll find those sweeps of white sand backed by machair grassland, speckled with rainbow-hued wildflowers in June.

Trip plan: Concentrate on a handful of the 100-plus islands and skerries. Fly to Benbecula or Stornoway (or catch the ferry from Ullapool) and roam Lewis and Harris, or sail to South Uist from Oban or Mallaig. You can also fly from Glasgow to Barra, landing on the beach at low tide.

Need to know: By June, Scotland's midge season is underway; however, breezes deter midges, and the Outer Hebrides' west coasts suffer much less than the Highlands.

Other months: Nov-Mar – dark, cold, wet; Apr-May & Oct – reasonably sunny; Jun-Sep – warm, increasingly wet.

The Tolmin Gorge in Triglav National Park

© Luca Bortolossi / 500px

JULIAN ALPS
SLOVENIA

→ **Why now? Roam mountain trails in warm sunshine.**

In this land of spectacular mountains, lakes and rivers, one of Europe's most forested countries, it's no coincidence that Slovenes are so keen on outdoor activities. And the Julian Alps, where the 2684m (8806ft) Mt Triglav is surrounded by 840 sq km (324 sq miles) of national park, are the focus of this action. The spring–summer transition month of June, when the mercury soars to around 25°C/77°F, is the time to get outside, whether swimming in picture-perfect lakes Bled or Bohinj, rafting the Soča River or canyoning the Grmečica gorge. Hiking is also huge here: it's said that every Slovenian should climb Triglav at least once, but you could also dip into the low-level, circular Julian Alps Trail, totalling 260km (162 miles) and affording tremendous views of the peaks, plus access to village accommodation, cultural insights and places to fuel up on excellent Slovenian cuisine and wines – universally high in quality but low in price.

Trip plan: Fly to Ljubljana or Venice (an easy drive west), then either tackle some of the Julian Alps Trail or explore from a handy base – Kobarid or Bovec for the Soča Valley, Kranjska Gora or Mojstrana for the Sava Valley, or any of the settlements in the Bohinj Valley.

Need to know: Lakeside Bled is a perennial honeypot town – book well ahead, or consider staying a little way outside, for example in Ribno.

Other months: Dec-Mar – winter, good snowsports; Apr-Jun – spring, wildflowers; Sep-Oct – autumn, warm, fiery foliage; Jul-Aug – high summer, crowds.

HVAR
CROATIA

Why now? Enjoy an Adriatic island ahead of the hordes.

Croatia's islands are hardly secret anymore. The beaches, the turquoise waters, the Venetian architecture, the seafood, the wine – all are acclaimed across Europe. Some 20,000 visitors a day descend on Hvar's eponymous capital in July and August – but come in June and you can enjoy guaranteed sunshine before the crowds arrive and demand for accommodation soars. June is peak lavender season, too, when hillsides are swathed in the purple blooms; and is the start of the Hvar Summer Festival, with a lively line-up of alfresco music and other cultural events. Sure, you might spend most of your time on the coast, perhaps swimming off bar-lined Palmižana on the nearby islet of Sveti Klement, or at Hvar's little Jagodna, where you'll even find sand (most beaches are rocky or pebbly). But don't miss the historic delights of Hvar Town, from a Venetian cathedral to Croatia's oldest theatre, or the atmospheric alleys of Stari Grad on the north coast. And be sure to settle into a traditional *konoba* (tavern) for *hvarska gregada* (fish stew) and a crisp local white wine.

Trip plan: Ferries sail from Split, which has a busy international airport, to Hvar Town and Stari Grad several times daily in June.

Need to know: Stay in Hvar Town for nightlife, or Stari Grad, Vrboska or Jelsa for a quieter time and lower prices.

Other months: Nov–Apr – cool, reduced services; May-Oct – hotter, warm seas.

© DaLiu / Shutterstock

EASTERN
FINLAND

Why now? Watch brown bears foraging in the forest.

If you go down to the woods today, you'd better go in disguise – or, at least, duck into a well-camouflaged hide and keep quiet. The 2000 or so brown bears shambling around Finland's taiga (boreal) forests are most active in June, and the long days of summer provide the best opportunities for watching and photographing them. The lakes and woods lining Finland's eastern border with Russia are bustling with wildlife, including a large proportion of the country's bears, plus wolves, wolverines, flying squirrels, rare endemic Saimaa ringed seal and birds such as mighty white-tailed eagles. The region's many wildlife centres offer hides where you can join experienced local guides to watch for these creatures, which are more active in the small hours – hike into the forest in late afternoon, and prepare for an adrenaline-charged night watching mainland Europe's largest land predators foraging and playing; if you're really lucky, you'll see a female bear with young cubs.

Trip plan: Fly to Helsinki, then head to Kajaani for the bear-watching hides, or drive north alongside the Russian border, stopping at Lake Saimaa and some forest hides. Various specialist tour operators offer guided or self-drive wildlife-watching itineraries.

Need to know: Finland sees almost constant daylight during June; the best times for watching mammals are usually the darkest hours of the sepia-hued 'night'.

Other months: Oct-Apr – cold, often snowy; May-Sep – light, bears active.

GRASSE
FRANCE

Why now? Use uncommon scents in the capital of perfume.

The ancient town of Grasse, nudging the French Riviera in southeastern Provence, was long famous for the wrong kind of smell: the stink of tanning leather. Local artisans began masking the smell of their renowned gloves with scent, and the Grasse perfume industry was born. Today, the tanneries are long gone and the surrounding countryside is speckled with jasmine, lavender, mimosa, orange trees and roses, yielding essential oils for the 30 or so perfumeries now operating in the town, which include the likes of Chanel and Dior. Sunny June, when *centifolia* (cabbage) roses bloom, is the ideal time to discover the scent-makers' secrets. Nose along to the wonderful Musée International de la Parfumerie to learn about the industry, visit one of the most venerable perfume houses – Fragonard, Galimard or Molinard – to create your own fragrance in a short workshop, or join a multi-day perfume-making course.

Trip plan: Grasse itself is surrounded by sprawling suburbs; if not taking a residential course, base yourself in nearby Cannes or in one of the surrounding, more attractive Riviera villages. Wherever you stay, explore the gorgeous Provençal countryside by car or bike.

Need to know: An aromatic alternative to Grasse is the Provençal village of Forcalquier, where the Artemisia Museum, housed in the medieval Couvent des Cordeliers, offers perfumery workshops.

Other months: Nov-Mar – cool, wet; Apr-May & Oct – pleasantly warm; Jun-Sep – hot, dry (Jasmine Festival in Aug).

FRISIAN ISLANDS NETHERLANDS

Terschelling on a quiet day

→ **Why now? Go mudlarking in midsummer.**

For an alternative, much more vigorous kind of mud therapy, head to the Frisian Islands off the north coast of the Netherlands: Vlieland, Terschelling, Ameland and Schiermonnikoog, four long, flat sandbars separating the Wadden Sea from the open North Sea. Here, experienced guides lead mudlarks on immersive (literally and figuratively) *wadlopen* (mud-walking) expeditions, with participants sometimes sinking waist-deep in the squelch – challenging and hugely uplifting in this mesmerising landscape of vast skies and far horizons, populated by wading birds and seals. It's most enchanting in the long days of June, when the weather warms but before tourist numbers peak in July and August. The islands themselves offer a variety of attractions, from the empty beaches and dunes of Schiermonnikoog National Park to pavilions and cafés on Vlieland and Terschelling. That latter island is transformed for 10 June days into an alfresco venue for the groundbreaking Oerol arts festival – expect acrobatics, open-air theatre, interactive installations and more, with audience participation de rigueur.

Trip plan: Ferries sail to Terschelling and Vlieland from Harlingen, to Ameland from Holwerd, and to Schiermonnikoog from Lauersoog. The best way to explore the islands is by bike; cycle hire is widely available.

Need to know: Wadlopen forays are possible only with a guide and with the right tide and weather conditions – the decision on whether a walk will happen is usually made the night before a planned excursion.

Other months: Nov-Mar – cold, dark; Apr-Oct – mud-walking possible (islands very busy Jul-Aug).

GREENLAND

Why now? Explore a wild frontier in the endless midsummer days.

'When you've seen the world, there's always Greenland.' So goes the old travellers' expression – and after you've experienced the otherworldly light of June, when day never fades to night, you'll understand why. Austerely beautiful Greenland is the world's biggest island, rendered bigger still by transport logistics: with barely any roads, travel between the small, scattered communities usually involves a boat or helicopter ride – cheap, this isn't. But it also isn't like anywhere else. You can immerse yourself in the traditional lifestyles of Inuit communities, watch breaching whales in Disko Bay and browsing musk ox near Kangerlussuaq, and breathe the scent of pure Arctic ice as you hike or kayak isolated fjords such as Ilulissat (home to the vast Sermeq Kujalleq glacier) or traverse the mountains of eastern Greenland.

Trip plan: Realistically, you'll want to plan a trip with a knowledgeable tour operator who can book international flights (probably to the main settlement, Nuuk), as well as accommodation and internal transport. Most itineraries focus on the (relatively) well-trodden west coast; the east coast is wilder, more sparsely populated and perhaps even more rewarding.

Need to know: Biting insects can become annoying later in summer (July and August). Bad weather can stymie travel plans at any time, so be flexible.

Other months: Nov-Apr – winter, husky sledding; May & Oct – colder, less reliable weather; Jun-Sep – mildest weather, easiest travel.

Colourful Tasiilaq is, improbably, Greenland's seventh largest town

PICOS DE EUROPA
SPAIN

→ **Why now? Spot rare birds of prey in the mountain sunshine.**

Think vulture and you probably picture a bald, wrinkly, squabbling specimen. The bearded vulture, though, is altogether different: with a 3m (10ft) wingspan, orange chest, black facemask and red eye-rings, plus that characteristic 'beard', the raptor also known as a lammergeier is mesmerising. Long persecuted, bearded vultures are resurgent in the Picos de Europa thanks to a novel reintroduction project – and June is a wonderful time to spot them soaring above the gleaming limestone crags of this spectacular national park in northern Spain. Watch for them as you hike the trails, or visit the open-air vulture feeding site above Covadonga, a small town renowned as the site of the 8th-century battle that began the so-called 'reconquest' of Spain. Look for other birds of prey – griffon and Egyptian vultures, honey buzzards and golden eagles – as well as (if you're incredibly lucky) wolves. You'll want to work up a hunger (and a thirst): the food and drink of the Asturias region are tremendous, particularly traditional *queso azul* (blue cheese), *fabada* (pork and bean stew) and *sidra* (cider).

Trip plan: Santander and Asturias are the nearest airports, and Santander is also accessible by ferry from Cork, Plymouth and Portsmouth. Public transport within the Picos is limited; hiring a car (or hiking) is the best option.

Need to know: Another good place to spot bearded vultures is Ordesa y Monte Perdido National Park, over to the east in the Aragon Pyrenees.

Other months: Dec-May – snow on higher trails; Jun-Sep – warm, dry; Oct-Nov – cooler, wetter.

A typical Picos view, characterised by limestone crags and placid lakes

BERLIN
GERMANY

Dip into Berlin's 30m-long Badeschiff, converted from a barge on the River Spree

© Mark Read / Lonely Planet

Why now? Enjoy parklife and performances in this leafy city.

Just three decades ago, Berlin was split by the infamous wall between west and communist east. Today, the reunified city is one of the coolest and friendliest European capitals, with hip bars galore; it's also surprisingly green, with more than 2500 parks and gardens. Explore the cultural highlights in warm, sunny June: centuries of international heritage on Museumsinsel (Museum Island), the more recent history of Checkpoint Charlie, the Jewish Museum and Holocaust Memorial, or the magnificent rebuilt Reichstag. June is chock with festivals, cultural happenings and carnivals, from street parades and science events to open-air opera and folk music. But spare some time for parklife, too. Tiergarten is the biggie, stretching west from Brandenburg Gate to the zoo. At weekends head to Mauerpark (literally, 'Wall Park') in hip Prenzlauer Berg, buzzing with buskers, flea-market stalls and even open-air karaoke sessions. Or go southwest past Charlottenburg to Grunewald ('Green Forest') and romantically landscaped Pfaueninsel ('Peacock Island').

Trip plan: Berlin has two airports, both around 30min from the city by bus: Schönefeld to the south, and Tegel to the northwest.

Need to know: The view from the dome of the Reichstag is spectacular, but advance booking is essential.

Other months: Dec-Feb – winter, very cold; Mar-May – warming, can be wet; Jun-Sep – summer, pleasantly warm; Oct-Nov – autumn, cooler, colourful foliage.

BEYOND BERLIN

POTSDAM · 29KM (18 MILES) · Palaces, museums and parks in the 'German Versailles'

ORANIENBURG · 32KM (20 MILES) · Museum at former Sachsenhausen concentration camp

RHEINSBURG · 88KM (55 MILES) · Magnificent riverside renaissance castle

LÜBBENAU · 92KM (57 MILES) · Punt on the canals of the Spreewald

Contemplating
Helgeland's
Svartisen Glacier

ARCTIC NORWAY

→ **Why now? Snap the light fantastic in the land of the Midnight Sun.**

In midsummer, Norway's far north is bathed in an endless light – from mid-May to late July, the sun doesn't dip below the horizon. You'll want every second of daylight to drink in the scenery – and to shoot it: with the so-called 'golden hour' lasting half the day, now's the perfect time to hone your camera-craft. Various courses offer tuition in photographing the colourful fishing villages and craggy ridges of the Lofoten Islands and less-visited Senja to the north. Focus on traditional red rorbuer (cabins) from Hamnøy Bridge on the Lofoten island of Flakstadøy, climb the peak of Barden to shoot the shark-fin peak of Segla framed by glistening fjords, or head to Tungeneset for vistas of the Devil's Jaw peaks on Senja. Alternatively, simply roam the empty roads, stopping to capture whatever grabs your attention. Watch out, too, for soaring sea eagles, savour fine fish and seafood, and explore Tromsø, the region's lively hub, with its cosy pubs, diverse museums, Toblerone-shaped Arctic Cathedral and annual Midnight Sun Marathon.

Trip plan: Tromsø has an international airport. Buses and the Hurtigruten ferry link towns, but self-drive's the easiest way to reach isolated fishing villages on Senja, the Sami centres of Kautokeino and Karasjok, and Europe's northernmost tip near Nordkapp.

Need to know: June is peak season in Tromsø – book accommodation in advance.

Other months: Nov-Apr – largely dark, cold; May-Oct – reliably above freezing (Midnight Sun mid-May to late Jul).

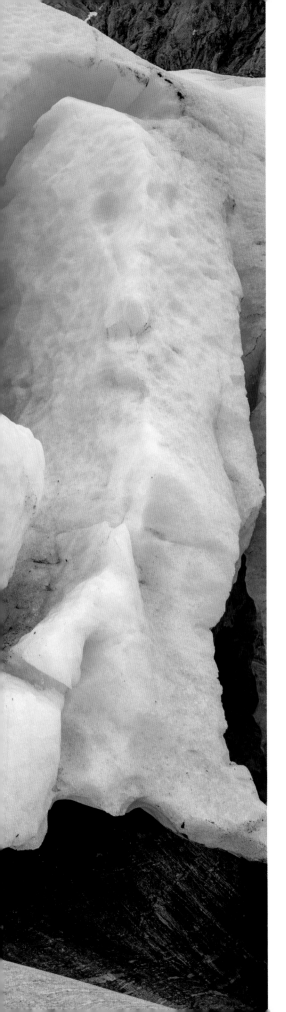

Wild horses in the
Andorran mountains

ANDORRA

→ **Why now? Get healthy among the Pyrenean peaks**

It's not French. It's not Spanish. It's something in between – both literally and figuratively. Andorra, the diminutive principality with the big mountains, is sandwiched between heavyweight neighbours, but has a flavour all of its own. Taste it for yourself in June, when the sun smiles on Pyrenean meadows, hiking trails lined with kaleidoscopic wildflowers and peaks soaring up to nearly 3000m (9842ft). Andorra is perfect for family adventures, with a packed menu of activities on offer in spring and summer, from mountain-biking, horseriding and ziplining to via ferrata climbing, canyoning and kayaking. And to revitalise weary legs after those adventures, call in for a soak, a hammam steam or a massage at the innovative Caldea, southern Europe's largest thermal spa complex; its location in Andorra La Vella, the compact capital, means you can combine treatments with some retail therapy, including duty-free shopping.

Trip plan: Andorra has neither an airport nor a rail system, so you'll have to fly to a nearby airport then use buses or hire a car; it's a 3hr bus journey from Barcelona airport, or 2hr 30min from Toulouse. Seasonal flights sometimes serve Lleida (Catalonia), from where buses take around 3hr. Allow at least three days to roam the mountains and relax at Caldea.

Need to know: Though not an EU member, Andorra uses the euro (€). The official language is Catalan, though French and Spanish are widely spoken.

Other months: Dec-Apr – cold, good skiing; May-Sep – warm, sunny (busiest late Jul & Aug); Oct-Nov – cooler.

Plaza Azoguejo and its Roman aquaduct attest to a storied past

SEGOVIA SPAIN

 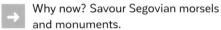

→ **Why now? Savour Segovian morsels and monuments.**

It's not all about the aqueduct – but as water features go, few are more dramatic than Segovia's. The magnificent stone structure, 28m (92ft) high and with some 167 arches, was built around AD 100 when this central Spanish city was a Roman powerhouse. Over the following centuries Segovia gained an array of astonishing Romanesque churches and the enchanting Alcázar – originally Moorish, rebuilt as a fairytale castle, today all Disney-esque castellations and turrets, regal staterooms and moats. Despite these marvels, Segovia remains a relatively hidden delight; lingering in the shadow of Madrid (some 30min to the south), it's an ideal city-break destination in sunny June, with culture and cuisine in spades. To find out about the latter, visit the small but tasty Museo Gastronómico, exploring the region's specialities, before browsing the menus of the many excellent eateries. There's roast suckling pig and lamb, *cocido* (chickpea stew), local mushrooms and *judiones de la granja* (large white beans), trout and Castilian garlic soup. Save room for dessert – particularly *ponche segoviano*, the city's famed caramelised marzipan layer cake.

Trip plan: Madrid has the nearest international airport. Trains from Madrid reach Segovia's Guiomar station, 5km (3 miles) from the historic centre, in less than 30min.

Need to know: The feasts of St John and St Paul are celebrated with nine days of music, theatre and children's activities towards the end of June, when the town gets very busy.

Other months: Nov-Mar – cool; Apr-May & Oct – pleasantly warm, wetter; Jun-Sep – hot and dry.

The Church of the Saviour on Spilled Blood is St Petersburg's most dazzling church

ST PETERSBURG
RUSSIA

 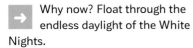

→ **Why now?** Float through the endless daylight of the White Nights.

This great city, founded on the Neva River by Tsar Peter the Great in 1703, was always designed to impress. Its palaces, museums and theatres are still as grand today as its early masters (and mistresses) envisaged, and in midsummer, when the sun never sets and St Petersburg is bathed in a luminous glow 24/7, it looks that much more romantic – busy with visitors, expensive, but magical nonetheless. During the *belye nochi* (White Nights), roughly from the second week in June to the start of July, St Petersburg is a whirl of opera, ballet, music and general *zhizni radost* (joie de vivre). Stroll alongside the Neva and into the Summer Garden, watch the bridges open and the fountains of the Peterhof gush.

Trip plan: You could spend a week wandering the riverbank, parks and streets, but at minimum make time for St Petersburg's grand palaces and churches, the incredible State Hermitage Museum in the white, green and gold Winter Palace, and the monuments of the Peter and Paul Fortress.

Need to know: Visitors must obtain a Russian visa, usually through a tour agency or via an invitation from a hotel, before arriving. Prices soar during the White Nights.

Other months: Dec-Mar – dark, freezing, magical; Apr-Sep – warm, bright; Oct-Nov – cold, grey.

(R): Grand crags on
the Prosecco road;
(B): Medieval Asolo

© Matt Munro / Lonely Planet

VENETO ITALY

→ **Why now? Bike or hike the
Prosecco Road.**

There's a hot fuss about fizz in the
foothills of the Dolomites north of Venice.
The slopes between Conegliano and
Valdobbiadene are striped with *ciglioni*
('hogback' hills), small plots of vines on
narrow grassy terraces producing some of
Italy's best bubbles: prosecco recognised
with DOCG status. You can drive between
100 or so wineries along the 50km (31
mile) La Strada del Prosecco (Prosecco
Road), or – even better – explore on foot
or by bike, perfect in early summer before
the mercury really soars. This region is
legendary among cyclists for its rolling
countryside and quiet backroads, and a few
days of pedalling between vineyards and
tastings is a wonderful way to appreciate
both scenery and oenology. Of course,
there are ample reasons to deviate off the
official route, perhaps to visit the lovely
medieval hilltop town of Asolo, take a cool
dip in Revine Lake, or admire the historic
covered wooden bridge (and nearby grappa
distillery) in Bassano del Grappa.

Trip plan: Fly to Venice, less than 1hr by car
or train from Conegliano; some low-cost
airlines serve Treviso, which is 20min away
by rail. Several tour operators offer guided
or self-guided walking and cycling tours of
the so-called Prosecco Hills, but it's easy
enough to organise for yourself.

Need to know: Naturally, driving or cycling
after drinking alcohol is dangerous and
illegal. Savour your fizz back at your hotel.

Other months: Nov-Apr – cool, wet; May-
Jul & Sep-Oct – warm, good cycling; Aug
– very hot.

© Leoks / Shutterstock

LISBON
PORTUGAL

→ **Why now? Indulge in fine wine, food and fado in the late Iberian spring.**
There are few major European cities where you can plant yourself on a sunny terrace outside a hip café, surrounded by historic architecture, and be confident you won't get stung for an overpriced coffee or beer. Lisbon is the exception – but though it's one of the best-value major cities in Europe, the Portuguese capital feels anything but cheap. Food and drink –

A popular 1930s tram makes short work of Castle Hill

© Jonathan Stokes / Lonely Planet

...m and festivals create a friendly buzz. The Feast of St Anthony sees the city go sardine-crazy, but at any time you'll likely inhale the aroma of someone grilling fish on an Alfama street corner. To explore, take tram 28 – vintage style, touristy but fabulous – on a tour of the city, then tram 15 to see the Torre de Belém and Jerónimos Monastery, and to try the finest *pasteis de nata* (custard tarts) at Antiga Confeitaria de Belém.

Trip plan: The Lisbon metro runs from the airport into the city centre. For convenience and character, pick accommodation in the Alfama, Baixa or Bairro Alto districts.

Need to know: Trams 28 and 15 are favourite rides for pickpockets; there's no need for paranoia, just awareness and sensible precautions. The city explodes into action during its fabulous pre-Lenten Carnaval.

Other months: Oct-Mar – winter rains; Apr-Sep – warm and dry.

BEYOND LISBON

CASCAIS · 26KM (16 MILES) · Beaches, great surf, vibrant nightlife

SINTRA · 27KM (17 MILES) · Fairy-tale palaces, subtropical gardens, lush forests

MAFRA · 40KM (25 MILES) · Extravagant monastery-palace, beautiful parkland

ÓBIDOS · 72KM (45 MILES) · Moorish city walls, labyrinthine alleyways

July

WHERE TO GO WHEN

CHALLENGE MYSELF

I WANT TO

TAKE ME OUT FOR...

- FOOD
  - ENGELBERG, SWITZERLAND P172
  - ALTA BADIA, ITALY P167
- DRINK
  - LA RIOJA, SPAIN P161

Sample strudel in the Alta Badia

Rioja is world-famous for its wine

TAKE ME TO TOWN

- ART & CULTURE
  - VAUCLUSE, FRANCE P163
  - VERONA, ITALY P175
- NIGHT-LIFE & HEDONISM
  - ANTWERP, BELGIUM P159
  - NOVI SAD, SERBIA P169

Rave through summer nights in Serbia's Novi Sad

RELAX/INDULGE

See rows of nodding sunflowers in France's Vaucluse region

DIAL IT DOWN

- WELLNESS
  - CURONIAN SPIT, LITHUANIA P159
- CHILLING
  - ADRIATIC ISLANDS, CROATIA P164
  - COMPORTA, PORTUGAL P173
  - OHRID, NORTH MACEDONIA P161

Macedonia's church of St John at Kaneo

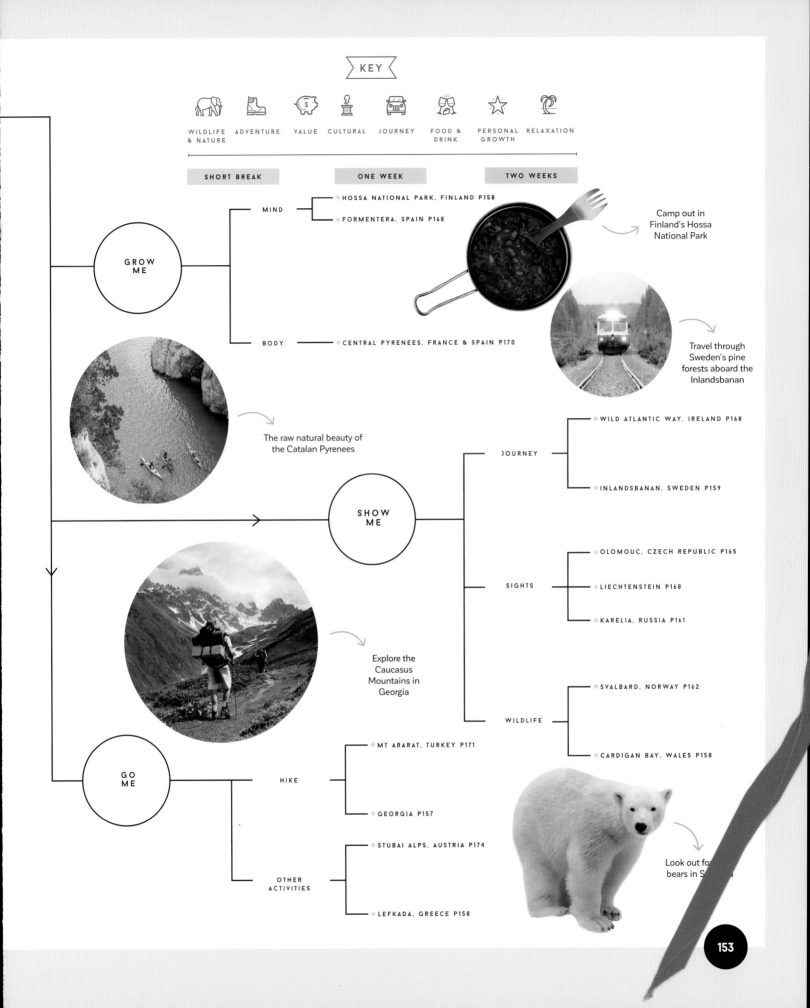

WILDLIFE & NATURE | ADVENTURE | VALUE | CULTURAL | JOURNEY | FOOD & DRINK | PERSONAL GROWTH | RELAXATION

SHORT BREAK | ONE WEEK | TWO WEEKS

GROW ME

MIND
- HOSSA NATIONAL PARK, FINLAND P158
- FORMENTERA, SPAIN P168

BODY
- CENTRAL PYRENEES, FRANCE & SPAIN P170

Camp out in Finland's Hossa National Park

Travel through Sweden's pine forests aboard the Inlandsbanan

The raw natural beauty of the Catalan Pyrenees

SHOW ME

JOURNEY
- WILD ATLANTIC WAY, IRELAND P168
- INLANDSBANAN, SWEDEN P159

SIGHTS
- OLOMOUC, CZECH REPUBLIC P165
- LIECHTENSTEIN P168
- KARELIA, RUSSIA P161

WILDLIFE
- SVALBARD, NORWAY P162
- CARDIGAN BAY, WALES P158

Explore the Caucasus Mountains in Georgia

GO ME

HIKE
- MT ARARAT, TURKEY P171
- GEORGIA P157

OTHER ACTIVITIES
- STUBAI ALPS, AUSTRIA P174
- LEFKADA, GREECE P158

Look out for bears in S[...]

EVENTS
IN JULY

ZOMER VAN ANTWERPEN
Antwerp, Belgium
A diverse calendar of music, dance, theatre and circus performances offers free or cheap entertainment during 'Antwerp Summer'.

VERONA OPERA FESTIVAL
Verona, Italy
Absorb performances by high-calibre singers and orchestras in the atmospheric setting of the Roman Arena.

MEDIEVAL DAYS
San Marino
Residents don medieval costume and practise historic activities during high summer – watch out for crossbow bolts.

WORLD BODYPAINTING FESTIVAL
Klagenfurt am Wörthersee, Austria
A pumping musical soundtrack accompanies this celebration of visual art using the human body as a canvas.

ISTANBUL JAZZ FESTIVAL
Istanbul, Turkey
This well-established, wide-ranging celebration of jazz, soul and blues spreads across the city, including paid events, music cruises and free concerts in the park.

EXIT FESTIVAL
Novi Sad, Serbia
Music-lovers from across Europe dance to big-name acts and DJs in the mighty Petrovaradin Fortress.

LES FÊTES DE GAYANT
Douai, France
A colourful cast of towering folkloric characters parades through the streets during the Festival of Giants.

WIFE-CARRYING WORLD CHAMPIONSHIPS
Sonkajärvi, Finland
For a quarter of a century, men have lugged spouses over an obstacle course in a hilarious and surprisingly nailbiting competition.

Late June to August — $

Late June to early September — $$

First Saturday in July — $$

Early July — $

Four days in early July — $$

Three weeks late June–mid July — $$

Three days in mid-July — $$

Late July — $$

July

Imposing and majestic, the Dolomites offer perfect hiking terrain

• DOLOMITES, ITALY

• ENGLEBERG, SWITZERLAND

• FORMENTERA, SPAIN

• PYRENEES, FRANCE/SPAIN

• ADRIATIC ISLANDS, CROATIA   • COMPORTA, PORTUGAL

• OHRID, NORTH MACEDONIA

Explore Saint Naum Monastery near Ohrid in North Macedonia

• CARDIGAN BAY, WALES

• CURONIAN SPIT, LITHUANIA

Sunflowers and lavender characterise France's Vaucluse in summer

• STUBAI ALPS, AUSTRIA

Scan the peaks for Alpine Ibex in the Stubai Alps

It's hard to decide which is bluer in Lefkada's sunshine; the sea or the paintwork

• VAUCLUSE, FRANCE

• LEFKADA, GREECE

• ANTWERP, BELGIUM

Bathing beauties; three cow walruses float in the surf of Hossa

• HOSSA NP, FINLAND

Find the heart of Sweden on the Inlandsbanan

• GEORGIA

• INLANDSBANEN, SWEDEN

• WILD ATLANTIC WAY, IRELAND

Ireland's famous Cliffs of Moher

• VERONA, ITALY

• OLOMOUC, CZECH REPUBLIC

• SVALBARD, NORWAY

• LIECHTENSTEIN

Sample La Rioja's finest local produce

• NOVI SAD, SERBIA

• KARELIA, RUSSIA

The wooden church on Kizhi Island in Karelia

• LA RIOJA, SPAIN

• MT ARARAT, TURKEY

Juliet frozen forever in the courtyard of her house in Verona

GEORGIA

→ **Why now?** Hike high-mountain meadows amid ancient monasteries.

Tucked away between the Black Sea and the high Caucasus, south of Russia, north of Turkey, Georgia is a land where stone watchtowers guard verdant valleys, ancient churches nestle beneath lofty peaks, and – so legend says – wine was first created 7000 years ago. While capital Tbilisi and the lowlands sizzle in high summer, July is ideal for hiking in trek-friendly regions such as Svaneti, Tusheti and Kazbegi (officially called Stepantsminda) – high trails are generally free from snow by now, and days are warmer and drier than in June (though, as in mountains everywhere, it pays to be prepared for all weather conditions).

Trip plan: Start in capital Tbilisi, its traditional balconied houses guarded by ancient Narikala Fortress. Head east into Kakheti for some wine-tasting, then into the peaks of the Caucasus around Kazbegi to discover remote churches, and west into the Svaneti region to trek high paths among villages guarded by medieval *koshkebi* (defensive stone towers). Descend to ancient Colchis (where, according to Greek myth, Jason found his golden fleece), and return to Tbilisi via the vast cave monastery of Vardzia.

Need to know: Check your government's travel advice before visiting the regions of Abhkazia and South Ossetia, which have declared independence.

Other months: Nov-Apr – highlands cold, snow on trails; May-Jun – warm, rainy; Jul-Aug – hot in lowlands, pleasant in mountains; Sep-Oct – warm, sunny.

Mountain goats are a common sight along the trails of Tusheti National Park

CARDIGAN BAY
WALES

→ **Why now?** Watch dolphins cavort in Cardigan Bay.

The coast of west Wales is a popular destination – for marine mammals as well as holidaying humans. In summer, the broad sweep of Cardigan Bay hosts Europe's largest population of bottlenose dolphins, some resident, others seasonal visitors, and numbering around 300 individuals. They're not shy, and as summer warms up, a boat trip offers a healthy chance of enjoying a close encounter, especially likely offshore of Cemaes Head or New Quay; hop on board from one of the attractive harbours at the southern end of the bay. The fun doesn't end with dolphins: grey seals haul out on rocks, and you might also spot harbour porpoises and seabirds such as guillemots and razorbills. On land, explore the Dylan Thomas connections at New Quay, roam ancient castles and churches, and fuel up on local treats – seafood, of course, but also excellent artisan cheeses.

Trip plan: Base yourself in one of Ceredigion's postcard-pretty coastal towns – New Quay, Aberaeron or Llangrannog – and spend a few days exploring. Or hike the coastal path – the Cardigan to Aberystwyth section (97km/60 miles) makes an achievable four- or five-day adventure.

Need to know: Dolphin-watching boat tours sail from New Quay, Aberaeron and the Teifi Estuary near Cardigan. You might also see dolphins from the coast – Mwnt is a good spot.

Other months: Oct-Feb – cool, wet; Mar-May – spring, boat trips running; Jun-Sep – warm, most dolphins in Cardigan Bay.

HOSSA NATIONAL PARK FINLAND

→ **Why now?** Refresh mind, body and spirit with a feast of forest bathing.

The Japanese concept of *shinrin-yoku* (forest bathing) might have the whiff of a new-age fad, but in Finland the benefits of immersion in leafy nature have long been cherished. Few places offer better opportunities than Hossa National Park, established in 2017 to celebrate the centenary of the country's independence. And independence is what you'll enjoy here: it's DIY nature therapy on your own terms, far from the stresses of modern life. Come in high summer to maximise daylight and warm sun. Hike or mountain-bike 90km (60 miles) of trails; swim, canoe or SUP the 100-plus pristine lakes and 3km/2 mile-long Julma Ölkky gorge; bed down under canvas, in log shelters or cottages; admire 4000-year-old rock art alongside Somerjärvi lake; pluck wild berries (the season starts now); and watch for bears, wolves, elk, wolverines and reindeer roaming the wild expanses. Mostly, though, simply find a spot among the trees where you enjoy the solitude, and let the stillness seep into your soul.

Trip plan: Isolation means a lack of public transport; realistically you'll need to drive to the park. The nearest airport is Kuusamo, about 80km (50 miles) to the north; Kajaani and Oulu are alternatives.

Need to know: In summer, Hossa can be buzzing – with visitors and insects. Pack heavy-duty bug repellent.

Other months: Nov-Mar – usually sub-zero, good cross-country skiing; Apr-May & Sep-Oct – cool, dry; Jun-Aug – warm, rainy.

LEFKADA
GREECE

→ **Why now?** Ride the waves by windpower.

Feel the need for speed? Meet Eric – the rather unlikely name given to the powerful thermal wind that sweeps down from the mountains into southwest Lefkada's Vasiliki bay on summer afternoons. Eric's the reason why this Ionian island is known as one of the world's top windsurfing locations, attracting beginners – who learn the sport in the gentle morning breezes – plus adrenaline-pumped freeracers and freestylers. July's a sweet spot, with hot sun, good wind and reliably dry days. Vasiliki itself is a winsome little town, with a good range of accommodation, plus tavernas and bars in which to revive and recount windsurfing adventures over wine, beer or ouzo. For a break from the board, relax on one of the beaches lining Lefkada's west coast – virtually one long strip of golden sand – sea-kayak or SUP along the shore, or head inland to mountain-bike amid gleaming white crags.

Trip plan: The nearest airport, Aktion, is on the mainland at Preveza, from where buses serve Lefkada town; Vasiliki is a 1hr bus ride further south.

Need to know: Regular summer ferries connect Lefkada with Kefallonia in under 2hr. At the very least, hop across to Lefkada's neighbouring island, pretty little Meganisi, to swim its turquoise coves.

Other months: Nov-Feb – winter, wet, facilities close; Mar-May – getting warmer and drier; Jun-Aug – hot, Eric wind; Sept-Oct – sea still warm.

CURONIAN SPIT
LITHUANIA

→ Why now? Discover an inspiring landscape of dunes and forests.

The narrow wisp of land stretching for nearly 100km (62 miles) along the southeast Baltic Coast was created by the giantess Neringa to protect the coast from a dragon. Well, that's the legend – and the landscape of the Curonian Spit is suitably magical, with 50m/164ft-high dunes, elk-browsed pine forests and pretty wooden villages. In the 19th century, it became a haven for German artists and writers seeking inspiration and peace – visit the summerhouse of Nobel laureate Thomas Mann, and admire the peninsula's generous helping of public sculpture and other artworks. Nurture your own creative streak among the wild landscapes in warm, sunny summer, ideally on two wheels: a wonderful cycle trail runs north from Nida, a former fishing village-turned-artists' colony at the southern end of Lithuania's share of the spit, and in the shadow of the most spectacular dune, Parnidis.

Trip plan: The nearest airport is at Palanga, 30km (19 miles) north of Klaipėda, from where frequent ferries make the short hop across to Smiltynė at the northern end of the Curonian Spit. Buses serve Klaipėda from Vilnius, Kaunas and Kaliningrad.

Need to know: Summer can be buggy, with swarms of biting insects – bring repellant. The southern half of the spit is within the Russian enclave of Kaliningrad – don't try crossing the border without a visa.

Other months: Oct-May – cool, wet, many facilities closed; Jun-Sep – warm, long days, sometimes rainy.

ANTWERP
BELGIUM

→ Why now? Enjoy bargain Belgian alfresco action.

Many things in this thrumming historical hub of the Low Countries are high: the culture, the fashion and, in many respects, the prices. Fortunately, July offers a respite for your wallet via Zomer van Antwerpen (Antwerp Summer), a diverse and densely packed calendar of music, dance, theatre and circus performances that takes over the city from late June through August – many are free, while others charge 'democratic' (ie bargain) prices. Of course, there's plenty more to pack into a short break: Rubens masterworks in his house-museum and within the spectacular Onze-Lieve Vrouwekathedraal; city-wide medieval and Art Nouveau architectural gems; hedonistic clubs and summer pop-up bars in parks and along the river. Long renowned as a trading centre for diamonds and, more recently, cutting-edge fashion, Antwerp offers dangerously addictive shopping, too.

Trip plan: Antwerp's spectacular fin-de-siècle Central Station is a destination in itself – arrive by train if possible (easy, with ample services from across Europe, many via Brussels). The airport is just 5km (3 miles) southeast of the city centre.

Need to know: Antwerp is also jam-packed with events during August – Pride, music festivals, Museum Night, even a Rubens Fair – so forward planning is even more important than in July.

Other months: Dec-Feb – dreary; Mar-May – variable, getting warmer; Jun-Sep – warm, plentiful events; Oct-Nov – mild, wet.

INLANDSBANAN
SWEDEN

→ Why now? Discover one of the globe's least-known great railway journeys.

Sure, you know about the hip coastal cities and wintry wonders. But there's another side to Sweden that few foreign visitors experience – the inside. Explore the diverse charms of the interior aboard the Inlandsbanan railway, chugging for 1300km (808 miles) along the country's spine between Kristinehamn on Lake Vänern and Gällivare in Lapland. There are faster ways of travelling, of course, but aboard this summer-only route you'll absorb the contrasts between south and north, pausing along the way. Fish in Vänern's glittering waters, discover traditional folk culture in Dalarna, hike the mountains of Härjedalen, spot fabulous wildlife (a bear-watching excursion is a highlight), meet Sami people in their canvas villages and taste the freshest local foods in Vilhelmina, and cross the Arctic Circle at Jokkmokk and experience the otherworldly twilight of the Midnight Sun.

Trip plan: The route between Kristinehamn in the south and Gällivare in the north is broken into three timetables, connecting in Mora and requiring an overnight in Östersund. Theoretically you could complete the journey in two days – but better to take at least a week. A two-week Inlandsbanan Card is good value.

Need to know: The trains have toilets, and snacks and coffee are available, but it's not possible to move between carriages.

Other months: Mid-Dec to late Apr – Snötåget train connects Östersund with Mora; Jun to mid-Aug – Inlandsbanan runs

(A) Macedonia's Bay of Bones; (L) Wine barrels in La Rioja; (R) A wooden church on Kizhi Island, with 22 birch bark domes

© jorisvo / Shutterstock

160

OHRID NORTH MACEDONIA

Why now? Enjoy lakeside chilling, cuisine and culture.

Big-ticket lakes in the likes of Italy bag the headlines for beauty and history, but for an alternative aquatic break, head southeast to this compact Balkan state's historic showpiece, jutting into a gorgeous mountain-ringed mere. The Old Town of Ohrid, mentioned in the fourth century BCE as Lychnidos ('City of Light'), boasts Byzantine frescoed churches, Ottoman merchants' houses and an impressive Hellenistic amphitheatre; head around the shore to find the reconstructed Bronze-Age settlement at the Bay of Bones and the 10th-century Sveti Naum Monastery. And it's not all past glories: today, beaches draw visitors to swim and chill – perfect in high summer, when the town also rings to the sound of music, theatre and vocal performances during the annual festival (from 12 July). Feed body as well as soul at one of the Old Town restaurants serving delectable local trout.

Trip plan: Ohrid receives flights from several European cities. Alternatively, capital Skopje is a 2hr 30min drive northeast; Tirana in Albania is a little closer. There are plentiful guesthouses and hotels in Ohrid town, while resorts and public beaches line the shore to the south – the village of Trpejca is an appealing option, its narrow, shingly beach backed by restaurants and bars.

Need to know: The mountain village of Galičnik, about 50km (31 miles) north of Ohrid, is the venue for an extraordinary wedding festival each July.

Other months: Dec-Feb – often sub-zero; Mar-May & Oct-Nov – cooler, quieter; Jun-Sep – reliably warm.

LA RIOJA SPAIN

Why now? Wake up and smell the Tempranillo.

The compact region of La Rioja somehow crams 500-plus wineries into its modest area, between Bilbao, Zaragoza and Madrid in northern Spain. In July, the vineyards striping the craggy Ebro River Valley are verdant and lush, and among them you'll find traces of past settlers – remains betray inhabitation from Neolithic times, through Moorish occupation to medieval Christian settlement. This is a slow-paced region, rich in history – and viticulture: tastings are a must. Visit the venerable, château-style wineries clustered around Haro in the Rioja Alta; elsewhere, Rioja Alavesa is more contemporary – architects Gehry and Calatrava had a hand in the design of Marqués de Riscal and Ysios wineries. Logroño, La Rioja's capital, is packed with bars serving cheap, tasty pintxos (tapas), ideal for soaking up the fruity reds.

Trip plan: Make a leisurely loop around La Rioja. Visit Haro's bodegas, head east to Briones for its ruined castle and the lowdown on rioja at Vivanco, and do a pintxos-crawl along Logroño's Calle del Laurel. On the return, stop at medieval Laguardia, below the Sierra de Cantabria; Calatrava's wave-like Ysios winery is nearby. Remember: don't drink and drive!

Need to know: Bilbao airport is 130km (81 miles) north of Haro, a convenient gateway to the region.

Other months: Nov-Mar – cold, stark, crisp; Apr-May – green; Jun – warm, Haro's 'wine war'; Jul-Aug – hot; Sept-Oct – warm, harvest.

KARELIA RUSSIA

Why now? Cruise toward the Arctic past historic churches and wild landscapes.

The Republic of Karelia, stretching along the Finnish border in far northwest Russia, is a wild land of finger lakes, swamps and forests, shaped by the last ice age and still subject to the whims of extreme weather: the White Sea–Baltic Canal, linking St Petersburg with the Arctic and constructed by forced labour during Stalin's rule, can only open for a few months each summer. July is the warmest month to take an inland cruise through this spectacular region. On Lake Ladoga, admire the Valaam archipelago's 14th-century Monastery of the Transfiguration; at Lake Onega, visit the open-air museum of Kizhi Island, dominated by onion-domed wooden churches; discover traditional culture and wildlife on the Karelian taiga (boreal forest). You could also venture far north to the White Sea's Solovetsky Islands, among historic monasteries and sobering Soviet-era prison camps.

Trip plan: Package cruises typically sail between Moscow and St Petersburg via Lake Ladoga and Kizhi Island/Lake Onega. Theoretically it's possible to continue up the canal to the White Sea, but realistically it's better to take the train from St Petersburg or Petrozavodsk on Lake Onega to Kem, and catch a boat from there to the Solovetsky Islands.

Need to know: Weather is unpredictable even in summer, and biting insects rife among the lakes. Ensure you have the correct visa before visiting Russia.

Other months: Nov-Apr – very cold; late May-Oct – White Sea–Baltic Canal open.

Three bull walruses
in the Svalbard
archipelago

Nodding sunflowers
and rows of lavender;
Provence at its
prettiest

SVALBARD NORWAY

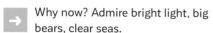

→ **Why now? Admire bright light, big bears, clear seas.**

In the high Arctic, the window of opportunity for cruising is open only briefly: the northernmost shores and most remote fjords of the chilly Svalbard archipelago are accessible by sea for only a month or two each summer. But it's a window worth seeking out. In July, the seas are mostly clear of ice, the temperature 'soars' to a (relatively) balmy 5°C (41°F) and the sun shines for weeks on end – morning, noon and (mid)night – enabling 24-hr sightseeing. Expedition cruise vessels plough past the islands' jagged mountains and creaking glaciers, while expert guides keep watch for wildlife: walrus colonies, herds of reindeer, Arctic foxes, seals, whales of all sorts and, of course, polar bears.

Perhaps 3000 of the huge white predators stalk Svalbard and the surrounding Arctic region; in summer, when the ice breaks up, the bears stay close to the coast. Board a small Zodiac boat and explore the shoreline for the chance of a close encounter.

Trip plan: Fly via Oslo to Longyearbyen on Spitsbergen, Svalbard's main island, from where one- or two-week cruises depart; itineraries and activities are dictated by weather and sea conditions.

Need to know: For the more adventurous, tall-ship vessels glide around Svalbard under sail. It's also possible to cruise from mainland Norway to Spitsbergen.

Other months: Sept-Mar – Northern Lights (Nov-Mar very cold); Apr-Aug – Midnight Sun (boat trips May-Sept).

VAUCLUSE
FRANCE

→ **Why now? Enjoy a purple patch amidst lavender and high drama.**

Swathes of gold festoon this western Provençal département in July – no, not sandy beaches (there's no coastline in the Vaucluse), but blooming sunflower fields. Blossoms are big in high summer – lavender purples hillsides in the Luberon area, too – as is culture: from July, Avignon throngs with theatre-lovers who flock here for the renowned annual festival, packed with big-name performances. But while that walled city's histrionics and history demand to be discovered – don't miss the world's largest Gothic palace, Disney-tastic 14th-century Palais des Papes, and the picturesque medieval demi-bridge Pont St-Bénézet – it's the surrounding countryside that's really alluring. Look beyond the floral fields to wine wonderland Châteauneuf-du-Pape, the Roman theatre at Orange, the dramatic limestone crags of the Dentelles de Montmirail and mighty Mont Ventoux, nemesis of many an intrepid road cyclist emulating the epic hairpin climbs of the Tour de France.

Trip plan: Avignon is best accessed by train, with excellent high-speed services from French and international stations – it's under 3hr from Paris and Geneva, 4hr from Barcelona, less than 6hr direct from London. Local buses serve Provençal destinations, or consider hiring a bike to explore the countryside.

Need to know: Avignon is incredibly busy during the festival – book accommodation well in advance.

Other months: Nov-Feb – cold, mistral winds; Mar-May & Oct – pleasant, quiet; Jun-Sep – hot, busy.

163

ADRIATIC ISLANDS
CROATIA

→ **Why now? Escape the crowds on car-free isles.**

The Dalmatian coast is hardly hush-hush. Its warm, turquoise waters, terracotta-tiled towns and idyllic islands attract visitors from near and far in high summer. But there's still peace to be found on car-free isles where the gentle hum of an electric cart is the loudest road noise. In July, the hottest, driest month, head to the Elafiti Islands in southern Dalmatia, where on traffic-free Lopud you'll find one of the finest sandy beaches on the coast, Šunj (pronounced 'shoon-je'); make time to admire spectacular art in the Franciscan Monastery's St-Mary-of-the-Cave Church, roam the ruins of grand merchant houses, and climb to the ruined Ragusan fortress for spectacular views. Or sail to Zlarin ('Golden Island') off Šibenik, famed as one of the sunniest on the Adriatic, to pedal quiet tracks, kayak empty coves or simply lounge in the sun between seafood feasts.

Trip plan: Ferries sail from Dubrovnik to Lopud several times daily in high season, taking just under 1hr. For Zlarin, fly to Split or Zadar, then head for Šibenik for the 25min onward ferry journey.

Need to know: Lopud receives day-trippers from Dubrovnik in high summer, but crowds thin after boat trips depart; stay overnight to experience the islands at their tranquil best.

Other months: Oct-Feb – cool, wet, facilities sparse; Mar-Apr – few tourists, Easter festivities; Jul-Aug – hot, dry, busy; May-Jun & Sep – warm, quieter.

The Franciscan monastery on Lopud Island

© robertharding / Alamy Stock Photo

OLOMOUC CZECH REPUBLIC

Olomouc's astronomical
clock puppets

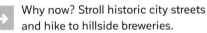

→ **Why now? Stroll historic city streets and hike to hillside breweries.**

While visitors cram the medieval streets, squares, bridges and monuments of Prague, head east instead to Olomouc, its gorgeous old centre reflecting its role as capital of Moravia from the 12th century. Explore the cobbled core on foot, starting at Horní náměstí (Upper Square), dominated by the extraordinary, Unesco-listed Baroque Trinity Column and the 14th-century town hall, complete with astronomical clock (albeit the current model is some six centuries younger than Prague's). Climb the tower of fortress-like, 15th-century St Moritz Cathedral for sweeping views across the town, then follow your eyes east to the Baroque St Michael's Church and the magnificent Romanesque Archbishop's Palace. There are plenty of chances to take a break from history, of course: stroll lovely Bezručovy sady riverside park, and refuel in the many pavement bars and restaurants – with a big student population, the city has great café culture and nightlife. Feeling brave? Order Olomoucký sýr, reputedly the country's stinkiest cheese.

Trip plan: Olomouc is on an international mainline railway, accessible from airports at Prague (around 2hr), Brno and Ostrava (1hr).

Need to know: For a refreshing day-trip, make the short hop east to Štramberk, a classic Moravian town on the slopes of Bílá hora (White Mountain), with a ruined castle and excellent brewery.

Other months: Nov-Mar – often sub-zero; Apr-May & Sep-Oct – comfortable; Jun-Aug – warm.

© Andrash-J / Getty Images

165

ALTA BADIA
ITALY

→ Why now? Sample superb cuisine amid marvellous mountains.

If the Dolomites are the Alps at their most magnificent, the Alta Badia valley in South Tyrol promises the Dolomites at their tastiest. This jagged array of deep valleys, high plateaus and piercing pinnacles in northern Italy echoes with poignant history: between 1915 and 1918, Italian and Austro-Hungarian forces fought amid these unforgiving peaks, and today you can hike routes such as the Kaiserjäger to discover their trenches and gun emplacements. Alta Badia is renowned for its skiing, but in summer the cable cars and mountain huts reopen to serve hungry hikers, cyclists, paragliders and trail-runners instead – the region is spangled with Michelin stars, but even simple refuges dish up good-value but top-notch cuisine (think mountain cheeses, pasta and strudels). For an extra adrenaline buzz, tackle the challenging via ferrata ('iron roads') climbs, a method of traversing vertiginous rock faces via rungs and cables.

Trip plan: The nearest airports are at Innsbruck, Verona and Venice. La Villa, San Cassiano (St Kassian) and Corvara make excellent bases from which to explore the peaks and valleys.

Need to know: The South Tyrol region was part of the Austro-Hungarian empire till WWI. Many place-name signs are in both Italian and German, and you'll hear those languages spoken plus, possibly, a third: Ladin, a venerable Romance tongue descended from ancient Latin.

Other months: Dec-Mar – great skiing; Apr-May & Oct – quieter, less accessible; Jun-Sep – warm, best for hiking and outdoor pursuits.

A land of contrasts: Lago di Carezza and the Val di Funes

© Matt Munro / Lonely Planet

LIECHTENSTEIN

→ **Why now?** Explore every corner of this compact Alpine principality.

Famous for banks, false teeth (it reputedly produces 20% of the world's dentures) and simply for being small, Liechtenstein is a blink-and-you'll-miss-it stop on many central European tours. That's an oversight that this bijou nation sandwiched between Austria and Switzerland aims to remedy, luring in visitors by way of developments such as the Liechtenstein Trail. This 75km (46 mile) route was launched in 2019 to celebrate the country's tercentenary, and links into a countrywide network of trails that cover a total of 400km (248 miles) – pretty impressive when you consider that Liechtenstein is less than 25km (15 miles) long. With the warmest weather arriving in July, now's the time to lace up and explore the country in depth via the meandering north–south trail. You'll see castles – capital Vaduz's 12th-century fortress and the hilltop medieval bastion at Balzers – but also Rhine-side fields and hillside vineyards, chocolate-box villages and workaday towns. The country buzzes with cultural events in July, too.

Trip plan: The closest airports are at Friedrichshafen (Germany) and Zurich, both an hour's drive from Vaduz. Allow three or four days for the Liechtenstein Trail.

Need to know: For testing trekking, tackle the vertiginous 12km (7 mile) hike from Fürstensteig to the Drei Schwestern.

Other months: Dec-Mar – cold, skiing at Malbun; Apr-May & Oct-Nov – chilly, quiet; Jun-Sep – fairly warm, hiking season.

WILD ATLANTIC WAY IRELAND

→ **Why now?** Tackle a magnificent coastal drive during long summer days.

Irish weather is notoriously unpredictable, but in July – typically the country's warmest month – you can at least rely on the light: 18 hours each day, enabling you to sightsee (or pub-crawl) until 11pm. This is a great time to roam the Wild Atlantic Way, some 2500km (1553 miles) of road snaking along Ireland's west coast between Kinsale in County Cork and the Inishowen Peninsula in County Donegal. The waymarked route showcases some of Ireland's finest scenery, including Mizen Head (the island's most southwesterly point), the soaring Cliffs of Moher, fjord-side Killary Harbour and Malin Head, the Way's most northerly point. Start in Cork for good eating; trace the scenic Ring of Kerry and Dingle Peninsula; listen to live music in the bars of Galway; seek surf in Sligo and stories of the Spanish Armada in Grange; and, if you're here on Reek Sunday (last in July), join the pilgrimage up Croagh Patrick, Ireland's holiest mountain.

Trip plan: Cork Airport is the closest to the drive's southern terminus, while City of Derry Airport is near the northern end. Allow two weeks to trace the whole route, making time for diversions and absorbing the legendary craic.

Need to know: Drive south to north, so you're always closest to the ocean for the best uninterrupted views.

Other months: Nov-Feb – wettest, bracing; Mar-May & Sept-Oct – mild but often damp; Jun-Aug – warmest, long days.

FORMENTERA SPAIN

→ **Why now?** Dive or snorkel electric-blue Mediterranean waters.

You want the science behind the spectacularly clear waters off Formentera? Well, the vast posidonia seagrass meadows on the bed of the Mediterranean, protected within Parc Natural de Ses Salines, are the miracle aquatic cleansers. But you probably don't need to know that – suffice to say that, with underwater visibility of around 50m (164ft), a range of submarine walls, arches and wrecks to explore and (particularly from July) balmy waters, this smallest of the Balearic Islands is a dream destination for learning to scuba. Head for the dive centres at La Savina, don mask, snorkel and fins, and boat out to sites such as El Arco and Es Banc to meet moray eels, seahorses, grouper, barracuda and more while mastering breathing, buoyancy and the other key diving skills. As Ibiza is loud and full-on, so Formentera is laidback, renowned since the 1960s for its slow pace. Post-dive, soak up the rays on the 6km (4 mile) strand at Platja de Migjorn, browse the hippy markets at El Pilar de la Mola, and sip a sundowner at Es Pujols.

Trip plan: There's no airport on Formentera. Frequent ferries (30min) sail from Ibiza Town.

Need to know: Unsurprisingly, fresh fish is a delicious treat in Formentera – rao is a local favourite. Italians arrive en masse in August.

Other months: Nov-May – cool, some services closed or less frequent; Jun-Oct – hot (rainier from Sep).

NOVI SAD
SERBIA

→ **Why now? Enjoy culture and clubbing in Serbia's seductive second city.**

Looking for full-throttle dance tunes and live music? Come to Novi Sad in July. Looking for cutting-edge art and historic gems? Come to Novi Sad in July. After the rains of June have eased, you can enjoy both sides of the 'Athens of Serbia', brimming with stately architecture from its heyday as a 'free royal city' after the mid-18th century. For four days at the start of July, the hefty Petrovaradin Fortress is thronged with music-lovers from across Europe dancing to big-name acts and DJs during the EXIT Festival. For the rest of the month, the city reclaims its easygoing charm. Explore that mighty crag-top citadel and numerous excellent museums and galleries, sip coffee and taste Balkan specialities in alluring pavement cafés, and relax on the sandy, 700m/2297ft-long Štrand (beach), lapped by the Danube. It's a great time to get active, too: pedal a stretch of the Danube Cycle Path that runs for nearly 3000km (1800 miles) alongside the river, or hop south to Fruška Gora National Park, Serbia's oldest, to

Street life at its prettiest: Novi Sad's main square, Trg Slobode

© Reinhard Schmid / 4Corners Images

stroll among artisan wineries and historic monasteries, some dating from the 15th century.

Trip plan: Serbian capital Belgrade, which has the closest airport, is a 1hr bus ride to the south (1hr 45min by train).

Need to know: Unsurprisingly, flights and accommodation are at a premium during EXIT – book well in advance.

Other months: Nov-Mar – cold; Apr-May & Oct – pleasant; Jun-Sep – consistently warm and sunny.

BEYOND NOVI SAD

SREMSKI KARLOVCI • 12KM (7 MILES) • Village famous for its local wines and Baroque edifices

FRUŠKA GORA • 20KM (13 MILES) • Serbia's oldest national park, its rolling hills peppered with monasteries

BELGRADE • 94KM (58 MILES) • Serbia's gritty, exuberant capital city

SUBOTICA • 105KM (65 MILES) • Leafy, laidback town with sugar-spun Art Nouveau marvels

CENTRAL PYRENEES
FRANCE & SPAIN

Kayak through the spectacular Congost de Montrebei in the Catalan Pyrenees

→ **Why now? Enjoy outdoor pursuits in a mountain playground.**

If the Alps are Europe's mountain model – the tall, leggy pin-up – the Pyrenees are the girl/boy next door: athletic, no-nonsense, truly loveable. There's no artificial glamour: towns and traditional stone-built villages perched amid glorious mountain scenery are the real deal, providing bases for a range of outdoor activities – the alfresco gym par excellence. Here you can hike and cycle high-altitude trails (the GR10 follows the entire range on the French side, the GR11 on the Spanish), canyon craggy gorges, and abseil, kayak or raft, resting up in lovely guesthouses and restaurants that provide cosy boltholes in which to sleep and refuel before the following day's adventures. In July, the weather is pretty consistent, high paths are free from snow and outdoor facilities are ready for action. In France, the Parc National des Pyrénées has the wildest stretches for active adventures – Barèges makes a good centre. In Spain, consider medieval villages like Vielha near Parc Natural de Posets-Maladeta in Aragón, or Sort (great for river rafting) for the Parc Nacional d'Aigüestortes i Estany de Sant Maurici in northern Catalonia.

Trip plan: Toulouse and Lourdes/Tarbes airports are most convenient for the central Pyrenees in both France and Spain.

Need to know: A number of tour operators offer adventure holiday packages based in villages in the French and Spanish Pyrenees, many aimed at families with kids.

Other months: Dec-Feb – winter, skiing; Mar-Jun – spring (snow on passes till mid-Jun); Jul-Sep – summer; Oct-Nov – autumn, weather variable.

If you make it this far you're nearly there: high camp at Mt Ararat National Park

© Westend61 GmbH / Alamy Stock Photo

© Artur Debat / Getty Images

MT ARARAT TURKEY

→ **Why now? Summit Turkey's highest mountain.**

Ağrı Daği, as the Turkish call Ararat, is reputedly the peak on which Noah's Ark came to rest after the Biblical flood. It's also magnificent in its own right – a monumental, permanently snow-capped, double-volcanic-coned mountain that soars to 5137m (16,854ft). Climbing isn't an easy task: even in July (which, along with August, enjoys the most stable weather for the ascent), expect icy temperatures at night, howling winds at the summit and a breathless, exhausting final haul –crampons are essential. But the rewards are incandescent, with spectacular views east into Armenia; the wider region, which long ago lay within the much larger ancient kingdom of Armenia, still retains fascinating sites from that era, such as the medieval Akdamar Kilisesi (Church of the Holy Cross) on Lake Van.

Trip plan: The usual base for Ararat summit attempts is Doğubayazıt; fly to Van (usually via Istanbul), from where you can drive the 170km (106 miles) to Doğubayazıt in 2–3hr. Climb only with a reputable local mountain guide; tour packages ranging from four to eight days are available.

Need to know: The climb should be attempted only by fit climbers with crampon experience. A special permit is required, usually included in a package tour – book at least two months in advance, and be aware that access may be restricted at short notice.

Other months: Oct-Feb – cold, blizzards common; Mar-Apr – skiing; May – rain and hail; Jun-Sep – warmest months, trekking season (Jun often rainy).

The Titlis glacier towers majestically above Engelberg

ENGELBERG
SWITZERLAND

→ **Why now? Tackle a cheese-powered trek through Alpine meadows.**

Why do we love hiking in the mountains so much? Is it the views of craggy peaks and glaciers, the fresh Alpine air, the wildflower-spangled meadows? Those, for sure – but mostly it's the appetite-boosting properties of walking. And in the heavenly village of Engelberg (literally 'Angel Mountain') in central Switzerland, guarded by mighty Mt Titlis, you can combine two great pleasures: cheese and treks. Between June and October, eight artisan dairies along the 45km (28 miles) of the Alpkäse (Alpine Cheese) Trail showcase their produce to hungry hikers – and warm July is the ideal month to roam the high paths. Start at the Show Cheese Factory in Engelberg's 12th-century monastery and loop around the valley. There's more high-octane adventure in the area, too, with fine mountain-biking, bungee-jumping, via ferrata climbing, paragliding and a vertigo-inducing Cliff Walk.

Trip plan: Zurich is the most convenient airport with rail connections to Engelberg via Lucerne (which is, being in Switzerland, efficiently connected by train to much of the rest of the country and, thence, wider Europe). Allow a week to hike the Cheese Trail and explore this spectacular region.

Need to know: In western Switzerland, Gruyères, famed for its lip-smacking namesake cheese, also has a Sentier des Fromageries (Cheesemakers' Path) covering 13km (8 miles).

Other months: Dec to early Apr – ski season; mid-Apr to May & Nov – some facilities closed; Jun-Oct – warm, cheese trail open.

Beaches like
Carvalhal are still
under the radar –
for now

COMPORTA PORTUGAL

→ **Why now? Barefoot luxury at the cognoscenti's Iberian 'secret'.**
Whispers about this near-legendary scimitar of sand began to circulate a few years ago, stoked by sightings of pop stars and designers – Madonna, Christian Louboutin, Philippe Starck – and rumours of pristine beaches and a boho vibe with virtually no visible tourism development. Today, though the Herdade da Comporta (as the finest stretch of the beaches stretching south of the Tróia Peninsula is officially known) is hardly a secret, it's still arguably Iberia's most unspoilt beach destination, preferred by those for whom the Algarve's coast has become too commercialised. Backed by cork oaks, rice-fields and the Reserva Natural do Estuário do Sado, in which bottlenose dolphins frolic and storks fish, the hinterland is verdant even in high summer, when Lisboetas and international celebs still (discreetly) descend on the seven coastal villages' low-key beach bars, boutiques and restaurants – unsurprisingly, given local bounty, seafood risottos are favourites.

Trip plan: Public transport is a non-starter here. Fly or catch the train to Lisbon, then drive to Setúbal for the ferry to Tróia, where the golden crescent begins. Accommodation tends to be pricey; book ahead for high season.
Need to know: This is ideal country for exploring on horseback, trotting inland among rice-fields and dunes, and up to the estuary to watch storks and dolphins.
Other months: Oct-May – cool, quiet; Jun-Sep – sunny, dry.

173

STUBAI ALPS
AUSTRIA

→ **Why now? Cool off on high trails amid mighty mountains.**

In high summer, Austria's hills are alive – with the sound of cowbells, kids and chomping, rather than swooshing skis. Amid the warm, sunny Alps, there are balmy lakes and pools to swim in, splendid mountains to climb (or ascend by cable car) and flowery, cow-grazed meadows to run through, Maria von Trapp-style. Austrian cuisine is ideal fuel for activities such as rafting, climbing, canyoning and ziplining, on offer across the range: try speck (cured ham), and the excellent local cheese (käse) and cake (kuchen). And since ski resorts aim to attract off-season guests, there are good deals to be found, too. Where to head? Try the glorious valleys of the Tyrol, south of Innsbruck. Our top tip: venture to the peaceful, picture-perfect Stubai Valley, hiking high trails between the Austrian Alpine Club's network of huts (open roughly mid-June to September) to sleep right amid the mountains.

Trip plan: Fly or take a train to Innsbruck, then catch the bus (20min) or – for a slower slice of mountain romance – hop on a tram to Fulpmes, from where cable cars run up to the high trails. Allow a week or more for a hut-to-hut circuit.

Need to know: For high-octane thrills, head to Igls, where the Olympic Bobsleigh chute opens from May to mid-October.

Other months: Nov-Apr – snowy, skiing; May-Jun & Oct – quiet, mild; Jul-Sep – warm, best hiking weather.

Ruminating Tyrolean brown cattle and the Grawa waterfall are just two reasons to visit this alluring area

© Gerhard Zwerger-Schoner / Getty Images

© agustavop / Getty Images

VERONA ITALY

→ **Why now? Absorb opera and history in balmy summer climes.**

'Shall I compare thee to a summer's day?' To continue the Shakespearean quote, Verona in July is both lovely and (fairly) temperate – though it's rapidly heating up. It may be rather overshadowed by near-neighbour Venice to the east, but Verona is a relaxed and absorbing city to visit in summer. Wander among its medieval palazzos and loggias, pausing to gaze longingly up at the balcony in the reputed Casa di Giulietta (Juliet's House – *Romeo and Juliet* is largely set in Verona), and explore its Roman remains – the arena reverberates from late June with the sounds of the annual opera festival. Food and drink are an obsession in Verona, and it's a great place to taste some of Italy's best gelato, plus fine wines, pumpkin ravioli and thick bigoli pasta – this handsome city provides nourishment for the body as well as the mind.

Trip plan: Verona receives low-cost flights from across Europe, and has a busy railway station; frequent trains reach Venice in just over 1hr, making it easy to combine the two cities.

A focus on fresh ingredients makes Verona a foodie delight

© Alice Martini / Getty Images

Need to know: Accommodation is at a premium during the Opera Festival (late June through August); book well in advance, or visit earlier in the month.

Other months: Nov-Mar – cool, unreliable weather; Apr & Oct – shoulder season, weather often pleasant; May-Sep – summer, busy.

BEYOND VERONA

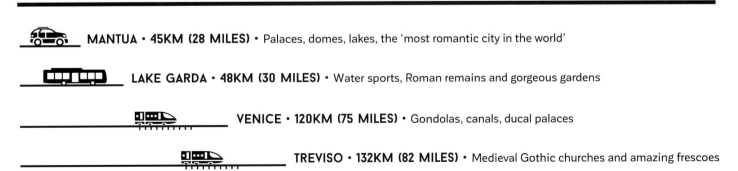

MANTUA • 45KM (28 MILES) • Palaces, domes, lakes, the 'most romantic city in the world'

LAKE GARDA • 48KM (30 MILES) • Water sports, Roman remains and gorgeous gardens

VENICE • 120KM (75 MILES) • Gondolas, canals, ducal palaces

TREVISO • 132KM (82 MILES) • Medieval Gothic churches and amazing frescoes

August

WHERE TO GO WHEN

CHALLENGE MYSELF

I WANT TO

TAKE ME OUT FOR...

FOOD
- ROMSDALEN VALLEY, NORWAY P194
- COASTAL BELGIUM P183

DRINK
- PENEDÈS, SPAIN P182
- EGER, HUNGARY P197

TAKE ME TO TOWN

ART & CULTURE
- GDAŃSK, POLAND P186
- DUNDEE, SCOTLAND P193

NIGHT-LIFE & HEDONISM
- LOCARNO, SWITZERLAND P189
- LÜBECK, GERMANY P197

RELAX/ INDULGE

DIAL IT DOWN

WELLNESS — CENTRAL AUSTRIA P183

CHILLING
- ALBANIAN RIVIERA P185
- PELION PENINSULA, GREECE P195
- MINHO, PORTUGAL P185

Penedès grapes, not quite ripe for the picking

Feast on herring in Norway

The historic centre of Gdańsk

The spa town of Bad Ischl in Austria

Postcard perfect: the Madonna del Sasso Church above Locarno

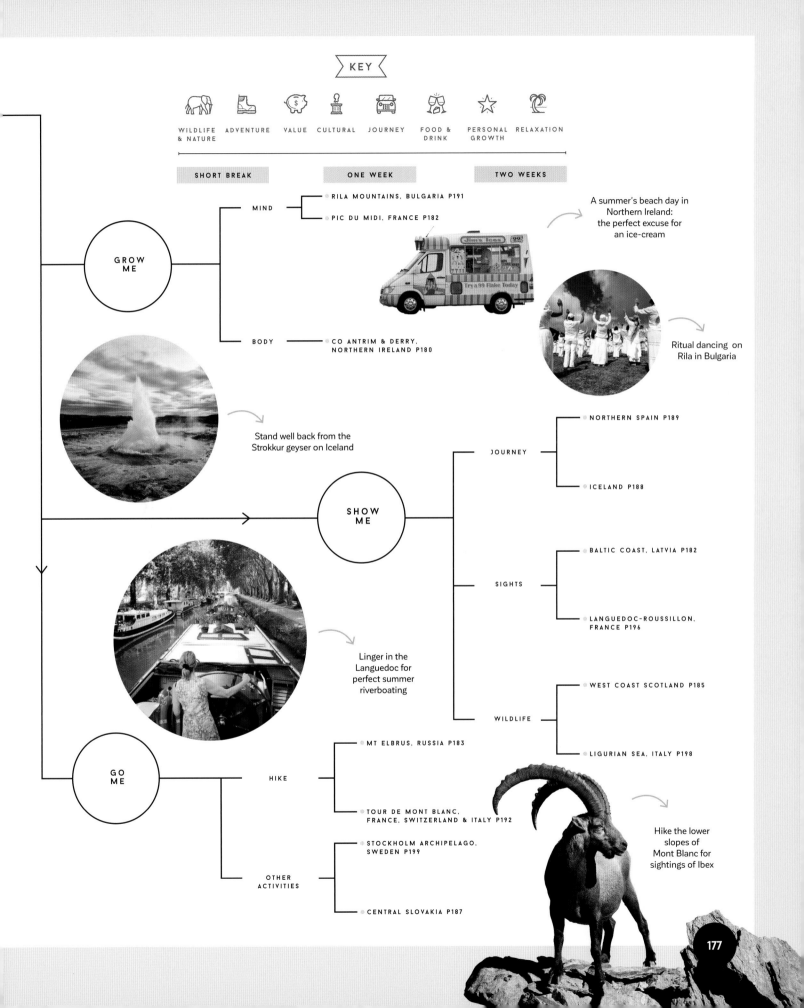

WILDLIFE & NATURE · ADVENTURE · VALUE · CULTURAL · JOURNEY · FOOD & DRINK · PERSONAL GROWTH · RELAXATION

SHORT BREAK · ONE WEEK · TWO WEEKS

GROW ME

MIND
- RILA MOUNTAINS, BULGARIA P191
- PIC DU MIDI, FRANCE P182

BODY
- CO ANTRIM & DERRY, NORTHERN IRELAND P180

A summer's beach day in Northern Ireland: the perfect excuse for an ice-cream

Ritual dancing on Rila in Bulgaria

Stand well back from the Strokkur geyser on Iceland

SHOW ME

JOURNEY
- NORTHERN SPAIN P189
- ICELAND P188

SIGHTS
- BALTIC COAST, LATVIA P182
- LANGUEDOC-ROUSSILLON, FRANCE P196

WILDLIFE
- WEST COAST SCOTLAND P185
- LIGURIAN SEA, ITALY P198

Linger in the Languedoc for perfect summer riverboating

GO ME

HIKE
- MT ELBRUS, RUSSIA P183
- TOUR DE MONT BLANC, FRANCE, SWITZERLAND & ITALY P192

OTHER ACTIVITIES
- STOCKHOLM ARCHIPELAGO, SWEDEN P199
- CENTRAL SLOVAKIA P187

Hike the lower slopes of Mont Blanc for sightings of Ibex

EVENTS
IN AUGUST

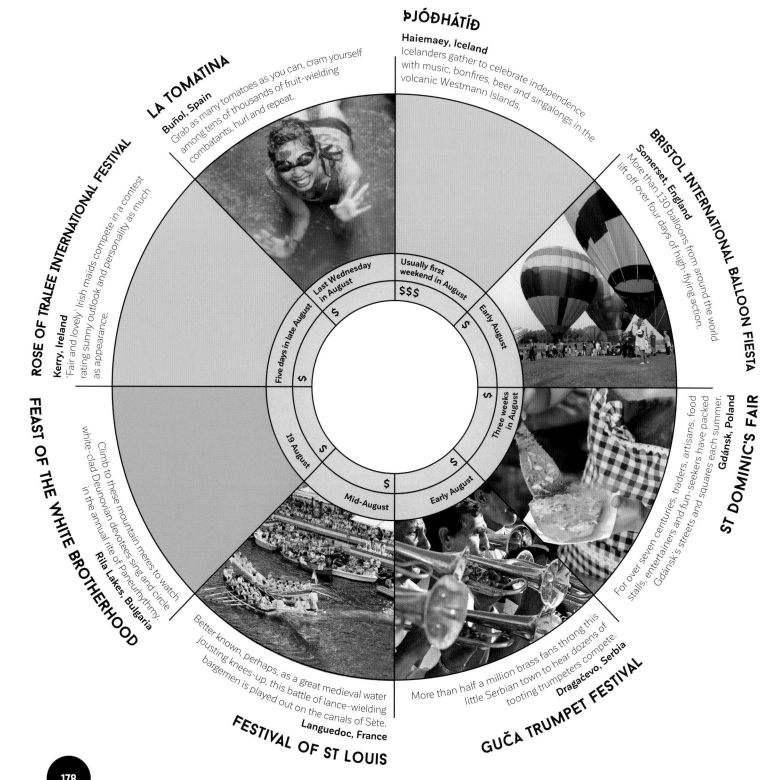

ÞJÓÐHÁTÍÐ

Haiemaey, Iceland
Icelanders gather to celebrate independence with music, bonfires, beer and singalongs in the volcanic Westmann Islands.

LA TOMATINA

Buñol, Spain
Grab as many tomatoes as you can, cram yourself among tens of thousands of fruit-wielding combatants, hurl and repeat.

ROSE OF TRALEE INTERNATIONAL FESTIVAL

Kerry, Ireland
'Fair and lovely' Irish maids compete in a contest rating sunny outlook and personality as much as appearance.

BRISTOL INTERNATIONAL BALLOON FIESTA

Somerset, England
More than 130 balloons from around the world lift off over four days of high-flying action.

FEAST OF THE WHITE BROTHERHOOD

Rila Lakes, Bulgaria
Climb to these mountain meres to watch white-clad Deunovian devotees sing and circle in the annual rite of Paneurhythmy.

ST DOMINIC'S FAIR

Gdánsk, Poland
For over seven centuries, traders, artisans, food stalls, entertainers and fun-seekers have packed Gdánsk's streets and squares each summer.

FESTIVAL OF ST LOUIS

Languedoc, France
Better known, perhaps, as a great medieval water jousting knees-up, this battle of lance-wielding bargemen is played out on the canals of Sète.

GUČA TRUMPET FESTIVAL

Dragačevo, Serbia
More than half a million brass fans throng this little Serbian town to hear dozens of tooting trumpeters compete.

Last Wednesday in August — $

Usually first weekend in August — $$$

Five days in late August — $

Early August — $

19 August — $

Three weeks in August — $

Mid-August — $

Early August — $

VERY FAMILY FRIENDLY

Stockholmers head to colourful summerhouses in August

LANGUEDOC, FRANCE

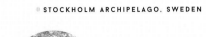

STOCKHOLM ARCHIPELAGO, SWEDEN

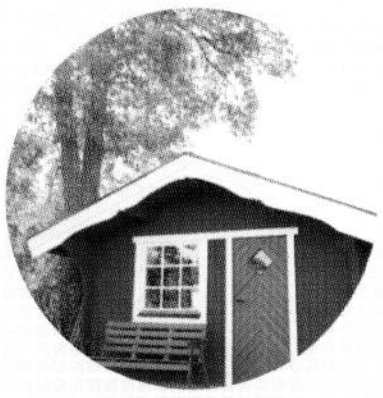

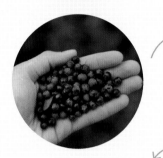

WEST COAST SCOTLAND

Norway's blueberries are at their juiciest best in August

DUNDEE, SCOTLAND

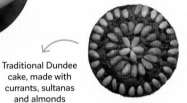

Traditional Dundee cake, made with currants, sultanas and almonds

ROMSDALEN, NORWAY

NORTHERN IRELAND

PELION, GREECE

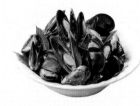

ALBANIAN RIVIERA

BALTIC COAST, LATVIA

A bowl of steaming *moules* is a Belgian speciality

COASTAL BELGIUM

Get a bird's-eye view of Neptune's Fountain on Long Market in Gdańsk

GDÁNSK, POLAND

CENTRAL AUSTRIA

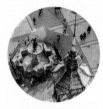

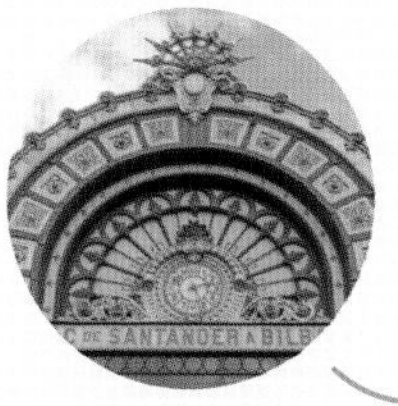

NORTHERN SPAIN

The facade of Bilbao's Abando train station

EXPENSIVE BUT WORTH IT

GOOD VALUE

LIGURIA, ITALY

ICELAND

Liguria's Corniglia in Cinque Terre

LÜBECK, GERMANY

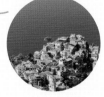

LOCARNO, SWITZERLAND

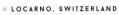

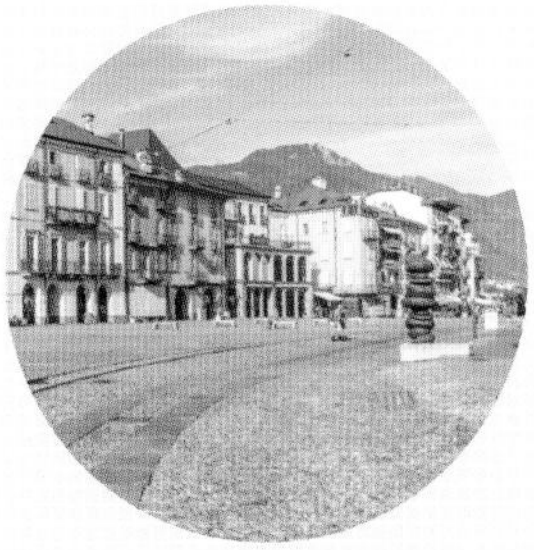

Locarno's lakeside promenade

Head for the hills; thousands of Russians do in summer

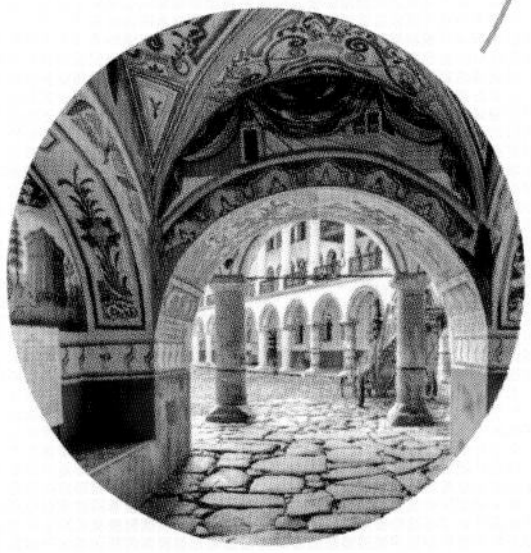

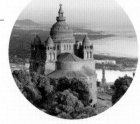

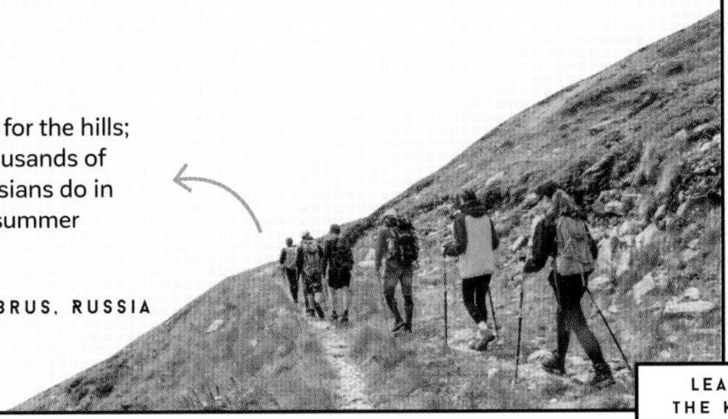

MT ELBRUS, RUSSIA

The elegant colonnades and colourful frescoes of Bulgaria's Rila Monastery

RILA MOUNTAINS, BULGARIA

PIC DU MIDI, FRANCE

EGER, HUNGARY

CENTRAL SLOVAKIA

MINHO, PORTUGAL

PENEDÉS, SPAIN

Admire the architecture in Viana do Castelo, in Portugal's Minho region

MONT BLANC, FRANCE/ITALY/SWITZERLAND

LEAVE THE KIDS AT HOME

CO ANTRIM & DERRY
NORTHERN IRELAND

→ **Why now? Ride the waves, whatever your level of experience.**

On the north coast of Ireland, swells roll in off the North Atlantic onto sweeps of sand, providing superb conditions for surfing. Arguably the most tempting stretch is Benone Beach, 10km (6 miles) of golden grains; not only does this huge swathe of shore provide plenty of room for all comers, even in busy August when the water's (relatively) warm and the sun plentiful, but it's well set up for beginners, kids and those with special requirements – a beach wheelchair and wheelchair surfboard are available. The action continues around the coast, with the right-hand break at neighbouring Castlerock, clean barrels at Portrush, dramatic cliff views at Whiterocks Beach and secluded surf at White Park Bay. If you need a break (!) from the waves, the extraordinary Giant's Causeway is just a hop away, as are the famed whiskey distillery at Bushmills and the seabirds and shipwrecks of craggy Rathlin Island.

Trip plan: Castlerock and Portrush are both around 90min from Belfast by train, and buses run further along the coast. Surf schools at Benone Beach and Portrush offer lessons and hire gear including SUPs and kayaks; accommodation options run from campsites and glamping to B&Bs, self-catering and hotels.

Need to know: There's surf here year-round and many schools stay open through the winter. Call ahead to book hire equipment – some places trim services at quiet times.

Other months: Oct-May – water cold, strong surf; Jun-Sep – warmest.

The otherworldy basalt columns of the Giant's Causeway

PIC DU MIDI
FRANCE

Why now? Gaze at celestial fireworks in the heart of the Pyrenees.

Scan the heavens on a clear night in mid-August and you might witness a spectacular lightshow: the Perseids meteor shower, sparking dozens of shooting stars in the upper atmosphere. The Perseids are active between mid-July and late August each year, peaking around 12 August. Head for a dark-sky reserve where you can also admire the Milky Way in between meteors. The Pic du Midi, in the central French Pyrenees, is one such reserve, with a historic (now high-spec) observatory at 2877m (9439ft); visit during the day to learn about celestial phenomena and admire the mountain panorama, or at night for an immersive astronomical experience. Even if you don't make it up to the observatory, this region – popular with skiers in winter but peaceful in summer – offers stellar stargazing opportunities, not to mention tremendous hiking: the GR10 long-distance trail meanders nearby. Find a campsite, mountain refuge or apartment in a quiet village, and simply look to the skies.

Trip plan: Shuttle-buses run from Lourdes to La Mongie, from where cable cars run up to the observatory. The nearest airports are at Lourdes/Tarbes, Toulouse and Pau; Lourdes has good train connections.

Need to know: Avoid visiting at full moon – it hinders views of the meteors.

Other months: Dec-Mar & Jun-Oct – observatory open; Apr-May & Nov – observatory may be closed.

BALTIC COAST
LATVIA

Why now? Roam wild Baltic shores with an edge-of-the-world vibe.

With some 300km (187 miles) of largely empty shoreline – much of it white sand, backed by wooded hills and ridges – you might wonder why Latvia's western coast isn't more developed. The answer lies in the communist era, when this was the western Soviet frontier, a strategic area from which locals were squeezed. Today it's a mesmerising region to roam on sunny August days: sometimes sombre, sometimes seductive, always spectacular. Coastal settlements range from rapidly gentrifying Ventspils to gritty, grungy Liepāja (great for alternative music) and a host of small fishing villages studding isolated stretches where you're sure to find a beach all to yourself. To really get away from it all, head north to Slītere National Park and Kolka, the headland where the Baltic meets the Gulf of Rīga, to hike or bike among towering dunes, woods and sea, and munch smoked fish bought in traditional fishing villages such as Vaide, Košrags and Mazirbe, where you can also learn about near-extinct Livonian culture.

Trip plan: Most visitors arrive on the west coast from Rīga; buses trace the coastline to Kolka and run inland to Ventspils and Liepāja, but hiring a car makes travel quicker and easier; given the flattish coastal terrain, you might also consider cycling.

Need to know: Accommodation in smaller spots, such as around Kolka, is sparse and sometimes simple – book ahead.

Other months: Oct-May – cold (often sub-zero Jan-Feb); Jun-Sep – warm, long days.

PENEDÈS
SPAIN

Why now? Cool off with a chilled cava in Catalonia.

Who doesn't love a wine region? Cruising through vine-covered hills between cellar doors, interspersing sips of fine tipples with tapas and cheese, learning about local varietals and terroir – and when it's beneath glorious blue skies and blazing sun, everything tastes so much the better. The Penedès denominación packs in more than 100 producers and cellars in a compact area 30km (19 miles) west of Barcelona, best known for its sparkling cava – big names such as Freixenet and Codorníu are based here, along with smaller boutique operations. It's also blissfully easy to combine sipping with sand-lounging after your grape escape: the venerable resort of Sitges is just 20km (12 miles) south of attractive Vilafranca del Penedès, at the heart of the region, and fine beaches such as Garraf and Castelldefels are a short hop along the coast.

Trip plan: Barcelona tour companies offer day-trips including visits to a handful of bodegas (wineries), with tastings and tapas. For a DIY trip, take one of the frequent trains from Barcelona Sants station to Sant Sadurní and Vilafranca (journey time 1hr). There are hotels in Vilafranca, plus cases de pagès (country houses) with accommodation nearby; this is also the place to hire bikes for a little two-wheeled exploring.

Need to know: Grapes aren't just for wine: outfits such as Cellers Avgvstvs Forvm produce acclaimed vinegars you can taste on your tour.

Other months: Nov-Apr – cool but pleasant, quiet, some facilities closed; May-Oct – warm, rain increasing.

COASTAL BELGIUM

Why now? Trundle the world's longest tram route and taste delectable seafood.

Belgium might not be your obvious go-to destination for a beach break. But with an almost unbroken 70km (44 mile) stretch of white sand fringing the North Sea, perhaps it should be – and around the turn of the 20th century it lured fashionable holidaymakers to its resorts. Today the Belgian coast is studded with attractions – aquariums, theme parks, watersports – all accessible aboard the Kusttram (Coastal Tram). This venerable tram line, established in 1885, is the world's longest, stretching 67km (42 miles) between De Panne in the west and Knokke-Heist in the east. August, the warmest month, is a great time to ride the rails, with a host of events including a fireworks festival in Knokke-Heist and, at De Haan, a celebration of prawns – these delicious crustaceans are a speciality here. On summer weekends you can ride a vintage tram from the depot at De Panne.

Trip plan: Ostend, in the centre of the Belgian coast, is 75min from Brussels by train, and under 15min from Bruges.

Need to know: You can get information and tickets at Kustlijnwinkels offices, which operate reduced hours outside July and August. One-, three- and five-day passes offer good value; or choose a combined ticket including attractions.

Other months: Nov-Mar – cool; Apr-Jun & Sep-Oct – pleasant, quiet; Jul-Aug – warmest, busiest.

MT ELBRUS
RUSSIA

Why now? Enjoy the views from the highest point in Europe.

Europe's highest point looms in the Caucasus in Russia's far south: the western of the twin peaks of Elbrus (its name, derived from Persian, means 'Two Heads') soars to 5642m (18,510ft). This volcanic mountain is almost 1000m higher than nearby prominences, providing astounding views from the top. Though not a technical ascent, it's generally considered to be tougher than, say, Kilimanjaro, with strong winds and changeable weather – a rewarding challenge for experienced, fit climbers. Though its slopes are popular with skiers in winter and hikers in summer, the summit-climb season runs only June to October. Even if you're not aiming for the top, the Elbrus Gondola will carry you up 3847m (12,621ft) of the mountain's flanks, and various walks in the area offer fine views – for example, to Donguz-Orunkel Lake on Mt Cheget or along the Terskol Valley to a hanging glacier.

Trip plan: Allow a week for acclimatisation and the long summit day of 10-plus hours on your feet, depending on your route. Book with a local or international trekking operator. The closest airport is at Nalchik, around 100km (62 miles) east, from where *marshrutky* (minibus taxis) run to Terskol.

Need to know: Tensions can run high at the nearby Georgian border; check the current security situation with your government's foreign office. You'll need a Russian visa and a permit for the summit ascent.

Other months: Nov-May – skiing; Jun-Oct – climbing season.

CENTRAL AUSTRIA

Why now? Spa yourself happy amid glorious mountain scenery.

To find wellness in Austria, look for the Bad in everything – at least, in place names: if it starts Bad, it's a spa town. A dense cluster of saunas, treatment centres and thermal waters studs a broad swathe of central Austria east and south of Salzburg, most with a suitably uplifting backdrop of Alpine peaks, meadows and valleys. The focus varies subtly from place to place. In Bad Aussee, expect a healthy diet plus outdoor activity, in line with the concepts of Kneipp therapy. The benefits of brine have been promoted in stately Bad Ischl since it received the imperial seal of approval in the mid-19th century. Natural hot springs feed the action at Bad Gastein, with forest bathing and barefoot walking added to the mix in neighbouring Bad Hofgastein, which hosts one of Europe's largest thermal spa complexes. But you won't want to stay inside during the long, warm days of August: roam the picturesque paths circling the Salzkammergut's sparkling lakes, pedal mountain-bike trails above Bad Gastein, or take an invigorating dip in an alpine tarn.

Trip plan: Fly or travel by train to Salzburg, from where most spa towns are accessible by bus or train.

Need to know: It's mandatory to sauna naked in Austria, even in mixed-sex saunas. Don't try to keep your swimsuit on, and be prepared to use towels strategically.

Other months: Nov-Apr – cold, good skiing; May & Oct – chilly, many facilities closed; Jun-Sep – sunny, warm.

(A) Albania's Borsh beach; (L) Sea kayaking along West Scotland's Solway coast; (R) Portuguese *caldo verde* soup

184

ALBANIAN RIVIERA

→ **Why now?** Sizzle on the sand at lesser-known Ionian Sea swathes.

While not quite the hidden gem that it was at the turn of the millennium, when empty beaches and truly bargain prices abounded, Albania's glorious southern shoreline remains a treat for those in search of sun, sand and seafood. Saranda is now a fully fledged party town, its esplanade lined with bars. For quieter resorts, head up the coast to Himara, flanked by a scattering of good beaches (try Potami, just to the south). In August, you're guaranteed sun, balmy water and temperatures nudging 30°C (86°F); unsurprisingly, loungers and beach umbrellas are at a premium but you can still seek out peaceful patches of sand at spots such as Palasa, Borsh, pebbly Bunec and the islands off Ksamil. Or head over the epic Llogara Pass to Vlora Bay, where you'll find more resorts and boat trips to isolated beaches at the end of the Karaburuni Peninsula. For a break from sand-lolling, head to the archaeological site of Butrint, where Greek, Roman and Byzantine ruins, some dating back 2500 years, are crammed onto a knobbly headland.

Trip plan: From Corfu, which receives international flights and ferries from the Italian port of Brindisi, daily fast-ferries reach Saranda in 30min.

Need to know: ATMs are rare along the coast – stock up on Albanian lekë when you can, and carry a reasonably ample supply of cash.

Other months: Nov-Mar – cool, transport and facilities sparse; Apr-May & Oct – pleasant, many campsites close; Jun-Sep – hot, busy.

WEST COAST SCOTLAND

→ **Why now?** Paddle warm seas on a wild kayaking adventure.

Europe's first long-distance paddling route, the Scottish Sea Kayak Trail, is a true epic, tracing the fractal inlets of the west coast some 500km (310 miles) from the Isle of Gigha off the Kintyre Peninsula to the Summer Isles near Ullapool. August, when weather is relatively settled and the seas warm(ish), is a sensible time to tackle this adventure – and as a boon, the midges that plague the Highlands in summer are kept at bay by sea breezes. Wild camping on remote beaches, paddling beneath craggy cliffs, watching the huge dorsal fins of basking sharks slice through the waves near Ardnamurchan Point, spotting otters, seals, eagles and seabirds – this is the untamed Scotland of legend. Though experienced kayakers will paddle upwards of 25km (15 miles) per day and could cover the entire trail in three weeks, most will tackle a shorter section: the central stretch around Mallaig, between Oban and the Kyle of Lochalsh, is tipped by those in the know, passing imposing castles and gleaming-white beaches.

Trip plan: Glasgow is the nearest city to the southern end of the route, Inverness is closest to the central section and northern terminus; both are still some way from the trail.

Need to know: Careful planning (plus experience and good equipment) is required for self-guided trips; various companies offer guided tours along sections of the route, mostly with wild camping.

Other months: Oct-Apr – cool, wet, many facilities closed; May-Sep – relatively warm, long days.

MINHO
PORTUGAL

→ **Why now?** Tuck into the tasty green heart of old Portugal.

Where do Portuguese holiday at home? Those in the know savour staycations in the birthplace of the kingdom: the northerly Minho region, a land of verdant hills, traditional culture and fabulous flavours. The Minho is noted for its *vinho verde*, literally 'green wine', released just a few months after harvest. As well as those fruity drops (Loureiro and Alvarinho are our picks), the cuisine is delectable, too – the Minho was designated as a European Region of Gastronomy in 2016. There are plenty of local specialities. In Ponte de Lima, Portugal's oldest town, find a restaurant overlooking the Roman bridge and savour *arroz de sarrabulho* – rice cooked in pig's blood and studded with various pork morsels (tastier than it sounds) – and *caldo verde*, a hearty kale soup. Monkfish, sea bass and bream are fish favourites, along with bacalhau – salt cod, a staple throughout the country. Work up an appetite strolling historic towns such as Braga, Guimarães and Viana do Castelo, where magnificently diverse architecture recalls the wealth of adventurous merchants who made their fortunes during the Age of Discovery and in the subsequent colonial era.

Trip plan: Porto is a 1hr train ride from Braga, from where buses serve other towns in the Minho.

Need to know: Note that portion sizes in most restaurants are huge – even 'single' servings are often ample for two people. Guimarães and Viana do Castelo both host spectacular traditional festivals in August – book ahead for those dates.

Other months: Oct-May – cool, wet; Jun-Sep – warm, driest.

185

© kavalenkau / Shutterstock

GDAŃSK POLAND

The historic centre of Gdańsk from St Mary's Cathedral

→ **Why now? Browse the stalls at one of Europe's largest open-air fairs.**

The historic core of this ancient Baltic port, lovingly restored after WWII devastation, is now back to its 17th-century prime. Magnificent townhouses, city gates and churches provide a picturesque backdrop to the summertime St Dominic's Fair, packing the city with traders, artisans, food stalls and entertainers and held almost continuously for 750 years. For the first three weeks of August, a busy programme of theatre, music and circus entertains visitors ambling between stalls selling everything from amber and antiques to beer and burgers. Gdańsk isn't just one city, though; it's part of the Trojmiasto (Tri-City), which also includes seaside Gydnia and Sopot to the north. Once you've imbibed the highlights of Gdańsk's annual cultural

beano and explored its historic core, make the most of August sunshine and head to Sopot's beaches, bars and nightclubs.

Trip plan: Spend a couple of days exploring the old sections of the city, plus a day (and night) on the coast in Sopot. If possible, add a day or two to explore northern Pomerania – at least as far as the enormous fortress at Malbork, Europe's largest Gothic castle.

Need to know: Don't leave Gdańsk without tasting its most unusual drink, Goldwasser – an aniseedy liqueur gleaming with flecks of real gold leaf. Book accommodation far in advance for St Dominic's Fair.

Other months: Dec-Feb – very cold, picturesque in snow; Mar-Apr & Oct-Nov – cool; May-Sep – pleasant, busy events calendar.

A hiking trail with views across the Tatra mountains

CENTRAL SLOVAKIA

→ **Why now?** Roam high trails and rugged gorges in wildlife-rich landscapes.

Take a north-south slice through Slovakia just east of centre, and you've a cross-section of all that makes this perky republic an alluring summer destination for active types. The High Tatras mountains attract hikers, bikers and wild swimmers, plus wildlife watchers seeking a glimpse of the bears and wolves that amble and prowl through the upper regions. In the central plain, there are fascinating historic sites to discover, such as the Renaissance-era walled town of Levoča, the vast ruined fortifications of 12th-century Spiš Castle and open-air Liptov Village Museum at Pribylina. And to the south, Slovenský Raj ('Slovak Paradise') National Park is a wooded wonderland of gleaming limestone gorges, mountain trails and forest roamed by wildcats, roe deer, boar and birdlife. The food is hearty, the beer and wine cheap, the locals friendly, the scenery spectacular – the quintessential central European combo for a summer week or two.

Trip plan: Poprad, which has an international airport, is a convenient base for exploring the High Tatras, Slovenský Raj National Park, Spiš Castle and Levoča. Stay in the city's attractive old quarter, Spišská Sobota, a short walk from the newer centre and train station.

Need to know: Learn about the history and wildlife of the High Tatras at the TANAP Museum in Tatranska Lomnicá, from where funicular railways continue into the mountains.

Other months: Nov-Mar – skiing; Apr & Oct – quiet, hiking possible in lower areas; May-Sep – warm, rainiest in midsummer (high-level trails open mid-Jun to Sep).

© Martins Vanags / Shutterstock

187

© Robin Kamp / 500px

Natural wonders:
Skógafoss waterfall
and Strokkur geyser in
Iceland

ICELAND

➡️ **Why now? Delve into Iceland's otherworldly interior.**

When NASA wanted to train their astronauts for lunar conditions, they sent them to Iceland – and a visit to the island's desolate interior reveals why. It's as starkly beautiful as you could imagine, and experiences harsh conditions for much of the year; August is the optimum – indeed, almost the only – time you can penetrate its lava fields, volcanic craters and jagged rockscapes. A few historic routes wind through the inner highlands creating shortcuts between the north and south, with some sections accessible only with the toughest of 4WDs. The effort is rewarded with vistas of a muscular, fascinating and unique landscape, featuring turquoise hot-water Lake Víti in vast Askja caldera, and the the mountain known as the 'Queen of the Mountains', Herðubreið. There's fine hiking for the hardy, too.

Trip plan: Fly to Reykjavík, hire the toughest 4WD vehicle you can find, and stock up with plenty of supplies – there's not much in the interior! The least challenging route is the Kjölur, crossing rivers over bridges rather than fords – it even carries a scheduled bus during the summer, via Geysir and Gullfoss.

Need to know: Numerous huts across the interior offer accommodation, but they get booked up quickly over summer. As an alternative, consider the Arctic Coast Way, a thus-far relatively undiscovered touring route (launched in 2019) that snakes along the northern shore.

Other months: Oct-Apr – cold, dark; May-Sep – relatively clement (most inland routes open Jul-Aug).

© Roc Canals Photography / Getty Images

LOCARNO
SWITZERLAND

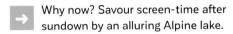

→ **Why now? Savour screen-time after sundown by an alluring Alpine lake.**

The lakes of northern Italy grab the lion's share of attention – but even though Switzerland's share of Maggiore amounts to just the northern nubbin, it's a compact delight. Locarno, near its terminus, is a semi-tropical delight, with a feel more Med than mountains (though with wonderful views of surrounding peaks), largely because of its phalanxes of palm trees charged by bountiful sunshine. Spend hot days exploring historic churches and monuments – don't miss the 15th-century Santuario della Madonna del Sasso or Castello Visconteo – hiking surrounding hills, roaming botanical gardens, cooling off with a lake swim or taking in the impressive falconry displays at Falconeria Locarno. Then enjoy balmy nights with alfresco movie-going: for over 70 years, big-name

© eltravo / Shutterstock

Locarno's centre offers a beguiling mix of Med and mountains

directors, actors and cineastes have flocked here each August for Locarno's Film Festival: 11 days of screenings, talks and competitions, with innovative new releases screened in the Piazza Grande.

Trip plan: Locarno is about 2hr 30min by train from both Milan and Zurich, the closest airports. Accommodation is at a premium during the film festival – book well in advance.

Need to know: Frequent ferries sail up and down Lake Maggiore, so it's easy to venture south into Italy to admire some of the magnificent gardens – perhaps the opulent confections and terraced gardens of Count Borromeo's Baroque palazzo on Isola Bella.

Other months: Nov-Mar – cold; Apr-May & Oct – cool but pleasant; Jun-Sep – warm, sunny.

NORTHERN SPAIN

→ **Why now? Ride the slow train along the north Spanish coast.**

If you need to get somewhere in a hurry, forget FEVE. This idiosyncratic service, running on remnants of the old Spanish narrow-gauge railways (hence the acronym, short for Ferrocarriles Españoles de Vía Estrecha), is the very definition of slow travel, trundling between the Basque Country art hub of Bilbao and Ferrol in Galicia, with branches accessing Gijón, Oviedo and Santander. This train is definitely all about the journey, its boxy

little carriages traversing dramatic scenery alongside the Atlantic Coast to the north and the looming Picos de Europa and Cantabrian mountains to the south. There's the chance to stop at any number of small towns and villages to sample local Asturian *sidra* (cider) and *queso azul* (blue cheese), Galician *pulpo* (octopus) and of course pintxos (tapas), or to cool off with a dip at a seaside spot on the Bay of Biscay.

Trip plan: Handy air hubs include A Coruña in the far west and Bilbao in the east, with Asturias and Santiago de Compostela

alternative access points. Euskotren services (also slow) link Bilbao with San Sebastian and Hendaye on the French border, so it's possible to arrive via Biarritz. Allow a week for the Bilbao-Ferrol traverse. Buy tickets at stations.

Need to know: An eight-day trip aboard the Orient Express-style Transcantábrico tourist train, between Bilbao and Santiago de Compostela, offers a luxurious all-inclusive alternative.

Other months: Nov-Apr – cooler, wetter; May-Oct – hot, drier.

RILA MOUNTAINS
BULGARIA

→ **Why now? Tune in to the spirit of lakes and mountains.**

Venture to the mirror-like Seven Rila Lakes on 19 August and you may hear a celestial chorus, with a circle of white-clad people moving in the synchronized ritual of Paneurhythmy – usually translated as 'dance of life', really more like t'ai chi. These are Deunovians, members of the so-called White Brotherhood, a spiritual movement founded in Bulgaria in the early 20th century emphasising unity between humans and nature. Whether or not you buy into that philosophy, you'll surely feel the power of the moment and the location – and exploring the Rila Mountains in sunny summer offers ample opportunities for nature immersion plus mental and physical refreshment. A cable car climbs to the lakes, but better to ascend under your own steam – hike up from villages such as nearby Govedartsi

via wildflower-strewn meadows, perhaps summiting 2729m (8954ft) Malîovitsa or 2925m (9797ft) Musala, highest peak in the Balkans. For an extra spiritual surge, visit Rila Monastery, enveloped in a forested valley to the south and covered with vivid frescoes.

Trip plan: The Rila Lakes are about 80km (50 miles) south of Sofia, which has a busy international airport. Hiking guides and local tour operators offer guided and self-guided hikes through the Rila Mountains.

Need to know: Weather in the mountains can change rapidly, and temperatures drop significantly at night: bring wet-weather gear, and warm clothes if sleeping in a mountain refuge (recommended).

Other months: Oct-May – cold, snow at high levels; Jun-Sep – warmest, driest.

(L) The Orthodox Rila Monastery; (R) A ritual dance on Rila mountain

Stock Photo

TOUR DE MONT BLANC FRANCE, SWITZERLAND & ITALY

 Why now? Hike high trails in the Alpine sunshine.

The highest mountain in the Alps looks spectacular from any angle – so why not view it from them all? The idea of hiking a circuit around Mont Blanc isn't new: Horace Bénédict de Saussure set out with friends to trace the loop in 1767, and since Victorian times it's become the benchmark for Alpine trails. The higher passes are snow-free for only a dozen or so weeks between June and September; expect to meet dozens of other trekkers in high summer, when the weather is relatively settled and warm (though be prepared for rain, wind and even freak snow). Typically, hikers start from Les Houches and walk in an anticlockwise direction, heading through France, Italy and then Switzerland to cover the most popular 170km (106 mile) route. Chamonix (France), Courmayeur (Italy) and Champex (Switzerland) are the main hubs: stock up on local delicacies such as bread, cheese, cured meats and more.

Trip plan: Geneva is the most convenient airport, with buses to Les Houches running several times a day. Trains run from Paris and Geneva to St-Gervais-Les-Bains, from where local trains serve Les Houches. Most trekkers take between nine and 14 days to complete the circuit.

Need to know: If walking the route clockwise rather than anti-clockwise, it's advisable to start at Champex rather than Les Houches to avoid beginning with a daunting ascent.

Other months: Nov-May – cold, snow on trails; Jun & Oct – paths may be snow-free; Jul-Sep – paths clear, busiest.

DUNDEE
SCOTLAND

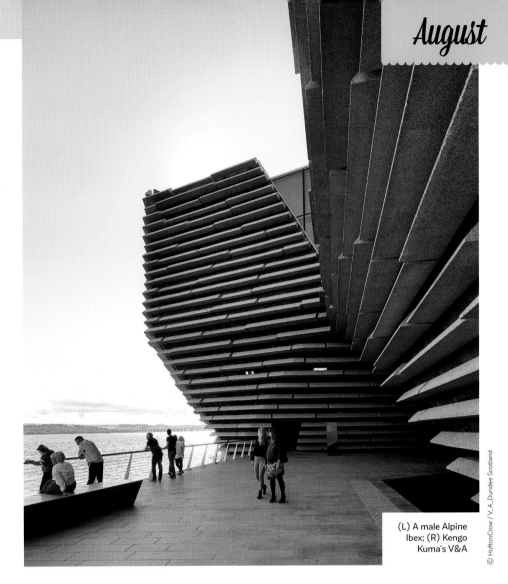

Why now? Spend sunny days discovering Scotland's newest capital of cool.

In August, Edinburgh is flooded with culture-seekers packing venues during the annual Fringe festival. For a quieter alternative, take an August break in Dundee – Scotland's sunniest city and, since the launch of an ambitious regeneration programme, arguably its hippest. Having dispelled the air of neglect following the end of its 'jute, jam and journalism' heyday, it's now home to an enviable roster of cultural venues, including cutting-edge Dundee Contemporary Arts. The cultural scene was further bolstered by the 2018 opening of the V&A, Scotland's first design museum; the centrepiece of the revitalised waterfront area, it's set in a spectacular building created by Japanese architect Kengo Kuma. With traditional pubs, music bars and speakeasies, plus a huge student population, nightlife is buzzing; and the eating scene gets better by the moment – though don't miss old-school local classics such as Dundee cake and the Arbroath smokie, a tasty smoked haddock.

Trip plan: Dundee has an airport (though serving limited destinations) and is around 1hr 30min from Edinburgh by train. Spend a couple of days exploring the city, and ideally add visits to the seaside at Broughty Ferry and to stately Glamis Castle just to the north.

Need to know: The city's Dundee Law isn't a TV drama but a 174m/571ft-high hill affording great views over city and the Firth of Tay.

Other months: Nov–Mar – cold, dark; Apr-May & Oct – fairly pleasant; Jun-Sep – warm.

(L) A male Alpine Ibex; (R) Kengo Kuma's V&A

© HuftonCrow / V_A_Dundee Scotland

BEYOND DUNDEE

 GLAMIS CASTLE • 19KM (12 MILES) • Scottish Baronial castle and legendary setting for Shakespeare's *Macbeth*

 ARBROATH • 27KM (17 MILES) • Seaside town and fishing harbour, home of the famous Arbroath smokie

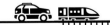 **CAIRNGORMS NATIONAL PARK • 85KM (53 MILES) •** Wild mountain landscape of granite and heather

 EDINBURGH • 100KM (62 MILES) • Reach the Scottish capital by train in under 90 minutes

ROMSDALEN VALLEY NORWAY

→ **Why now?** Tackle twisting mountain roads and forage fabulous wild foods.

Enshrined in Norway's soul (and law) is the Allemannsretten – literally 'every man's right' – the freedom to roam, wild-camp and forage on non-enclosed land across the country. There's little to compare with the flavours of fish you've hauled yourself from a fjord, mushrooms hand-harvested from the forest, or berries plucked from bushes on mountain hillsides. August is prime fruit season, when blueberries, lingonberries and rare 'mountain gold' cloudberries are ripe for picking. It's also one of the few months when the 11 hairpins of western Norway's most thrilling highway, the Trollstigen ('Troll's Ladder'), are snow-free and navigable. This is the time to explore the Romsdalen Valley and surrounding area around Åndalsnes, skirting fjords, gawping at waterfalls and hiking into the wilds to feast on nature's bounty. Tackle Route 63, part of the National Scenic Route which includes Trollstigen and slightly less adrenalin-surging Ørnevegen ('Eagle Road'), as well as jaw-dropping, World Heritage-listed Geirangerfjord, 90km (56 miles) to the south.

Trip plan: Molde has the nearest airport, some 1hr by car drive from Åndalsnes; Ålesund is a 2hr drive. Better to arrive by train along the beautiful Romsdalen Valley, or by boat aboard a Hurtigruten ship cruising the coast.

Need to know: In general, foraging of wild foods is permitted on public land, but special rules apply to cloudberries in certain regions – check locally before picking.

Other months: Mid-Oct to May – snow; Jun to mid-Oct – Trollstigen open.

© Simon Bajada / Lonely Planet

A basket of freshly picked lingonberries

Laidback Plaka beach
on the Pelion Peninsula

© Iosif Lucian Bolca / Alamy Stock Photo

PELION PENINSULA GREECE

→ **Why now? Cool off in balmy waters or traditional hillside villages.**

Sure, you could bake on busy beaches on a Greek island. But in sizzling August, head instead for cool Pelion, the gnarled finger curling into the Aegean to tickle the Sporades. There's a range of coastal resorts, mostly more isolated and peaceful than elsewhere: try Horto or Milina on the sheltered west coast, southerly Platanias, or busier Horefto, Agios Ioannis and cute Damouhari near beautiful Fakistra beach on the east coast. The mountainous interior oozes natural and cultural appeal – this is where mythical centaurs came to carouse – with ancient cobbled paths linking traditional villages where you can admire church frescoes, sip grape-based, rakı-like *tsipouro* in the shade of venerable plane trees, and savour local specialities such as *spetsofaï* (pork-sausage stew), *fasoladha* (butter bean soup) and lamb in lemon sauce. Up here, the air's a good few degrees lower than on the coast, and in summer you can board the narrow-gauge To Trenaki loco that chugs from Ano Lehonia to Milies, running daily in July and August.

Trip plan: The nearest airport is at Thessaloniki, a 3hr bus or train ride from the gateway to the Pelion, Volos. Athens and Preveza are alternatives.

Need to know: Many of the Pelion's *arhontika*, stately stone-built mansions in hill villages, have been converted into characterful guesthouses – book ahead in high summer.

Other months: Nov-Apr – cool, snow on mountains; May & Oct – pleasant, To Trenaki runs weekends; Jun-Sep – very hot at the coast.

The oldest working canal in the world at its verdant best: the Canal du Midi

LANGUEDOC-ROUSSILLON
FRANCE

Why now? Cruise between the historic gems of southwest France.

Barge-lovers bless the name of Pierre-Paul Riquet, the 17th-century mastermind behind the Canal du Midi. Meandering for 241km (150 miles) between the Mediterranean and Toulouse, his epic achievement paved (or, rather, dug) the way for watergoing holidaymakers who today chug between Sète, near Béziers, and the Garonne river. August is a mixed blessing: it promises sunny days, festivals and markets, but also crowds – it's the month when France holidays en masse. The answer? Play it cool: plan no more than a few hours' on the move each day, allowing time to enjoy the magnificent citadel at Carcassonne, the old centre (and sausages) of Toulouse, the cathedral and Roman heritage of Narbonne, plus countless opportunities for wine tasting and feasting.

Trip plan: Béziers, Carcassonne and Toulouse all have airports. Choose between self-drive boat hire or a crewed barge – some are extremely luxurious (and commensurately pricey), with excellent food, wine and excursions. Allow a week to pootle from the coast to Carcassonne, another to reach Toulouse.

Need to know: Locks on the Canal du Midi open 9am-7pm, and close for lunch 12.30-1.30pm. There can be queues for locks at busy times. Consider hiring a bike to pedal sections of the canal for a leg-stretching break from the boat.

Other months: Late Nov-Dec – canal closed for maintenance; Jan-Mar – few boats or facilities available; Apr-May & Oct – cooler, some facilities closed; Jun & Sep – warm, quieter; Jul-Aug – hot, busy.

EGER
HUNGARY

Why now? Explore an opulent Baroque city and winery-hop between cellars.

Tucked away in the hills of northern Hungary, Eger (pronounced 'egg-air') is an elegant, lively city that wins everyone's heart, perfect for a city break in sunny August. Dominated by the hefty hilltop castle that held out against Ottoman invaders in 1552, and which rings to martial cries during the historical festival in mid-August, Eger's streets are lined with lavish Baroque architecture. Far from being a staid museum piece, though, it's a vibrant city with a buzzing events calendar, great nightlife and some renowned wines, the latter best enjoyed via a half-hour stroll to the so-called 'Valley of Beautiful Women' (Szépasszony Völgy). Though not quite as visually alluring as it sounds – it's really a row of wine cellars just west of the centre – this is the place to taste famed Egri Bikavér (Bull's Blood) red and a trio of other local tipples in dozens of close-packed cellars. Clear the head with a hike or bike ride in the beech-clad, cave-riddled Bükk Hills just to the northeast.

Trip plan: Eger is a 2hr train or bus from Budapest, a little more from Debrecen, both of which receive international flights.

Need to know: College dorms host travellers during the summer holidays (Jun-Aug), providing good budget accommodation – book through the tourist office.

Other months: Nov-Mar – cold, quiet; Apr-May & Oct – warm, ample events; Jun-Sep – hot.

Lübeck Old Town and the River Trave bask in the sun

LÜBECK GERMANY

Why now? Explore the 'Venice of the Baltic' in festival season.

Normally, you'd be wary of a place claiming such a grandiose tag – but this graceful old city, centred on an oval island in the river Trave, has the cultural chops to back up the marketing mantra. Still wreathed in architectural glory from its medieval heyday as epicentre of the powerful Hanseatic League, the Altstadt (Old Town) is a fascinating place to wander. Venture between the bulky, witch-hatted twin towers of the 15th-century Holstentor (city gate) to admire the 13th-century Rathaus (Town Hall), Gothic Marienkirche and numerous galleries and museums centred on the Hanseatic League and on Nobel laureates Thomas Mann and Günter Grass. Sweet-toothed travellers should make a beeline for Café Niederegger to taste its renowned marzipan; the almond confection was first created in Lübeck, and has been perfected here over more than two centuries. In early August, the city rings to the sound of music and other performances during the ten-day Duckstein Festival held along the banks of the Trave.

Trip plan: Hamburg, which has the closest airport, is a 45min train ride from Lübeck. The city has a good range of accommodation at all price points.

Need to know: Just 20km (12 miles) north of the old city, and reachable via a 20min train journey, Travemünde has a broad, sandy beach.

Other months: Nov-Mar – cold; Apr-May & Oct – cooler, quieter; Jun-Sep – pleasantly warm.

197

LIGURIAN SEA
ITALY

→ **Why now? Dolphin-watch with a purpose in the Mediterranean.**

Seeing a dolphin cresting in the waves can be the encounter of a lifetime – and one that might be becoming rarer. Make your wildlife-watching a little more meaningful by joining a project investigating cetaceans in the Pelagos Sanctuary for Mediterranean Marine Mammals, a diamond-shaped protected reserve bordered by Liguria, Tuscany, Corsica and the Côte d'Azur, and encompassing part of the Ligurian Sea. Boarding a research boat, you'll work alongside scientists logging sightings and recording and analysing visual and acoustic data relating to eight species – including Risso's, striped and bottlenose dolphins, plus sperm, pilot and fin whales. August, a month of sunshine and warm seas, is a fine time to contribute to important studies aiming to understand more about the populations, behaviour and movements of species about which little is currently known. And, of course, it's a wonderful time to be afloat in the northern Med...

Trip plan: Research boats commonly depart from San Remo in southwest Liguria; by train, the port is 1hr east of Nice, 2hr from Genoa, the two closest airports.

Need to know: Several agencies arrange placements with NGOs including the Tethys Foundation, generally with a minimum one-week commitment; check out feedback from previous volunteers before booking. Other cetacean projects operate in locations such as Croatia.

Other months: Oct-Apr – cool; some species migrate from the Ligurian Sea; May-Sep – research season.

Rugged and remote, the Cinque Terre coastline hosts playful dolphins at this time of year

© Justin Foulkes / Lonely Planet

STOCKHOLM ARCHIPELAGO
SWEDEN

→ **Why now? Island-hop the coastal capital on long summer days.**

Less a city, more a wooded archipelago that happens to host some important buildings, Sweden's capital is unreasonably attractive – and never more so than in sunny August, when the sun glints on the water and the many parks beckon. Stockholm has enough cultural attractions to pack several days, from the cobbled alleys of Gamla Stan (Old Town) to exceptional contemporary galleries and museums (including open-air Skansen), while the sleek modern shopping district of Nordmalm offers ample welcoming cafés and restaurants for the all-important *fika* (coffee and cake break). It's easy to roam the 14 main islands on foot, or by bike or metro, but there are tens of thousands more islets and rocks in the archipelago that are best explored by ferry, on a boat cruise or – better yet – by kayak. Watch for ospreys, beavers and grey seals in various choice spots around the archipelago.

Trip plan: Arlanda airport is only 20min from the city by express train, or 40min by bus. With ample bike lanes, cycling's a great way to get around. Guided and self-guided sea-kayaking tours explore the archipelago.

Need to know: Even in summer, bring warm layers for evenings, when temperatures can drop to 10°C (50°F). Things get quieter after Swedish school summer holidays end in the second half of August.

Other months: Dec-Feb – winter, holiday markets; Mar-May – spring, cooler and cheaper; Jun-Aug – summer, warm, busiest; Sep-Oct, cooler, autumn colours.

Placid waters by the hamlet of Bruket

© Matt Munro / Lonely Planet

BEYOND STOCKHOLM

DROTTNINGHOLM PALACE • 14KM (9 MILES) • Grand palace on the 'Queen's Islet', still the royal residence

SIGTUNA • 46KM (29 MILES) • Sweden's first town, historic wooden buildings, nearby Skokloster Castle

MARIEFRED • 50KM (31 MILES) • Picturesque town, Gripsholm castle, steamboat journey from Stockholm

UPPSALA • 64KM (40 MILES) • Charming city, Bronze-Age burial mounds, huge cathedral

September

WHERE TO GO WHEN

CHALLENGE MYSELF

I WANT TO

TAKE ME OUT FOR...

FOOD
- BOHUSLÄN COAST, SWEDEN P216
- BOLOGNA, ITALY P217

DRINK
- STUTTGART, GERMANY P209
- JEREZ DE LA FRONTERA, SPAIN P209

Try fresh crayfish on Sweden's Bohuslän Coast

Soak up festival vibes at Stuttgart's Cannstatter Volksfest

TAKE ME TO TOWN

ART & CULTURE
- VESZPRÉM, HUNGARY P219
- SAN MARINO P209

NIGHT-LIFE & HEDONISM
- BRAGA & GUIMARÃES, PORTUGAL P206
- BRISTOL, ENGLAND P223

Sunset on one of Braga's elegant plazas

RELAX/ INDULGE

Get a dose of culture in Veszprém, Hungary

DIAL IT DOWN

WELLNESS
- SOUTHERN STYRIA, AUSTRIA P213

CHILLING
- AEOLIAN ISLANDS, ITALY P220
- TURQUOISE COAST, TURKEY P218

Monte dei Porri, one of Salina's twin volcanoes on the Aeolian Islands

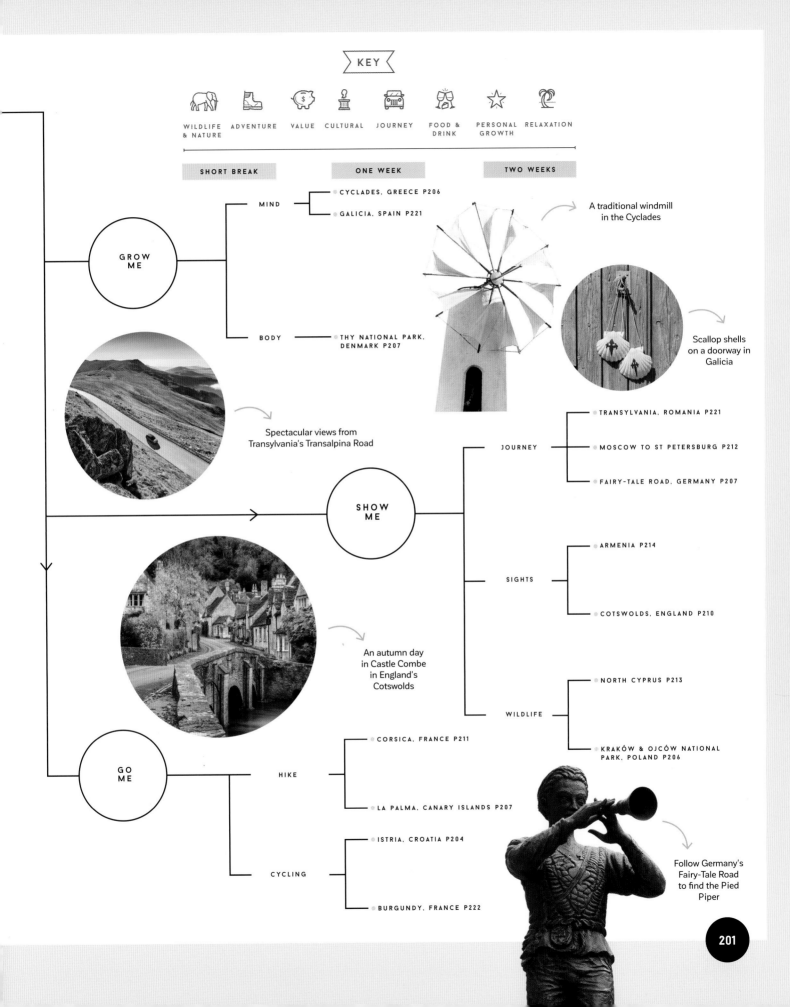

KEY

| WILDLIFE & NATURE | ADVENTURE | VALUE | CULTURAL | JOURNEY | FOOD & DRINK | PERSONAL GROWTH | RELAXATION |

SHORT BREAK   **ONE WEEK**   **TWO WEEKS**

GROW ME

MIND
- CYCLADES, GREECE P206
- GALICIA, SPAIN P221

BODY
- THY NATIONAL PARK, DENMARK P207

A traditional windmill in the Cyclades

Scallop shells on a doorway in Galicia

Spectacular views from Transylvania's Transalpina Road

SHOW ME

JOURNEY
- TRANSYLVANIA, ROMANIA P221
- MOSCOW TO ST PETERSBURG P212
- FAIRY-TALE ROAD, GERMANY P207

SIGHTS
- ARMENIA P214
- COTSWOLDS, ENGLAND P210

WILDLIFE
- NORTH CYPRUS P213
- KRAKÓW & OJCÓW NATIONAL PARK, POLAND P206

An autumn day in Castle Combe in England's Cotswolds

GO ME

HIKE
- CORSICA, FRANCE P211
- LA PALMA, CANARY ISLANDS P207

CYCLING
- ISTRIA, CROATIA P204
- BURGUNDY, FRANCE P222

Follow Germany's Fairy-Tale Road to find the Pied Piper

201

EVENTS
IN SEPTEMBER

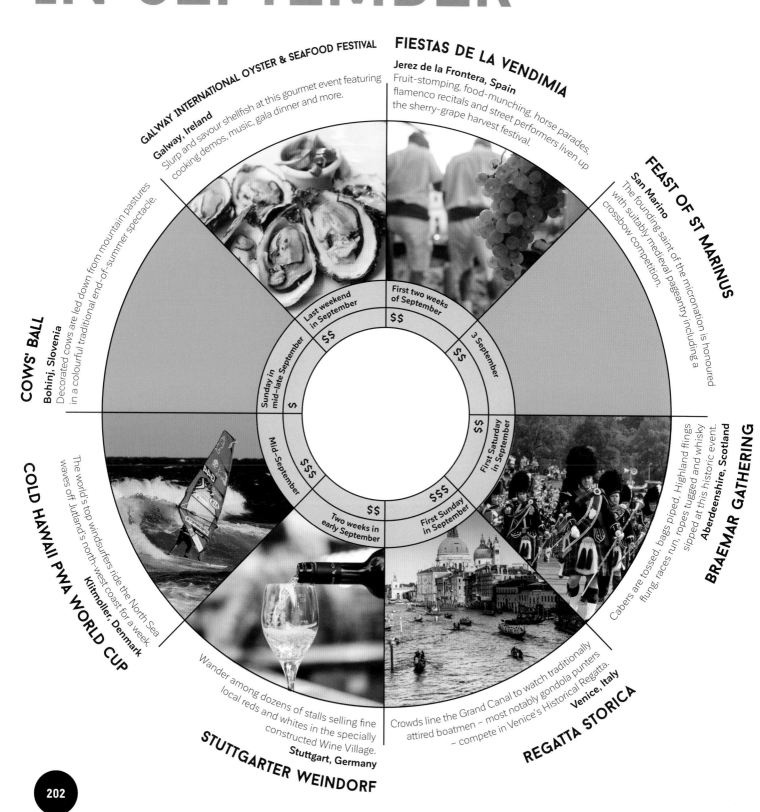

GALWAY INTERNATIONAL OYSTER & SEAFOOD FESTIVAL
Galway, Ireland
Slurp and savour shellfish at this gourmet event featuring cooking demos, music, gala dinner and more.

FIESTAS DE LA VENDIMIA
Jerez de la Frontera, Spain
Fruit-stomping, food-munching, horse parades, flamenco recitals and street performers liven up the sherry-grape harvest festival.

FEAST OF ST MARINUS
San Marino
The founding saint of the micronation is honoured with suitably medieval pageantry including a crossbow competition.

COWS' BALL
Bohinj, Slovenia
Decorated cows are led down from mountain pastures in a colourful traditional end-of-summer spectacle.

BRAEMAR GATHERING
Aberdeenshire, Scotland
Cabers are tossed, bags piped, Highland flings flung, races run, ropes tugged and whisky sipped at this historic event.

COLD HAWAII PWA WORLD CUP
Klitmøller, Denmark
The world's top windsurfers ride the North Sea waves off Jutland's north-west coast for a week.

STUTTGARTER WEINDORF
Stuttgart, Germany
Wander among dozens of stalls selling fine local reds and whites in the specially constructed Wine Village.

REGATTA STORICA
Venice, Italy
Crowds line the Grand Canal to watch traditionally attired boatmen – most notably gondola punters – compete in Venice's Historical Regatta.

Last weekend in September — $$
First two weeks of September — $$
3 September — $$
Sunday in mid-late September — $
First Saturday in September — $$
Mid-September — $$$
Two weeks in early September — $$
First Sunday in September — $$$

VERY FAMILY FRIENDLY

FAIRY-TALE ROAD, GERMANY

CORSICA

BOHUSLÄN COAST, SWEDEN

Scoot through the streets in the Aeolian Islands

AEOLIAN ISLANDS, ITALY

Admire the splendour of autumn in the Cotswolds

SAN MARINO

COTSWOLDS, ENGLAND

When in Corsica... drink Colomba, a local beer brewed with a pinch of wild herbs

BRISTOL, ENGLAND

TURQUOISE COAST, TURKEY

CYCLADES, GREECE

NORTH CYPRUS

Sail in the Cyclades sunshine

Istria produces some of the world's best olive oil

TRANSYLVANIA, ROMANIA

Bran Castle in Romania – commonly known as Dracula's Castle

ISTRIA, CROATIA

VESZPRÉM, HUNGARY

EXPENSIVE BUT WORTH IT

GOOD VALUE

THY NP, DENMARK

LA PALMA, SPAIN

ARMENIA

Embrace slow travel aboard a barge in Burgundy

SOUTHERN STYRIAN, AUSTRIA

Don't miss Armenia's magnificent Noravank monastery

BOLOGNA, ITALY

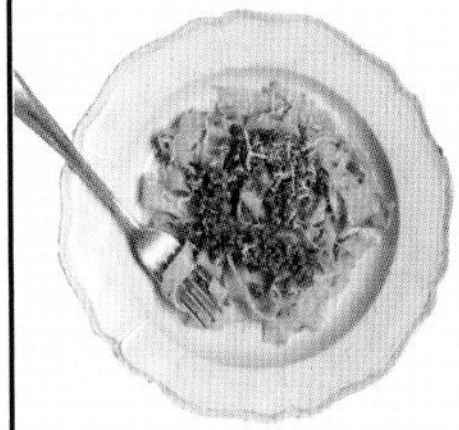

Chow down on bolognese in its birthplace

BRAGA & GUIMARÃES, PORTUGAL

BURGUNDY, FRANCE

JERÉZ DE LA FRONTERA, SPAIN

MOSCOW-ST PETERSBURG

KRAKÓW & OJCÓW, POLAND

Bag a bagel in Kraków

STUTTGART, GERMANY

Sweet treats: a gingerbread heart on sale at Cannstatter Volksfest

Travel the tram in St Petersburg

GALICIA, SPAIN

LEAVE THE KIDS AT HOME

203

ISTRIA
CROATIA

→ **Why now? Pedal a culinary and cultural cycling odyssey.**

Overflowing with asparagus, olives and oysters, there are few tastier destinations than Istria, the triangular peninsula nudging into the Adriatic in far northwest Croatia. And there are few tastier times to explore Istria than September, when grapes are harvested and truffles ripen beneath the forest floor. Bank calorie credits by cycling between feasts: there's relatively easy pedalling along the coast, where tourist numbers are thinning in September, and where you can roam the lovely Venetian port of Rovinj and admire Pula's impressive Roman amphitheatre. But for the real gastro treats, crank up the calf muscles and explore the truffle-centric hilltop settlements of medieval Motovun, Buzet and tiny Hum in the north, and the wine regions around Buje and Momjan to the northwest – white Malvasia and red Teran are top local tipples. Easing you into your edible odyssey is the Parenzana Trail cycle route, following 123km (77 miles) of disused railway line between Trieste in Italy and Poreč on the Istrian coast, with a short stretch in Slovenia.

Trip plan: There are international airports at both ends of the Parenzana – Trieste to the north, just over the border between Slovenia and Italy; and Pula at the Istrian peninsula's southern tip. Allow at least a week to cycle between the two, longer to explore Croatia's hilly interior.

Need to know: Numerous events across Istria celebrate truffle season in autumn – head to Buzet on the second Saturday in September to watch a giant truffle omelette being cooked (and chomped) during the festivities of Buzetska Subotina.

Other months: Nov-Mar – cool; Apr-Jun & Sep-Oct – pleasantly warm on the coast; Jul-Aug – very hot, busy.

Heaven scent: Freshly harvested olives and black and white Buzet truffles

CYCLADES
GREECE

Why now? Sail between whitewashed fishing villages and gorgeous beaches.

You've seen the postcard pictures: views across whitewashed, blue-roofed Oia on Santorini, fishing boats bobbing at anchor in a traditional harbour, empty coves with limpid water. Sure, you can book a package tour to an island such as party-central Mykonos, Naxos or Paros, or take the island-hopping route on local ferries. But consider trying a different tack – literally: sail amid the Cyclades, scattered jewel-like across the Med southeast of Athens. In September, the meltemi wind that blows fiercely through these islands in high summer subsides, and conditions become increasingly safe for newbie sailors. Temperatures are still balmy, and seas calm, but prices and visitor numbers fall. Travelling under sail allows you to tailor your course to match your interests: find hiking trails, snorkelling spots, peaceful tavernas or beach clubs – whatever floats your boat!

Trip plan: Numerous sailing schools based in Saronic Gulf islands such as Porós and Aegina offer courses; cruise from there southeast to the Cyclades isles – perhaps to Santorini via Kythnos, Serifos and Sifnos, up to Paros for hillside villages, beaches and windsurfing, Naxos for diving, or one of the Little Cyclades to get off-grid.

Need to know: Hotels, tavernas and other services on most islands close from mid-October to Orthodox Easter.

Other months: Nov-Mar – cool, sleepy; Apr & Oct – mild; May-Sep – hot, busiest (meltemi wind strongest Jul-Aug).

KRAKÓW & OJCÓW NATIONAL PARK POLAND

Why now? Fall for dazzling autumn foliage.

Kraków's history is visible in overlapping layers, from the medieval marvels of the Old Town and Wawel Hill, with its magnificent castle and cathedral, to the Jewish heritage of the Kazimierz district and sobering reminders of WWII atrocities at Schindler's Factory and nearby Auschwitz. But while Kraków's drawcard is its rich cultural heritage, nearby natural history comes to the fore in September. Ojców National Park lies just 15km (9 miles) northwest – and it's a pocket gem, particularly in autumn when its oaks, birches and hornbeams glow fiery gold and traffic-light red among dramatic limestone outcrops and ravines. Combine city and country for a memorable short break: roam Kraków's streets, then take to the park's hiking trails, investigating its 400-plus caves, pretty Ojców village and two 14th-century fortresses – grand Pieskowa Skała and the Gothic ruins of Kazimierz – as well as watching for badgers, beavers and ermine among the woodland.

Trip plan: Minibuses depart Kraków five times daily for the 35min journey to Ojców National Park. Or you could cycle; the ride should take around 1hr 30min.

Need to know: Kazimierz and Pieskowa Skała Castles are two of a chain of 25 bastions linked by the Szlak Orlich Gniazd ('Trail of the Eagles' Nests'), a hiking and cycling route covering 163km (101 miles).

Other months: Nov-Mar – very cold; Apr-May – spring; Jun-Aug – warm; Sep-Oct – pleasant, autumn colours.

BRAGA & GUIMARÃES
PORTUGAL

Why now? Imbibe history, wine and top-notch food on a double-city break.

One buzzing university town chock with monumental medieval masterpieces, hip bars and exceptional cuisine is a rare travel treat; two cities within bar-hopping distance, rivalling one another for history and nightlife – that's a dream double-city break. Bigger Braga, founded by the Romans and traditional capital of the Minho region, has the burly medieval Sé – the country's oldest cathedral – while Guimarães is guarded by a 1000-year-old castle, reputed birthplace of the first king of Portugal, Afonso Henriques, and the crenelated hilltop Paço dos Duques (Dukes' Palace). Between them, the two cities host nearly 20,000 students, and enough cafés, bars and venues to keep them all entertained. By September, the students have returned but prices are dipping – an ideal time to explore fascinating heritage by day and enjoy warm evenings sipping local *vinho verde* ('green wine').

Trip plan: Porto, with its busy international airport, is 1hr from both Braga and Guimarães by bus or train; buses link the two in 30min. Nearby highlights include the viewpoint atop 617m (2024ft) Penha peak, and the extraordinary Baroque staircase at Bom Jesus do Monte, 5km (3 miles) east of central Braga.

Need to know: Arteries not clogged enough after your dinner main? Order *pudim do Abade de Priscos*, a richly delicious crème caramel devised by a 19th-century Abbot of Priscos, just southwest of Braga – the recipe involves at least 15 egg yolks, a chunk of lard and a heap of sugar.

Other months: Oct-May – cool, wet; Jun-Sep – summer, warm, drier.

FAIRY-TALE ROAD GERMANY

→ **Why now?** Follow a German trail of Grimm tales.

Two centuries ago, a pair of brothers from Hanau, near Frankfurt, published *Kinder- und Hausmärchen* (Children's and Household Tales), their first edition of folk stories featuring the likes of Cinderella, Rapunzel, Hansel and Gretel, Snow White and Rumpelstiltskin. You'll meet these characters and more along the Fairy-Tale Road (Märchenstrasse), a 600km (373 mile) curated driving route through central Germany, visiting beautiful Baroque towns and quaint villages, plus sites and landscapes connected to the stories the Grimms collected – castles and churches, cities and forests. Drive the route in September, after children return to school but with still-warm days and autumn colours heating up. At Hamelin, you'll be overrun with rats – stuffed, baked, painted on pavements – in honour of the Pied Piper. And at Sababurg, you can admire the 'Sleeping Beauty' castle, now a hotel.

Trip plan: Hanau, the southern terminus, is 15min by train from Frankfurt, while Buxtehude, at the northern end, is 40min from Hamburg. Spend at least a week on the road, allowing ample time for stops.

Need to know: The route splits between Marburg and Hamelin, with multiple alternatives in several places.

Other months: Dec-Mar – cold (Christmas markets Dec); Apr-May – spring blooms; Jun-Aug – warm, busy; Sep-Nov – cooling, quieter.

THY NATIONAL PARK DENMARK

→ **Why now?** Master the waves in Denmark's top surfing spots.

Drifting dunes, Bronze Age burial mounds, WWII-era bunkers, red deer and otters: Thy is Denmark's so-called last wilderness, a glorious national park fringing a 55km (34 mile) stretch of Jutland's northwest coast. But Thy is also 'Cold Hawaii', as surfers dub the stretch of coast around Klitmøller which encompasses the country's finest breaks. September marks a time of transition, between the mellow swells of summer and the bigger breaks of winter, but when sea temperatures are still relatively balmy. Surf instructors take beginners out to the Reef and the Bay off Klitmøller, or to Wind Mill at Hanstholm (also great for SUP jaunts), while the sandy shore at Agger has left- and right-hand breaks for all levels. Advanced board-riders come later in the year to tackle the fast barrels at Fisherman's Corner at Hanstholm. But whatever the length of your board or surf CV, there's a break to suit.

Trip plan: Public transport to Thy from the nearest cities, Aalborg and Aarhus, is limited – hiring a car is the best way to explore. Klitmøller and nearby Nørre Vorupør are convenient places to stay, with guesthouses and campsites; most people arrange accommodation through surf camps.

Need to know: This coast is the windiest in Western Europe, and windsurfers descend on Klitmøller for the Cold Hawaii PWA World Cup in mid-September, when it's particularly sensible to book accommodation in advance.

Other months: Oct-May – big waves, cold water; Jun-Sep – better for beginners.

LA PALMA CANARY ISLANDS

→ **Why now?** Enjoy stellar hiking through verdant valleys and volcanic calderas.

The dinky northwesterly outpost of the Canaries is reputedly the steepest island in the world. Unsurprisingly, it offers some of the most dramatic hiking in this volcanic archipelago – and with around 1000km (621 miles) of footpaths, there's a diverse array of options. September promises reliable sunshine but thankfully cooling temperatures, as well as improved availability of accommodation after the main summer peak. In the south, trails cross crispy black lava flows to the lighthouse and saltpans at Fuencaliente. Running north along the island's spine is the Ruta de los Volcanes (Route of the Volcanoes), with dramatic views to coasts on east and west. The highlight is the full-day trek down through the vast Caldera de Taburiente crater, through rocky ravines and Canarian pine forests. The streets of capital Santa Cruz de La Palma are also made for walking, lined with enticing Renaissance churches, vintage pharmacies and 18th-century mansions. Beaches – mostly black volcanic sand – provide post-hike relaxation.

Trip plan: Allow a week to hike the Caldera de Taburiente and the other trails around Los Llanos de Aridane, as well as the southern volcanic coastal region (including the Ruta de los Volcanes), and for pottering around Santa Cruz.

Need to know: La Palma was the first designated Unesco Starlight Reserve – views of the night sky are fabulous. Visit the Gran Telescopio Canarias for astronomical insights, or book a stargazing tour with a specialist local operator.

Other months: Oct-May – cool and rainy, pleasant for hiking; Jun-Sep – summer, hot.

(A) Guaita Castle atop San Marino;
(L) Sweet treats in Stuttgart; (R) The
Palomino grape harvest gets underway
in Jerez de la Frontera

SAN MARINO

→ **Why now?** Discover the world's oldest sovereign state.

Never heard of St Marinus, patron saint of bachelors? A brief resume: born 18 centuries ago in what's now Croatia, he became a stonemason, then moved to live in a cave on Monte Titano near the northeast Italian coast. Oh, and in AD 301 he founded the micronation today called San Marino: entirely surrounded by Italy, this enclave of just 61 sq km (23 sq miles) is the fifth-smallest country in the world, and reputedly the oldest republic. On 3 September each year, the founding saint's day is celebrated in San Marino with pageantry (and a crossbow competition), but in any case it's a fine month to clamber the eponymous capital city's steep streets and capture panoramic views from the dramatically perched medieval mountaintop fortresses of Torre Guaita and Torre Cesta, pausing to munch the local variety of *piadina*, stuffed local flatbreads. Visit before mid-September to experience the pomp of the daily changing of the guard in the Piazza della Libertà.

Trip plan: The gateway to and accommodation hub for San Marino is the Italian seaside resort of Rimini, a 40min ride away by bus. Bologna, which has the nearest airport, is about 1hr by train from Rimini.

Need to know: Too puffed to tackle the steep ascent up into Città di San Marino? Catch the funicular from Borgo Maggiore at the bottom of Monte Titano. And don't call locals Italian – they're proudly Sammarinese.

Other months: Nov-Mar – cold; Apr-May & Sep-Oct – pleasant, quiet; Jun-Aug – hot, busy.

STUTTGART
GERMANY

→ **Why now?** Discover the city where drinking and driving really do mix.

The capital of Baden-Württemberg has always been a high-horsepower place. Founded in AD 950 as a stud farm (Stuotgarten) for war horses, it's famed today as the home of Mercedes-Benz and Porsche – but as autumn approaches, attention turns from steering wheels to wines and steins. For 12 days till the second Sunday in September, the Stuttgarter Weindorf ('Wine Village') takes over the centre, with dozens of stalls selling local Trollinger reds and white Rieslings along with traditional Swabian food. Then, at the end of the month, the drinking heats up again with the Cannstatter Volksfest, a buzzing beer festival second only to Munich's, selling mainly local brews. There's no shortage of opportunities to indulge between those events, in bars and cafés as well as cosy Weinstuben (wine bars) and restaurants. The museums of the big two car manufacturers are must-sees, of course, but don't miss the Baroque Neues Schloss, the Roman remains around the Schlossplatz (castle square), and the city's excellent museums and art galleries.

Trip plan: Allow at least two days to enjoy Stuttgart's attractions, plus another day to visit the palaces at Ludwigsburg, some 20min by car to the north, and more if you plan on exploring the vineyards in the surrounding hills.

Need to know: Besenwirtschäften ('broom taverns'), pop-up inns serving house wines and home-cooked meals, open for just 12 weeks each year, usually from autumn – to find one, follow the brooms!

Other months: Nov-Apr – cold; May-Aug – warm, wettest; Sep-Oct – cooler, wine festivals.

JEREZ DE LA
FRONTERA SPAIN

→ **Why now?** Sink a sherry or three and browse the bodegas.

Think sherry is an old-fashioned Christmas-only tipple? Think again. In its hometown, the fortified wine named for the Andalucían city of Jerez de la Frontera is complex, varied and delicious – and perhaps best savoured during the Fiestas de la Vendimia. To coincide with the harvest of the sherry grapes – Palomino, Pedro Ximénez and Moscatel – this festival in the first two weeks of September features fruit-stomping, food eating, horse parades and street performers. Expect music too, especially flamenco, which reputedly originated in the city. At any time, though there are many handsome and historic bodegas (wineries) to explore in the city centre, most offering tours. Visit the cavernous storehouses and modern tasting rooms at González–Byass (makers of the best-selling Tio Pepe) or sip sherry in the cathedral-like cellars of Bodega Lustau. Then hit the characterful bars of the old centre, where you can sample bargain dry *finos* and smoky-sweet *olorosos* accompanied by authentic flamenco tunes. Make time, too, to explore city's fine Moorish Alcázar and flamboyant cathedral, all under the sizzling sun of southern Spain.

Trip plan: Allow two days in Jerez. A longer sherry-tasting tour could also take in oft-overlooked El Puerto de Santa María, Chipiona (good for beaches) and Sanlúcar de Barrameda or Trebujena, both close to the wetlands of Parque Nacional de Doñana.

Need to know: Jerez is a 1hr 15min train journey from Seville.

Other months: Nov-Mar – coolest; Apr-May – warm, pleasant; Jun-Aug – very hot; Sep-Oct – hot, wine festivals.

Rooms with a view: the clifftop citadel on the Mediterranean

© joe daniel price / Getty Images

COTSWOLDS ENGLAND

Autumn arrives in Wiltshire's Castle Combe

Why now? Explore idyllic English villages in early autumn sunshine.
In the golden light of September, the Cotswolds seem to ooze honey. This land of rolling hills ('wolds'), hiding wool towns and stone hamlets in their clefts and valleys, has long attracted urbanites seeking an idealised English idyll. Visit in September not just to miss the heaviest onslaughts of coach parties, but also to enjoy the countryside at its finest, and to admire the leaves beginning to spark into their fiery autumn finery in the wonderful arboretums at Westonbirt and Batsford. True, this region is hardly an undiscovered gem: chocolate-box favourites such as Castle Combe and Bourton on the Water can be thronged with tourists. But it's not hard to find peace, especially if you're prepared to stretch your legs: a comprehensive network of footpaths laces the region, while the 164km (102 mile) Cotswold Way traces the escarpment, linking charming towns and villages strung along the route between Chipping Campden and Bath.

Trip plan: If you're not hiking, choose a base from which to explore: Broadway in the north, perhaps, for quirky Snowshill Manor, Batsford Arboretum and peaceful Stanway, with its magnificent Jacobean mansion; or Tetbury to the south, for antiques, historic Malmesbury Abbey and Westonbirt Arboretum.

Need to know: Many attractions, particularly those managed by the National Trust, close or have reduced opening November–April.

Other months: Nov-Mar – cold; Apr-Oct – mostly warm.

CORSICA
FRANCE

→ **Why now?** Hike the Île de Beauté at its beautifully un-busiest.

There's barely a straight road on the wildly rumpled Mediterranean isle of Corsica. Tarmac has to twist around mountains and through the herby maquis scrubland that blankets the interior, and in high summer seemingly the whole of France decamps to the gorgeous shores of the 'beautiful isle'. Better wait till September, when the air and sea are still warm, and the beaches – arguably Europe's best – are quieter. This is also the time to lace up your hiking books and venture into the seemingly impenetrable interior on trails such as the tough but epic GR20: tackle the whole 180km (112 miles) or just a section. Alternatively, book a villa in the hills, crack open a Pietra beer, nibble brocciu cheese and simply contemplate the wilderness. But spare a few days to explore the precipitous, cliff-perched town of Bonifacio; feel the mafioso vibe in hilltop Sartène; hit the history trail in lively Ajaccio, birthplace of Napoléon Bonaparte; or tour the tiny fishing ports of offbeat Cap Corse.

Trip plan: With one week, concentrate on one area: the north (Calvi, Île Rousse, Bastia) or south (Propriano, Bonifacio, Porto-Vecchio). Walking the whole GR20 takes around 15 days.

Need to know: The island's two main airports are at Ajaccio and Bastia. Ferries sail to Corsica from France and Italy; journey time is 4–6hr.

Other months: Nov-Mar – cool, some facilities close; Apr-Jun & Sept-Oct – warm, quieter; Jul-Aug – hottest, busiest.

MOSCOW TO ST PETERSBURG
RUSSIA

→ **Why now?** Cruise between two great cities in 'granny's summer'.

Summer sees St Petersburg packed with visitors enjoying its *belye nochi* (White Nights) and cultural jewels: the artistic marvels of the Hermitage Museum, mighty Peter and Paul Fortress, the dizzying mosaics of the Church of the Saviour on Spilled Blood, and the grand edifices lining Nevsky Prospekt. Meanwhile, Muscovites retreat from the heat to country *dachas*, leaving the Kremlin and St Basil's Cathedral to tourists. Best come in September, when Moscow cools and its trees are aflame with autumn hues, and when St Petersburg's crowds thin, but before the *rasputitsa* ('sludge') season arrives. Enjoy *Babie Leto* ('granny's summer'), a pleasantly warm time to visit both cities on a twin-city Volga River cruise – itineraries usually include stops to admire the historic wooden architecture in the open-air museum on Kizhi Island, the beautiful churches of Uglich and traditional village houses at Mandrogui.

Trip plan: Cruises typically take around five or six days to travel between Moscow and St Petersburg; add at least two days at either end to explore these cities.

Need to know: Most nationals require a visa for entry to Russia, obtained in advance of arrival; but visitors arriving on a cruise ship or ferry can stay up to 72hrs visa-free. Visa information can change at short notice, though, so check well before travel.

Other months: Nov-Mar – very cold; Apr & Oct – cold, wet; May & Sep – pleasant; Jun-Aug – warm, busy.

NORTH CYPRUS

→ **Why now? Seek sun, sand, turtles and time travel.**

Visiting the northern half of divided Cyprus is a bit like holidaying in the 1970s. It might lack a certain slickness, but there's also a pleasing lack of development. Some of the Med's most unspoilt sands are here, especially along the wild Karpas Peninsula (Karpaz in Turkish), where you're more likely to see donkeys and turtles than other people. Indeed, both loggerhead and green turtles visit northern Cyprus' shores regularly and, from June to late September, the Society for the Protection of Turtles runs guided, eco-sensitive night tours to view them nesting from its base at Alagadı Beach, just east of Kyrenia's comely harbour. September is a particularly fine time to visit: the crowds have gone but weather and waters are still warm. It's ideal

(L) The Church of the Saviour on Spilled Blood; (R) Spot the sea turtles amid the pebbles

for hiking between ruined Crusader castles in the Kyrenia range or strolling the well-preserved ancient city of Salamis. Don't miss North Nicosia/Lefkoşa, the world's only divided capital. Amble the minaret-speared streets before passing a checkpoint for a weird wander into the bullet-scarred no man's land that separates the island's Turkish north and Greek south.

Trip plan: Flights to Ercan Airport (North Cyprus) route via mainland Turkey. Spend a week mixing beaches, marine life, ruins, castles and traditional villages.

Need to know: Turtle-watching should be booked in advance; tours last from around 8pm until 5.30am.

Other months: Nov-Mar – cool, wettest; Apr-May & Sept-Oct – warm, quieter; Jun-Aug – hottest, busy.

© Kirill Greshnov / Getty Images

SOUTHERN STYRIA AUSTRIA

→ **Why now? Roam a route of wine and wellness.**

Meandering along Austria's southeastern border is a range of verdant hills lined with vines – and meandering through these hills and vineyards is the Southern Styria Wine Road, a 70km (44 mile) route between Ehrenhausen and Leutschach linking top producers of Welschriesling, Gelber Muskateller and Sauvignon Blanc whites. Whether you roam by car, bike or on foot, the joy isn't just in the grapes – wellness vies for your attention, too. As well as a host of spas with saunas, pools, massages

and other therapies, look out for activities utilising the region's natural bounty: wild herbs, apples, grapes, pumpkins and elderberries are all used in spa treatments, while cookery classes share tips for healthy eating. In September, summer rains ease, autumn colours begin to flame and the hills are alive with the sounds of clacking *klapotetz* (wind-powered bird-scarers) and grape-harvest festivals. From this month, too, you can savour Sturm – still-fermenting new wine, delicious with roast chestnuts.

Trip plan: Trains run from regional capital Graz to Ehrenhausen in under 1hr. Though

the Wine Road is relatively short, allow a week to dawdle between wineries, taverns and spas – perhaps hike or bike instead of driving.

Need to know: Fuel up at traditional Buschenschänke, taverns in wineries serving Brettljause, a wooden platter of bread, cheeses and smoked meats, paired with local tipples and fruit juices.

Other months: Dec-Feb – cold; Mar-May – warming, getting wetter; Jun-Aug – warm, wettest; Sep-Nov – cooler, drier, autumn colours.

ARMENIA

→ Why now? Explore the world's oldest Christian country in temperate early autumn.

Armenia does ancient like almost nowhere else. This little-visited crossroads of continents is a landlocked nation packed with churches, monasteries and caravanserais (inns) dating from the 1st century AD, and relics stretching back even further, including the Karahunj (Zorats Karer) standing stones, reputedly dating back some 7000 years. More than that, the dramatic backdrop of the Caucasus, with snow-capped Mt Ararat peering across the Turkish border, matches Armenia's turbulent history. The weather is starting to cool in September, after sweltering high summer (when temperatures can top 40°C/104°F), but it's still warm enough for hiking the hills; this is the driest month, too. From capital Yerevan's chilled café culture to the troglodyte village of Old Khndzoresk and hilltop monasteries such as Geghard, Tatev and Noravank, it's a mesmerising,

diverse land that's not quite like anywhere else. The wine's not bad, either.

Trip plan: Fly to Yerevan and head south to Noravank, Tatev and Karahunj, then work your way north skirting Lake Sevan (stopping to admire the field of Khachkars – engraved cross-stones – at Noratus cemetery) and to explore the forested hills around Dilijan. Many add a visit to Georgia, just to the north.

Need to know: If you've time, fit in a side-trip to the self-proclaimed state of Nagorno-Karabakh (Artsakh), a fascinating enclave of Armenian heritage within Azerbaijan – but check the safety situation before travelling.

Other months: Dec-Feb – winter, very cold; Mar-Jun – spring, pleasant temperatures and wildflowers; Jul-Aug – high summer, very hot; Sep-Nov – autumn, cooler days.

The view of Mt Ararat from the Khor Virap monastery

BOHUSLÄN
COAST SWEDEN

→ **Why now? Think pink along Sweden's seafood-crazy coastline.**
Love shellfish? The world's your oyster on the Bohuslän coast, north of Gothenburg (Göteborg) on Sweden's west coast. This tessellated shoreline, noted for its pink granite rocks, is also known for producing Sweden's finest seafood. September marks the start of lobster season, the perfect time to explore the 8000 or so islands and rocky islets along the coast, sampling the local 'Big Five': langoustines, prawns, mussels, oysters and, of course, those rubicund, big-clawed crustaceans. Join a 'seafood safari' with fishermen from Smögen to catch, cook and consume your own, or – even better – hire a kayak or canoe and paddle among colourful fishing villages such as Gullholmen, Käringön and Fiskebäckskil, stopping off to test-taste the area's welcoming eateries: try Salt och Sill in charming Klädesholmen.

Trip plan: Gothenburg, Sweden's perky second city, is the gateway to the Bohuslän coast, with ample international flights. From there, travel is easiest with your own vehicle, though cycling around local centres is a great idea. Islands are linked to the mainland by bridges or short ferry rides.

Need to know: Don't be alarmed if someone proposes *fika* – Swedes are partial to these regular pauses for coffee and cake.

Other months: Nov-Apr – cold, often snowy; May & Sep-Oct – pleasant, quieter; Jun-Aug – sunny, busiest.

(L) Akvavit shots and fresh langoustine;
(R) The medieval cityscape of Bologna

© Matt Munro / Lonely Planet

BOLOGNA ITALY

→ **Why now? Indulge yourself in one of Italy's tastiest cities.**

This isn't the time or place for dieting. Bologna's nickname, La Grassa ('the fat one'), gives you an idea of what to expect; home of ragù (aka bolognese), this is Italy's bulging belly, where life seems to revolve around food. September – when the weather is still warm enough for outdoor eating – means the start of autumn produce: mushrooms, pumpkins, game and chestnuts. These flavours join an array of other great ingredients gracing the menus of the city's lauded restaurants and down-to-earth trattorias, as well as the market stalls and delis of the Quadrilatero, Bologna's historic gourmet food district. Another Bologna nickname is La Dotta ('the learned one'), a nod to what's reputedly Europe's oldest university; thanks partly to its large student population, the city is awash with lively bars, too. Work off some calories strolling the historic centre via the Piazza Maggiore, Neptune Fountain and the Archaeological Museum, and by climbing the 498 steps of the Torre degli Asinelli or, just southwest of Bologna, ambling through 666 *portici* (arches) to

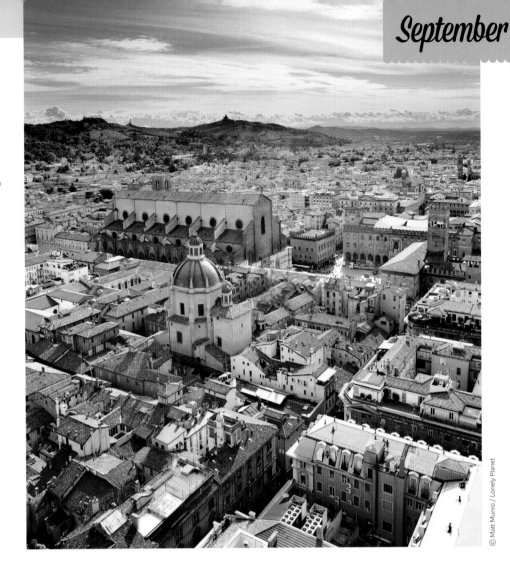

© Matt Munro / Lonely Planet

reach the hilltop sanctuary of the Madonna di San Luca.

Trip plan: After exploring Bologna, consider adding foodie visits to the nearby town of Parma (1hr away by car), which hosts its annual Prosciutto di Parma Festival in early September, and Modena (30min), to visit a maker of the town's most celebrated product: balsamic vinegar.

Need to know: Bologna's airport is 8km (5 miles) northwest of the city.

Other months: Dec-Mar – cool, quiet; Apr-Jun – warm; Jul-Aug – hot, busy; Sept-Nov – warm, harvest, food festivals.

BEYOND BOLOGNA

MARANELLO • 40KM (25 MILES) • Take a turbocharged spin around the birthplace of the legendary Ferrari

RAVENNA • 80KM (50 MILES) • Town famous for its dazzling Early Christian mosaics

PARMA • 100KM (62 MILES) • The city that gave the world Parma ham and Parmesan cheese

CINQUE TERRE • 136KM (85 MILES) • Five medieval villages set amid dramatic coastal scenery

TURQUOISE COAST TURKEY

> **Why now? Sail the Aegean or Med aboard a traditional gület.**

If diving off the wooden deck of a twin-masted sailing boat into the impossible blue of the Mediterranean is your idea of heaven on a hot day, you're not alone. Back in the 1920s, renowned Turkish writer Cevat Şakir Kabaağaçlı took to hiring local sponge-divers' boats to cruise along the so-called Turquoise Coast from Bodrum on what he called 'Blue Voyages'. Over the following decades, increasing numbers of Turkish and foreign tourists recognised the appeal, and today a wide range of vessels – some more traditional, some built specifically for the cruises – ply the waters along Turkey's Aegean and Mediterranean coasts from Bodrum, Marmaris and Fethiye, stopping to visit ancient sites such as Letoön and Patara, and to swim, lounge on a beach, eat and drink. It's a perfect holiday for families, too. By September, temperatures (and tourist numbers) are happily subsiding, but the water's still bathwater-warm and the sites as alluring as ever.

Trip plan: Dalaman is the nearest international airport to both Marmaris and Fethiye; Bodrum has its own airport. Book ahead to ensure a place on a quality boat. International tour operators offer one-week packages and longer trips.

Need to know: Not all gülets use their sails. Check in advance whether your chosen vessel will be powered by wind or a diesel motor.

Other months: Nov-Apr, cool, increased chance of rain; May-Oct – dry and warm.

A gület near the sunken remains of a Lycian town off the coast of Kekova

© Mark Read / Lonely Planet

Age-old statues watch the centuries go by in Veszprém

© Madrugada Verde / Shutterstock

VESZPRÉM HUNGARY

→ **Why now? Explore the recurringly regal 'City of Queens'.**

One of Hungary's oldest towns is also one of its least visited – at least, by foreign tourists. Hungarians know the joys of a break in Veszprém, spread across five hills and dominated by its imposing walled Vár (castle district), and so did royals in days gone by: in the Middle Ages this was the seat of the queen's household, hence its 'City of Queens' nickname. Among the historic treasures in the Vár, accessed via cobbled Óváros tér, are the needle-sharp Fire Lookout Tower, the stately Bishop's Palace and the 13th-century frescoes of the Gizella Chapel. There are plenty of cultural offerings, too: museums and galleries in the castle's House of Arts include the Constructivist and Abstract works of the Vass László Collection. In September,

after the crowds of high summer have dissipated, it's also hard to resist the allure of beach-lounging and watersports at Lake Balaton, just 15km (9 miles) south; or the leafy trails of the Bakony Hills in the Veszprém surrounds.

Trip plan: Veszprém is around 1hr 30min from Budapest by train or bus. Spend a day or two exploring the old city, adding time hiking the Bakony Hills, for splashing in Lake Balaton or taking the thermal waters at the lakeside resort of Balatonfüred.

Need to know: Veszprém celebrates Michaelmas (29 September) with an annual fair in the castle, with dances, handicrafts, food and drink.

Other months: Dec-Feb – often sub-zero; Mar-Apr & Oct-Nov – cool; May-Sep – warm, Lake Balaton swimming.

(A) Lipari old town;
(B) Rocky Salina in
the Aeolians

AEOLIAN ISLANDS
ITALY

Why now? Sail between grumbling volcanoes and cute coastal towns.
You don't want to meet Iddu when he's in a bad mood: he's got quite the temper, roaring and spitting fire when enraged. Iddu, of course, is a volcano – a local nickname for Stromboli, still periodically belching rocks and steam. Climbing his flanks after dark is an electrifying experience, and becoming a little less busy in September. Most visitors aren't just cone rangers: they come to the Aeolian Islands for peaceful coves and warm Mediterranean waters (still around 25°C/75°F), to roam whitewashed villages blooming with oleander and bougainvillea, and to tuck into delicious seafood washed down with orangey, sweet Malvasia wine from Salina. These volcanic islands have different characters: Lipari has a bustling port guarded by a walled fortress, the Castello; Panarea has Bronze Age remains and an exclusive, upmarket clientele; Vulcano has eggy-smelling fumaroles and thermal waters.

Trip plan: The nearest airport is Sicily's Catania a 3hr train ride from Milazzo, the gateway to the Aeolians: from here, you can board a traditional-style caïque to explore the islands by sail, or catch hydrofoils or slower ferries. Allow a week to visit Vulcano, Lipari, Salina, Panarea and Stromboli, longer if you want to add on little Filicudi and Alicudi, or to discover Sicily's historic sites and hike on Etna.

Need to know: Hiking on sulphur-scented Vulcano is relatively unchallenging, but Stromboli can be dangerous – only climb with an authorised guide and adhere to all instructions.

Other months: Nov-Mar – cool, wet, cheaper, ferries more limited; Apr-May – pleasant, often misty; Jun-Aug – hot, dry, busy; Sep-Oct – warm, increased rain and winds.

GALICIA SPAIN

→ **Why now? Hike the perfect pilgrimage past empty beaches.**

The appeal of Spain's verdant northwestern province is summed up in four Cs: coast, culture, cuisine and camino. Galicia's beaches are among Spain's least developed (try dune-backed Playa de la Lanzada or sandy Praia As Catedrais, sprinkled with towering rock formations), and the crowds subside after the summer peak – you'll still enjoy warm, sunny days in September, despite a little more rain. Galician cuisine is exceptional, particularly seafood like *pulpo gallego* (tender Galician octopus), as well as Padrón peppers and the curious breast-shaped queixo de tetilla cheese – and history abounds, not least in capital, Santiago de Compostela. For many, this atmospheric city is the ultimate goal: endpoint of the Camino de Santiago pilgrimage route, which starts in St-Jean Pied de Port across the Pyrenees in France. September is a great time to hike part (or all) of the route; the pilgrim hostels are less crowded so there's a choice of places to bed down, and the days are still long. Stretch your legs, still your spirit and expand your mind (and, possibly, waistline).

Trip plan: Covering 780km (485 miles), the full Camino Frances across northern Spain takes around 30 days to walk. For access to Galicia's north- and west-coast beaches and other towns (Pontevedra, A Coruña), fly to Santiago.

Need to know: Santiago has a range of characterful accommodation. At the end of your camino, consider splurging on a night at the Parador de Santiago, the heritage hotel overlooking the cathedral, built in 1499 – pilgrims are eligible for special rates.

Other months: Nov-Mar – cold, wet, facilities close; Apr-Jun & Sept-Oct – warm, quieter; Jul-Aug – hottest, busiest.

Possibly the world's most beautiful road?

TRANSYLVANIA ROMANIA

→ **Why now? Explore Transylvanian castles via the 'world's best road'.**

Whatever you think of TV car buff Jeremy Clarkson, he knows about driving. So when he proclaimed the Transfăgărăşan Hwy the 'world's best road' on *Top Gear*, petrolheads sat up straight. This lofty route, 90km (56 miles) of jinking bends and high passes, was constructed over four years on the orders of dictatorial former ruler Nicolae Ceauşescu, to provide a cross-mountain military route between the Romanian regions of Transylvania and Wallachia. September's the time to traverse its hairpins: the weather's temperate (snow closes the road between October and June) and autumn colours set hillsides ablaze. Driving north to south, you'll pass the cascades of Bâlea waterfall and climb to mirror-like Lake Bâlea, continuing to the crag-top ruins of Poenari Castle, a key lair of Vlad Ţepeş (aka 'the Impaler', inspiration for Stoker's Dracula), and descending to visit the royal tombs in 16th-century Curtea de Argeş Monastery.

Trip plan: Fly to Bucharest and embark on a loop lasting at least a week to ten days. Head north to Baroque Braşov and nearby Bran Castle, veer northwest to medieval Sighişoara (reputed birthplace of Vlad Ţepeş), then south to Sibiu, from where you can tackle the Transfăgărăşan before returning to Bucharest.

Need to know: The Transfăgărăşan lures keen cyclists – if you're feeling energetic, you can traverse sections tackled by riders in the Tour of Romania, staged in mid-September.

Other months: Nov-Mar – sub-zero, best wildlife-tracking, castles magical in snow; Apr-May & Oct – slightly warmer; Jun-Sep – warm, Transfăgărăşan open.

BURGUNDY
FRANCE

→ **Why now? Plot a pedal-powered grape escape during harvest season.**
Life's pretty red and white in Burgundy – Pinot Noir and Chardonnay, to be precise, the two grape varieties that dominate France's most venerable wine region, where viticultural heritage stretches back centuries to Roman occupation. Explore Burgundy's rolling hills in *vendange* (grape harvest) season, when you'll also enjoy ideal conditions for pedalling Le Tour de Bourgogne (Tour of Burgundy). This cycling circuit comprises some 800km (500 miles) of *voies vertes* (traffic-free greenways), canal towpaths and quiet country lanes linking the region's most alluring attractions: Dijon's medieval core, Beaune's spectacular Hôtel-Dieu des Hospices, the ancient monastic complex of Abbaye de Fontenay, the châteaux of Ancy-le-Franc and Tanlay. If the full circuit is too long, pick a subsection: perhaps part of the flat 240km (149 mile) leg along the Canal de Bourgogne, or the 206km (128 mile) stretch of the Canal du Nivernais between Auxerre and Decize. For a wine-centric section, tackle the Voie des Vignes route between Beaune and Santenay (just 22km/14 miles), or simply pootle off among Burgundy's vine-striped hillsides.

Trip plan: Dijon, Auxerre and Mâcon are the main gateways, all with busy railway stations. Allow two weeks for the full Tour de Bourgogne circuit.

Need to know: Though not part of the Tour of Burgundy, the Grande Traversée du Morvan offers testing mountain-biking among the verdant peaks and valleys of the region's Parc Naturel Régional du Morvan.

Other months: Nov-Mar – cold, wet; Apr-May & Oct – cooler, quieter; Jun-Sep – reliably warm.

(B) A serene scene on the Canal de Nivernais;
(R) A surfer in the waves of the Bristol Channel

222

BRISTOL
ENGLAND

→ **Why now?** Explore the Mild West's artsy, eatsy indoor-outdoor city.

You know the headline acts: Massive Attack, Banksy, Wallace and Gromit, that bloke out of The Office. 'Brizzle' is an artistic ideas incubator, but there's much more to see and do than discover new bands, artists, restaurants, bars and shows. On sunny September days, action stations beckon: SUP around the Floating Harbour past Brunel's magnificent *SS Great Britain* or surf epic breaks at The Wave's inland artificial break. Raining? Check in at the world-class museums and galleries (engaging local history at M Shed, Arnolfini for contemporary arts), or shop the boutiques and one-offs around Christmas Steps and Clifton. And when the sun goes down, the action heats up, with alfresco music at events across the city, and short films screened at Encounters Film Festival. Catch a performance at the gorgeous Old Vic – the oldest continuously operating theatre in the English-speaking world – or cutting-edge Tobacco Factory, head to Stokes Croft for edgy bars, great food and cultural happenings, and hear diverse music just about everywhere.

© Susan Walker / Getty Images

Trip plan: Allow at least two days for the city, scooting around the Floating Harbour and taking in an exhibition or two, an evening performance and some fine food. If time permits, add a day in elegant Georgian Bath, just a 15min train ride away.

Need to know: In a packed calendar of annual events, the Bristol Balloon Fiesta in early August is perhaps the most popular – book accommodation in advance.

Other months: Dec-Mar – cold, dark; Apr-May & Oct-Nov – cooler, wetter, quieter; Jun-Sep – warm, lively.

BEYOND BRISTOL

 BATH • 21KM (13 MILES) • Town with exquisite Roman and Georgian architecture, hipster hang-outs and swish spas

 CHEDDAR GORGE • 32KM (20 MILES) • Enormous ice-age canyon riddled with subterranean caverns

 STONEHENGE • 64KM (40 MILES) • Britain's most iconic archaeological site

 EXMOOR NATIONAL PARK • 112KM (70 MILES) • Wild moorland encompassing coast and countryside

October

WHERE TO GO WHEN

I WANT TO

CHALLENGE MYSELF

TAKE ME OUT FOR...

- **FOOD**
  - COPENHAGEN, DENMARK P241
  - UMBRIA, ITALY P233
- **DRINK**
  - TOKAJ, HUNGARY P243
  - CHAMPAGNE, FRANCE P233

Enjoy Scandi café culture in Copenhagen

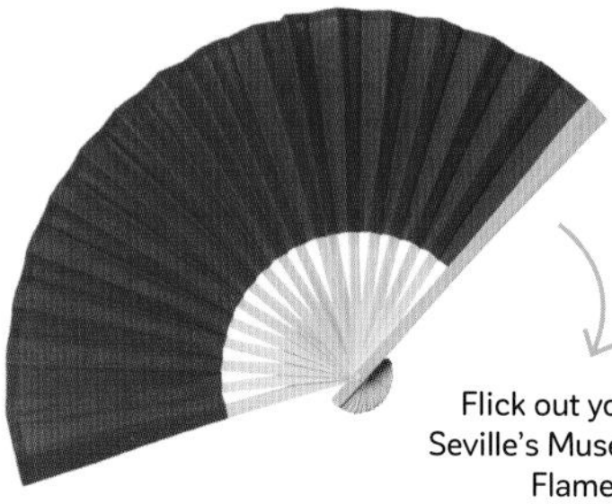

Flick out your fan at Seville's Museo del Baile Flamenco

TAKE ME TO TOWN

- **ART & CULTURE**
  - SPLIT, CROATIA P231
  - SEVILLE, SPAIN P235
- **NIGHT-LIFE & HEDONISM**
  - BELGRADE, SERBIA P230
  - MARSEILLE, FRANCE P247

Soak up still-warm autumn sun in Marseille

RELAX/ INDULGE

Natural spas and family-friendly fun at Slovenia's Lake Bled

DIAL IT DOWN

- **WELLNESS**
  - SLOVENIA P235
- **CHILLING**
  - DODECANESE, GREECE P246
  - SOUTHERN SARDINIA, ITALY P239

Take a beach-hopping tour of the Dodecanese

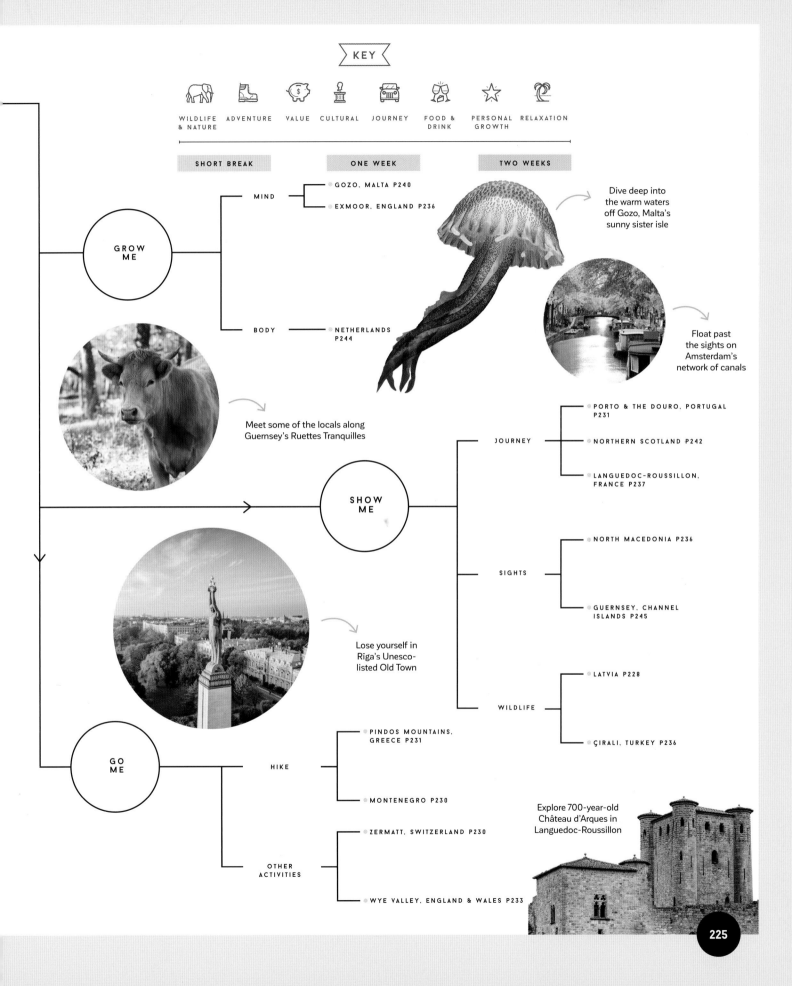

KEY

WILDLIFE & NATURE   ADVENTURE   VALUE   CULTURAL   JOURNEY   FOOD & DRINK   PERSONAL GROWTH   RELAXATION

SHORT BREAK   **ONE WEEK**   **TWO WEEKS**

GROW ME

MIND
- GOZO, MALTA P240
- EXMOOR, ENGLAND P236

BODY
- NETHERLANDS P244

Dive deep into the warm waters off Gozo, Malta's sunny sister isle

Float past the sights on Amsterdam's network of canals

Meet some of the locals along Guernsey's Ruettes Tranquilles

SHOW ME

JOURNEY
- PORTO & THE DOURO, PORTUGAL P231
- NORTHERN SCOTLAND P242
- LANGUEDOC-ROUSSILLON, FRANCE P237

SIGHTS
- NORTH MACEDONIA P236
- GUERNSEY, CHANNEL ISLANDS P245

WILDLIFE
- LATVIA P228
- ÇIRALI, TURKEY P236

Lose yourself in Riga's Unesco-listed Old Town

GO ME

HIKE
- PINDOS MOUNTAINS, GREECE P231
- MONTENEGRO P230

OTHER ACTIVITIES
- ZERMATT, SWITZERLAND P230
- WYE VALLEY, ENGLAND & WALES P233

Explore 700-year-old Château d'Arques in Languedoc-Roussillon

EVENTS
IN OCTOBER

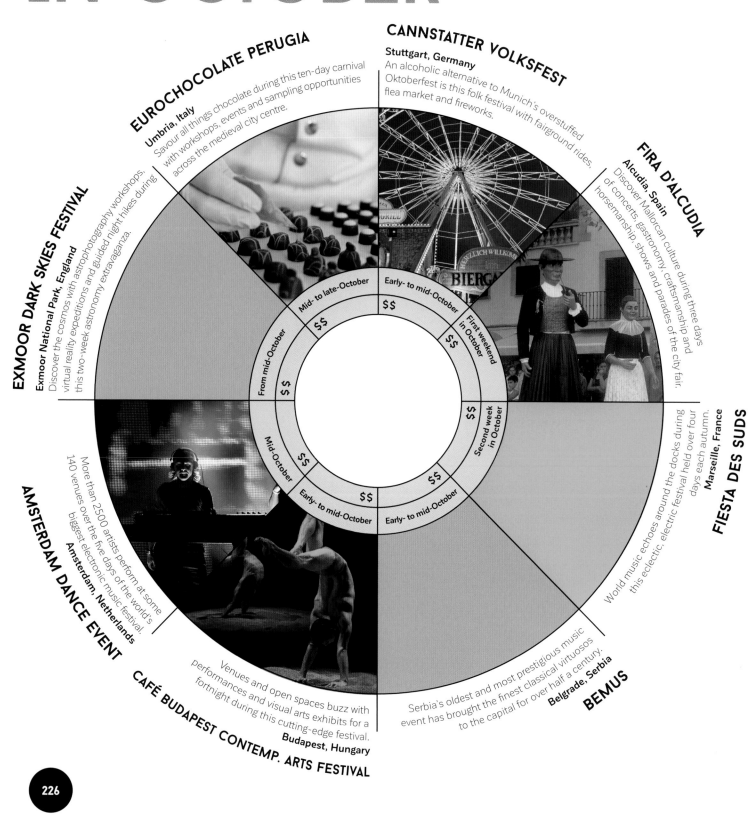

EUROCHOCOLATE PERUGIA

Umbria, Italy
Savour all things chocolate during this ten-day carnival with workshops, events and sampling opportunities across the medieval city centre.

CANNSTATTER VOLKSFEST

Stuttgart, Germany
An alcoholic alternative to Munich's overstuffed Oktoberfest is this folk festival with fairground rides, flea market and fireworks.

EXMOOR DARK SKIES FESTIVAL

Exmoor National Park, England
Discover the cosmos with astrophotography workshops, virtual reality expeditions and guided night hikes during this two-week astronomy extravaganza.

FIRA D'ALCUDIA

Alcudia, Spain
Discover Mallorcan culture during three days of concerts, gastronomy, craftsmanship and horsemanship, shows and parades of the city fair.

FIESTA DES SUDS

Marseille, France
World music echoes around the docks during this eclectic, electric festival held over four days each autumn.

AMSTERDAM DANCE EVENT

Amsterdam, Netherlands
More than 2500 artists perform at some 140 venues over the five days of the world's biggest electronic music festival.

CAFÉ BUDAPEST CONTEMP. ARTS FESTIVAL

Budapest, Hungary
Venues and open spaces buzz with performances and visual arts exhibits for a fortnight during this cutting-edge festival.

BEMUS

Belgrade, Serbia
Serbia's oldest and most prestigious music event has brought the finest classical virtuosos to the capital for over half a century.

Mid- to late-October — $$
Early- to mid-October — $$
First weekend in October — $$
From mid-October — $$
Second week in October — $$
Mid-October — $$
Early- to mid-October — $$
Early- to mid-October — $$

VERY FAMILY FRIENDLY

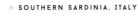

SOUTHERN SARDINIA, ITALY

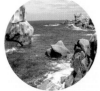

GUERNSEY, CHANNEL ISLANDS

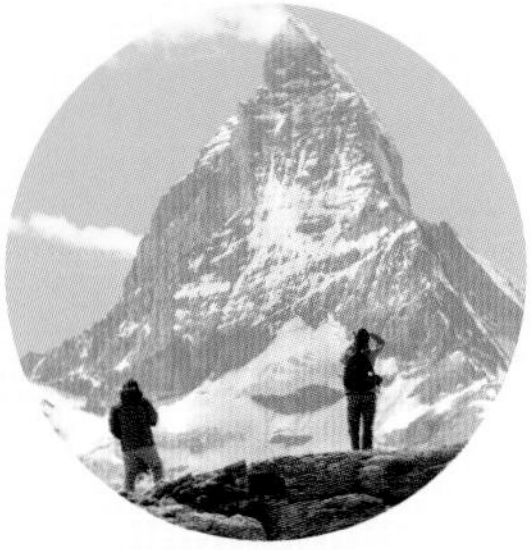

Sardinia's stunning southern coastline is largely crowd-free in October

Seek out Umbria's lesser-known gems, from Gubbio to Assisi

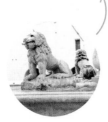

UMBRIA, ITALY

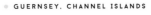

WYE VALLEY, ENGLAND/WALES

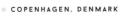

ZERMATT, SWITZERLAND

EXMOOR, ENGLAND

Meander below the Matterhorn before the big snows set in

Tour the bars and restaurants of Split's spectacular Diocletian's Palace

ÇIRALI, TURKEY

DODECANESE, GREECE

SPLIT, CROATIA

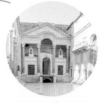

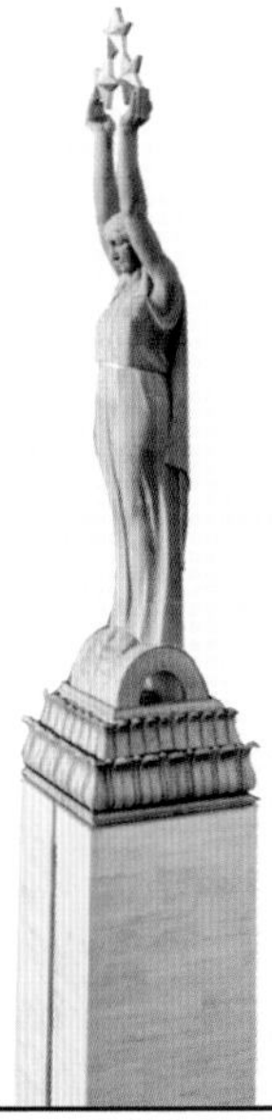

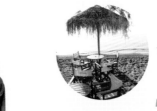

NETHERLANDS

Enjoy some last-minute beach time in the balmy Dodecanese

October in Rīga means Old Town charm and a buzzing Restaurant Week

LATVIA

MONTENEGRO

LANGUEDOC-ROUSSILLON, FRANCE

SLOVENIA

EXPENSIVE
JT WORTH IT

GOOD VALUE

GOZO, MALTA

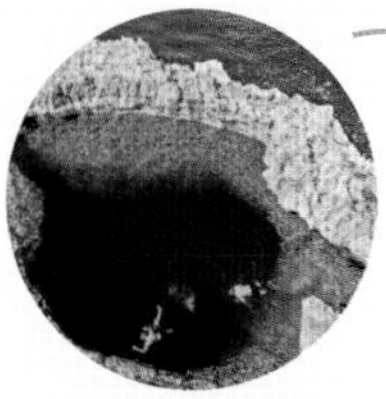

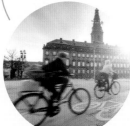

Gozo's limpid waters are perfect for diving and snorkelling – even in October

NORTHERN SCOTLAND

Hop on a bike to sample Copenhangen's New Nordic nosh

COPENHAGEN, DENMARK

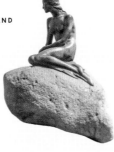

MARSEILLE, FRANCE

Pop some bottles in the home of Champagne

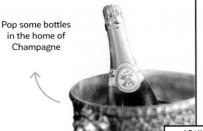

CHAMPAGNE, FRANCE

SEVILLE, SPAIN

See Seville's Real Alcázar without the summer crowds

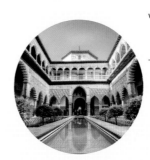

NORTH MACEDONIA

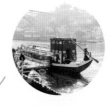

PORTO & DOURO, PORTUGAL

Take a boat trip along the Douro as the riverside vineyards turn autumnal gold

PINDOS MOUNTAINS, GREECE

TOKAJ, HUNGARY

Zip around Belgrade's Old Town aboard the iconic Tram 2

BELGRADE, SERBIA

LEAVE THE KIDS AT HOME

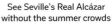

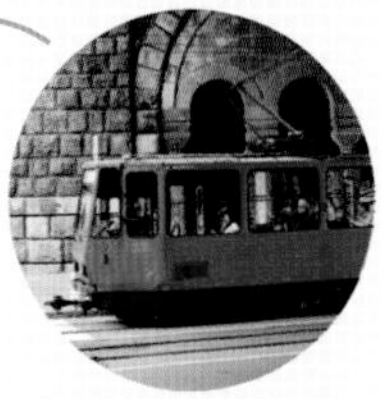

LATVIA

→ Why now? Embrace the autumnal outdoors.

Quick! The weather isn't yet baltic in the Baltics – October is a last-gasp chance to wander Latvia's wonderful wild places in warmish weather: the days are still a reasonable length, winter winds haven't started to blow and autumn colours are at their best. Head to Gauja National Park, where you can admire medieval castles and misty waterways set against a sea of yellow-gold trees; there are hiking trails aplenty, from short leaf-peeping strolls to long routes along the Gauja River. Alternatively, head to Ķemeri National Park to strap on a pair of bog shoes and tramp through this unique environment; in autumn, the birding is brilliant. Both parks are within easy reach of capital Rīga, whose handsome Unesco-listed Old Town is worth exploring at any time; and in mid-October, Rīga Restaurant Week sees a range of restaurants offer creative multi-course menus for low prices, usually utilising the seasonal bounty of mushrooms, berries, fish and game.

Trip plan: Trains from Rīga to Ķemeri take around 50min; the park is 3km (2 miles) from Ķemeri station. The Rīga–Valka rail line goes through Gauja National Park, stopping at access points such as Sigulda (1hr 15min) and Cēsis (2hr). Fares are cheap.

Need to know: Trips on the Gauja River, by boat or canoe, are possible whenever the water is ice-free.

Other months: Nov-Mar – cold, snowy; Apr-Jun – warming (cruise season May-Sep); Jul-Aug – hot, busy; Sep-Oct – mild, quiet.

Golden hues in
Gauja National Park

MONTENEGRO

→ **Why now? Hit the heights.**
Don't pack away the hiking boots just yet – thanks to their southerly latitude, the mountains of Montenegro remain open and awesome for ambling until November. And what mountains: the highest are within Unesco-listed Durmitor National Park, a cluster of dark, serrated summits (of which 48 soar to over 2000m/6065ft) scattered with pine forest, lush meadows and glittering glacial lakes, and home to all manner of wildlife, from birds to bears; there's also good walking amid the peaks and primeval forests of Biogradska Gora National Park. Coastal high-points such as mounts Orjen and Lovćen offer sweeping views of the Adriatic – mix hikes here with dips in the azure sea, which remains beautifully inviting throughout October, and is wonderfully crowd-free. A week's walking could include an ascent of Rumija, on the south coast; hiking in the Kučka Krajina range near capital Podgorica; admiring the autumn colours around Mt Bjelasica in Biogradska Gora; and varied trekking in Durmitor, with the chance to stand atop Bobotov Kuk (2523m/8277ft), the country's highest peak.

Trip plan: The most convenient airports are at Podgorica and Dubrovnik (Croatia). Ferries sail from Bari in Italy to Bar in Montenegro once-weekly in October (more frequently in summer).

Need to know: Bobotov Kuk is a strenuous but not technical climb, though the final step to the peak requires you to use fixed cables.

Other months: Nov-Mar – cold, skiing possible; Apr-Jun & Sep-Oct – warm, less crowded; Jul-Aug – hot, busy.

BELGRADE
SERBIA

→ **Why now? Make merry, Balkan style.**
Forget New York: the Serbian capital is the city that never sleeps. Every night is a Friday here – an attitude to fun-seeking that springs from the 1990s Balkan War, when locals turned to banging tunes and hedonism to keep spirits up. October sees the shift from summer to winter clubbing season, with the action moving from the *splavovi* (floating clubs on Belgrade's rivers) to the city centre hotspots. There are venues that cater to all tastes – house, techno, turbo-folk, R'n'B, pop, rock, trance, jazz... If none of those suit, October also brings BEMUS, the Belgrade Music Festival. Founded in 1969, it's Serbia's oldest music event, celebrating the best in classical performance. There's plenty to do during the day, too: amble around Belgrade Fortress, the Stari Grad (Old Town) and along the banks of the Danube. Admire art at the National Museum, explore the regenerated Savamala creative district and get a history fix at the Museum of Yugoslavia and Marshal Tito's Mausoleum.

Trip plan: Allow two or three days. The centre is walkable, but don't miss a ride on Tram 2, the iconic, Czechoslovakian-built streetcar that makes an 8km (5 mile) loop around the Old Town, via some of the most interesting neighbourhoods.

Need to know: Look out for *kafanas*, traditional taverns or coffee-houses serving food and drinks from early to late.

Other months: Nov-Mar – cold; Apr-Jun – warm (club season starts Jun); Jul-Aug – hot, festivals; Sep-Oct – cooler, lively.

ZERMATT
SWITZERLAND

→ **Why now? Hike late, ski early.**
October is a bit in-betweeny in the chocolate-box alpine resort of Zermatt, but there's still potential for having all manner of adventures. For a start, it's possible to ski here year-round: Zermatt's Matterhorn Glacier Paradise operates Europe's highest lifts and has 21km (13 miles) of pistes, 14 training runs (spot world-class athletes preparing for winter), a snow park for freestylers, a snow machine that can pump out powder even in warmer weather and eye-watering views of one of the continent's most iconic mountains. Ski from mid-October to the end of November to take advantage of Ski Test, when the pistes are quiet and well-prepared, and you can try out the latest models of skis. Another October advantage is that it's still possible to hit some of Zermatt's 400km (250 miles) of hiking trails. Pick a forest route, such as the Larch Trail, to amble amid yellow-gold trees. Or join a guided, crampon-strapped hike up the Breithorn (trips run to mid-October).

Trip plan: Be flexible and realistic – you might luck out with a dump of autumn snow or be stuck with poor conditions. Zermatt is beautiful either way. Combine it with neighbouring Saas Fee, which offers a ten-month ski season (slopes open from mid-July).

Need to know: In the summer/autumn ski season, slopes are only open until midday.

Other months: Dec-Apr – snow, skiing; May & Nov – shoulder months, conditions not ideal; Jun & Oct – outdoor potential; Jul-Sep – warm, good hiking.

© kaband / Shutterstock

PINDOS MOUNTAINS
GREECE

→ **Why now? Follow bear tracks through the forests.**

Most people come to Greece for its beaches, not its bears. But the mainland's mountainous north has a sizeable population of the big, brown ursines, as well as wolves, deer, golden eagles and other species. Icing on the cake: in October (which can still hit 20°C/68°F), the beech forests will be both brimful of edible mushrooms and blazing with autumn colours. A pretty place to start is Nymfaio, a postcard-perfect village of neat stone houses and cobbled lanes, on the slopes of Mt Vitsi. Just outside is a network of hiking trails as well as the Arcturos sanctuary, which looks after rescued and orphaned bears – close-ups guaranteed. For the possibility of wilder encounters, head further west into the Northern Pindos National Park. Join park rangers on hikes into the bear-roamed valleys, looking for paw-prints and scat, taking in the fresh air and spectacular summits. Stop, too, at historic Kastoria – home to many old mansions and a Byzantine Museum – and its namesake lake, a great spot for birding: look out for pygmy cormorants, white pelicans and night herons.

Trip plan: The Pindos region is a 2hr drive west of Thessaloniki. For the best experience, head out with a wildlife guide.

Need to know: Choose bear-watching activities with care: 'baiting' to attract bears is not considered a responsible practice.

Other months: Dec-Feb – cold, potentially snowy; Mar-May – warm, quiet; Jun-Aug – hot; Sep-Nov – cooling, good for hiking/bear activity.

PORTO & THE DOURO
PORTUGAL

→ **Why now? Float down the Douro at its most intoxicating.**

The Douro Valley is the godfather of wine production. Listed by Unesco for its uniquely beautiful viticultural landscape, it's one of the world's oldest wine regions: the Portuguese Denominação de Origem Controlada (DOC) system was authenticating the provenance of the wine here 200 years before the French began their AOC. Take a boat trip down the Douro River and you're assured a fine drop, as well as unrolling pastoral scenes – particularly delightful in autumn, when the sun is still warm and the grape-heavy vines turn golden. You'll cruise past traditional *rabelos* (cargo boats), tiny towns plastered with azulejo tiles and numerous *quintas* (wineries) where you can stop for delicious tastings. Tumbling down hills at the Douro's mouth is historic Porto, first settled by the Romans and now Portugal's second-largest city. The old, narrow-streeted Ribeira district is a must, as is Vila Nova de Gaia on the opposite bank, brimful of port-wine houses.

Trip plan: Spend a few days in Porto, before a week-long river cruise to Vega de Terron, on the Spanish border and 2hr by road from Salamanca.

Need to know: The Douro's best sites are not right by the river; road transfers from boat docks are required. A train also runs down the valley.

Other months: Nov-Mar – cool, barren; Apr-Jun – warming, blossom; Jul-Aug – hottest; Sep-Oct – warm, harvest.

SPLIT CROATIA

→ **Why now? Dip into Dalmatian life.**

Come autumn, Croatia's tourist season is almost spent. But Split – the country's second-largest city – remains lively year-round, and is the perfect place to sink into local life while the temperatures are still balmy (average highs of 20°C/68°F) but crowds smaller and accommodation significantly cheaper. The big draw here is Diocletian's Palace, one of the most impressive Roman monuments on the planet, a vast set of ruins now filled with shops and bars. Also worth a look are the medieval sculptures in the Cathedral of St Domnius, the Meštrović Gallery (a seaside villa packed with impressive art) and, just outside, Klis Fortress, a medieval bastion brought to world attention as a Game of Thrones location. When you're cultured out, hit the coast. Split sits between dramatic mountains and the sparkling Adriatic, still warm enough for paddling in October. Head to the bar above Bačvice beach to join locals sipping coffee.

Trip plan: Spend a few days in Split, then consider a Dalmatian coast sailing trip. The season runs to the end of October (winds are moderate, the weather still warm), and yachts can be chartered from Split, with prices lower than in peak summer.

Need to know: Though services are reduced from October to May, Jadrolinija ferries still run from Split to destinations such as Hvar Island and Dubrovnik.

Other months: Nov-Mar – cool; Apr-May & Sept-Oct – warm, shoulder months, fewer ferries; Jun-Aug – hottest, busiest.

(A) Wye Valley's Tintern Abbey, founded by Cistercian monks in 1131 CE;
(L) Assisi, overlooked by the Rocca Maggiore fortress;
(R) Fizz chilling in Arlaux

WYE VALLEY
ENGLAND & WALES

→ **Why now? Forage amid fall colours.**
The River Wye – which straddles the border between England and Wales, winding lazily from the Cambrian Mountains to the Severn Estuary – is wonderful in autumn. Flanked by protected woodland, the valley blazes in October, providing picturesque scenes of red-gold trees reflected in the mist-hung waterway. Particularly good autumn-colour spots include the Cyril Hart Arboretum (home to over 200 species of trees), the limestone slopes around the Gloucestershire village of St Briavels, the surrounds of medieval Tintern Abbey and atop the old hill fort at Symonds Yat, where the river bends majestically between forested cliffs. Possibilities for crisp, leaf-kicking walks are plentiful, too – from short riverside strolls to sections of Offa's Dyke National Trail, which follows the ancient earthwork. And if it's a little chilly, all the better. This area is well replete with cosy pubs for post-walk warm-ups, ranging from traditional and log-fired to Michelin-starred fancy. Or find your own supper on a foraging walk, hunting for mushrooms, nuts, sloes and berries.
Trip plan: There are train stations at Lydney, Chepstow and Gloucester. The easiest way to explore is by car.
Need to know: The Forest Food Showcase at Speech House (first Sunday in October) celebrates everything edible, with cookery demos, foraging sessions, stalls, crafts and music.
Other months: Nov-Feb – cold, quiet; Mar-May – spring flowers; Jun-Aug – warm, good canoeing; Sep-Oct – cooler, fruitful.

UMBRIA ITALY

→ **Why now? Gorge on a glut of local goodies.**
Autumn fruitfulness doesn't come more marvellously mellow than in Umbria – Tuscany's lower-key neighbour is beautiful and bounteous in this season. Its rolling hills and walled hill towns like Orvieto, Amelia and Narni are bathed in golden light and free of crowds. Its tables are overspilling with incredible local produce: lentils, beans and mushrooms, chestnuts and black truffles, bright saffron and *olio novello* (new oil) from the olive harvest. A range of *cacciagione* (game) dishes fill the menus, including *cinghiale* (wild boar) and *fagiano* (pheasant). And the grape harvest is in full swing, making it a fascinating time to follow the wine routes of the Strada del Sagrantino, visiting vineyards and medieval villages for tastings. And then there's the chocolate. Every October, Umbria's provincial capital Perugia hosts Eurochocolate, a celebration of all things cocoa – not least Baci, the choc-hazelnut confection that hails from the city. The 10-day festival sees events, workshops and sampling opportunities across the well-preserved medieval centre.
Trip plan: Perugia has a small airport; other nearby access points include Florence and Pisa. Car hire is almost essential for exploring. Include visits to Spoleto, with a Roman amphitheatre and fine frescoed churches, medieval Gubbio and Assisi (of St Francis fame).
Need to know: For a lovely rural base, stay in an *agriturismo*, self-catering accommodation within working farms.
Other months: Nov-Mar – chilly; Apr-Jun & Sep-Oct – pleasant weather, uncrowded; Jul-Aug – hot, busy.

CHAMPAGNE
FRANCE

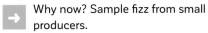

→ **Why now? Sample fizz from small producers.**
For the most effervescent autumn, head to Champagne. This sparkling, vine-covered region of northern France is fabulous in October, especially if you want to combine tastings of the big-name brands – the Dom Pérignons, Krugs and Taittingers – with visits to more boutique wineries. By now, the busy harvest should be over, so independent winemakers running tiny-but-interesting vineyards will have time to show you around. Plus the colours are on the turn, leaving the fields glowing glorious shades of rust and gold. Champagne has five main regions. Historic Reims, with its magnificent cathedral and basilica, is the best base for the Montagne de Reims, where you can sample full-bodied champagnes. Head to Épernay, nestled into vine-clad hillsides to the south, to walk the Avenue de Champagne and explore both the Vallée de la Marne and the chardonnay-focused Côte des Blancs. Stay in Troyes, the ancient capital of the Champagne-Ardennes, to access the lesser-known vineyards of the Aube and Côte de Sézanne.
Trip plan: Reims is 45min by train from Paris; Épernay is a little further south. Driving between wineries isn't ideal; book taxis or join a guided tour.
Need to know: Eat a good breakfast – tastings can start as early as 10am and you might find yourself drinking all day. Cellar tours and dégustations should be booked in advance.
Other months: Nov-Mar – cooler, rainier; Apr-Oct – warm, driest, grape season.

Seville's flair spans Plaza de Espana, tapas bars, Casa de Pilatos and flamenco... *olé!*

SEVILLE SPAIN

→ **Why now? See the sites in the sunshine.**

Autumn? Pah! Seville hits temperatures in October that many a European city would be proud of in summertime – think highs of 26°C (79°F). Indeed, this is a beautiful month, ideal for sightseeing: the steaming heat has abated but it's still warm enough for T-shirt walks along the Guadalquivir River and evenings spent hopping between alfresco tapas bars. There's much to see, starting with the Real Alcázar, the astonishing royal palace complex, with its Mudéjar architecture and glorious gardens. Then there's the world's largest Gothic cathedral with its commanding belltower, the exquisitely tiled mansion of Casa de Pilatos and some excellent museums. Indeed, don't miss the Museo del Baile Flamenco, where you can learn all about this passionate, flamboyant dance and catch a live performance.

Trip plan: Walking is the best way of getting around. Hop between districts: Barrio de Santa Cruz is Seville's medieval, maze-like Jewish quarter; riverside El Arenal, to the west, has lots of buzzing bars; El Centro is a hub of narrow shop-lined streets and squares; to the north is Alameda de Hércules, one of the coolest districts, packed with chic bars and cafés; atmospheric Triana is the home of flamenco and ceramic tiles.

Need to know: Consider getting around by bike. Seville's Sevici bike-sharing scheme is extensive, and the city has around 130km (80 miles) of well-marked bike lanes.

Other months: Nov-Feb – mild; Mar-May & Oct – warm, pleasant; Jun-Sep – baking hot.

Slovenia's woodlands promise fabulous forest-bathing

SLOVENIA

→ **Why now? Unwind amid autumnal nature.**

Just being in Slovenia is like a mega-dose of *shinrin-yoku* – the country is 60% tree-covered so you always feel like you're forest bathing. In autumn, that means bathing in astonishing fall colours, not least around fairytale Lake Bled. But wellness seekers will find more specific ways to soothe their souls: Slovenia has many natural spas that can ease ailments and warm you up should the October weather turn wintry. They're great value, too. The magnesium-rich spring at Rogaška Slatina, in Slovenia's Savinja region, has been healing the sick since it was discovered in the 17th century. People still come to sip the metallic waters and check in for detoxes; the surrounding hills are splendid for hikes and bikes, too.

Nearby Terme Olimia is also therapeutic, and good for both families (there's a fun water park) and hipsters, who might prefer the adults-only spa with its swim-up bar and 'Naked Nights'. Alternatively, try the town of Laško. The healing waters here have been known of since Roman times; it's also home to the country's oldest brewery – combine a brewery tour and a beer-butter massage.

Trip plan: From Ljubljana, it's 1hr 30min by car or 3hr 30min by train to Rogaška, and 1hr by car or 1hr 30min by train to Laško.

Need to know: It's usual to remove all clothing before entering a sauna; always sit on a towel.

Other months: Nov-Mar – cold, snowy; Apr-Jun – warm, wildflowers; Jul-Aug – hottest; Sep-Oct – still balmy.

© mpaniti / Shutterstock

ÇIRALI TURKEY

➜ Why now? Chill out with baby turtles.

There are few better October beach spots than serene Çıralı. This sweeping bay, within the Olympos Bey Mountains Coast National Park, still sees air temperatures reach 26°C (79°F) and the water around 25°C (77°F), while the trees flanking the sand start to put on a colourful turn. Even better, because this is a protected area, development is minimal and the wildlife profuse: almost 865 plant species, 72 species of birds and a range of mammals such as bobcat, caracal and wolf. It's also an important nesting spot for loggerhead turtles – from May these endangered sea creatures haul up onto the sand-pebble beach to lay their eggs; in September and October, the eggs hatch. Wake at dawn and you may be lucky enough to watch the little'uns dash for the sea. It's also a good crowd-free month for hiking bits of the 500km-long (311 mile) Lycian Way, which passes through Çıralı; for visiting the ancient site of Olympos, with its Roman theatre and Ottoman fortifications; and to marvel at the extraordinary Chimaera, where natural flames lick out of the rocks.

Trip plan: Antalya airport is 100km (62 miles) away. Buses run to Çıralı Junction.

Need to know: Turtle nests are protected by cages: do not disturb. Volunteers monitor nests; for a chance to see baby turtles, arrange to visit with a warden.

Other months: Nov-Mar – cool, facilities close; Apr-Jun – warm, quiet; Jul-Aug – hot, busiest; Sep-Oct – turtle hatchlings, warm.

EXMOOR ENGLAND

➜ Why now? Gaze at glittering skies.

The hilly moorlands of Exmoor are out of this world in autumn. Not only is the sea warm, the heather and gorse in full flower and the trees fiery, but the skies above are heavenly. In 2011 Exmoor was designated Europe's first International Dark Sky Reserve, on account of its low levels of light pollution and its commitment to keeping it that way. Across the national park, and especially within the core dark sky zone – including Holdstone Hill, County Gate and Wimbleball Lake – the stargazing is some of the best in the country; on clear, moonless nights the glow of the Milky Way is easily seen. Even better, autumn brings the annual Exmoor Dark Skies Festival (mid-October to early November), an astronomy extravaganza that encompasses planetarium sessions and virtual reality expeditions into the solar system, astrophotography workshops and guided night hikes. You can even head out on a dusk safari – as well as spotting constellations, you might hear red deer stags bellowing for a mate. As well as coinciding with rutting season, the festival overlaps with the peak of the Orionid meteor shower (20–23 October), so keep a look out for shooting stars.

Trip plan: Buses cross Exmoor between Dulverton and Minehead, and run along the coast between Minehead and Barnstaple.

Need to know: Free Dark Skies Pocket Guides are available at national park centres. Telescopes can be hired.

Other months: Nov-Feb – cold, dark; Mar-May – spring flowers (walking festival May); Jun-Aug – warmest; Sep-Oct – deer rut, autumn colours.

NORTH MACEDONIA

➜ Why now? Make a cool cultural meander.

North Macedonia remains one of Europe's least-known destinations. But this complex, compact and culturally rich nation is gradually starting to catch on. With the mercury still hitting 18°C (64°F), October offers comfortable touring weather without the other tourists. Start in capital Skopje, with its Ottoman-era Čaršija bazaar and castle, and mixed-up Modernist and faux-Neoclassical architecture. Then take a scenic drive through Mavrovo National Park, stopping at the fine Sveti Jovan Bigorski monastery. Further south lies alluring Ohrid, a historic little town on the shores of an eponymous lake, its shores home to frescoed churches, the Sveti Naum Monastery and fascinating Museum of Water – Bay of Bones, which tells of the prehistoric peoples that used to live here on pile houses, floating on the water. Continue to Pelister National Park, for autumnal walks and village visits to try local food. Nearby is Bitola, where you can visit the Roman ruins of Heraclea Lyncestis and a heap of lively cafés. Wind back towards Skopje via the picturesque Tikveš region, where wine has been produced since the 4th century BCE. The main towns are Kavadarci and Negotino, good bases for tours and tasting.

Trip plan: Allow a week to 10 days. Hire a car or join a tour – public transport is limited and rural regions are well worth visiting.

Need to know: ATMs are not widespread; withdraw local currency in Skopje.

Other months: Nov-Mar – cold, wettest; Apr-May & Oct – warm, quieter; Jun-Sep – hottest, busiest.

LANGUEDOC-ROUSSILLON
FRANCE

→ **Why now? Tour castles without the crowds.**

Stretching from the Mediterranean up into the Pyrenees, the Languedoc's Aude region is a glorious mix of forests, lagoons, peaks, caves, hilltop châteaux and chilling history: it was here, in the Middle Ages, that the heretical Cathars hid (ultimately unsuccessfully) from Papal persecution. It's a macabre tale, but a fascinating reason for a road trip, bike or hike through 'Cathar Country' – especially good in shoulder-season October, when fellow tourists are fewer on the ground. Between Med-side Port-la-Nouvelle and the upland town of Foix, discover a landscape littered with limestone outcrops, vineyard-cloaked slopes, high pastures, plunging ravines and former Cathar castles: the peak-perched ruins of Quéribus, cliffside Roquefixade, the prow-like fort of Peyrepertuse and mighty Montségur where, in 1244, the Cathars made their last stand. Visiting the fairytale turrets of Carcassonne is also a must.

Trip plan: There are airports in Nîmes, Montpellier, Carcassonne, Perpignan and Béziers; Nîmes is 3hr by train from Paris. If you're hiking, allow around 12 days to cover the 250km-long (155 mile) Sentier Cathare ('Cathar Way'). With a car, allow around five days for exploring.

Need to know: Languedoc-Roussillon is the world's biggest wine region. In the Aude, look out for Blanquette de Limoux, the oldest fizz, made here since the 16th century.

Other months: Nov-Mar – coldest, some businesses closed; Apr-Jun & Sep-Oct – warm, quiet, good for walking; Jul-Aug – hot, crowded.

© Karnavalfoto / Shutterstock

The medieval citadel of Carcassonne glows in the evening sunshine

SOUTHERN SARDINIA
ITALY

→ **Why now? Find warm seas and lower prices.**

As Sardinia gears down for the season, so can you. A visit in October – when highs still bust 20°C (68°F) and the Med is still balmy – will be good value and relaxing. The south is reliably a few degrees hotter than the north, and where capital Cagliari provides a lively contrast to the semi-hibernating beach spots. Medieval Cagliari deserves a few days – visit the churches, the Pisan towers and the archaeology museum, and loll in pretty piazzas. Then hit the coast road east, calling at an unfurling of tourist-free coves: Villasimius, Costa Rei and Ogliastra are beauts. Veer inland to the lush Monte dei Sette Fratelli, a wild haven of strawberry trees, holm oaks, wild boar and hiking trails. Further north is the Nuraghe Su Naraxi at Barumini, among the largest of the island's prehistoric nuraghic stone villages. Then head west of Cagliari, visiting the Phoenician ruins of Nora before flopping onto the dazzling beaches of the Costa del Sud. Chia is best for windsurfing, birdwatching and walks along the dunes.

Trip plan: Fly into Cagliari. Hire a car and allow a week to explore.

Need to know: Detour north of Barumini to the mountain village of Aritzo for the Sagra delle Castagne (Chestnut Fair; late October), where locals go nuts for nuts.

Other months: Nov-Mar – cool, wetter; Apr & Sep-Oct – lower prices; May-Jun – clear, warm; Jul-Aug – hot, busy.

Sardinia's spectacular coastline

Snorkelling in Gozo's
gin-clear Blue Hole

GOZO MALTA

→ **Why now? Dive into still-warm waters.**

Welcome to the best dive site in Europe: the waters off Malta – and specifically its smaller sister isles of Gozo and Comino – offer the finest sub-aqua action on the continent. The diving is diverse and colourful, with everything from shallow reef dives to deep and technical dropoffs; Gozo alone has 80-plus dive sites. The visibility is generally brilliant – from 20m to 70m (65–230ft) – and the underwater topography is dramatic, with an array of caves, chimneys, swim-throughs, walls and wrecks to explore. The sea is still warm in October (around 23°C/73°F), and the winter storms haven't yet set in. Beginners can come to learn – there are plenty of dive schools – and those with experience can try challenging dives such as Booming Cave, Double Arch and a range of wrecks, many dating from WWI and WWII. The most popular site is the Blue Hole, a dramatic shore-dive that plunges down a deep, sheltered rock tube. The marine life is abundant, from schools of glittery barracuda to grouper, cuttlefish and conger eel, spider crabs, Mediterranean parrot fish and giant bioluminescent pyrosomes.

Trip plan: One-day sample dives are open to everyone (aged ten-plus). Allow four days to compete the PADI Open Water scuba course. Explore on land too, from Gozo's traditional villages to its 5500-year-old Ġgantija Temples.

Need to know: The Malta–Gozo ferry takes 25min.

Other months: Dec-Apr – cool; May-Jun & Oct-Nov – warm, uncrowded; Jun-Sept – hot, dry, busiest.

COPENHAGEN
DENMARK

Edvard Eriksen's *Little Mermaid*, in pole position on Copenhagen's harbour

© Pocholo Calapre / Shutterstock

→ Why now? Tuck in to Nordic nosh.

Achingly cool Copenhagen is the epicentre of both Scandi design chic and the New Nordic food revolution – nowhere is food more creative, sustainable or seasonal than here, whether it be in Michelin-starred kitchens or farm-shop cafés. October, with its autumnal bounty, is a great month to eat local. So, as well as wandering the fall-fiery gardens at Rosenborg Castle, viewing Viking treasures at the Nationalmuseet and enjoying amazing art at nearby Louisiana, be sure to eat well. Start at Torvehallerne KBH, Copenhagen's mouthwatering food market, which serves up everything from organic porridge to splendid *smørrebrød* (open sandwiches). Make reservations well in advance for hot culinary tickets such as Noma, Kadeau or Gemyse. Then take a foodie walking tour to find out where locals get their coffee and pastries, and graze Nørrebro, the city's most multicultural neighbourhood, where hip boutiques sidle up next to craft-beer bars and cool cafés. Finish at Kødbyen, the city's Meatpacking District, to drink like a Dane.

Trip plan: Copenhagen's hotels tend to be cheaper between summer and Christmas. Allow three days here, including sightseeing at Slotsholmen island and Nyhavn harbour, and spooky fun at Tivoli: the city's 19th-century amusement park is in Halloween mode from mid-October.

Need to know: The second Friday in October is Kulturnatten ('Culture Night'), when many museums and galleries open late and run events.

Other months: Nov-Mar – chilly (Christmas markets Dec); Apr-May & Oct – quieter, cooler; Jun-Sep – sunny, lively, busy.

BEYOND COPENHAGEN

 MALMÖ · 40KM (25 MILES) · Øresund Strait bridge provides a speedy link to Sweden

 ELSINORE · 45KM (28 MILES) · Setting of *Hamlet*, home of Kronborg Castle

OSLO · 510KM (317 MILES) · Reach the Norwegian capital with a 17-hour ferry trip via scenic fjords

KANGERLUSSUAQ · 3219KM (2200 MILES) · Greenland, Denmark's distant territory, is a five-hour flight

NORTHERN SCOTLAND

→ Why now? Drive empty, ravishing roads.

The NC500 is Britain's answer to the Pacific Coast Hwy, an 830km (516 mile) drive that hugs the Scottish seashore, skirting the North Highlands via Ullapool, John O'Groats, Dornoch and Inverness. Autumn is a magnificent time to make a road trip here: with summer crowds (and midges) gone, the roads are quieter, while the Highlands are blushing with autumn colours and reverberating to the sounds of the deer rut. Shorter days and dark skies also heighten your chances of spotting the 'mirrie dancers', as locals call the Northern Lights. Pick stops based on your interests. En route lie dramatic glens and mountains (consider bagging one of the Munros), frothing sea caves, surf beaches and white-sand bays. There are Iron Age standing stones, heritage centres and romantic castles (both intact and in ruins), plus legend-laced lochs and rivers great for rafting and fishing. Cosy lodges, roaring fires and whisky tastings will keep you warm whatever the weather.

Trip plan: Inverness, easily accessible by plane and train, is the best starting point. Take a week to 10 days to make the loop. Roads can be winding, so allow more time than you think you'll need.

Need to know: Many attractions close over winter. Some shut at the end of September, but many – Dunrobin Castle, Strathnaver Museum – are open until the end of October. Check before visiting.

Other months: Nov-Mar – snow possible, quiet; Apr-May – spring wildlife; Jun-Aug – busiest, long days, warm, whale-watching; Sep-Oct – quieter, rutting deer, autumn colours.

A stag surveys the Scottish Highlands' Knoydart Peninsula

TOKAJ HUNGARY

→ **Why now? Sample the wine of kings.**

The wine region of Tokaj, in Hungary's northeastern corner, is officially glorious: in 2002, Unesco added it to its list of World Heritage Cultural Historic Landscapes, one of only a few viticultural areas to achieve this acclaim. A breathtaking mélange of extinct volcanoes, forested slopes, small villages, characterful wine cellars and sweeping vineyards, it both looks and tastes great. Sweet, golden wines have been produced here since the 15th century from bone-dry Aszú grapes; there's also a fine line in appley dry whites. Try a few on a wine tour – route maps are available in Tokaj's tourist office. Picturesque Tarcal, just west, is the gateway to the wider wine region, from where you can visit various *pincék* (private cellars). For sheer size, head to the vast, 600-year-old Rákóczi Cellar; Patricius is one of Hungary's most beautiful vineyards, where first-class wines come with magnificent views. At Tokaj-Oremus in Tolcsva you can taste super-sweet and syrupy Eszencia, made from Aszú grapes and said to have magical properties. Once you've drunk your fill, try other available activities: there's fine cycling, hiking, horse riding and boating to be done amid these intoxicating hills.

Trip plan: Trains to Tokaj run from Budapest (3hr 45min) and Debrecen (2hr).

Need to know: When wine tasting in Tokaj, move from dry to sweet grapes: from Furmint to Szamorodni to Aszú.

Other months: Nov-Mar – cold, quiet; Apr-Jun & Sept-Oct – warm, wine festivals; Jul-Aug – hot.

243

NETHERLANDS

→ **Why now? Be at one with your barge.**

There's something soothing about pootling along at swan speed aboard a Dutch canal boat, watching a world of waving grass, windmills, lakes, dunes and historic cities glide by. It's a little like a moving meditation. And the waterways will be even more meditative in autumn, as the weather cools and the end of the cruising season draws near – it lasts roughly from April to the end of October, and outside this period some canals are closed entirely. The Netherlands has a network of waterways covering some 5000km (3100 miles), so where to boat? For the most relaxing trip, try northerly Friesland. Life runs at a slower pace in this rural region of lakes and traditional villages. Boats can be hired in Hindeloopen, on Lake IJssel, and sailed via spots such as seaside Workum, the medieval town of Elburg, bustling Huizen, charming Utrecht and matchless Amsterdam – there's no better way to experience the capital than by floating along the mighty canal ring circling its handsome centre.

Trip plan: Allow seven to 10 days. Load a bike onto your barge for the option to cycle waterside trails and explore deeper into the countryside.

Need to know: Lock-keepers operate all locks and raisable bridges. Keep loose change to hand – there's a small charge to pass through locks.

Other months: Nov-Mar – cold, some canals closed; Apr-May & Sep-Oct – canals open, warm, quieter, cheaper; Jun-Aug – hottest, busiest.

GUERNSEY CHANNEL ISLANDS

→ Why now? Feast on food and history.

Closer to France but distinctively British, charming little Guernsey – second-biggest of the Channel Islands – offers an unexpectedly powerful historic punch. Its location has put Guernsey right in the middle of some big moments: the shoreline not only boasts a range of tempting coves, bays and beaches, but also the 800-year-old fortress of Castle Cornet and a scattering of Martello towers, built to keep Napoleon away and subsequently repurposed by the Germans, who occupied the island during WWII. October is a lovely month for sightseeing, with Guernsey's narrow roads and even narrower Ruettes Tranquilles (country lanes) free of crowds and the temperatures mild for the British Isles (average highs of 17°C/63°F). Wander the Regency-grand streets of St Peter Port, visit handsome Hauteville House (designed by Victor Hugo) and visit the Neolithic Dehus Dolmen, which dates to around 3500 BCE. Also make time to eat – local produce is good, especially during Tennerfest (October to early November), when restaurants across the island offer great-value menus.

Trip plan: Guernsey has an airport. There are also year-round ferry services from the UK, Jersey and France. The best way to get around is by bus or bike.

Need to know: UK sterling can be used on Guernsey, but Channel Islands pounds are not accepted in the UK.

Other months: Dec-Mar – coolest; Apr-Jun – warm; Jul-Aug – hottest; Sep-Nov – mild, cooler evenings.

DODECANESE
GREECE

> **Why now? Enjoy last-minute island-hopping.**

Autumn is awesome in the Dodecanese: this is when you'll find the southeasterly island group offering largely good weather, lower prices, warm seas and fewer visitors, as well as plenty of facilities that haven't yet shut for winter. The diverse Dodecanese is good for hopping, with good inter-island ferry connections (including to nearby Turkey) and a network of small boats serving smaller islands, so you can mix up towns, beaches, historic sites and offbeat hangouts – this archipelago has both islands that see hordes of holidaymakers and specks that see barely a soul. Rhodes is the biggie, but interesting islands on which to linger include spectacular pebble-beached Symi (an easy trip from Rhodes); tiny, eco-pioneering Tilos, which strives to run on renewable energy; authentic Karpathos, which has managed to retain its strong traditional culture in the face of tourism (don't miss Olymbos, the hilltop village that's like a living folklore museum); and little-known Astypalea, with its quiet coves, castle-topped capital and vine-filled valleys.

Trip plan: Start in Rhodes, which has an airport. Alternatively, the ferry from Athens to Rhodes takes 16–18hrs. Hop northwards from Rhodes towards Patmos, the northernmost of the Dodecanese. Allow at least a week, two if you can.

Need to know: The easiest way to reach Karpathos, southwest of Rhodes, is a 1hr flight from Athens; the ferry to Karpathos from Rhodes takes 4–5hrs.

Other months: Nov-Apr – cool, closed up, fewer ferries; May-Jun & Sept-Oct – sunny, warm, services open; Jul-Aug – hot, busy.

(A) Karpathos retains a strong local culture; (B) Monastery of St John, Patmos

© Matt Munro / Lonely Planet

MARSEILLE
FRANCE

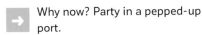

→ **Why now? Party in a pepped-up port.**

History-soaked Marseille – first founded by the Greeks in around 600 BCE – has long had a somewhat unsavoury reputation. But since the instigation of the largest regeneration project in southern Europe, not to mention its 2013 tenure as European Capital of Culture, the multicultural Provençal port has cleaned up its image. The once dilapidated Docks des Suds area is now home to the flagship Museum of European and Mediterranean Civilisations, designer shops and buzzing concert venues, while abandoned tobacco factories have become culture and craft-beer hubs. Soak up the old-new ambience in still-balmy October (average highs 21°C/70°F). Take the ferry to fortress island Château d'If (immortalised in the Dumas' *Count of Monte Cristo*). Wander the bohemian quarter, with its cool bars, street art, galleries and restaurants, and seek out the nightspots around the Vieux Port and Rue Sainte or Rue d'Endoume. Or time your visit for the 4-day Fiesta des Suds (early or mid-October), when an eclectic mix of world music blasts from the docks.

Marseille's picturesque Le Panier district

Trip plan: Allow two days in the city, then visit the ravishing cliffs and bays of the Parc National des Calanques (off-limits in high summer due to fire risks); excursions by boat and kayak are possible.

Need to know: Most Marseille museums close on Mondays.
Other months: Dec-Mar – mild, quiet; Apr-Jun – warm; Jul-Aug – hottest, busiest; Sep-Nov – still warm, cooler evenings.

BEYOND MARSEILLE

 **AIX-EN-PROVENCE · 30KM (18 MILES) ·** A pocket of Parisian chic deep in Provence

 ST-TROPEZ · 100KM (62 MILES) · Sizzling jetset favourite

 GRASSE · 131KM (81 MILES) · Town that has been synonymous with perfumery for centuries

 SARDINIA · 468KM (290 MILES) · A ferry connects Marseille with Sardinia's beaches and outdoor adventures

© Matt Munro / Lonely Planet

November

WHERE TO GO WHEN

CHALLENGE MYSELF

I WANT TO

TAKE ME OUT FOR...

FOOD
- PIEDMONT, ITALY P257
- TOULOUSE, FRANCE P271

DRINK
- HIGHLANDS, SCOTLAND P263

Warm up with a foodie foray around Toulouse

November is one of the quietest times to see Florence's Galleria dell'Academia and Michelangelo's *David*

TAKE ME TO TOWN

ART & CULTURE
- ATHENS, GREECE P265
- FLORENCE, ITALY P259

NIGHT-LIFE & HEDONISM
- ROTTERDAM, NETHERLANDS P254
- CORK CITY, IRELAND P255

Take an architecture tour of Rotterdam

RELAX/ INDULGE

Explore Malta's honey-hued towns and cities

DIAL IT DOWN

WELLNESS — WESTERN TURKEY P261

CHILLING
- TENERIFE, CANARY ISLANDS P270
- MALTA P267

Have Pamukkale's summer-packed terraces to yourself in winter

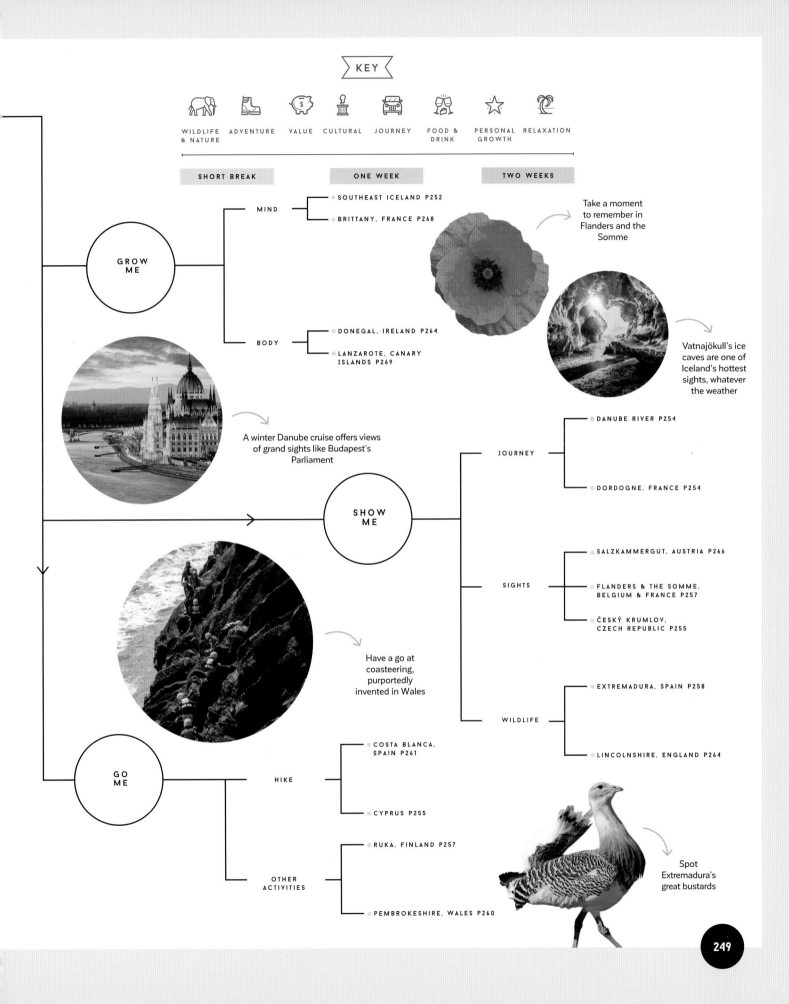

WILDLIFE & NATURE ADVENTURE VALUE CULTURAL JOURNEY FOOD & DRINK PERSONAL GROWTH RELAXATION

SHORT BREAK   ONE WEEK   TWO WEEKS

GROW ME

MIND
- SOUTHEAST ICELAND P252
- BRITTANY, FRANCE P268

BODY
- DONEGAL, IRELAND P264
- LANZAROTE, CANARY ISLANDS P269

Take a moment to remember in Flanders and the Somme

Vatnajökull's ice caves are one of Iceland's hottest sights, whatever the weather

A winter Danube cruise offers views of grand sights like Budapest's Parliament

SHOW ME

JOURNEY
- DANUBE RIVER P254
- DORDOGNE, FRANCE P254

SIGHTS
- SALZKAMMERGUT, AUSTRIA P266
- FLANDERS & THE SOMME, BELGIUM & FRANCE P257
- ČESKÝ KRUMLOV, CZECH REPUBLIC P255

WILDLIFE
- EXTREMADURA, SPAIN P258
- LINCOLNSHIRE, ENGLAND P264

Have a go at coasteering, purportedly invented in Wales

GO ME

HIKE
- COSTA BLANCA, SPAIN P261
- CYPRUS P255

OTHER ACTIVITIES
- RUKA, FINLAND P257
- PEMBROKESHIRE, WALES P260

Spot Extremadura's great bustards

249

EVENTS
IN NOVEMBER

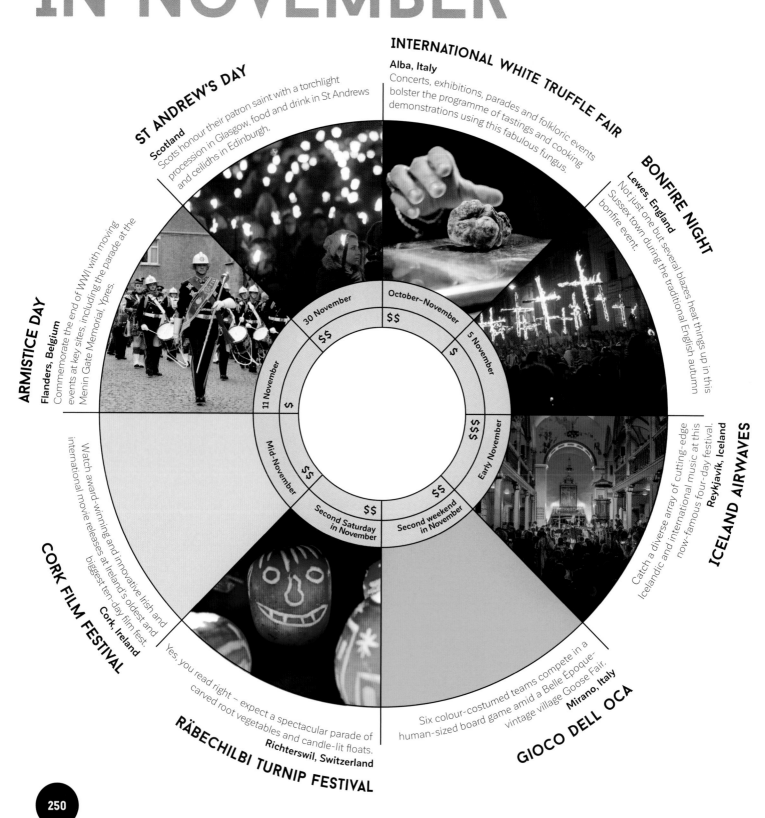

ST ANDREW'S DAY
Scotland
Scots honour their patron saint with a torchlight procession in Glasgow, food and drink in St Andrews and ceilidhs in Edinburgh.

INTERNATIONAL WHITE TRUFFLE FAIR
Alba, Italy
Concerts, exhibitions, parades and folkloric events bolster the programme of tastings and cooking demonstrations using this fabulous fungus.

BONFIRE NIGHT
Lewes, England
Not just one but several blazes heat things up in this Sussex town during the traditional English autumn bonfire event.

ARMISTICE DAY
Flanders, Belgium
Commemorate the end of WWI with moving events at key sites, including the parade at the Menin Gate Memorial, Ypres.

ICELAND AIRWAVES
Reykjavík, Iceland
Catch a diverse array of cutting-edge Icelandic and international music at this now-famous four-day festival.

CORK FILM FESTIVAL
Cork, Ireland
Watch award-winning and innovative Irish and international movie releases at Ireland's oldest and biggest ten-day film fest.

RÄBECHILBI TURNIP FESTIVAL
Richterswil, Switzerland
Yes, you read right – expect a spectacular parade of carved root vegetables and candle-lit floats.

GIOCO DELL OCA
Mirano, Italy
Six colour-costumed teams compete in a human-sized board game amid a Belle Époque-vintage village Goose Fair.

Inner wheel labels:
- 30 November — $$
- October–November — $$
- 5 November — $
- 11 November — $
- Early November — $$$
- Mid-November — $$
- Second Saturday in November — $$
- Second weekend in November — $$

VERY FAMILY FRIENDLY

EXPENSIVE BUT WORTH IT

GOOD VALUE

LEAVE THE KIDS AT HOME

Head to Lapland's Ruka for early winter snowfall

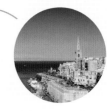

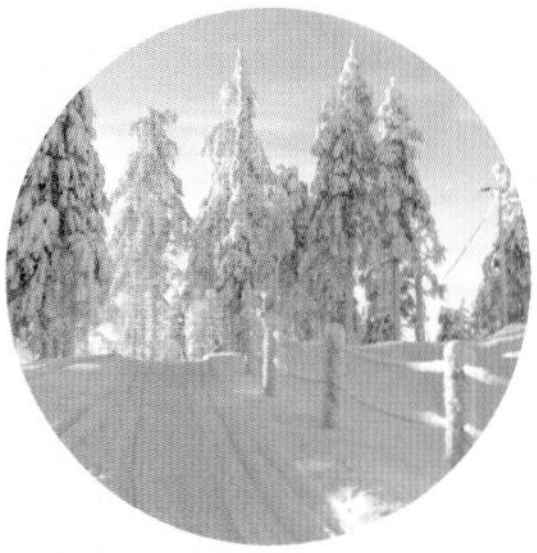

- RUKA, FINLAND
- PEMBROKESHIRE, WALES
- LINCOLNSHIRE, ENGLAND

As temperatures dip, Hallstatt cranks up its wintry charm

- SALZKAMMERGUT, AUSTRIA

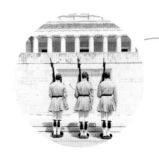

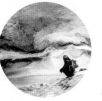

Vatnajökull glacier produces awesome icy formations each winter

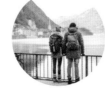

- SOUTHEAST ICELAND
- BRITTANY, FRANCE

- TENERIFE, SPAIN
- MALTA

Malta's pint-sized capital can be comfortably explored on foot

- CYPRUS

Beat the summer crowds and see Athens as it settles into winter

- WESTERN TURKEY
- ATHENS, GREECE
- ROTTERDAM, NETHERLANDS

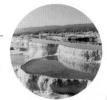

Take a winter warmer in the ancient outdoor pools at Pammukkale, Turkey

- TOULOUSE, FRANCE

Tuck in to some fortifying comfort food in Toulouse

- FLORENCE, ITALY

Cruise down the 'blue' Danube

- CORK CITY, IRELAND

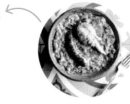

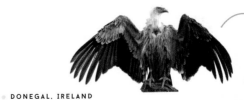

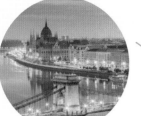

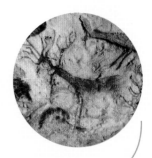

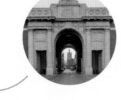

- FLANDERS, BELGIUM

The Menin Gate is one of Flanders' many moving WWI memorials

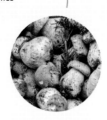

- HIGHLANDS, SCOTLAND
- DANUBE RIVER

- DORDOGNE, FRANCE
- LANZAROTE, SPAIN

November is prime time to see eagles cruising the Extremadura skies

- ČESKÝ KRUMLOV, CZECH REPUBLIC
- DONEGAL, IRELAND
- EXTREMADURA, SPAIN
- COSTA BLANCA, SPAIN
- PIEDMONT, ITALY

Find mushrooms in Piedmond, from perfect porcini to truffles

Step back to prehistory in the Dordogne's Lascaux caves

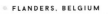

SOUTHEAST ICELAND

🐘 🥾 ☆

→ **Why now? Enter a world of ice.**
Iceland is not short of epic scenery.
It has huffing volcanoes, glaciers as big as countries, thunderous waterfalls, spewing geysers and all manner of weird rocks and steaming fissures. But from November to March it is also has something else: natural ice caves. When the temperature drops and conditions are deemed safe, tours start running to seek out these sparkling caverns – some remain year after year, while new ones are regularly created, carved out by the spring-summer meltwater. Vatnajökull, Europe's largest glacier, is a hot spot for spectacular ice formations. The huge, vivid-turquoise Crystal Cave, near Jökulsárlón glacier lagoon, has been around for a while and is easy to reach; others may require an exhilarating crampon-strapped hike before you get to clamber inside. As well as Vatnajökull, other ice-cave areas include Langjökull and Mýrdalsjökull.

Trip plan: Ice caves and glaciers must not be explored without a knowledgeable local guide. Join a two- or three-day guided tour of southeast Iceland that combines glacier adventures with classic sites such as the black-sand beach at Vík, Seljalandsfoss waterfall and Eyjafjallajökull volcano. Spend a night in Reykjavík and visit the Perlan, which has an ice-cave exhibition. Keep a look out for the Northern Lights, too.

Need to know: The super-cool four-day Iceland Airwaves music festival is held in Reykjavík in early November.

Other months: Oct-Mar – cold, dark, aurora sightings more likely; Apr-May & Sep – warmer; Jun-Aug – warmest, busiest, long days.

Inside an ice cave at the spectacular Vatnajökull, Europe's largest glacier

DANUBE RIVER

→ **Why now?** Cruise serene waters through quieter cities.

The continent-cutting Danube may not be Europe's longest river, but it's arguably the most significant, passing through a string of venerable capitals (Vienna, Budapest, Bratislava, Belgrade) and allowing the transport of goods from the North Sea to the Black Sea. Cruising it in November is a good choice: water levels are generally stable, the fares are cheaper, and the ports are less crowded and beginning to look festive – in many cities, Christmas markets, with their warming glühwein and hot sausages, open from the middle of this month. You can escape the chill in the museums and palaces you pass en route. Be sure to bring warm layers so you can stand on deck to see scenic stretches such as the Danube Bend (near the Hungarian city of Visegrád), Austria's castle-strewn Wachau Valley and the Iron Gate Gorge.

Trip plan: Cruises range from seven to 16 days, though three-night tasters are also possible. A typical week-long cruise on the Upper and Middle Danube might run from Nuremberg to Budapest via ports such as Passau in Germany and Vienna in Austria.

Need to know: Lower Danube cruises are also possible. These usually start in Budapest and sail through Croatia, Serbia and Bulgaria to the Black Sea in Romania.

Other months: Jan-Mar – no/few cruises; Apr-May – warmer, floods may affect sailings; Jun-Aug – hot, busy, low water levels; Sep-Nov – cooler, cheaper, reliable water; Dec – Christmas markets.

ROTTERDAM
NETHERLANDS

→ **Why now?** Embrace the city of innovation.

After being decimated by bombs during WWII, riverside Rotterdam – the largest port in Europe – made the decision to rebuild looking forwards not back. The result? A modern city of innovative architecture, known as 'Manhattan on the Maas', ideal for a New York-ish weekend without the transatlantic flight. Rotterdam has no weather extremes; November is as good a time as any to explore its art scene and café culture. Start with a guided architecture tour to view the highlights, from the Modernist Van Nelle Fabriek building to Rem Koolhaas's 2013 De Rotterdam, a 'vertical city' of three interconnected towers (incorporating a cocktail bar). Another must-see is the Markthal, an enormous arch of an indoor market with a fruit-and-veg-painted ceiling and stalls selling top produce. Foodies should also find the Fenix Food Factory, an old shipping warehouse turned market that's packed to its beams with local-roast coffee, stroopwafels and craft beer. For more beer and a lively night out, head to Witte de Withstraat, the main bar street.

Trip plan: Allow three days. Buy an OV Chipkaart travel card to save money on the city's trams, metros, buses and waterbuses.

Need to know: Don't miss the masterpieces by Bosch, Brueghel, Rubens and Rembrandt at the Museum Boijmans van Beuningen.

Other months: Oct-Mar – cold, quiet; Apr-May & Sep – warm, uncrowded; Jun-Aug – warmest, busiest, most festivals.

DORDOGNE
FRANCE

→ **Why now?** Tour a ravishing region on empty roads.

This historically rich region of southwest France, centred on a leafy river that zigzags amid hill towns and entrancing châteaux, is perennially popular. Which is why an off-season November visit has its pluses. While the weather might be hit-and-miss, the roads – horribly bunged-up in summer – will be traffic free, enabling an easier road-trip between the sites. Hire a car and plot a route. While some attractions close for winter, most of the chateaux – such as rock-top Castelnaud and well-preserved Beynac – stay open, as do the incredible rock art sites of Lascaux and Font-de-Gaume. Good restaurants in bigger towns keep serving too. The foodie hub of Sarlat is a must. The markets here, brimful of local goodies such as mushrooms, walnuts and duck conserves, run year-round. Also pay a visit to the Écomusée de la Truffe in Sorges, where it's possible to taste truffles at any time, and watch a truffle-hunting demo during the harvest season (which starts in December).

Trip plan: The Dordogne's capital is Périgueux, but the best access airport is Bergerac.

Need to know: Some accommodation closes for winter; hotels that remain open often slash prices. If hiring a gîte, check that heating is included.

Other months: Nov-Mar – cold, truffles; Apr-Jun – warm, quieter; Jul-Aug – hot, busy; Sep-Oct – mild, harvest.

CORK CITY
IRELAND

→ Why now? Raise a glass to the movies.

Ireland's second city has heaps of history and a fine location, set on an island in the River Lee. But, honestly, most come for the craic. Cork is liberal, cosmopolitan and comfortable in its own skin, with a sizeable student population that keeps things lively and dynamic. But it also has a healthy respect for older ways, as evidenced by the thriving traditional music scene: gigs are held at theatres, clubs and bars citywide. Wander the compact centre of narrow lanes and you won't go far before hearing tunes flooding out of many a door. The food scene is one of the country's best too, thanks to some excellent local produce – beef, seafood, dairy. Graze your way around the English Market, which has been officially trading since 1788; look out for unusual specialities such as *drisheen* (blood sausage), buttered eggs and *battlebord* (dried salted fish). November could give you any weather, but you won't mind if you're holed up in a pub, tapping your toes to a band. This month also sees the Cork Film Festival – Ireland's largest movie fest – take over town for ten days, with an eclectic programme of local, national and international cinema.

Trip plan: Cork Airport is 8km (5 miles) south of the city. Dublin is 3hr away by bus.

Need to know: Don't order Guinness; locally brewed Murphy's and Beamish are the stouts of choice here.

Other months: Dec-Feb – wet, bracing; Mar-May & Sep-Nov – relatively mild, quiet; Jun-Aug – warm, busy, long days.

CYPRUS

→ Why now? Seek sun, surf and sites.

Southerly Cyprus clings to summer longer than most of Europe, which makes savouring warm days – potentially 20°C/68°F – possible even in November. Plus the crowds are gone and the prices are lower; it's ideal as long as you're not after wild nights out – Cyprus in November is more about exploring. Start in year-round-lively Nicosia (Lefkosia), with its historic centre, art galleries and museums, buzzy café scene and divisive Green Line (cross the no man's land to visit both the Greek south and Turkish north sides). Next, head for the mountains: the Troödos will be cloaked in late-autumn colour and cool for hiking – the hills are riddled with trails. Here you'll also find fine frescoed churches and monasteries, and traditional villages with atmospheric tavernas serving local wines. Then set a course for the coast: perhaps Pissouri Bay near Lemesos for wild wintry surf; the sands near the clifftop ruins of ancient Kourion; or kayaking along the rocky headland of Cape Greco National Park. Consider adding a visit to the salt lakes at either Akrotiri or Larnaka, where flamingoes might be spotted from November to spring.

Trip plan: Larnaka is the main airport. The easiest way to get around is to hire a car. Allow one week to explore the island.

Need to know: If you want to explore both the Greek and Turkish sides, it is best to hire separate cars on either side of the border.

Other months: Nov-Mar – mild, quiet; Apr-May & Sep-Oct – warm; Jun-Aug – hot.

ČESKÝ KRUMLOV
CZECH REPUBLIC

→ Why now? Start to feel festive away from the masses.

Prague is so pretty – but so overrun, virtually all year round. November, when winter officially begins, is one of the quietest months for exploring the capital's comely cobbles. But if you'd still prefer an alternative, consider Český Krumlov instead. Deep in the Bohemian countryside, this Unesco-listed town is a sort of mini Prague, with its Old Town square, Gothic, Renaissance and Baroque architecture and dominating 13th-century castle, all clustered alongside the Vltava River. It sees its fair share of tourists too, though many are deterred by November's chill. The cold can be spectacular, though, with frost rimming the window panes and perhaps snow cloaking the surrounding hills. The best view is from the top of the Castle Tower, which remains open even after the castle interior has closed for the season. Spend time wandering the old centre, stopping in cosy taverns for Czech staples: goulash, steamy dumplings, hearty soups – all perfect for fuelling freezing days. If time allows, combine Český Krumlov with nearby České Budějovice, which has a huge main square and a maze of narrow alleys; it's also the home of Budvar beer, and brewery tours run year-round.

Trip plan: Český Krumlov is 180km (112 miles), or a 3hr bus ride, south of Prague.

Need to know: Ice hockey is one of the most popular sports in the Czech Republic. The season runs from September to March – catch a game at the Budvar Arena in České Budějovice.

Other months: Nov-Mar – cold, quieter; Apr-May & Sep-Oct – warm; Jun-Aug – hottest, busiest.

(A) Cross-country skiing in Ruka; (L) Tyne Cot Cemetery in Flanders; (R) Piedmont pleasures

© The Tourist / Alamy Stock Photo

256

BLU DI MOCCA

RUKA
FINLAND

→ **Why now? Get an early piste fix.**
Do you really, really need to ski? Then get thee to Ruka! On account of its extremely northerly location and usually reliable dumps of snow, this Finnish resort boasts the longest non-glacier ski season in Europe. Its slopes usually open in October (though are best from November onwards) and don't close until May – bank on around 220 days of skiing and snowboarding action per year. Cute, car-free Ruka village is an especially good base for families: it has the biggest beginner area in the country and a good network of lifts, and offers a range of other activities from sleigh rides, tobogganing and husky-sledding to ice-fishing snowmobiling, river-floating (yes, even in winter) and traditional Finnish saunas. The downhill slopes, 35 in all, are never that crowded; most of them are floodlit, so you can ski during the 24hr darkness of polar night. When you're done, tuck into a Lappish wild-food dinner and après-ski cocktails – though Ruka is small, there are a few places to party. Keep an eye out for the Aurora Borealis too.

Trip plan: Book a week in a cosy log cabin in Ruka, mixing downhill skiing with excellent cross-country trails and other snowy activities.

Need to know: Ruka is 800km (497 miles) from Helsinki. It is a 1hr flight from Helsinki to Kuusamo Airport, some 25km (15 miles) from Ruka.

Other months: Oct-Apr – winter, snow activities, aurora; May – thawing; Jun-Sep – warmer, Midnight Sun.

FLANDERS & THE SOMME BELGIUM & FRANCE

→ **Why now? Be humbled by the horrors of war.**
We're not going to lie, the weather in western Belgium is far from lovely in November: on average it's the wettest month, and temperatures hover around 7°C (44°F). But that seems quite fitting for a sobering tour of the region's WWI battlefields, the grim climate aping the grimness of what happened here, just over a century ago. Start in the town of Ypres, home to a handsome market square and the In Flanders Fields museum. A Last Post ceremony is held at the Menin Gate Memorial at 8pm daily, or consider timing your trip for Armistice Day (11 November) when a commemoration parade and other events are also held. From Ypres, explore the wider area: Tyne Cot, the world's largest Commonwealth military cemetery; the Sanctuary Wood (Hill 62) Museum, home to some of the last surviving WWI trenches; and the Messines Ridge British cemetery. Over the French border, visiting the sites of the Somme, the bloodiest of battles, is especially moving – get context at the Historial de la Grande Guerre museum, view the crater-pocked grasslands at Newfoundland Park and pay your respects at the Thiepval Memorial and Museum.

Trip plan: Ypres is 1hr 35min by train from Lille, around 2hr from Brussels. The nearest station to Thiépval is Albert, 1hr from Lille. Allow three days.

Need to know: Some sites are difficult to reach by public transport. Consider an organised tour – a knowledgeable guide will add to the experience.

Other months: Nov-Mar – cold, damp; Apr-May & Sep-Oct – warmer, quiet; Jun-Aug – hottest, busiest.

PIEDMONT
ITALY

→ **Why now? Feast on fantastic fungi.**
Bordered by France and Switzerland, the northwestern region of Piedmont sits beneath the Alps and a little apart from the rest of Italy. It doesn't draw the same crowds as Tuscany, yet has similarly sylvan countryside, hilltop towns and foodie-ness. This is especially true in autumn when Piedmont's wild mushrooms abound, its red Nebbiolo grapes are harvested and its white truffles – the world's most expensive fungi – come into season. Other specialities include excellent beef, arborio rice and traditional cheeses (try crumbly Castelmagno). Head to Alba, a cluster of medieval towers and Baroque and Renaissance palaces. It has splendid restaurants and, throughout October and November, a truffle festival, celebrating the region's 'white gold' – chefs create dishes using truffles and there are musical events and historical re-enactments. Also venture into the forested Langhe hills to join a truffle hunt and visit tiny cantinas to taste the region's fine Barbaresco and Barolo wines.

Trip plan: Fly to Turin, visit the city's museums and churches, then head to rural Piedmont. A hire car is handy for reaching smaller villages. Allow a week.

Need to know: Alba is 65km (40 miles) south of Turin; trains make the journey in 1hr 45min, buses in 2hr.

Other months: Dec-Mar – cold, skiing; Apr-May – warming, quiet; Jun-Aug – very hot; Sep-Nov – warm, harvest.

EXTREMADURA SPAIN

A griffon vulture; just one of Extremadura's feathered friends

➜ **Why now? Spot a bevy of birds.**

With its scorching climes, Extremadura is only for the brave in high summer. It's far better to wait till autumn to venture to this wild and remote inland swathe of Spain, when the mercury won't rise above 15°C (59°F) and the birds are back in numbers. Extremadura is one of the country's most important over-wintering sites – species such as great bustards, black-bellied sandgrouse and large numbers of lapwings, larks, golden plovers and other small birds flock to the rolling plains of the Spanish steppe. November is also a great month for catching glimpses of golden, Spanish imperial and Bonelli's eagles, commonly seen flying over the rocky valleys that cut through the gilded autumnal woodland. One of the greatest spectacles is the dense concentration of common cranes – the largest in Europe – which gather on the irrigated farmland. The region's reservoirs also harbour huge numbers of ducks, while Monfragüe Natural Park is the place to look for griffon vultures as well as other raptors – and otters.

Trip plan: The best access airports are Madrid, Lisbon and Seville. The historic town of Trujillo, birthplace of conquistador Francisco Pizarro, makes a good base; allow time to explore its medieval castle.

Need to know: During the spring and summer, you can do some urban birding in Trujillo: the main square is home to breeding swifts, white storks and one of Europe's highest concentrations of lesser kestrels.

Other months: Nov-Feb – cool, overwintering birds; Mar-May – warm, migrant/breeding birds; Jun-Aug – very hot, dry; Sep-Oct – cooler, migrant birds.

Brunelleschi's magnificent cathedral dome can't fail to impress

FLORENCE
ITALY

→ **Why now? Appreciate art without others.**

Weigh it up: would you rather see Florence soaked in sunshine but jam-packed with tourists? Or risk a bit of weather to have the sites more to yourself? November is one of the least-busy months in this Tuscan treasure. That means smaller queues and the ability to admire the art and architecture at your own pace rather than being swept through with the crowds. Nowhere will this be more appreciated than at the Galleria degli Uffizi, the splendid palazzo packed with Renaissance masterpieces by all the greats: Giotto, Botticelli, Michelangelo, Da Vinci, Raphael, Titian, Caravaggio. Then there's the Duomo, the A-list cathedral with the iconic red dome – you should have a bit more space on the spiral staircase that leads up onto the roof. Also, enjoy quieter visits to the Galleria dell'Accademia (home to Michelangelo's *David*), the exquisite 14th-century Palazzo Vecchio and the unsung Museo di San Marco, with its Fra' Angelico frescoes – all indoor, weather-proof, world-class sites.

Trip plan: Florence has an airport. Pisa, 80km (50 miles) west, is another useful entry point. Allow four days to see the city sights.

Need to know: Mix high culture with winter-sport fun at the Winter Park. This complex, comprising a ski slope, ice-skating rink and more, opens just outside the city from late October to March.

Other months: Dec-Mar – chilly, quiet (Carnival Feb/Mar); Apr-May & Oct-Nov – warm, less busy; Jun-Sep – hot, crowded.

© RossHelen / Shutterstock

PEMBROKESHIRE
WALES

➔ **Why now? Jump into wild waters.**
The adrenalin-pumping pursuit of coasteering – scrambling up sea cliffs, swimming along ledges, clambering through rock arches, exploring caves and gullies, and leaping into the waves – was allegedly invented along the southwest coast of Wales, making this the place to give it a try. It's a beautiful spot too, encompassed within Pembrokeshire Coast National Park. Here, the shore is a dramatic jumble of coves, crags, precipices and astonishing undeveloped beaches. In winter it's at its most dramatic, as wild Atlantic swells smack the shore, creating fizzing cauldrons. Yes, you might need more robust kit – thick wetsuits, neoprene socks, hoods and gloves – but heading out with an experienced guide and plunging in is nothing short of exhilarating. It's a good time for cobweb-blowing walks too. A national trail runs right along the Pembrokeshire coast for 299km (186 miles); the section around the cliffs at Cemaes Head and Marloes Peninsula might also reward with sightings of grey seals and their pups.

Trip plan: Tenby, St Davids, Fishguard and Newport all make good bases. Most of the coastal bus services continue running over winter (albeit on reduced timetables) making it easier to plan linear walks.

Need to know: Coasteering is open to everyone (over the age of eight), even non-swimmers – buoyancy jackets are provided.

Other months: Nov-Mar – cold, quiet, dramatic; Apr-May & Sep-Oct – warm (puffins in spring); Jun-Aug – warmest, busiest.

Coasteering was allegedly invented here. Not for you? The hikes are grand too

COSTA BLANCA
SPAIN

→ **Why now? Walk off the winter blues.**

Its beach resorts might be largely shut up for winter, but there's still plenty of fun to be had on Spain's southerly Costa Blanca. Or rather, just inland. The dramatic Sierra de Aitana range, which rises up behind Benidorm, has some of the most temperate weather in Europe, with mild winters (highs of 15–20°C/59–68°F) and more than 300 days of sunshine a year – ideal for an off-season walking trip. These are handsome mountains, where limestone peaks, needles, ravines and amphitheatres rise to provide fine views of distant hilltop castles and across to the Mediterranean. The trails largely follow old mule and shepherds' tracks, and range from gentle slopes to scrambly scree. Highlights include the route up Aitana (at 1558m/5111ft, the sierra's highest peak), the climb to the summit of the Puig Campana (for the best panoramas), the descent of the Barranc de la Canal gorge and the Bernia walk, which runs along a ridge that looks more like Scotland than Spain. Look out for profuse birdlife as you walk.

Trip plan: Fly to Alicante. Base yourself in a village pensión for quick access to the trails.

Need to know: Add a visit to the cliff-teetering village of El Castell de Guadalest. A 30min bus ride from Benidorm, its medieval streets are rammed in peak season, but will be quieter in November.

Other months: Nov-Apr – mild, quiet; May & Sep-Oct – warm; Jun-Aug – hottest, busiest.

Enjoy the terraces of Pamukkale without the summer crowds

© Gu / Getty Images

WESTERN TURKEY

→ **Why now? Warm up in an ancient spa.**

Humans have been enjoying the thermal, mineral-rich waters at Hierapolis and Pamukkale since the 2nd century BCE. Now, Pamukkale's brilliant-white travertine terraces and warm pools, which tumble down a valley-side, are one of Turkey's most-visited sites. November, however, is the quietest month, meaning you can explore without hordes of others. And if it gets cold, you can warm up in the water. Enter Pamukkale via the south gate, as soon as it opens – most people visit on a long day-trip from the coast, but you'll enjoy a more relaxed visit if you stay overnight in Pamukkale village or nearby Denizli. Walk through the formations along the travertine path; allow plenty of time, and wear a swimming costume under your clothes – it's possible to bathe. Then visit the well-preserved ruins of the Greco-Roman city of Hierapolis, including the baths, temple, necropolis and impressive theatre. While in the area, detour to the little-visited ancient ruins of Afrodisias and Laodicea too.

Trip plan: Denizli has an airport, though it's a 45min shuttle-bus ride from the town. The more central Denizli train station has services from Izmir (4hr 30min) and Selçuk (3hr); a bus from Antalya to Denizli takes 3hr. Minibuses run from Denizli to Pamukkale (30min); taxis are also available.

Need to know: To prevent damage, you must walk around Pamukkale barefoot. Wear shoes that are easy to remove.

Other months: Dec-Feb – chilly, snow possible; Mar-May – warm; Jun-Aug – hottest, dry, busiest; Sep-Nov – quiet, warm.

HIGHLANDS
SCOTLAND

 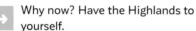

→ **Why now? Have the Highlands to yourself.**

A swirl of mist, moorland glowing in the dawn light and, perhaps, the anguished bellow of a stag angling for a fight – late-autumn mornings in the Scottish Highlands are an atmospheric affair. Indeed, travel there this month and you might catch the end of the red deer rut, when the males joust with their impressive antlers to secure control over the females. Whether you explore by 4WD or on foot, it certainly adds an extra frisson to the already breathtaking lochs, glens and moors. There are festivities at the end of the month too – 30 November is St Andrew's Day, when Scotland's patron saint is celebrated. And while it might be chilly, tourist season is over, making it a good time for quieter sightseeing: Stirling, Eilean Donan Castle, Glen Coe, Fort William. Warm up with a wee dram, and tuck into fantastic seasonal food: Scottish oysters and lobster, and plentiful pheasant, grouse and other game.

Trip plan: Fly to Inverness to loop northern Scotland, taking in dramatic landscapes, lochs and castles. Add on wildlife safaris – for instance, to the hidden glens of Lochaber (near Fort William) or the hills around Loch Torridon.

Need to know: November sees the start of salmon-spawning season – they might be seen swimming upstream, leaping out of the water.

Other months: Dec-Mar – cold, snow possible; Apr-May – quieter, blooming; Jun-Aug – warmest, long days, midges; Sep-Nov – autumn colours, deer rut.

(L) Kilchurn Castle and Loch Awe; (R) Sunrise at Quiraing on the Isle of Skye

A seal at Donna Nook National Reserve

© Andy Rouse / Getty Images

LINCOLNSHIRE ENGLAND

Why now? Peer at seal pups.
Every winter thousands of grey seals start hauling themselves onto the sandbanks at Donna Nook National Nature Reserve – one of the largest and most accessible breeding colonies in the UK – to give birth to a new generation of white fluffy pups. A viewing area at the foot of the dunes is open from dawn till dusk, from late October until mid-December (dependent on seal numbers), so you can watch from a non-intrusive distance. Wardens are on hand to provide information, and close-ups are virtually guaranteed. Also scan the mudflats and saltmarshes for birdlife including fieldfares and flocks of starlings.
Trip plan: Donna Nook is 60km (37 miles) east of Lincoln. Combine a visit to the

nature reserve with a stay in the historic city, which is home to a fine Gothic cathedral that was once the tallest building in the world; the cathedral owns one of the four surviving copies of the 1215 Magna Carta, which is on view in Lincoln Castle.
Need to know: Donna Nook gets busy during seal season. Visit during the week if possible, when the reserve is quieter – the car parks and narrow lanes leading to the site can become congested at weekends. Visitors must stay behind the fence; seals must not be touched or fed.
Other months: Nov-Dec – cold, seal-viewing, starlings; Jan-Mar – cold; Apr-May – wading birds; Jun-Aug – warmest, summer birds; Sep-Oct – overwintering birds.

DONEGAL
IRELAND

Why now? Catch crashing waves.
Zip up that 6mm wetsuit! With its consistent Atlantic swells, the rugged, wild-west coast of County Donegal is the surfing capital of Ireland, and November is one of the best months for intermediates and pros to get in the water. It's a little cold – though preferable to later in the winter, when sea temperatures have dipped further – but the waves are worth it. The beach at Rossnowlagh is best for beginners. There's a world-class reef break, The Peak, at Bundoran; reliable breaks at Tullan Strand and more challenging waves at Inishowen, Dunfanaghy and Dungloe. To see brave (maybe crazy) dudes tackle enormous swells, head to Mullaghmore. Compact Bundoran is the main hub, home to multiple surf schools. It has its share of closed-for-the-season arcades, but also a laidback surfy vibe and some great little pubs and cafés. There are also plenty of prime clifftop spots for watching the ocean smashing the shore.
Trip plan: Bundoran is the southernmost point in Donegal – from here, head north on the scenic Donegal Bay Drive, which passes the sea cliffs of Sliabh Liag, the heritage town of Ballyshannon, lively Donegal Town and the mountain valleys and bays of Kilcar and Carrick.
Need to know: The nearest airports are at Donegal, Derry and Knock. Dublin Airport is a 3hr drive away.
Other months: Jan-Mar – good surf, water/air coldest; Apr-May – consistent swells; Jun-Aug – waves best for beginners, warmest; Sep-Dec – big waves.

ATHENS GREECE

→ **Why now? Run or roam amid the ruins.**

Athens is utterly ancient, the heft of its main sites unmatched in any European capital. It can sometimes feel like all of history lies here. Yet it also has a good dose of modern cool. In November, it's quite literally cool too, with temperatures averaging 10–18°C (50–64°F) – ideal for sightseeing without the summer sweat and crowds. Must-sees include the Acropolis and its state-of-the-art museum, the Temple of Olympian Zeus and the ancient Agora (the birthplace of democracy). For a more modern marvel, visit the Renzo Piano-designed Stavros Niarchos Foundation Cultural Center, home to the Greek National Opera, cultural performances and a fragrant park with Med views. Most fun, though, is exploring Athens' neighbourhoods: the colourful backstreets of Pláka, the taverna-filled districts of Monastiráki and lively Psyrrí, where you can hop between bars until the small hours. Don't miss a sundown ascent of Lykavittos Hill (either by foot or funicular) for one of the best views over the city.

Guards at the 1930s Tomb of the Unknown Soldier, by sculptor Fokion Rokthe

© Adrienne Pitts / Lonely Planet

Trip plan: Allow at least three days. The centre is very walkable, but plan to do your sightseeing in the morning – in the offseason, many sites close by early afternoon.

Need to know: In 490 BCE, Pheidippides sprinted from Marathon to Athens to announce the Greek army's victory over the Persians; today's Athens Marathon is run along the same route, in early November.

Other months: Dec-Feb – cool, wettest; Mar-May & Oct-Nov – warm, cheaper; Jun-Sep – sweltering, busy.

BEYOND ATHENS

  PIRAEUS • 15KM (9 MILES) • The Mediterranean's biggest port and a hotspot for seafood restaurants

 MT PARNITHA NATIONAL PARK • 20KM (13 MILES) • National park with hiking trails, caves and wildlife

HYDRA • 75KM (46 MILES) • The only Greek island free of wheeled vehicles

 SANTORINI • 300KM (186 MILES) • The star of the Cyclades, with whitewashed buildings and dazzling views

SALZKAMMERGUT
AUSTRIA

Waterside Hallstatt, a Unesco World Culture Heritage site

➜ **Why now? Welcome the winter.**
It's all starting to get a little bit fairytale-festive in the lake-dotted environs around Salzburg. As the mercury plunges, the first flakes of snow fall, the lights are strung, the glühwein stirred. Indeed, winter officially starts hereabouts in November, when the Salzkammergut Winter Card launches (valid 1 November–30 April), offering reduced prices on a range of activities, from warming dips in the spa towns of Bad Ischl and Bad Mitterndorf to indoor attractions like the old Salt Mine in Altaussee. It also saves money on boat trips on the Wolfgangsee – just one of the area's 67 lakes. Waterside Hallstatt – once dubbed 'most beautiful lake town in the world' – is a good base, with its romantic lanes, sky-piercing church, coffeehouses, museums (including the World Heritage Museum) and mountain backdrop. From here you can hike into the hills (in boots or snowshoes), take sleigh rides and reach warming thermal baths and pools.

Trip plan: Hallstatt is a 45min drive from Salzburg. The quickest way by public transport is to take a bus from Salzburg to Bad Ischl, from where trains run to Hallstatt station, on the opposite side of the lake from the village; the scenic Hallstatt ferry connects the two.

Need to know: The Salzkammergut Winter Card is free for visitors staying at least three nights in the region.

Other months: Nov-Apr – cold, snowy, winter activities; May-Jun & Sept-Oct – warm, quiet; Jul-Aug – hottest, busiest.

© Boris Stroujko / Alamy Stock Photo

MALTA

→ **Why now? Mix Med sunshine and marvellous sights.**

Tiny Malta has a lovely Mediterranean climate – it's still toasty warm in November, when much of Europe shivers. Indeed, with temperatures around 21°C (70°F) and seas holding on to the last of the summer's heat, hitting the quiet beaches of sister-isles Gozo and Comino remains viable. Combine lazing around in the mild climes with some sightseeing – Malta's tiny size means you can pack a lot in while also taking it easy. Spend time exploring Unesco-listed capital Valletta and the walled former capital Mdina, known as the 'Silent City', a fascinating collection of churches, museums and medieval alleyways. Visit the ancient underground burial chambers of the Hal Saflieni Hypogeum and the clifftop prehistoric temples of Ħaġar Qim and Mnajdra. Walk along the Dingli Cliffs, take a boat ride to the Blue Grotto and kick back on the beach at Golden Bay. Finish with a day trip to Comino's Blue Lagoon, a preternaturally sapphire sea pool, overcrowded in summer but serene off-season.

Trip plan: Allow a week. Hiring a car is useful; if relying on buses, base yourself in Valletta, Naxxar, Sliema or St Julian's for the best range of connections.

Need to know: Head over to Gozo, 25min by ferry, to catch Mediterranea, the island's annual festival of culture, featuring history, art, crafts and music events from late October to early December.

Other months: Dec-Mar – cool; Apr-Jun & Oct-Nov – warm, uncrowded; Jul-Sep – hot, dry, busy.

The port city of St-Malo and its impressive medieval château

BRITTANY
FRANCE

♟ 🌴 ☆

→ **Why now? Live a life more literary.**
Are you one of those people who, when it's cold outside, just wants to curl up with a good book? Then try Bécherel. This pretty Brittany 'little town of character', a former textile-making hub clustered around the ruins of a 12th-century castle, was designated France's first Book Town in 1989. Now it has around 15 bookshops; some specialise in particular subjects, others have cosy cafés, all encourage browsing. The Maison du Livre cultural centre is open year-round, while a secondhand book market is held on the first Sunday of every month. Thanks to its flax and hemp heritage, Bécherel has also been named France's first City of Paper, and it's possible to take a one-day calligraphy class here with a local expert (available October-June). Bécherel isn't big, so combine a bookish break here with brisk sea-air walks along the ramparts of St-Malo, slurping fresh oysters by the waterfront in Cancale and wandering around the half-timbered old town of Dinan.

Trip plan: Ferries arrive at St-Malo, which also has a train station (journeys to Paris take just over 3hr). Buses run from St-Malo to Bécherel (1hr) via Dinan.

Need to know: Rennes, the capital of Brittany (30min by car from Bécherel) hosts the TNB theatre festival over three weekends in November.

Other months: Nov-Mar – chilly, quiet; Apr-Jun & Sept-Oct – warm, fewer tourists (book festival Easter); Jul-Aug – hottest, crowded.

© Rebecca Cole / Alamy Stock Photo

The otherworldly landscape of Lanzarote

LANZAROTE CANARY ISLANDS

→ **Why now? Work out in winter warmth.**

Lanzarote's beautiful beaches – both soft yellow sand and rugged black rock – are a strong temptation, even in November, when temperatures can still hit 23°C (73°F) and the sea is still warm. But what the northernmost, easternmost Canary isle really excels at in winter is providing an outdoor playground when the rest of the continent is off-puttingly chilly. A self-declared European Sports Destination, Lanzarote lures runners, triathletes, golfers,

surfers, sailors and more, who come to train in the warm, sunny weather. As such, the facilities (gear hire, sport hotels) are excellent. The terrain is particularly appealing to cyclists. This wild, volcanic island, slapped by the deep-blue ocean, provides dramatic rides on quiet roads that are hilly rather than mountainous, including routes through the lunar-like weirdness of Timanfaya National Park. Be prepared for strong gusts though – there's a reason why so many windsurfers and kitesurfers will also be found holidaying here. A good base

is Costa Teguise (where the annual Iron Man is held every spring), which is halfway down the east coast, offering easy access to both Timanfaya and the northern peaks.

Trip plan: Arrecife airport is on the east coast, 15km (9 miles) from Costa Teguise.

Need to know: Cycle hire is easy to arrange. Many companies will deliver bikes to your resort; some offer additional services such as guided tours, training camps and roadside assistance.

Other months: Dec-Feb – mild, busy; Mar-Jun – warm, dry; Jul-Aug – hottest; Sep-Nov – pleasant, cooler evenings.

Coastal colours and the
rock formations of Teide
National Park in Tenerife

TENERIFE
CANARY ISLANDS

→ **Why now? Revel in proper sunshine.**
Tenerife has long welcomed
sunseekers year-round – average daytime
temperatures hover around 24°C (75°F)
even now. Realistically, this is the only place
in Europe you can plan a beach holiday
in November. Plus there are few school
holidays this month, so you can expect an
adults-only break (and cheaper prices).
The big tourist resorts are in the south;
better to head north instead, perhaps to
the historic town of Puerto de la Cruz or
the beaches around Los Gigantes and
Puerto de Santiago in the west. If you can
drag yourself off the beach, you'll find
the weather ideal for walking. At 3718m
(12,199ft), Mt Teide is Spain's highest peak
and the world's third-largest volcano; it's
a challenging five-hour hike (or a short
cable-car ride) up to its snowy summit.
But the island has a varied array of trails
– including routes through the northwest
pine forests, ridge walks among the laurels
of the Anaga Mountains and the traverse of
spectacular Masca Gorge – and excellent
infrastructure for trekkers, with a good bus
network and plentiful accommodation.

Trip plan: Tenerife has two international
airports. The most convenient base for
walking is Puerto de la Cruz.

Need to know: Microclimates can be
dramatically different even in adjacent
valleys. If you don't like the weather in one
spot, shift a few miles and you'll likely find
sunshine.

Other months: Dec-Feb – mild, snow
possible on Teide; Mar-May – warm,
wildflowers; Jun-Sep – hot, sunny; Oct-Nov
– warm, uncrowded.

© RossHelen / Getty Images

© John_Walker / Shutterstock

TOULOUSE
FRANCE

Hearty cassoulet elevates sausage and beans to new gastronomic heights

© River Thompson / Lonely Planet

→ **Why now? Eat and be merry.**

France's fourth-largest city, home to one of the biggest universities outside Paris, is a lively proposition even in November. Known as 'La Ville Rose' (the Pink City) on account of its blush-coloured brickwork, it has a gorgeous Old Quarter chock-full of warm cafés, bars and restaurants serving local specials – not least *cassoulet*, the hearty slow-cook of pork, duck confit, lamb, white beans and Toulouse sausage that is tailormade for cold days. Indeed, the food here is renowned. Markets showcase regional produce all year; don't miss the 100-year-old Marché Victor Hugo and the bistros upstairs. The grand Place du Capitole makes a good starting point for a walk through the pedestrianised Vieux Quartier, and bracing strolls along the River Garonne and Canal du Midi. Visit the 11th-century Basilica of St Sernin, the huge Jacobin Convent and the Abattoir (now a museum of contemporary art). Also gen up on aviation history: Airbus is based here and there are a number of aeronautical attractions, including Aeroscopia, where you can board a Concorde, and the space-exploration displays at Cité de l'Espace.

Ultimately, this is a city with a warm vibe whatever the weather.

Trip plan: Toulouse is well connected. TGV trains link it to cities including Bordeaux (2hr), Marseille (4hr) and Paris (5hr).

Need to know: The ski resorts of the Pyrenees are only 1hr 30min away by car.

Other months: Nov-Mar – cold, quieter; Apr-May & Sep-Oct – warm; Jun-Aug – hottest, busiest, most festivals.

BEYOND TOULOUSE

 **ALBI · 76KM (47 MILES)** · Provinicial town where artist Henri de Toulouse-Lautrec was born in 1864

 **CARCASSONNE · 95KM (59 MILES)** · Fortified city perched on a hilltop and bristling with battlements

 **ANDORRA · 185KM (115 MILES)** · Tiny country punching above its weight in sky-reaching peaks

 BARCELONA · 253KM (157 MILES) · The ever-lively Catalonian capital

December

WHERE TO GO WHEN

I WANT TO

CHALLENGE MYSELF

TAKE ME OUT FOR...

- **FOOD**
  - ● LYON, FRANCE P295
  - ● LVIV, UKRAINE P288
- **DRINK**
  - ● LIÈGE, BELGIUM P278
  - ● ALSACE, FRANCE P281

Take to the ice on the skating rink in Warsaw's Old Town square

Vibrant Borscht is a Ukrainian staple

TAKE ME TO TOWN

- **ART & CULTURE**
  - ● BRNO, CZECH REPUBLIC P288
  - ● TALLINN, ESTONIA P284
  - ● BRATISLAVA, SLOVAKIA P288
- **NIGHT-LIFE & HEDONISM**
  - ● WARSAW, POLAND P279
  - ● MILAN, ITALY P289

Warm up with a hot chocolate in frosty Tallinn

RELAX/ INDULGE

Korasida Beach is one of Evia's most beautiful sandy stretches

DIAL IT DOWN

- **WELLNESS** ── ● BLACK FOREST, GERMANY P290
- **CHILLING**
  - ● EVIA, GREECE P278
  - ● CORFU TOWN, GREECE P279

Take a snowy hike through the Black Forest

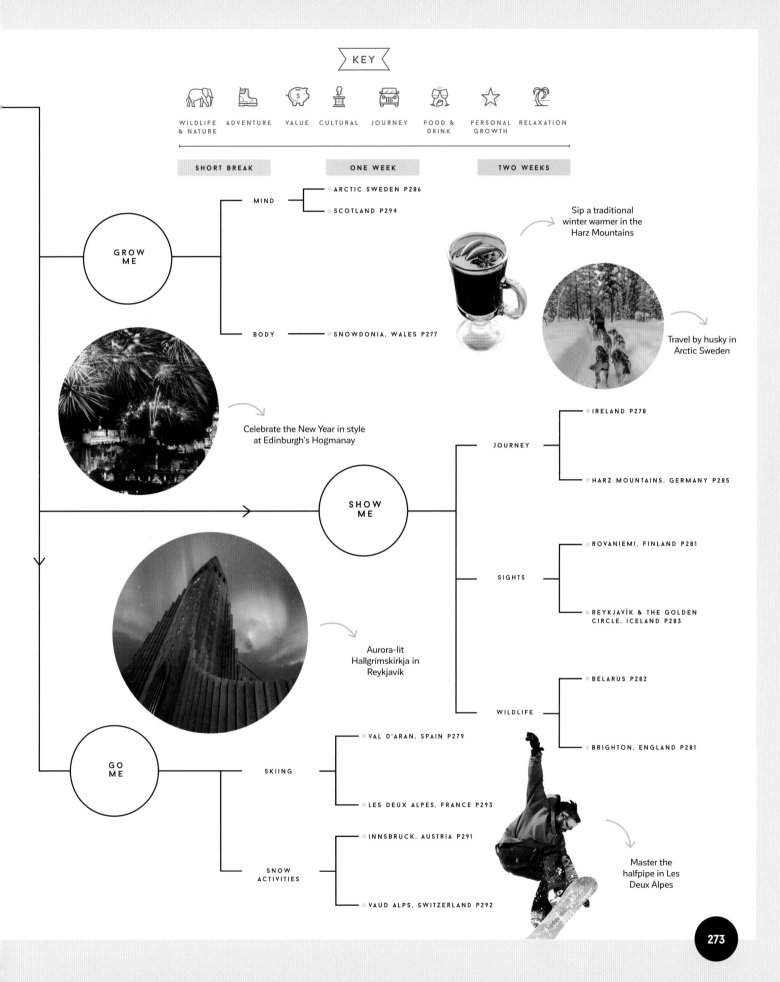

KEY

WILDLIFE & NATURE   ADVENTURE   VALUE   CULTURAL   JOURNEY   FOOD & DRINK   PERSONAL GROWTH   RELAXATION

SHORT BREAK   ONE WEEK   TWO WEEKS

GROW ME

MIND — ARCTIC SWEDEN P286
— SCOTLAND P294

BODY — SNOWDONIA, WALES P277

SHOW ME

JOURNEY — IRELAND P278
— HARZ MOUNTAINS, GERMANY P285

SIGHTS — ROVANIEMI, FINLAND P281
— REYKJAVÍK & THE GOLDEN CIRCLE, ICELAND P283

WILDLIFE — BELARUS P282
— BRIGHTON, ENGLAND P281

GO ME

SKIING — VAL D'ARAN, SPAIN P279
— LES DEUX ALPES, FRANCE P293

SNOW ACTIVITIES — INNSBRUCK, AUSTRIA P291
— VAUD ALPS, SWITZERLAND P292

Sip a traditional winter warmer in the Harz Mountains

Travel by husky in Arctic Sweden

Celebrate the New Year in style at Edinburgh's Hogmanay

Aurora-lit Hallgrímskirkja in Reykjavík

Master the halfpipe in Les Deux Alpes

EVENTS
IN DECEMBER

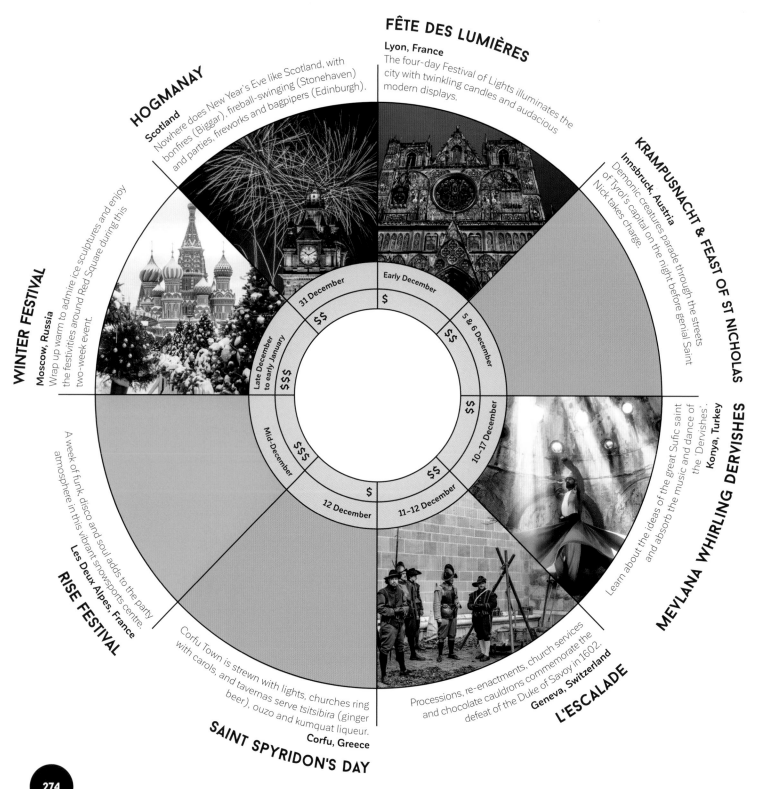

FÊTE DES LUMIÈRES
Lyon, France
The four-day Festival of Lights illuminates the city with twinkling candles and audacious modern displays.

HOGMANAY
Scotland
Nowhere does New Year's Eve like Scotland, with bonfires (Biggar), fireball-swinging (Stonehaven) and parties, fireworks and bagpipers (Edinburgh).

KRAMPUSNACHT & FEAST OF ST NICHOLAS
Innsbruck, Austria
Demonic creatures parade through the streets of Tyrol's capital on the night before genial Saint Nick takes charge.

WINTER FESTIVAL
Moscow, Russia
Wrap up warm to admire ice sculptures and enjoy the festivities around Red Square during this two-week event.

MEVLANA WHIRLING DERVISHES
Konya, Turkey
Learn about the ideas of the great Sufic saint and absorb the music and dance of the 'Dervishes'.

RISE FESTIVAL
Les Deux Alpes, France
A week of funk, disco and soul adds to the party atmosphere in this vibrant snowsports centre.

L'ESCALADE
Geneva, Switzerland
Processions, re-enactments, church services and chocolate cauldrons commemorate the defeat of the Duke of Savoy in 1602.

SAINT SPYRIDON'S DAY
Corfu, Greece
Corfu Town is strewn with lights, churches ring with carols, and tavernas serve tsitsibira (ginger beer), ouzo and kumquat liqueur.

Early December — $

31 December — $$

5 & 6 December — $$

Late December to early January — $$$

10–17 December — $$

Mid-December — $$$

$ — 12 December

$$ — 11–12 December

ROVANIEMI, FINLAND

LIÈGE, BELGIUM

Corfu's kumquat liqueur is a
local speciality

CORFU, GREECE

EVIA, GREECE

Swoosh down snowy
mountains in Les
Deux Alpes

ARCTIC SWEDEN

BRIGHTON, ENGLAND

VAL D'ARAN, SPAIN

INNSBRUCK, AUSTRIA

LES DEUX ALPES, FRANCE

Wake up early to see
daybreak over Iceland's
Gullfoss waterfall

Tallinn's Alexander Nevsky
Cathedral is topped with
onion domes

SNOWDONIA, WALES

ALSACE, FRANCE

TALLINN, ESTONIA

Eat sweet *Kugelhopf*
in Alsace

HARZ MOUNTAINS,
GERMANY

WARSAW, POLAND

LYON, FRANCE

REYKJAVÍK & GOLDEN CIRCLE, ICELAND

Step aboard a steam
train in the Harz
Mountains

BRNO, CZECH REPUBLIC

SCOTLAND

Take in panoramic
views in the Black
Forest

IRELAND

LVIV, UKRAINE

Edinburgh's Hogmanay
celebrations are the stuff
of legend

BLACK FOREST,
GERMANY

BRATISLAVA, SLOVAKIA

Gape at the
facade of Milan's
Gothic Duomo

VAUD ALPS, SWITZERLAND

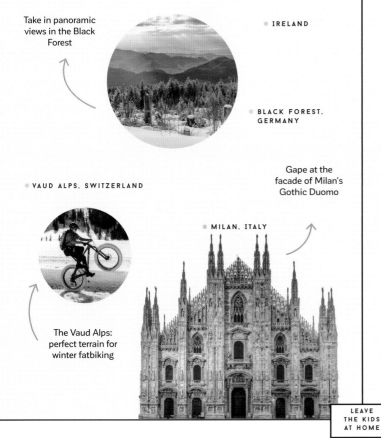

MILAN, ITALY

Wander the
handsome streets
and squares
of Lviv

The Vaud Alps:
perfect terrain for
winter fatbiking

BELARUS

Keep your eyes peeled for
sightings of wolves
in Belarus

SNOWDONIA
WALES

→ **Why now? Have an adventure, above ground or below.**

The clue's in the name: SNOWdonia. This varied national park in northern Wales – a dramatic assemblage of mountains, glittering coastline, lakes, ancient woodland and roaring waterfalls – could well be powder-smothered in December. There will certainly be some weather. But that doesn't need to stop thrill-seekers who take the proper precautions. There are companies that specialise in winter walking, who will teach you skills such as basic mountain safety, navigation and using crampons before leading you out on crisp, crowdless hikes. And Snowdonia's dam-controlled National White Water Centre is open to rafters year-round (wetsuits compulsory). This area used to be a mining hotspot; now, abandoned industrial sites are providing opportunities for subterranean exploration, including abseiling, zip-lining, boating, climbing and trampolining underground.

Trip plan: Bangor is the region's major rail hub. Connections run to Betws-y-Coed and Blaenau Ffestiniog. Having a car is useful. The village of Beddgelert is a charming base for exploring the national park; bigger Betws-y-Coed and Llanberis are less attractive but have more facilities.

Need to know: Some Snowdonia attractions close for winter, but several remain open –including the area's seven castles, the Inigo Jones Slateworks and the fairytale/bonkers village of Portmeirion.

Other months: Nov-Mar – cold; Apr-May – warming, wildflowers; Jun-Aug – warmest; Sep-Oct – warm, autumn colours.

Sunrise over Y Lliwedd Mountain

LIÈGE BELGIUM

→ **Why now? Feel as festive as possible.**

Want to turn the festive dial up to 11? Look no further than Liège. The gritty Wallonian city is not only home to the oldest Christmas market in Belgium, but has been designated the official European Capital of Christmas. Every December, its historic Old Town becomes more Santa-centric than Lapland. Three separate Christmas villages spring up; as well as food trucks, craft stalls and sparkling lights, each has its own mayor, carol singers and entertainment. There's also a skating rink, puppet nativity, big wheel, sledging run and a sound-and-light show in the St Paul Cathedral. Market must-trys include oval-shaped Liège waffles (which have caramelised sugar lumps hidden inside), *boulets à la liégeoise* (meatballs in rich gravy), a shot or two of *peket* (a potent spirit made with juniper berries) and a range of local craft beers. This is a pretty cheap city to drink in, and feels authentically local even when the markets are in full flow. The narrow lanes around the Rue du Pot d'Or are the nightlife centre; head also to the down-to-earth Outremeuse quarter.

Trip plan: Liège is connected via rail to hubs including Bruges (2hr), Brussels (1hr) and Cologne (1hr).

Need to know: Every Sunday, from October to April, the Musée Tchantchès on Liège's Outremeuse island holds a puppet show about Tchantchès, the city's mascot.

Other months: Nov-Mar – cold (Christmas markets Dec); Apr-May & Sep-Oct – warm; Jun-Aug – hot (Outremeuse Festival Aug).

EVIA GREECE

→ **Why now? Plot a Hellenic holiday.**

December isn't your typical month for a Greek island jaunt. But Evia isn't your typical Greek island. The country's second-largest isle, it has glittering Aegean beaches, a mountainous interior, ancient sites and great food, but is largely overlooked by foreign tourists. Athenians love it, though – only an hour away from the capital, Evia provides locals with a handy urban escape (and is subsequently heaving on summer weekends). It won't be so busy in winter, but Evia's large size and location ensures a sizeable year-round population, so it doesn't turn into a ghost island. Temperatures (average highs of 15°C/59°F) might not be bikini-friendly but are mild enough for beach strolls, plus proper hikes and bikes – the island has some excellent trails. There's plenty to see, too, including ancient Eretria and the accompanying museum, the Convent of Agios Nikolaou Galataki with its 16th-century frescoes and the historic centre, promenade and seafood tavernas of capital Halkida. If you get chilly, head to Edipsos, Greece's oldest thermal spa, where more than 75 different hot springs and numerous health spas offer treatments.

Trip plan: Ferries run from Oropos and Rafina to Evia. The island is also linked to the mainland by two bridges. Halkida is halfway down the west coast.

Need to know: Be aware of Evia's size. Driving end to end takes four to five hours.

Other months: Dec-Feb – cool, quiet; Mar-May & Oct-Nov – warm, cheaper; Jun-Sep – sweltering, busy.

IRELAND

→ **Why now? Soak up some ancient history.**

There's something mystical about Ireland, an air of magic that goes way beyond the leprechaun clichés. Our early pagan forbears clearly felt the same, as the island is rich in Neolithic spiritual sites. The stand-out is the Unesco-listed Brú na Bóinne in County Meath, a cluster of monumental burial mounds that pre-dates Stonehenge; just after sunrise on the mid-December winter solstice, light shines down into the passage at the site's Newgrange tomb and illuminates the main chamber. Tickets to be inside for the phenomenon are hard to secure, but December – quiet and pub-cosy – is still an interesting time to make a tour of ancient Ireland. Luck out with a bright day, with low winter sunshine glowing on the stones, and there's nothing better. Combine Newgrange with visits to sites such as the Stone of Destiny and the Hill of Tara (alleged former seat of the High Kings of Ireland); the huge prehistoric cemetery at Carrowmore (overlooked by Queen Maeve's Cairn, possible burial place of the Celtic monarch); the megalithic complex of Carrowkeel; and the wild island of Inishmore (Inis Mór), home to many monuments.

Trip plan: Newgrange is 60km (37 miles) north of Dublin. Start in the capital (including a visit to Trinity College to see the 9th-century Book of Kells). Hire a car.

Need to know: Entry to Newgrange for solstice is decided on a lottery system; results are announced in September.

Other months: Nov-Mar – cool, damp; Apr-May & Sep-Oct – mild, quieter; Jun-Aug – warmest, busiest.

WARSAW POLAND

→ **Why now?** Eat, drink and be merry – on a budget.

After the devastation of WWII, there was virtually no Warsaw left – though wandering the splendidly reconstructed centre these days, that's almost impossible to believe. It also seems like the Polish capital is still celebrating its survival: Warsaw bubbles with energy, and locals know how to enjoy themselves, even in the dark days of winter. Every night of the week you'll find people packing out inexpensive milk bars (traditional, canteen-style cafes) cool coffee shops, cocktail lounges, craft-beer pubs and vodka dives. At this time, Christmas markets – notably in the old Market Square – add mulled wine to the mix, along with craft stalls and a skating rink. Warsaw's attractions are equally inexpensive, and most are free on at least one day a week: see amazing art in the National Museum (free Tuesdays), celebrate the titular Polish composer at the Fryderyk Chopin Museum (Wednesdays), get a history hit at the Museum of Warsaw (Thursdays) and face WWII horrors at the Warsaw Rising Museum (Sundays).

Trip plan: Warsaw has two airports. There are good local and international bus and train services.

Need to know: Take a bus out to the Wilanów Palace & Park, constructed in the 17th century and much embellished since. The Royal Garden of Light open-air exhibition (Nov-Feb) sees the gardens illuminated with millions of LEDs and light projections.

Other months: Nov-Mar – cold; Apr-May – spring flowers; Jun-Aug – hot, riverside beaches; Sep-Oct – warm (film festival Oct).

VAL D'ARAN SPAIN

→ **Why now?** Swoop in for reliable world-class skiing.

Turn your compass away from the Alps and settle on some Spanish skiing this December. The Val d'Aran, a singular and spectacular valley in the northern Pyrenees, is famed for its Atlantic climate and the quality of its snow. The ski season usually begins in November and runs until late April. The resort of choice is Baqueira Beret, Spain's biggest and classiest; former king Juan Carlos has a holiday home here. But despite its glamour, prices remain reasonable: the food and wine are inexpensive, the heli-skiing some of the cheapest on the continent. Baqueira Beret tops out at 2510m (8235ft) and offers around 150km (93 miles) of groomed terrain. There are good ski schools and facilities for beginners, some lovely long runs and some white-knuckle off-piste-ing for the experienced – not least the thrilling/terrifying Escornacrabes ('Where Goats Fall'). Base yourself in handy but unattractive Baqueira or choose one of the traditional medieval villages nearby, picture-perfect clusters of stone, slate and wood houses and Romanesque churches.

Trip plan: The nearest airport is Toulouse, 160km (100 miles) north and 2hr away by road. There is some public transport in the Val d'Aran (for instance, buses connect the villages between Vielha and Baqueira), but otherwise you'll need to rent a car.

Need to know: Reduced-price ski passes are available for the beginners' area.

Other months: Nov-Apr – reliable snow, skiing; May & Oct – shoulder months; Jun-Sep – warm, hiking.

CORFU TOWN GREECE

→ **Why now?** Explore a quiet isle and gorge on Greek hospitality.

Raise a glass to Saint Spyridon! This Ionian island's patron saint is celebrated on 12 December, which kicks off the run up to Christmas nicely. The capital, Corfu Town, will be strewn with festive lights, its 39 churches resounding with carols, its tavernas serving *tsitsibira* (traditional ginger beer), throat-warming ouzo and the island's unique kumquat liqueur. It's a great time to experience authentic Corfiot hospitality – other tourists will be thin on the ground. Unesco-listed Corfu Town makes the best winter base as it remains lively year-round. Flanked by two hills, each topped by a Venetian fortress, the charming whitewashed old centre is a dense maze of alleys where you'll find good restaurants, cute shops and impressive architecture, as well as locals going about their daily business. From here, explore more of the island, one of the greenest in Greece. The roads and beaches that are so busy in high season are now empty – take scenic drives, via evergreen olive groves, to pretty Paleokastritsa beach and the hilltop castle of Angelokastro, to traditional southern villages such as Lefkimmi, Argyrades and Afionas and north towards dramatic Cape Drastis.

Trip plan: Ferries to the island run from the mainland ports of Igoumenitsa and Patra.

Need to know: A mild winter day is perfect for hiking some of the Corfu Trail, a long-distance route covering 220km (137 miles).

Other months: Nov-Mar – cool, quiet; Apr-May – warm, green; Jun-Aug – hot, very busy; Sep-Oct – harvest, seas still warm.

(A) Starlings over Brighton Pier;
(L) Choose *choucroute* in Alsace;
(R) The Santa Village in Lapland, Finland

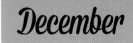

BRIGHTON
ENGLAND

→ **Why now? Watch a wonder of the wildlife world.**

A single starling isn't the most exciting sighting. But seeing tens of thousand of these glossy-black birds soaring and swerving together in a mesmerising, balletic display – known as a murmuration – well, that's one of nature's greatest spectacles. Murmurations occur over winter, with starling numbers tending to peak between December and January, when resident birds are joined by migrants from Europe. As many as 40,000 might be seen in the East Sussex seaside city of Brighton as they come in to roost at dusk. Wrap up warm and grab a spot along the seafront before sunset to catch their aerial acrobatics over the city's two piers; displays aren't guaranteed but can last around an hour. This is a fine way to end a day exploring the city. Brighton is a great place for Christmas shopping, especially in the alleyways of The Lanes, bohemian North Laine and under the seafront arches. Also pay a visit to the Royal Pavilion, a wedding cake of a building, topped with onion domes and stuffed with opulent chinoiserie and antiques; there's an ice rink here in winter.

Trip plan: Trains run to Brighton from London (1hr) and Gatwick airport (30min).

Need to know: Other good places to watch huge, whirling murmurations in the UK include Ham Wall and Shapwick Heath on the Somerset Levels, the Attenborough Nature Reserve in Nottinghamshire and, on the Welsh coast, from Aberystwyth's Royal Pier.

Other months: Nov-Feb – chilly, starlings; Mar-May – spring (Brighton Festival May); Jun-Aug – warmest, busiest (Brighton Pride Aug); Sep-Oct – mild, quieter.

ALSACE
FRANCE

→ **Why now? Find mixed-up festive flair.**

Alsace is, well, Alsatian. It's in France but hard up against Germany and Switzerland, giving it a distinctive, melting-pot flavour – not least in December, when Christmas comes to oh-so-pretty towns across the regions. Blush-pink Strasbourg, canal-laced Colmar, romantic Eguisheim, ancient Ribeauvillé... There's a stream of fairytale, candy-coloured, half-timbered, straight-out-of-a-storybook spots, all medieval ramparts and delicate church spires, that look impressively festive; each one hosts markets that are a touch Teutonic, a touch Gallic, all delicious. Fill your belly with everything from Munster cheese and fresh pretzels to bacon-and-onion tarte flambée, Alsatian brioche, *choucroute* (a combo of sauerkraut, potatoes and sausage) and *pain d'épices* (spicy, cinnamon-laced gingerbread). The wine here is good too, featuring a range of spicy winter whites, light Pinot Noirs and fizzy Crémant d'Alsace. Head for the picturesque village of Riquewihr, which looks like it's been dropped straight out of the 16th century, where you can go wine-tasting year-round; finish each day in a traditional *winstub*, to knock back carafes at red-checkered tables while warming up with Alsatian dishes.

Trip plan: There's a good rail and bus network throughout Alsace. Major hubs include Strasbourg, Mulhouse and Colmar.

Need to know: Alsace's Vosges mountains are one the of best regions in France for cross-country skiing.

Other months: Nov-Mar – cold (Christmas markets Dec); Apr-May – warm, wildflowers; Jun-Aug – hottest, busiest; Sep-Oct – warm, wine harvest.

ROVANIEMI
FINLAND

→ **Why now? Visit Santa in his snow-clad grotto.**

Christmas comes but once a year. Except in Finnish Lapland, where you can immerse yourself in Yule for the full 365 days. The town of Rovaniemi proudly declares itself the 'official' home of Santa, and at nearby Napapiiri (Finnish for the Arctic Circle), there's a village dedicated to the cult of Claus. Naturally, the whole (unsurprisingly commercialised) shebang looks most festive in snowy December, when only those with a heart of ice could fail to be captivated by the magical ambience. And once your kids have met Santa and mailed a card from his post office, there's plenty to absorb the family in and around Rovaniemi for several days: husky sledding, tobogganing, reindeer safaris, cross-country skiing and a trio of interesting museums in the city itself, covering art, Arctic life and Finnish nature. As a bonus, this is a great place to watch the Aurora Borealis dance across the dark northern skies.

Trip plan: Fly to Rovaniemi via Helsinki. Suitably Arctic accommodation options, many in and around Santa Claus Village, include igloos of ice and glass, a snowhotel and a range of chalets, cabins and lodges.

Need to know: Temperatures can drop to -30°C (-22°F) in Lapland – bring plenty of warm clothes and thick-soled shoes; activity companies will usually provide overalls/outerwear.

Other months: Nov-Mar – very cold, snow activities, dark; Apr-May – transition to spring, days lengthening; Jun-Aug – summer, warmest, long days; Sep-Oct – autumn ('ruska') foliage.

Spot a grey wolf in Belarus... as well as beaver, bison, elk and lynx

© RonaldWJansen / Getty Images

BELARUS

Why now? Track lynx and wolves through wintry forests.

Little-known Naliboki Forest, in northwestern Belarus, has long been a refuge. During WWII, local partisans hid here when the country was being used as a battlefield between Russian and German armies; these days it's a haven not for people but for creatures, boasting one of the world's highest densities of lynx, elk, bison and eagles. You can go wildlife-spotting year-round – each season has its highlights – but the winter months, when snow cloaks the swamp and centuries-old woodland, are optimum for tracking lynx and wolf. Indeed, walk here with an expert naturalist, looking for prints in the powder and checking the camera traps dotted around the forest, and they say you have a 70% chance of seeing wolves, 30%

of seeing the rare cats. Other potential sightings include bison, elk and beaver – Naliboki is home to one of the densest Eurasian beaver populations on the continent – as well as a host of birds, from capercaillie to black grouse.

Trip plan: Naliboki Forest is around 50km (31 miles) west of Minsk. Stay at a traditional homestead within the forest and allow three/four days to explore with expert guides. Add on a day or two in Minsk to enjoy the Christmas markets, Soviet architecture and cosy cafés.

Need to know: A 30-day visa-free regime is in place for most visitors arriving in and departing from Minsk National Airport.

Other months: Nov-Apr – cold, snow, good tracking; May – wolf denning; Jun-Aug – kayaking, otters and beavers; Sep-Oct – deer rut.

Winter sunrise above Gullfoss waterfall in southwest Iceland

© Ultima_Gaina / Getty Images

REYKJAVÍK & THE GOLDEN CIRCLE
ICELAND

Why now? Embrace the dark side.
December days are pretty short in Iceland – around four or five hours long. But darkness certainly doesn't stop play. For a start, it provides an excellent black canvas against which to (hopefully) see the Northern Lights. Reykjavík will also be a-twinkle with decorated trees and fairylights, as festive fever takes over; head to Árbær Open Air Museum, which opens on weekends in December, its turf houses and churches set up to display old Icelandic Christmas traditions. The cold and dark don't stop Golden Circle tours either. You can still zip between the famed trio: fascinating Þingvellir National Park, the spewing Geysir geothermal fields and Gullfoss waterfall (enhanced by a cloak of ice). You can also book glacier hikes, snowmobile safaris, superjeep drives; you can even snorkel between the North American and Eurasian tectonic plates at Silfra – fed by glaciers, the water temperature varies little year-round, and you'll be snug inside a dry suit. If the cold does get too much, seek out one of Iceland's hot springs.

Trip plan: Arrange tours from Reykjavík. Spend a few nights away from the city lights for better odds of seeing aurora.

Need to know: Look out for jólahlaðborð, special Christmas buffets served in cosy restaurants and heaving with smoked lamb, gravlax and delicate, lace-like *laufabrauð* ('leaf bread').

Other months: Oct-Mar – cold to freezing, dark, aurora; Apr-May – warmer (whales May-Sep); Jun-Sep – long days, warmest, interior accessible.

283

(L) Russian
Orthodox Alexander
Nevsky Cathedral;
(R) Market knitting

TALLINN ESTONIA

 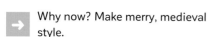

→ **Why now? Make merry, medieval style.**

While plenty of northern European cities host Christmas markets, few are blessed with such a perfect backdrop as Tallinn, one of Europe's best-preserved medieval centres. Its walled Old Town and Toompea Castle district are enchanting, especially in December when Tallin nestles under a blanket of snow, with festive lights strung along cobbled streets and the bonhomie of the annual Christmas market radiating from the craft stalls and enormous tree.

The days are short, the nights dark, but the atmosphere is genuinely charming – and the traditional food and drink, from black pudding to gingerbread, will warm your cockles. Also, various concert halls and churches echo with holiday mood music for most of the month – there's little more atmospheric than listening to carols in a candle-flickered nave as snow flutters outside. Tallinn is shaking off its reputation as a stag-weekend destination, but this is far from peak stag season anyway. Enjoy the city's great-value boutique hotels, fine

eateries and Christmas spirit without the bawdy disruption.

Trip plan: Spare time to explore the Old Town's many Gothic and Baroque gems, including the Town Hall, Toompea Castle, ancient Dominican Monastery and the many churches.

Need to know: The Christmas market runs from late November into early January.

Other months: Nov-Mar – cold; Apr-May & Sep-Oct – cooler, quieter; Jun-Aug – hottest, busy.

Full steam ahead: a historical steam train grinds its way up the Brocken Mountain

HARZ MOUNTAINS
GERMANY

→ **Why now? Ride a vintage railway though a winter wonderland.**

Spend December stepping into the pages of a German folk tale: the Harz Mountains are a place of myths, medieval villages, crooked spires, lovely lakes and mysterious forest – all of which look particularly Brothers-Grimm-beautiful under a sparkle of snow. Visit Wernigerode, with its Disney-like castle; gorgeous Goslar's Unesco-listed Rammelsberg Mines, with its bundle of half-timbered houses; and the cobbled lanes of Quedlinburg, another World Heritage site with an impressive tenth-century fortress. Warm up with mulled wine. Also, hop on the terrific old trains – the undulating Harz range is well suited to narrow-gauge railways, and several negotiate the region. The Brocken Railway grinds to the top of the Brocken (1141m/3743ft), the Harz's highest summit, where it's said witches gather, and which was used as a Soviet lookout during the Cold War; the views – of the surrounding peaks, of the loco's steam condensing in the chill air – are spectacular. Running from Quedlinburg, the nostalgic metre-gauge Selke Valley Railway provides glorious access deep into the Harz.

Trip plan: The closest major airports are Berlin, Hamburg, Hannover and Frankfurt. The main towns of the Harz are close together; base yourself in Wernigerode, the most central, and make day-trips.

Need to know: The Harz's summer hiking and biking paths become cross-country ski routes after snowfall; downhill skiing is limited.

Other months: Nov-Mar – cold, snow possible; Apr-May – spring flowers; Jun-Aug – hottest, busiest; Sep-Oct – cooling, autumn colours.

ARCTIC SWEDEN

→ **Why now? Sleep on ice beneath the Northern Lights.**

At the Swedish village of Jukkasjärvi, one degree of latitude north of the Arctic Circle, the sun never rises in the last three weeks of the year. In December, darkness is the dominant state – perfect for watching the swirling light show of the Aurora Borealis in inky skies. Jukkasjärvi is the home of the original Icehotel, carved anew each year from the pristine waters of the Torne River, where you can spend a night in a bed made of ice. It's also a base for cross-country skiing, husky sledding, snowmobiling, sleigh rides, meeting reindeer and learning about traditional Sami culture – magical for kids and grown-ups alike. Some 100km (62 miles) to the northwest, Abisko National Park is even further removed from the light, an otherworldly landscape offering arguably the world's best aurora-watching – head to the top of 900m (2953ft) Mt Nuolja for spectacular views of light and land.

Trip plan: Kiruna, 16km (10 miles) west of Jukkasjärvi and 20min away by car, has an airport, served by flights from Stockholm and international cities. Trains from Kiruna to Abisko take 1hr.

Need to know: The Northern Lights are sparked when charged particles from the sun hit the earth's atmosphere. Various websites offer reasonable forecasts based on solar activity.

Other months: Dec-Apr – winter, Icehotel open; May-Jul – warmer, Midnight Sun; Aug-Sep – autumn; Oct-Nov – cool, dark, good aurora-watching.

Huskies in the snow-covered forests of Jukkasjärvi

LVIV UKRAINE

→ **Why now?** Wake up and smell the coffee.

You've done Prague and Kraków. Now look to Lviv, perhaps one of the loveliest but most overlooked winter cities around. With barely a splotch of Soviet-ugly in sight, Lviv's medieval centre is perfectly preserved, with an array of fine Baroque buildings adding to the Unesco-listed mix. The festive market in the colourful square of Ploshcha Rynok is worth a visit: little cabins sell everything from handmade baubles to mulled wine, *shashlyky* (grilled-meat skewers) and traditional *mlyncy* (thick pancakes). This is a good time to indulge in the city's coffee culture too. Lviv is crammed with atmospheric cafés – some are Viennese fancy, others are rustically old school or hipster cool. Also head for Lviv Handmade Chocolate to indulge in devilishly good hot chocolate with a slab of *syrnyk*, the local take on chocolate cheesecake. Elsewhere, admire the city's many churches, catch a folklore performance at the opera house, visit the open-air Museum of Folk Architecture and Life (which puts on special displays in winter) and climb the 65m (213ft) tower of the Town Hall tower for the best views.

Trip plan: Lviv's airport is 7km (4 miles) west of the centre. Trains run to Kyiv (from 5hr), as well as international destinations.

Need to know: Most Ukrainians are Orthodox and celebrate Christmas on 7 Jan.

Other months: Nov-Apr – cold, quiet; May & Sep-Oct – warm, uncrowded; Jun-Aug – hottest, busiest.

BRNO
CZECH REPUBLIC

→ **Why now?** Descend to get out of the cold.

It can be brisk in Brno in December. But the Moravian city has a solution for escaping inclement climes: head underground, into the extensive network of corridors, crypts and cellars that lie beneath the old streets. Start at the Ossuary at the Church of St James, the second-largest ossuary in Europe, where over 50,000 bodies were once interred – creepily cool. Then enter a nuclear bunker: 10-Z, dug into the rock under Špilberk Castle, was designed to house 500 people in the event of an A-bomb apocalypse; fortunately it was never used, but you can tour the old tunnels. Finish in the Labyrinth under the Cabbage Market, where 212 stairs lead down to the cellars, used as storage by the merchants and as shelters during wars. Above ground, soak up the atmosphere at Liberty Square, the Cabbage Market, Moravian Square and Radnická Street, where stalls sell crafts and punch. Also see the sites, from the Old Town Hall to Unesco-listed Vila Tugendhat, a pioneering 20th-century house.

Trip plan: Brno has a small airport. Regular train and coach services run to Brno from Prague (2hr 30min), Bratislava (1hr 30min) and Vienna (2hr).

Need to know: The BRNOPAS tourist card includes free public transport, free or reduced entry to some attractions and skip-the-line privileges at Vila Tugendhat.

Other months: Nov-Feb – cold, snow possible; Mar-May – warming; Jun-Aug – hottest; Sept-Oct – mixed weather.

BRATISLAVA
SLOVAKIA

→ **Why now?** Discover a cultural, Christmassy capital.

Though Bratislava has only been a capital since Slovakia gained its independence in 1993, its roots go far deeper. The area was first inhabited in the 6th century; the earliest mention of the city's castle dates to AD 907. Which means there's plenty of history to pick over on a long winter weekend. Bratislava Castle, filled with impressive art, is a good starting point; its renovated ramparts give a good city overview too: look over the misty Danube, the medieval and Gothic Old Town, the Renaissance palaces, the concrete Soviet blocks. Learn more at the Museum of City History; there's a Viticulture Museum in the cellar where you can taste local wines. Just outside is handsome Hlavné nám, the main square, which becomes a cheery Christmas market in December. Next, walk the narrow streets of the historic centre, dropping into magnificent St Martin's Cathedral, warming up with dumplings, fried cheese and shots of *slivovica* (plum brandy) at an array of cafés and underground pubs. If you get a fresh-n-frosty day, head out for a bracing walk in the Bratislava Forest Park from the suburb of Koliba.

Trip plan: Allow two or three days, including out-of-town excursions to the Danubiana Meulensteen Art Museum and Devín Castle.

Need to know: Bratislava is well connected by rail. Regular trains run to Vienna (1hr), Prague (4hr 30min) and Budapest (2hr 45min).

Other months: Nov-Mar – cold; Apr-Jun – mild, blossom; Jul-Aug – hottest, busiest, festivals; Sep-Oct – warm, settled, autumn colours.

The Gothic Duomo; clamber across its roof for far-reaching views

MILAN ITALY

Why now? Enjoy a stylish spectacle.

December is dreary but cheery in cosmopolitan Milan. Any winter blues are counteracted by a range of festivities, not least the launch of opera season (early December) at spectacular La Scala. Tickets are almost impossible to secure, but the buzz and the beautiful people dressed up in their finery is worth savouring. December also sees the feast day of St Ambrose (7 December), Milan's patron saint, with a service in the Duomo; a visit to this vast Gothic-style cathedral, including a rooftop tour, is a must. Milan is renowned for its boutiques. There's high-class shopping to be done, of course: seek out designer brands in the Quadrilatero d'Oro neighbourhood, explore the Zaha Hadid-designed CityLife Shopping District. Or pay a visit to red-brick Castello Sforzesco, where the Obej Obej Christmas fair spills around the ramparts this month. Art buffs should head for the Pinacoteca di Brera, home to an impressive Renaissance collection. Da Vinci's *Last Supper* hangs in the Chiesa di Santa Maria delle Grazie.

Trip plan: Allow two/three days. Book tickets for *The Last Supper* at least a month in advance (closed 25 December). Cheap restricted-view tickets are available for La Scala performances; other reduced-price tickets go on sale 1hr before shows start.

Need to know: The best time to hit the streets is early evening (5-9pm), when the Milanese go out for aperitivo drinks and snacks.

Other months: Nov-Feb – cold, opera season (sales start Jan; Fashion Week Feb); Mar-Jun – busy; Jul-Aug – hot; Sep-Oct – warm (Fashion Week Sep).

BEYOND MILAN

 BERGAMO • 50KM (31 MILES) • Beguiling city with a tangle of tiny streets and a wealth of art and architecture

 LAKE LUGANO • 64KM (40 MILES) • Sparkling expanse with trails that wind along its shores

 GENOA • 120KM (74 MILES) • The home of *pesto genovese* – which tastes better here than anywhere else

 PISTOIA • 218KM (135 MILES) • A pretty, uncrowded Tuscan town rich in history and culture

© Olja Merker / Getty Images

BLACK FOREST
GERMANY

→ **Why now? Sink into hot spas and invigorating nature.**

The healing springs of Baden-Baden have long attracted the great and good – since being discovered by the Romans 2000-odd years ago, various celebs and royals have visited this well-to-do spa town for a jolt of wellness. Sitting in the foothills of the Black Forest, on the east bank of the Rhine, Baden-Baden remains a handsome retreat, with its colourful old buildings and 12 thermal springs spewing the hottest, most mineral-rich waters in Germany – perfect for a winter warm-up. Baden-Baden is also the northern gateway to the Black Forest region, one of the most romantic chunks of the country; being largely evergreen, the woodlands keep much of their namesake cloak year-round. Visit some of the prettiest towns you ever did see, all looking especially appealing in festive finery. Stop at picture-book Calw and the lively uni hub of Freiburg, which has a lovely Christmas market. Head down the Kinzig valley, dotted with medieval villages, and don't miss Triberg, birthplace of the Black Forest gâteau.

Trip plan: Allow a week. Spend one day driving the 60km (37 mile) Schwarzwaldhochstrasse ('Black Forest Highway') from Baden-Baden to Freudenstadt, which cuts a scenic route into the heart of the forest.

Need to know: Several airlines serve Baden-Baden/Karlsruhe airport. Baden-Baden train station has direct connections to cities including Strasbourg, Basel and Frankfurt.

Other months: Nov-Mar – cold, snow possible; Apr-May – spring flowers; Jun-Aug – hottest, busiest, festivals; Sep-Oct – warm.

Scramble the paths of the frozen forest before sinking into a thermal spring spa

© Andy Brandl / Getty Images

Seefeld, home to some of the best cross-country skiing in Europe

© Reinhard Schmid / 4Corners Images

INNSBRUCK AUSTRIA

→ Why now? Strike out into the snow.
Innsbruck looks like the innards of a snow globe in winter, its chocolate-box-pretty Old Town twinkling with fairylights, inhabited by mythical creatures and surrounded by the frosted Nordkette alps. The Tyrolean capital has not one but six Christkindl markets (running mid-November to early January), adding festive frivolity to the medieval centre; its alleys are also lined with effigies of folk characters. Spend a few days in town browsing the stalls, museums, grand Habsburg palace and Baroque cathedral, consume mulled wine and scented almonds, and take in the views from the Zaha Hadid-designed Bergisel Ski Jump. Then make a break for the great outdoors. Few cities offer such easy access to the mountains. Try the nearby resort of Seefeld, four-times host of the Winter Olympics and home to some of the best cross-country skiing in Europe. Around 280km (174 miles) of well-groomed trails (including floodlit trails for night skiing) wind around a cluster of five villages, with options for all levels. There are also 142km (88 miles) of cleared winter walking trails (snow shoes not required).

Trip plan: Fly to Innsbruck, from where Seefeld is 30min by car, 1hr by train.

Need to know: The Feast of St Nicholas is celebrated on 6 December; 5 December is Krampusnacht, when a hairy devil runs amok in the streets.

Other months: Dec-Apr – winter activities, snow; May-Sep – warm, outdoor activities; Oct-Nov – fall colours, cool, quietest.

Wheelie on a fatbike
then warm up with a
fondue or two

VAUD ALPS
SWITZERLAND

→ **Why now? Make fat wheeltracks in
the snow.**

Fatbikes look vaguely ridiculous. But,
thanks to the greater grip and stability
offered by their oversized puffy tyres, they
open up usually off-limits ice- and powder-
smothered terrain to keen cyclists. The
sport is beginning to take off, with a Global
Fatbike Day now celebrated annually in
early December. In the Alps, the Swiss
resort of Villars-Gryon/Les Diablerets is
pioneering the sport. It offers fatbike rental,
weekly night rides (that end with fondue)
and a dedicated 7km (4 mile) fatbike
slope, open from around mid-December
(or earlier, if snow conditions suit). If the
snow hasn't arrived on the lower slopes,
fun can still be found higher up at Glacier
3000. Skiing, snowshoeing, sledding and
husky-mushing are possible, or brave the
Peak Walk, a vertiginous suspension bridge
between two mountains. Warm up at the
Les Bains de Lavey thermal spa – nestled
at the foot of the Alps, it's fed by the hottest
spring in Switzerland.

Trip plan: The closest major airports
are Geneva (120km/74 miles), Zurich
(250km/155 miles) and Lyon (240km/149
miles). Trains/buses connect to Villars, with
changes at Aigle or Bex.

Need to know: The fatbike trail runs
between Bretaye and Villars; trains run to
Bretaye from Villars station. A one-day
Liberty Pass allows unlimited travel on the
train, so you can make multiple descents.

Other months: Nov – glacier skiing season
open (runs to May); Dec-Apr – snow, main
ski season; May & Oct – shoulder months;
Jun-Sep – summer activities.

Virtually guaranteed snowboarding, skiing and freeboarding for all levels

LES DEUX ALPES
FRANCE

 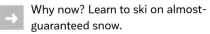

→ **Why now? Learn to ski on almost-guaranteed snow.**

Being reliable isn't usually considered sexy. Useful, but not sexy. Not so in Les Deux Alpes, which provokes passion in many a skier thanks to its alluringly predictable snow. There's glacier skiing virtually year round, but the lift system on the main mountain area gets moving from early December, opening up a winter playground said to number over 220km (137 miles) of pistes, with a top altitude of 3568m (11,706ft). It's especially exhilarating for beginners: unusually, the gentlest runs are at the top, while the lower valleys are the steepest and scariest; this means novices get to experience particularly varied and scenic slopes. There's plenty for snowboarders and freestylers, with a snowpark on the glacier, while the experienced can venture off-piste around the adjoining village of La Grave, where there's plenty of thrilling, crowd-free terrain to explore. The après-ski is also legendary, with 30-odd bars to crawl between. For a week in mid-December, the Rise festival adds extra funk, disco and soul to the mix.

Trip plan: The nearest airport and train station are in Grenoble, 70km (44 miles) northwest. Mont de Lans is the main resort village; lower down is the more traditional alpine village of Venosc.

Need to know: Book ski passes in advance for cheaper prices. Passes are free for under-fives and over-72s.

Other months: Dec-Apr – snow, skiing; May & Oct-Nov – quietest (glacier skiing open during late Oct-early Nov half term); Jun-Sep – warm, glacier skiing.

SCOTLAND

➜ **Why now? Celebrate the end of the year in the home of Hogmanay.**

Forget dropping balls or raising champagne glasses – the most inflammatory new year shindigs involve blazing barrels or torches paraded through Scottish towns. The traditional Hogmanay conflagrations reputedly stem from ancient Viking celebrations of the winter solstice, though some also claim they were intended to drive away evil spirits. The festivities come in a host of fiery flavours, with unique versions in different parts of Scotland. Inverness throws an alfresco party with music and fireworks; the people of Comrie in Perthshire light tall torches – birch poles topped with tarred rags – and Biggar builds a huge bonfire; in Stonehaven a piper leads a procession swinging fireballs, while in Dufftown, the 'malt whisky capital of the world', the annual Hogmanay ceilidh ends with drams of whisky in the town square. But the biggest bang is surely in Edinburgh, with a huge party in Princes Street, an outdoor concert and fireworks, and a lone bagpiper tooting in the new year from the castle ramparts.

Trip plan: Book ahead, turn up and be ready to celebrate!

Need to know: The town of Burghead ignores the Gregorian calendar and instead celebrates Hogmanay on 11 January with a parade of the *clavie* – a stave-filled barrel which is then set aflame on a nearby hilltop.

Other months: Nov-Apr – cold, dark; May-Jun – warming, bright; Jul-Aug – warmest, long days, busy; Sep-Oct – cool, driest.

Up Helly Aa Vikings prepare for Edinburgh's Hogmanay celebrations

© Iain Masterton / Alamy Stock Photo

LYON FRANCE

→ **Why now? Be dazzled and indulgent.**

Lyon might be France's second city, but it's the world's first when it comes to food – they say there are more restaurants per square metre here than anywhere else on the planet. These range from Michelin-starred spots creating nouvelle cuisine (a cooking style invented right here) to traditional Lyonnais *bouchons* (family bistros) serving calves' feet and tripe sausage. There are markets overflowing with Bresse chickens, St-Bonnet-le-Froid mushrooms, world-class cheeses and all sorts of offal. And there are traditional charcuteries, fromageries, chocolatiers, boulangeries... In winter, simply seek out the protection of the ancient *traboules* (passages built to shelter silk-weavers) and graze the eateries tucked within; the cold isn't really a problem if you're mostly inside eating, boutique shopping or perhaps taking a class at one of Lyon's many cookery schools. December dazzles too: early in the month, the four-day Fête des Lumières (Festival of Lights) illuminates the city, with both twinkling candles and audacious modern displays.

Trip plan: Allow three/four days for eating and sightseeing – explore the Old Town, the

Old meets new: the Festival of Lights Ferris wheel lights up Louis XIV in Place Bellecour

© Yanis Ourabah / Getty Images

numerous galleries and the museum at the Institut Lumière, which honours the local brothers who invented cinematography. Lyon could also be combined with a ski break – there are slopes only a 2hr drive away.

Need to know: Many markets, including Quai St-Antoine and Les Halles, are closed on Mondays.

Other months: Nov-Mar – chilly; Apr-May – warming, blooming; Jun-Aug – warmest, busiest; Sep-Oct – cooling, harvest.

BEYOND LYON

 **FLEURIE & MORGON · 54KM (34 MILES) ·** Heart of Beaujolais wine country

 GENEVA · 144KM (90 MILES) · Short hop to genteel lakeside Switzerland

 ARLES · 265KM (165 MILES) · South to Provence via River Rhone cruise

 PARIS · 321KM (200 MILES) · Just two hours by TGV from the capital

INDEX

Y

Z

PHOTOCREDITS

LONELY PLANET'S

WHERE TO GO WHEN EUROPE

Published in September 2020 by Lonely Planet
Global Limited CRN 554153
www.lonelyplanet.com
ISBN 978 18386 9040 3
© Lonely Planet 2020
10 9 8 7 6 5 4 3 2 1
Printed in China

Written by Sarah Baxter & Paul Bloomfield

Managing Director, Publishing Piers Pickard
Associate Publisher & Commissioning Editor Robin Barton
Editors Jessica Cole, Polly Thomas, Clifton Wilkinson, Yolanda Zappaterra
Art Direction Daniel Di Paolo
Layout Designer Jo Dovey
Print Production Nigel Longuet
Thanks to Tina García, Anna Tyler

Lonely Planet offices

AUSTRALIA
The Malt Store, Level 3, 551 Swanston Street,
Carlton VIC, 3053 Australia
Phone 03 8379 8000

UNITED KINGDOM
240 Blackfriars Road, London SE1 8NW
Phone 020 3771 5100

USA
Suite 208, 155 Filbert Street, Oakland, CA 94607
Phone 510 250 6400

IRELAND
Digital Depot, Roe Lane (off Thomas St),
Digital Hub, Dublin 8, D08 TCV4

STAY IN TOUCH lonelyplanet.com/contact

Paper in this book is certified against the Forest Stewardship Council™ standards. FSC™ promotes environmentally responsible, socially beneficial and economically viable management of the world's forests.